D1571767

# EXTREME FEAR, SHYNESS, AND SOCIAL PHOBIA

SERIES IN AFFECTIVE SCIENCE

*Series Editors*
Richard J. Davidson
Paul Ekman
Klaus Scherer

The Nature of Emotion
*Fundamental Questions*
edited by Paul Ekman and Richard J. Davidson

Boo!
*Culture, Experience, and the Startle Reflex*
Ronald Simons

Emotions in Psychopathology
*Theory and Research*
edited by William F. Flack Jr. and James D. Laird

What the Face Reveals
*Basic and Applied Studies of Spontaneous Expression*
*Using the Facial Action Coding System (FACS)*
edited by Paul Ekman and Erika Rosenberg

Shame
*Interpersonal Behavior,*
*Psychopathology, and Culture*
edited by Paul Gilbert and Bernice Andrews

Affective Neuroscience
*The Foundations of Human and Animal Emotions*
Jaak Panksepp

Extreme Fear, Shyness, and Social Phobia
*Origins, Biological Mechanisms, and Clinical Outcomes*
edited by Louis A. Schmidt and Jay Schulkin

# EXTREME FEAR, SHYNESS, and SOCIAL PHOBIA

Origins, Biological Mechanisms, and Clinical Outcomes

Edited by

Louis A. Schmidt

Jay Schulkin

New York     Oxford

Oxford University Press

1999

Oxford University Press

Oxford   New York
Athens   Auckland   Bangkok   Bogotá   Buenos Aires   Calcutta
Cape Town   Chennai   Dar es Salaam   Delhi   Florence   Hong Kong   Istanbul
Karachi   Kuala Lumpur   Madrid   Melbourne   Mexico City   Mumbai
Nairobi   Paris   São Paulo   Singapore   Taipei   Tokyo   Toronto   Warsaw

and associated companies in
Berlin   Ibadan

Copyright © 1999 by Oxford University Press, Inc.

Published by Oxford University Press, Inc.
198 Madison Avenue, New York, New York 10016

Oxford is a registered trademark of Oxford University Press

Library of Congress Cataloging-in-Publication Data
Extreme fear, shyness, and social phobia : origins, biological mechanisms,
and clinical outcomes / edited by Louis A. Schmidt, Jay Schulkin.
p.   cm. — (Series in affective science)
Includes bibliographical references and index.
ISBN 0-19-511887-1
1. Social phobia—Etiology.   2. Social phobia—Physiological aspects.
3. Social phobia—Animal models.   4. Bashfulness.   I. Schmidt, Louis A.
II. Schulkin, Jay.   III. Series.
RC552.S62E95   1999
616.85′225—dc21      98-51459

1  3  5  7  9  8  6  4  2

Printed in the United States of America
on acid-free paper

We dedicate this book
to the memory of
Kurt Schmidt and Billy Toth,
whose young lives abruptly ended
before they even began.

# Acknowledgments

One does not pursue knowledge in isolation. We would like to thank our friends, colleagues, and family members for their support along the way. We would also like to acknowledge the work and patience of the contributors to this volume. Finally, special thanks to the series editor Richard Davidson for his helpful suggestions and comments and to our senior editor, Joan Bossert, associate editor, Philip Laughlin, and production editor, MaryBeth Branigan, at Oxford University Press for their efforts.

# Foreword

Richard Davidson

One of our hopes for the Series in Affective Science is to feature cutting-edge interdisciplinary approaches to the study of emotion and emotion-related phenomena. This volume is the product of a collaboration between a developmental psychologist (Louis Schmidt) and a neuroscientist (Jay Schulkin), who bring together a diverse array of scholars representing developmental psychology, neuroscience and neurobiology, psychiatry, and clinical psychology to provide a review of the current state of knowledge on fear and its pathological expressions.

For the past decade, the study of fear has been an important project in research in the neuroscience of emotion. Inroads in the study of fear, which is conserved across mammalian species, have provided the most solid, consistently replicated facts about the circuitry of emotion that we have today. Two of the most common psychiatric disorders—anxiety and mood disorders—involve dysregulation of some sort in components of the fear system. The basic research at the animal level has provided important guideposts to the key elements of the circuitry that subserve fear and its related affective phenomena. The corpus of work has had a profound influence on the study of these phenomena at the human level. One of the most ubiquitous characteristics of fear at this level is the extraordinary range of individual variation across people in its expression. This salient human variability has catalyzed the search for its sources at the animal level.

The study of fear thus represents a remarkable advance in the science of emotion where continuous two-way interaction regularly occurs between scientists studying the phenomena in animals at more basic levels and those studying it in humans at more integrative levels. Schmidt and Schulkin palpably exemplify this two-way interaction, and their influence can be seen in their strategic choice of contributors who, like themselves, understand and appreciate the benefit of such interdisciplinary scholarship. As this book testifies, it is necessary to preserve this interdisciplinary approach to fully capture the complexity of this topic.

# Introduction

## Origins of the Book

The seeds for this book were sown some 3 years ago during weekly walks at night around northwest Washington, D.C., shortly after we were introduced by Nathan Fox. In addition to the physical exercise, the walks provided an outlet for intellectual discourse and an exchange of ideas. We would start off a typical evening covering disparate topics which ranged from Thomas Aquinas, William James, and Ludwig Wittgenstein to the neural basis of motivation and emotion to what it meant growing up as a Roman Catholic in southwest Baltimore and as a Jewish kid in the Bronx. It did not take long to realize that we both shared a mutual bond and friendship, a common passion for the human condition, and an insatiable thirst for the search for knowledge. We also soon discovered that we shared a common interest in understanding the phenomena of extreme fear and shyness, due largely to our discussions of Jerome Kagan's work at Harvard and the encouragement of Nathan Fox at Maryland.

This book reflects the interface of our two disparate worlds and training: one as a developmental psychologist and the other as a behavioral neuroscientist. The idea for the book emerged from a symposium (Schmidt, 1997) that we conducted at the 62nd Biennial Meeting of the Society for Research in Child Development (SRCD) in Washington, D.C., on integrating developmental, biological, and clinical perspectives of extreme shyness in children, at which some of the contributors to this book presented papers. The purpose of the book, similar to that of the symposium, is to bring together a number of people under one intellectual setting: namely, the attempt to understand the origins, developmental course, and outcomes of extreme fear and shyness.

## Historical Precedent and Contemporary Relevance

The study of temperament has a long and diverse history. To the early Greeks, individual differences in temperament originated from differences in bodily humors.

References to temperamental differences have surfaced in literary efforts over the years as well. Emerson wrote how temperament colors one's world. For pragmatists such as ourselves, temperamental differences are discussed along the lines of their functional utility to adaptation. Fear and shyness are temperamental qualities that have received much attention over the years, particularly within the last decade (see Kagan, 1994; LeDoux, 1996). Fear is a central state that is biologically rooted, that is conserved across mammals, and that serves an important function. The purpose of fear is to warn the organism about danger and to prepare the organism to avoid it. Fear is a property of the organism that is coded by genes and earmarked by experience.

There are a number of brain systems and regions that have been implicated in maintaining fear responses (see LeDoux, 1996). The key players appear to be the frontal cortex, the amygdala (particularly the central nucleus), the bed nucleus of the stria terminalis, the hippocampus, and the hypothalamic pituitary adrenal system (see Schulkin, McEwen, & Gold, 1994). The ability to regulate fear responses is important for negotiating a complex world.

Individual differences in the regulation of fear responses have been noted across mammals including rats, dogs, goats, nonhuman primates, and humans (Boissy, 1995). For some individuals, however, the ability to regulate normal fear in response to real or imagined socially evaluative situations becomes problematic, and what would normally be seen as adaptive responses may soon become maladaptive (Rosen & Schulkin, 1998). Such people are likely to have problems successfully interacting in a social world, which may contribute to their developing chronic problems such as social anxiety, social phobia, and depression (see Beidel & Turner, 1998).

## Outline of the Book

This book is divided into three major parts, with each part followed by a commentary on the chapters contained within that section. Part I is devoted to a discussion of the conceptual and developmental issues that surround extreme fear and shyness. In this section, we have assembled a group of developmental and personality psychologists. Here, we have focused on the origins and conceptual meanings of fear, shyness, and related constructs such as behavioral inhibition in children and adults, placing a particular emphasis on the biological mechanisms that underlie the development of extreme fear and shyness. The first two chapters in this section present conceptual issues related to fear and shyness in children. In chapter 1, Jerome Kagan discusses the conceptual meaning of behavioral inhibition in children and provides data from a series of ongoing empirical studies in his laboratory investigating this phenomenon. Ray Crozier in chapter 2 puts forth the notion that there may be different types of childhood shyness. In chapters 3 through 5, the focus is on the biological and environmental antecedents and correlates of extreme fear and shyness in human infants and children. Kathy Stansbury (chapter 3) presents evidence that adrenocortical activity is an important factor mediating the child's internal social milieu. In chapter 4, Louis Schmidt and Nathan Fox present data from a series of longitudinal studies that they have been conducting which suggest that there may be a distinct pattern of physiological responses which describes and characterizes different types of shy children. Richard Davidson and Maureen Rickman (chapter 5) describe data derived from electrocortical and neuroimaging studies which provide strong evidence for a possible neuroanatomical circuit underlying fear responses and shyness in humans. Mary Rothbart provides perspective and commentary on the five chapters contained in this section.

Part II is devoted to a discussion of the endocrine and neural bases of fear. In this section, we have assembled a group of neuroscientists who are doing research on the development of animal models of fear with implications for understanding the development of extreme fear and shyness in humans. In chapter 6, Lorey Takahashi and Ned Kalin provide an animal model of behavioral inhibition in rats, emphasizing the role of corticosteroids in the development of fear. Karim Nader and Joseph LeDoux (chapter 7) map the neural circuits that underlie fear responses in animals and examine the possible implications for understanding fear and shyness in humans. In chapter 8, Jay Schulkin and Jeffrey Rosen emphasize the role of elevated cortisol and corticotropin releasing hormone in the regulation of fear responses, placing a particular emphasis on the central nucleus of the amygdala and the bed nucleus of the stria terminalis. Bruce McEwen (chapter 9) describes the effects of hormones on brain development and how these effects have implications for understanding the development of both shyness and disease. George Chrousos and Philip Gold provide perspective and commentary on the four chapters in this section.

Part III is devoted to a discussion of the developmental course and clinical outcomes that surround extreme fear and shyness. In this section, we have assembled a group of psychologists, psychiatrists, and clinicians who work in the area of intervention and treatment of shyness and related social maladies. Deborah Beidel and Samuel Turner (chapter 10) provide data and a model that may shed light on the developmental course of shyness and social inhibition. In chapter 11, Jonathan Cheek and Elena Krasnoperova describe the development and outcomes associated with different types of shyness in adolescents and adults. In chaper 12, Elaine Aron presents evidence from her work with highly sensitive people and discusses its clinical relevance to understanding and treating shyness. Franklin Schneier (chapter 13) concludes this section by presenting the most current methods for treating shyness and anxiety-related problems in children and adults. Lynne Henderson and Philip Zimbardo provide perspective and commentary on the four chapters presented in this section.

New discoveries in developmental psychology and the neurosciences make this an exciting time in the study of extreme fear and shyness. Our hope is that this book will serve as a resource for researchers and students working in the areas of behavioral neuroscience, developmental and clinical psychology, psychiatry, and pediatric medicine.

Louis A. Schmidt                                          Jay Schulkin
Hamilton, Ontario                                    Washington, D.C.

April, 1999

*References*

Beidel, D. C., & Turner, S. M. (1998). *Shy children, phobic adults. Nature and treatment of social phobia.* Washington, DC: American Psychological Association.

Boissy, A. (1995). Fear and fearfulness in animals. *Quarterly Review of Biology, 70,* 165–191.

Kagan, J. (1994). *Galen's prophecy: Temperament in human nature.* New York: Basic Books.

LeDoux, J. E. (1996). *The emotional brain.* New York: Simon & Schuster.

Rosen, J. B., & Schulkin, J. (1998). From normal fear to pathological anxiety. *Psychological Review, 105,* 325–350.

Schmidt, L. A. (1997). *Childhood shyness: Interfacing the neurosciences, genetics, socialization, and psychopathology.* Symposium conducted at the 62nd Meeting of the Society for Research in Child Development, Washington, DC.

Schulkin, J., McEwen, B. S., & Gold, P. W. (1994). Allostasis, amygdala and anticipatory angst. *Neuroscience and Biobehavioral Reviews, 18,* 385–396.

# Contents

# Contributors

Elaine N. Aron (Ph.D., Pacifica Graduate Institute) is a research scientist in the Department of Psychology at the State University of New York at Stony Brook. Her research interests include adult temperament, sensitivity, and close relationships.

Deborah C. Beidel (Ph.D., University of Pittsburgh) is professor of psychology and codirector of the Maryland Center for Anxiety Disorders at the University of Maryland, College Park. Her research interests include the etiology and treatment of anxiety disorders in adults and children.

Jonathan M. Cheek (Ph.D., Johns Hopkins University) is professor of psychology at Wellesley College in Massachusetts. His research interests include the psychology of shyness, self-concept, and aspects of identity.

George P. Chrousos (M.D., Sc.D., Athens University) is chief of pediatric endocrinology at the National Institute of Child Health and Human Development, National Institutes of Health, Bethesda, Maryland. His research interests include endocrine mechanisms of stress and development.

W. Raymond Crozier (Ph.D., Keele University) is reader in psychology and education, University of Wales, Cardiff, United Kingdom. His research interests include shyness and its relation to embarrassment and the social psychology of creativity.

Richard J. Davidson (Ph.D., Harvard University) is the Vilas Professor of Psychology and Psychiatry and director of the Wisconsin Center for Affective Science and the W. M. Keck Laboratory for Functional Brain Imaging and Behavior at the University of Wisconsin. His research interests include affective neuroscience, the neural substrates of affective style, and mood and affective disorders.

Nathan A. Fox (Ph.D., Harvard University) is professor of human development and psychology and director of the Child Development Laboratory at the University of Maryland, College Park. His research interests include emotional development in infants and children and developmental psychophysiology.

Philip W. Gold (M.D., Duke University) is chief of the Clinical Neuroendocrinology Branch at the National Institute of Mental Health, National Institutes of Health, Bethesda, Maryland. His research interests include neuroendocrine regulation of stress and depression.

Lynne Henderson (Ph.D., Pacific Graduate School of Psychology) is a visiting scholar in the Department of Psychology at Stanford University and co-director of the Shyness Institute in Portola Valley, California. Her research interests include the treatment of shyness and self-conceptualizations in successful adaptation.

Jerome Kagan (Ph.D., Yale University) is the Daniel and Amy Starch Professor of Psychology at Harvard University. His research interests include temperamental differences in development and cognitive and emotional development in infants and young children.

Ned H. Kalin (M.D., Jefferson Medical College) is the Hedberg Professor and Chair of Psychiatry at the University of Wisconsin Medical School. His research interests include the ontogeny of stress-related behavioral and hormonal responses in primate and rodent species.

Elena N. Krasnoperova (Ph.D., Stanford University) is an organizational consultant in the private sector in Palo Alto, California. Her research interests include social anxiety and interpersonal approaches to depression.

Joseph LeDoux (Ph.D., State University of New York, Stony Brook) is the Henry and Lucy Moses Professor of Science at the Center for Neural Science at New York University. His research interests include emotion, memory, cognition, the limbic system, audition, animal behavior, and consciousness.

Bruce S. McEwen (Ph.D., Rockefeller University) is professor and head, Laboratory of Neuroendocrinology at Rockefeller University in New York. His research interests include brain plasticity and the effects of stress and hormones on the hippocampus, memory, and aging.

Karim Nader (Ph.D., University of Toronto) is a postdoctoral fellow at the Center for Neural Science at New York University. His research interests include neurobiological approaches to understanding the organization of emotions.

Maureen Rickman (Ph.D., University of Wisconsin-Madison) is an assistant research scientist in the Department of Psychology at the University of Wisconsin, Madison. Her research interests include the use of EEG in the study of emotion.

Jeffrey B. Rosen (Ph.D., Wayne State University) is assistant professor of psychology at the University of Delaware. His research interests include the neurobiology of fear and anxiety.

Mary K. Rothbart (Ph.D., Stanford University) is professor of psychology at the University of Oregon. Her research interests include the early development of attention and the role of infant temperament in early personality development.

Louis A. Schmidt (Ph.D., University of Maryland, College Park) is assistant professor of psychology at McMaster University in Canada. His research interests include socioemotional development in infants and young children, the neural basis of human emotion, developmental psychophysiology, and individual differences in temperament, particularly shyness subtypes.

Franklin R. Schneier (M.D., Cornell University Medical College) is associate professor of clinical psychiatry at the Columbia University College of Physicians and Surgeons and associate director of the Anxiety Disorders Clinic at the New York State Psychiatric Institute. His research interests include aspects of social phobia and panic disorder, including diagnosis, psychopharmacology, and brain imaging.

Jay Schulkin (Ph.D., University of Pennsylvania) is research professor of physiology and biophysics at Georgetown University in Washington, D.C., and research scientist at the Clinical Neuroendocrinology Branch of the National Institute of Mental Health, Bethesda, Maryland. His research interests include the neuroendocrine regulation of behavior, particularly fear and appetitive behavior.

Kathy Stansbury (Ph.D., University of California, Los Angeles) is assistant professor of psychology at the University of New Mexico, Albuquerque. Her research interests include the development of emotion regulation in normally developing and high-risk children and the role of psychoneuroendocrinology in this development.

Lorey K. Takahashi (Ph.D., Rutgers University) is assistant professor of psychiatry at the University of Wisconsin Medical School. His research interests include the neurobiology of stress and emotional behavior.

Samuel M. Turner (Ph.D., University of Georgia) is professor of psychology and codirector of the Maryland Center for Anxiety Disorders at the University of Maryland, College Park. His research interests include anxiety disorders in children and adults and behavior therapy.

Philip G. Zimbardo (Ph.D., Yale University) is professor of psychology at Stanford University and codirector of the Shyness Institute in Portola Valley, California. His research interests include effects of temporal perspective on behavior, cognition and emotion, and also madness and shyness.

# PART I

## THE PHENOMENA
## OF CHILDHOOD
## FEAR AND SHYNESS

Conceptual, Biological, and
Developmental Considerations

# 1

# The Concept of Behavioral Inhibition

Jerome Kagan

Scientists differ in their preferences for beginning their inquiries either with ideas or with phenomena. Psychology witnessed a relatively dramatic shift from the former to the latter style during the 1960s, when loyalty to the abstract concepts of psychoanalysis and learning theory faltered, and when many psychologists initiated their research by focusing first on behaviors, such as aggression or shyness, rather than on concepts, such as hostility or anxiety. This trend was helped by the positivism of the neurosciences and the influence of research on temperament in young children, which also focused on public behaviors such as crying, motor activity, or avoidance of novelty.

One source of variation that can be observed in every community in every culture is the degree to which children older than 1 year become quiet, serious, and withdrawn when they confront or interact with an unfamiliar adult or child. Longitudinal data from the Berkeley Guidance Study revealed that boys who displayed such shy behavior during childhood grew into adults who married, became parents, and established careers later than did their less shy counterparts. Although shy girls married at normative times, they were less likely than their less shy female peers to develop careers (Caspi, Elder, & Bem, 1988). A longitudinal study of New Zealand children revealed that about 15 percent of a large group of adults who had been rated as shy when they were 3 years old described themselves as cautious and avoidant of dangerous situations (Caspi & Silva, 1995).

Kenneth Rubin and his colleagues, who rely more often on behavioral observations of children in natural contexts than on questionnaires or ratings, make an important distinction between the child who plays alone and shows signs of anxiety and the equally solitary child who is actively engaged in activities. The latter child, who prefers to be autonomous, does not show signs of anxiety or uncertainty. These two kinds of children, both of whom appear to be isolated, should be distinguished (Coplan, Rubin, Fox, Calkins, & Stewart, 1994).

My colleagues and I regard shyness with unfamiliar children or adults as only one feature of a much broader temperamental category that we call *inhibition to the unfamiliar*. Children classified as inhibited, usually after the 1st birthday, re-act to very different classes of unfamiliar events with initial avoidance, subdued affect, or distress. The source of the unfamiliarity can be people, situations, or events. When the incentive is people, parents call the child shy; when the incen-tive is an unfamiliar situation, parents call the child timid; when the situation is an unfamiliar food, parents call the child finicky. Thus the concept of an inhibited child assumes that the individual can display an avoidant style in one or more un-familiar contexts. Membership in the category is not defined by one specific class of behavior, such as shyness with strangers. Thus only a proportion of shy children are properly classified as inhibited, and some children who are classified as in-hibited may not be shy with strangers. The behavior quantified cannot be separated conceptually from the hypothetical set of biological events that mediate the be-haviors. Because the detailed profile of shy behavior displayed by temperamen-tally inhibited children is not exactly like the profile of those who acquired their shy demeanor as a result of experience alone, we should not treat the predicate "shy" as an independent quality that is separable from the child's physiology, age, or life history.

The work on inhibited children began over 40 years ago at the Fels Research Institute in Yellow Springs, Ohio. The staff of the Institute had studied, longitudi-nally, 89 Caucasian children born between 1929 and 1939. The children had been observed from the early months of life through adolescence in naturalistic settings and were interviewed and tested when they became young adults (Kagan & Moss, 1962). The most provocative finding was that a small group of children who had been extremely fearful during the first 3 years of life, in home and in nursery set-tings, had retained some derivative qualities in young adulthood. Most of these fearful children became introverted and cautious adults.

Over 20 years later, Richard Kearsley, Philip Zelazo, and I were reflecting on a corpus of data gathered on 53 Chinese-American and 63 Caucasian infants who were participants in a study designed to assess the effects of day care on young in-fants (Kagan, Kearsley, & Zelazo, 1978). Some infants had attended an experimen-tal day-care center from 4 to 21 months of age, whereas others, matched on eth-nicity, had been reared at home. All children were observed on five occasions between 3½ and 29 months of age. To our surprise, the Chinese-American infants, whether reared at home or attending a day-care center, were more shy and fearful than the Caucasian infants. The former spent more time proximal to their mothers in unfamiliar settings and were wary when playing with unfamiliar children of the same age and sex. Many of the Chinese-American mothers characterized their chil-dren as apprehensive, using phrases like "stays close to me" and "dislikes the dark." The results of the Fels Longitudinal Study and the day-care investigation, separated by almost a quarter of a century, provoked the concept of the inhibited child.

We chose the term *inhibited* because it seemed less evaluative than the terms *anxious* or *fearful* and because it captured the restraint and timidity these children displayed in unfamiliar contexts. The term *inhibition*, which first appeared in nine-teenth-century reports of physiological investigations of the central nervous system, described the discovery, surprising at the time, that reflexes and autonomic responses can be slowed or even made to disappear. Inhibition seemed an appropriate term for these physiological phenomena, and the term had positive connotations. Nineteenth-century Europeans celebrated those adults who could control the strong emotions of sexuality and anger. Indeed, by the end of the century, many physicians in Europe believed that the primary cause of psychosis and criminality was a deficiency in inhibition that occurred because the higher brain centers of these individuals failed to control the lower ones.

It was left to Freud to reverse the evaluative meaning of inhibition in a serious way by substituting the repression of motives for the disappearance of reflexes. Sex was to be enjoyed rather than controlled, and, therefore, inhibition became an undesirable, rather than a desirable, characteristic. Freud pitted the well-being of society, which required inhibition of impulse, against the pleasures of the individual. Thus, in less than a century, the connotations of the word *inhibition* had changed from the celebration of those who were able to control their passions to sympathy toward those who were unable to enjoy life.

We began our first systematic studies of the inhibited child 20 years ago. Galileo and Kepler recorded their observations on the moon, stars, and planets because these entities were obvious and changes in their location over the year appeared regular. The behaviors that define the inhibited child are equally obvious. Diamond (1957) had written over 40 years ago that withdrawal from unfamiliarity was a temperamental trait, and the journals in psychology and psychiatry contained many reports that suggested that introversion was a heritable quality.

It is also important that no matter what mammalian species is observed, there is always genetically based variation within each species in the propensity to approach or to avoid unfamiliarity (Wilson, Clarke, Coleman, & Dearstyne, 1994). Schneirla (1959), who devoted most of his career to pursuing this idea, believed that the intensity of a stimulus was the most important determinant of whether an animal would avoid or approach it. Animals approach stimuli with low intensity and avoid those with high intensity.

## The Early Work

In our first study of this phenomenon 117 21-month-old Caucasian children, both first- and later born, were observed as they encountered unfamiliar people, objects, and situations in a laboratory setting. The 33 children who displayed consistent signs of fear and avoidance were classified as inhibited; the 38 children who showed the opposite tendency to approach the unfamiliar were called uninhibited. The remaining children, whose behavior was inconsistent, were not seen at later ages (Garcia-Coll, Kagan, & Reznick, 1984).

We also saw a second sample of 31-month-old children as they interacted with an unfamiliar child of the same sex and age. At the end of the play session with the other child, a woman dressed in an unusual costume—a plastic cover over her head and torso—entered and, after a period of silence, invited the two children to ap-

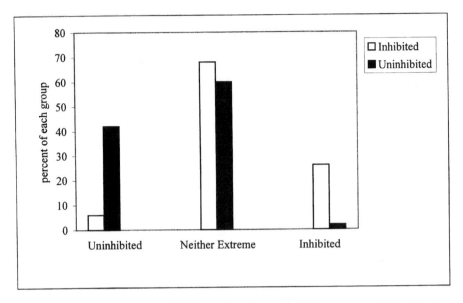

Figure 1.1. The percentage of children classified as inhibited or uninhibited in the 2nd year of life who were categorized as uninhibited, neither, or inhibited when they were 7½ years old. (Kagan, 1994)

proach her. About 15 percent of this group were very shy and timid with both the unfamiliar child and the strangely dressed adult stranger (Kagan, Reznick, & Snidman, 1988).

These children were assessed again when they were approximately 4, 5½, and 7½ years of age. About a quarter of the originally inhibited children were, at 7½ years of age, unusually shy, quiet, and timid. But only two children who had been inhibited when younger lost that quality completely and behaved as if they were uninhibited (Kagan, Reznick & Snidman, 1988) (see figure 1.1).

The children in the two samples were last evaluated when they were about 13 years old. Initially, they were tested by an unfamiliar female examiner and on a later occasion were interviewed by Carl Schwartz, a psychiatrist, who, along with the examiner, was unfamiliar with the child's prior behavior or temperamental classification. The most important result is that the phenotype of most children had not changed a great deal since age 7½. The children who had been inhibited earlier did not display a great deal of spontaneous conversation or smiling during the interview with the examiner or during the longer session with the psychiatrist. Two-thirds of the children who had remained inhibited from the 2nd year to the 7th year were still quiet, serious, and shy as adolescents; only five were affectively spontaneous.

Study of twins has suggested the possibility of an inherited basis for inhibition. Both Matheny (1983, 1990) and a team of investigators collaborating in a large twin study at the Institute for Behavioral Genetics at the University of Colorado have found that the heritability coefficients for inhibited behavior, based on direct observations, hover around 0.5 (Saudino & Kagan, in press).

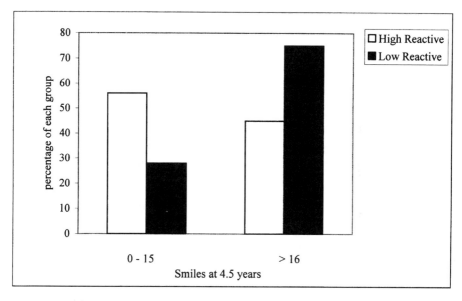

Figure 1.2. The percentage of high- and low-reactive infants showing low versus high smiling with the examiner at 4½ years of age. (Kagan, Snidman, & Arcus, 1998)

### Infant Predictions

In an attempt to discover the very early signs of inhibition, my colleagues and I observed a cohort of more than 450 healthy Caucasian infants when they were 4 months of age and assessed more than 250 of them when they were 14 and 21 months old (Kagan, 1994). About 20 percent of these infants showed frequent and vigorous limb activity combined with distress to visual, auditory, and olfactory stimuli. These infants, called high-reactive, were most likely to be inhibited when they encountered unfamiliar events in the laboratory at 14 and 21 months. When these children were 4½ years old, those who had been high-reactive were subdued during a 1-hour interview with an examiner and shy when they played with two unfamiliar children of the same age and sex. Specifically, they talked and smiled less frequently than those who had been low-reactive infants and, when playing with a peer, stayed closer to their mothers and stared at the unfamiliar children for longer periods of time (see figure 1.2). However, only 13 percent of the children who had been classified as high-reactive infants had been consistently inhibited, fearful, and subdued at 14 and 21 months and at 4½ years. But not one child who had been a high-reactive infant met the complementary criteria of minimal fearfulness in the 2nd year and affective spontaneity and sociability at 4½ years (Kagan, Snidman, & Arcus, 1998).

The parents of high-reactive infants reported that their children were extremely sensitive to criticism and became subdued or had tantrums when they were chastised (see figure 1.3).

A sample of 164 of these children was assessed in a variety of situations when they were between 6 and 8 years of age. The parents and teachers of the children

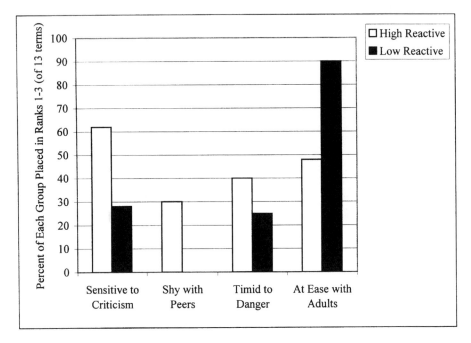

Figure 1.3. Percentage of high- and low-reactive children described by their mothers as possessing various traits at 4½ years of age. (unpublished data)

had been interviewed to determine which ones were showing signs of serious anxiety. The children who had been high-reactive infants were most likely to possess anxious symptoms at school age. Forty-two percent of the children who had been high reactives were classified as possessing anxious symptoms, compared with only 12 percent of the children who had been low-reactive. Further, those who had been high-reactive infants continued to display, at 7 years, an emotionally subdued, cautious, and reflective style (Kagan, Snidman, & Zentner, in press).

In one analysis, we compared 23 children who had been high-reactive infants and who had anxious symptoms with 27 children who also had been high-reactive as infants but did not have anxious symptoms. The two groups of 7-year-olds differed on three contemporary variables. The anxious children had higher sitting diastolic blood pressures, narrower faces, and greater cooling of the temperature of their fingertips when presented with the cognitive challenge of remembering series of digits. Further, these children had been very fearful when they were observed at 21 months. We then asked how many children met criteria for all four of these variables, where the criterion was a score above the mean for that variable for that child's gender. Forty percent of the high-reactives who were anxious but only one high-reactive–nonanxious child met all four criteria. The seven high-reactive children with anxious symptoms who met criteria for all four variables differed from the original group of 97 high-reactive infants. At 4 months, these seven infants displayed higher motor activity and irritability scores, higher and more stable heart rates as the battery began, and a larger decrease in heart rate to the onset of a taped sentence spoken by a female voice. This evidence suggests that

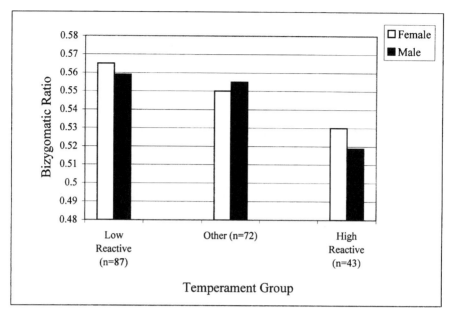

Figure 1.4. Ratio of width of face at the bizygomatic over length of face for the two temperamental groups and other children at 14 months. (Arcus & Kagan, 1995)

this small group of high-reactive infants who developed anxious symptoms were different from the other high-reactives when they were only 16 weeks old (Kagan, Snidman, & Zentner, in press).

## Physiological Differences

Inhibited and uninhibited children differ on a small number of theoretically relevant physiological variables. Other investigators have found that inhibited children show greater EEG activation on the right frontal area under resting conditions; most children show greater activation in the left frontal area (Calkins, Fox, & Marshall, 1996; Davidson, 1994). It is also of interest that high-reactive infants have narrower faces than low-reactive infants and that inhibited children have narrower faces than uninhibited children (Arcus & Kagan, 1995) (see figure 1.4). The fact that the facial skeleton is a significant correlate of inhibition implies the contribution of a set of genes that influences features as diverse as the growth of facial bone, ease of distressed arousal in infancy, and fear of the unfamiliar. It may not be a coincidence that inbred mouse strains such as A/JAX that are susceptible to inhibition of the growth of the palatal shelf following pharmacological doses of glucocorticoids during gestation are more fearful in an open field than other mouse strains such as C57 BL/6 that are less susceptible to the influence of this steroid on the growth of this facial bone (Thompson, 1953; Walker & Fraser, 1957).

There is also suggestive evidence that high-reactive–inhibited children have greater sympathetic reactivity than low-reactive–uninhibited children. For exam-

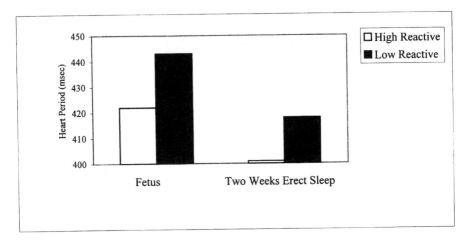

Figure 1.5. Heart period during the fetal era and at 2 weeks for children classified as high or low reactive at 4 months of age. (Snidman, Kagan, Riordan, & Shannon, 1995)

ple, at 5 and 7 years of age, inhibited children showed greater cardiac acceleration and larger changes in blood pressure to cognitive challenges. Moreover, more high-than low-reactive infants had high fetal heart rates 3 to 4 weeks before birth, as well as higher sleeping heart rates 2 weeks after birth while being held erect, but not when held supine (see figure 1.5). Spectral analysis of these sleeping heart rates at two weeks, which separates vagal from sympathetic influences to some degree, revealed that the high, compared with the low, reactive infants had greater power in the low frequency band (between .02 and .10 Hz) when held erect, suggesting greater sympathetic reactivity (Snidman, Kagan, Riordan, & Shannon, 1995). Di Pietro (1995) also found that fetuses with high heart rates were less likely to show positive affect when they were 6 months old. It is of interest that infants with highly variable heart rates, which usually reflect more vagal and less sympathetic activity, tend to approach, rather than avoid, objects (Richards & Cameron, 1989) and people (Fox, 1989) and to display more frequent facial expressions suggestive of a happy affect (Stifter, Fox, & Porges, 1989).

Unpublished data on 4- to 5-year-old children born either to a parent with panic disorder or to parents without anxiety or depression revealed that the former showed greater autonomic lability than the latter. Thus the existing evidence suggests that inhibited children display a specific behavioral and biological profile.

Although the data suggest that the construct of an inhibited child is likely to have some validity, most high-reactive infants did not become consistently inhibited children but, rather, became similar to average children. What terms shall we use, therefore, to describe the substantial group of high-reactives who did not become consistently inhibited older children? The decision as to what to call the children who change their outward behavioral profile is a function of the investigator's position on the debate between appearance and reality. Some scientists argue that we cannot ever know what is occurring in nature. Niels Bohr was skeptical about our ability to grasp whatever hidden whole lay behind what was observed, even though he agreed it was necessary to use words as conceptual aids to describe the invisible processes. But these words were conjectures to help understanding. If a 6-year-old is sociable, we cannot state that he is inhibited simply because he began life as a high-reactive infant.

Other scholars, for whom Einstein is the prototype, feel obligated to infer some critical processes, even though they are invisible to machines or to the human senses. Einstein trusted the human mind's capability of capturing the events that lay behind the measurement. Scientists who side with Einstein would argue that we do not violate any rules by speculating that sociable children who had been high-reactive infants are different from equally sociable children who had not been high-reactive.

I side with Bohr. To side with Einstein is to commit the error of awarding inhibition a Platonic reality—a thing in itself—that is a fiction. Hilary Putnam (1995) argues that when we talk of "ding an sich," we do not know what we are talking about. At present, it is probably wiser to pay attention to the behavior. There may come a time when the empirical substantiations of the concept intertwine. When that happens, the meaning of inhibition will reside in all of those threads, a victory that is now actualized for the biological concept of species.

## Conclusion

The return of the idea of temperament is an important development in the fields of developmental psychology, personality, and psychopathology. The histories of all the sciences are replete with examples of the progress that occurs when two or more previously isolated domains begin to study common problems with a shared vocabulary and common methods. The field of molecular biology is an example. Because the union provides new information for the partners, popular terms are refined, and ideas that have outlived their usefulness are eliminated. The idea of temperament unites both biology and developmental psychology.

The idea of temperament also will turn our attention to interactions. We should not expect children with different temperamental types to react in the same way to a given experience, and, therefore, we must invent constructs that capture that fact. There are very few incentives that provoke the same response in all children.

Finally, the return of temperamental ideas will recruit additional interest to emotional phenomena and alert psychologists to those events that have a primary effect on emotions, especially the families of emotions we call guilt, shame, fear, anxiety, sadness, and excitement. The individual variation in the frequency of occurrence and intensity of those affective states is influenced by temperament, along with the psychological constructions individuals create from their encounters.

*Acknowledgments*   This research was supported in part by a grant from the W.T. Grant Foundation.

*References*

Arcus, D. M., & Kagan, J. (1995). Temperament and craniofacial skeleton in children. *Child Development, 66,* 1529–1540.

Calkins, S. D., Fox, N. A., & Marshall, T. R. (1996). Behavioral and physiological antecedents of inhibited and uninhibited behavior. *Child Development, 67,* 523–540.

Caspi, A., Elder, G. H., & Bem, D. J. (1988). Moving away from the world. *Developmental Psychology, 24,* 824–831.

Caspi, A., & Silva, P. A. (1995). Temperamental qualities at age three predict personality traits in young adulthood. *Child Development, 66,* 486–498.

Coplan, R. J., Rubin, K. H., Fox, N. A., Calkins, S. D., & Stewart, S. L. (1994). Being alone, playing alone, and acting alone. *Child Development, 65,* 129–137.

Davidson, R. J. (1994). Asymmetric brain function, affective style, and psychopathology. *Development and Psychopathology, 6,* 741–758.

Diamond, S. (1957). *Personality and temperament.* New York: Harper.

Di Pietro, J. (1995, March). *Fetal origins of neurobehavioral function and individual differences.* Paper presented at the meeting of the Society for Research for Child Development, Indianapolis, IN.

Fox, N. A. (1989). Psychophysiological correlates of emotional reactivity during the first year of life. *Developmental Psychology, 25,* 364–372.

Garcia-Coll, C., Kagan, J., & Reznick, J. S. (1984). Behavioral inhibition in young children. *Child Development, 55,* 1005–1019.

Kagan, J. (1994). *Galen's prophecy: temperament in human nature.* New York: Basic Books.

Kagan, J., Kearsley, R., & Zelazo, P. (1978). *Infancy.* Cambridge, MA: Harvard University Press.

Kagan, J. & Moss, A. J. (1962). *Birth to maturity.* New York: Wiley.

Kagan, J., Reznick, J. S., & Snidman, N. (1988). Biological bases of childhood shyness. *Science 240,* 167–171.

Kagan, J., Snidman, N., & Arcus, D. (1998). Childhood derivatives of high and low reactivity in infancy. *Child Development, 69,* 1483–1493.

Kagan, J., Snidman, N., & Zentner, M. (In press). Infant temperament and anxious symptoms in school-age children. *Development and Psychopathology.*

Matheny, A. (1983). A longitudinal twin study of stability of components from Bayley's infant behavioral records. *Child Development, 54,* 356–360.

Matheny, A. (1990). Developmental behavior genetics. In M. E. Hahn, J. K. Hewitt, N. D. Henderson, & R. H. Benno (Eds.), *Developmental behavior genetics: Neural, biometrical, and evolutionary approaches* (pp. 25–38). New York: Oxford University Press.

Putnam, H. (1995). *Words and life.* Cambridge, MA: Harvard University Press.

Richards, J. E., & Cameron, D. (1989). Infant heart rate variability and behavioral developmental status. *Infant Behavior and Development, 12,* 45–58.

Saudino, K. J., & Kagan, J. (in press). The stability and genetics of behavioral inhibition. In R. N. Emde (Ed.), *The MALTS Longitudinal Study.*

Schneirla, T. C. (1959). An evolutionary and developmental theory of biphasic processes underlying approach and withdrawal. In M. R. Jones (Ed.), *Nebraska Symposium on Motivation: Vol. VII* (pp. 1–41). Lincoln: University of Nebraska Press.

Snidman, N., Kagan, J., Riordan, L., & Shannon, D. (1995). Cardiac function and behavioral reactivity in infancy. *Psychophysiology, 32,* 199–207.

Stifter, C. A., Fox, N. A., & Porges, S. W. (1989). Facial expressivity and vagal tone in five- and ten-month old infants. *Infant Behavior and Development, 12,* 127–137.

Thompson, W. R. (1953). The inheritance of behavior. *Canadian Journal of Psychology, 7,* 145–155.

Walker, B. E., & Fraser, F. C. (1957). The embryology of cortisone induced cleft palate. *Journal of Embryology and Experimental Morphology, 5,* 201–209.

Wilson, D. S., Clarke, A. B., Coleman, K., & Dearstyne, T. (1994). Shyness and boldness in humans and other animals. *Trends in Ecology and Evolution, 9,* 442–446.

# 2

# Individual Differences
# in Childhood Shyness

## Distinguishing Fearful and Self-Conscious Shyness

### W. Raymond Crozier

The recent surge of interest in shyness has led to a conception of shyness as related to fear and timidity, particularly in unfamiliar situations. Jerome Kagan's construct of inhibition, with its associated base of empirical research, has been very influential (see, for example, Kagan, 1994; see also Kagan, chapter 1, this volume). This research program has included studies of the identification of inhibition in infancy (reactions to novel situations have a key role in this); longitudinal studies of the life paths of inhibited infants (shyness and anxiety characterize a proportion of inhibited children); and studies of the psychophysiological correlates of inhibition (an emphasis on the involvement of the amygdala in fear states). Alternative perspectives on shyness, for example Schlenker and Leary's (1982) self-presentational model, also conceptualize shyness as a form of social anxiety. Extreme forms of shyness tend to be labeled as social phobia, a conception that also emphasizes the link between shyness on the one hand and fear and anxiety on the other. This conception of shyness has obviously had considerable heuristic value, as the contributions to this volume testify. The research it has elicited has also served to obscure an alternative conception of shyness, one that relates it more closely to shame.

## Shyness and Shame

The affinity between shyness and shame tends to be postulated by researchers who are interested in shyness as a state or emotion rather than as a temperament or trait. Thus Izard's (1971) theory defined shame-shyness as one of the fundamental emotions. More recently, there is growing interest in shame as a "self-conscious" emotion (Tangney & Fischer, 1995), alongside emotions such as humiliation, shyness, embarrassment, guilt, regret, and remorse. These emotions are regarded as "social" in the sense that they involve a negative evaluation of the self (or the prospect of such evaluation) by other people.

These approaches to shyness owe much to Silvan Tomkins's theory of emotion, which does not distinguish shyness, shame, and guilt from each other at the level of affect. Among the characteristics that they share, according to Tomkins, is a distinctive pattern of responses that includes a reduction in facial communication, with gaze aversion and lowering of the head (and hiding the face with the hands, particularly in childhood). It also includes blushing, which Tomkins characterizes as a response to heightened self-consciousness. Tomkins regards novel situations, particularly encounters with strangers, as a cause of shame, and, like Kagan, he draws on studies of animals, as well as human infants, to support this view. His description of the variability of infants' reactions to strangers is similar to that provided by Kagan:

> In human infants . . . there is no shyness until the infant can learn to distinguish the mother's face from the face of the stranger at which point he first begins not to smile, to look away and sometimes to cry and even to fall asleep. These reactions to the stranger by the infant are first of all reactions of not smiling. Infants appear to vary in what else they do when confronted with the stranger for the first time. Some infants cry, some turn their eyes away, some stare with intense interest at the unfamiliar face, some appear to freeze in fear. (Tomkins, 1963, p. 122)

Although the two theories are similar in their accounts of reactions to the stranger and in the age at which these reactions can be observed (i.e., in infancy), they differ in their accounts of the source of these reactions. For Kagan, inhibition is a reaction specifically to the unfamiliar, and this can include unfamiliar objects and environments and familiar people in strange contexts, as well as strangers. According to Tomkins, shame is produced by anything that inhibits interest and enjoyment; therefore, it can only be activated when interest and enjoyment are already being experienced. In the case of strangers, shame affect is activated when the excitement of exploration meets a "barrier [perhaps] because one is looked at by one who is strange, or because one wishes to look at or commune with another person but suddenly cannot because he is strange, or one expected him to be familiar but he suddenly appears unfamiliar, or one started to smile but found one was smiling at a stranger" (Tomkins, 1963, p. 123).

Of course, neither inhibition nor shame affect in itself constitutes shyness as it is understood by current psychological research, in which the term refers to a complex pattern of reactions to social situations. For example, the Stanford Shyness Survey (Zimbardo, Pilkonis, & Norwood, 1974) elicited personal accounts of the nature of shyness. Respondents to the survey reported cognitions, such as self-consciousness and apprehension about being negatively evaluated by others; behaviors, including quietness and tendencies to withdraw from social interaction; and physiological reactions, including increased heart rate, perspiration, and blushing. Although novel situations, including contact with strangers, were reported as an important source of shyness, so too were situations in which the individual is being evaluated or anticipates being evaluated: A student interacting with a professor or a subordinate worker with his or her manager may well experience shyness even though that person is familiar. These self-report data are supported by experimental evidence obtained by Asendorpf (1989) that showed that shyness is elicited by the anticipation of social evaluation, as well as by the unfamiliarity of the person with whom one expects to interact.

In similar fashion, shame is a complex pattern of cognitions, behaviors, and physiological reactions. It involves a dual role for the self: The self both evaluates and is the object of evaluation (Tangney, Miller, Flicker, & Barlow, 1996). Furthermore, the experience of shame requires that the person take another perspective on the self and evaluate his or her behavior as if through the eyes of another (Taylor, 1985). Such accounts are related to notions that shame is a loss of standing or loss of face; thus shame is linked to reputation, honor, and dignity.

These complexities raise many questions about the relationships among inhibition, shame affect, and shyness. Research has yet to establish the links between inhibition to the unfamiliar on the one hand and self-consciousness and concerns about being negatively evaluated by others on the other hand. There are also conceptual problems. As Asendorpf pointed out:

> Whereas inhibition toward strangers can be accounted for by a static temperamental trait, social-evaluative concerns are due to the nature of the social relationships that emerge in stable social settings. Because a relationship between two children cannot be reduced to the temperamental trait of one of them, children's inhibited behavior with *familiar* people cannot be fully accounted for by a temperamental trait (emphasis in original). (1993, p. 266)

There are methodological and empirical problems, too. Although the account of the origins of shame affect can be applied to the analysis of shyness-eliciting situations, this tends to be post hoc interpretation; there seems no clear way of identifying in advance either the sources of enjoyment or the barriers in the relevant social situations, for example, when the individual faces the prospect of evaluation.

Nevertheless, Tomkins's theory does draw attention to important (and neglected) aspects of shyness. First, there is at the core of his account a conflict between the positive and negative aspects of social interaction; such a conflict is included in several different theoretical accounts of shyness (e.g., Cheek & Briggs, 1990; Lewinsky, 1941; Schlenker & Leary, 1982). It serves to distinguish between shyness and such related constructs as introversion or lack of sociability (Cheek & Buss, 1981; Eysenck & Eysenck, 1969).

Second, the theory includes blushing as a characteristic reaction in shyness. The role of blushing is controversial in psychological accounts of shyness. For example, Buss (1980) argued that blushing was associated with embarrassment, not shyness. However, there is less controversy in lay perspectives: A substantial proportion of respondents to the Stanford survey reported that blushing was an element in their shyness. Tomkins's theory, as well as accounts of the "self-conscious emotions" more generally, regards self-consciousness and blushing as closely associated. This, too, accords with empirical evidence; for example, 85 percent of Stanford survey respondents alluded to self-consciousness in shyness. Blushing is a little-understood element of shyness. It is also problematic in research into embarrassment, and there is currently disagreement as to whether blushing is a central element in embarrassment, whether blushing occurs without embarrassment, whether blushing is an element in shame, and whether blushing can help to distinguish embarrassment from shame (Keltner & Buswell, 1997).

The relevance of blushing to this chapter is that it appears to be a reaction to social difficulties that is associated with self-consciousness but is *not* associated with heightened arousal mediated by the sympathetic nervous system. Blushing tends to be associated with reduction in heart rate in embarrassing situations; as Keltner and Buswell (1997, p. 257) point out in a review of empirical studies of physiological reactions to embarrassing situations , "In this study [Buck and Parke, 1972] and in subsequent research . . . embarrassment was associated with reduced heart rate, which may be the product of inhibited sympathetic and increased parasympathetic nervous system activity. . . . The heart rate deceleration of embarrassment is distinct from the elevated heart rate of . . . fear." Nevertheless, blushing is also problematic at the physiological level of explanation, and some research suggests that blushing may be mediated by sympathetic activity. Drummond (1989) reported that blushing in an embarrassing situation could be detected in the unaffected region but not in the damaged region of the faces of individuals who had a lesion to the sympathetic pathway to the face. Blushing requires further research before its role in shyness can be understood.

## The Dual Nature of Shyness?

Shyness thus embraces apprehension about being evaluated, as well as responses to novel situations. Its characteristic responses include not only wariness and avoidance but also self-consciousness and, perhaps, blushing. Comprehensive accounts of shyness will have to deal with all these aspects. One approach to accommodating all these elements is to suggest that shyness is not a unitary experience but refers to two distinctive experiences, fear and wariness on the one hand and shame and embarrassment on the other. Assigning a single term to two experiences may reflect "common sense" theories of social difficulties, psychological accounts of social anxiety, or both. Whether or not it is the case that the lay perspective tends to blur distinctions among different emotions, the trend in psychological research is to emphasize the differences among the self-conscious emotions rather than their similarities. For example, recent research into embarrassment suggests that embarrassment and shame may be distinct emotions (Keltner & Buswell, 1997; Miller, 1996). Moreover, Miller (1995) has argued that although shyness and embarrassment do share such components as public self-consciousness, they also differ from each other in important respects. For example, embarrassment is typically regarded as a reaction to a social predicament that has already arisen, whereas shyness is an anticipation of, and possibly a defensive strategy against, such predicaments. Differences are also argued at the trait level. For example, Miller (1995) reported a factor analysis of a set of scales measuring shyness, embarrassability, self-consciousness, self-esteem, and fear of negative evaluation, among others. Shyness and embarrassability had significant loadings on separate, uncorrelated factors: Shyness was represented, along with low social self-esteem, on a factor that was interpreted by Miller as low social self-confidence; embarrassability shared a common factor with fear of negative evaluation and social sensitivity, a factor interpreted as concern with social evaluation.

A second approach is to suggest a duality within shyness—either that it is a "common final pathway of two different kinds of inhibitory processes" (Asendorpf, 1993, p. 266) or that there are two forms of shyness, one related to fear and one related to self-consciousness (Buss, 1984, 1986).

Asendorpf argued, and provided empirical support, for the proposition that shyness can be triggered by two different kinds of social situations: those involving the individual interacting with strangers and those which have the potential for evaluation of the individual by others. His theory also included a developmental aspect. He argued that the self in early childhood is not sufficiently developed to support the kinds of thinking about the self or perspective-taking ability that is characteristic of self-consciousness:

> Young children below the age of four years seem incapable of the complex
> cognitive processes for two different kinds of inhibitory processes involved
> in Schlenker and Leary's (1982) approach to self-presentational behavior.
> The ability to take others' perspective and, more generally, to represent the
> relation between two people's views, emerges between the ages of 4–6
> years . . . and it is rather likely that looking at oneself from the perspective
> of others is an even more complex cognitive task that perhaps emerges
> even later. (Asendorpf, 1989, p. 483)

Buss (1984) adopted a stance that opposes the unitary nature of shyness advocated by Asendorpf. Buss proposed two distinct types, fearful shyness and self-conscious shyness. He distinguished between these in terms of immediate causes and affective reaction. Fearful shyness is elicited by novelty and intrusion into a social situation; self-conscious shyness is produced by formal situations and breaches of privacy and is also a result of being scrutinized and being uniquely different. The predominant affective components of the two types are, obviously, fear and self-consciousness. This theory also has a developmental aspect, related to the cognitive demands of self-consciousness. Fearful shyness emerges early in life and is associated with inhibition in new situations, including contact with strangers. This form does not require self-awareness of any degree of complexity, but the later-appearing self-conscious form is associated with heightened awareness of the self as a social object and the capacity to adopt a detached-observer perspective toward the self.

## Research into Fearful and Self-Conscious Shyness

### Identification of the Two Forms

Buss's thesis has attracted a small amount of empirical research. Bruch, Giordano, and Pearl (1986) classified young adults into the two types according to their profile of scores on measures of shyness, fearfulness, and public self-consciousness. Following a proposal made by Buss (1986, p. 45), fearful shyness was defined as shyness accompanied by scores 1 standard deviation above the mean fearfulness score and 1 standard deviation below the mean self-consciousness score. Conversely, self-conscious shyness was defined in terms of shyness accompanied by scores 1 standard deviation above the mean self-consciousness score and 1 standard deviation below the mean fearfulness score. There were some significant differences between the two groups thus formed; specifically, there was support (at least from respondents' retrospective reports on the onset of shyness) for the hypothesis that fearful shyness had an earlier onset than self-conscious shyness. Schmidt and Robinson (1992) adopted a similar approach to the classification of the two forms of shyness. They found that fearful shy participants had lower self-esteem than self-conscious shy participants and interpreted this trend to mean that the more enduring fear of negative evaluation of fearful shy individuals restricted their opportunities to develop social skills and self-efficacy. This interpretation finds support in the study by Bruch et al. (1986), who found that fearful shy participants obtained significantly lower scores than nonshy participants on a test of responses to hypothetical problematic social situations (the self-conscious group was not different from the nonshy group).

Despite the differences that have been demonstrated by operationalizing the two forms of shyness in this way, further research is hampered by the absence of reliable measures of the two forms. Indeed, one of the arguments against there being two forms is that studies of shyness questionnaires consistently find substantial correlations between existing measures (Briggs, 1988; Briggs & Smith, 1986). This argument is reinforced by the presence of a common factor that underlies shyness items drawn from different scales and by the absence of separate factors related to fearfulness and self-consciousness (Briggs & Smith, 1986). A further problem is that findings may be influenced by the contribution of self-consciousness scores to the identification of participants. For example, self-consciousness tends to have lower correlations with self-esteem than does shyness (Bruch, Hamer, & Heimberg, 1995), and this has to be kept in mind when interpreting self-esteem differences between fearful and self-conscious shy subjects.

## The Developmental Hypothesis

Little research has tested the hypotheses that fearful shyness is developmentally prior to the self-conscious type and that the emergence of the latter type is related to cognitive development, particularly development of the self-concept. One approach has been to examine age differences in children's conceptions of shyness. Crozier and Burnham (1990) interviewed 60 children aged from 5 to 11 years about shyness (as well as other experiences such as happiness and sadness). Their answers to questions were assigned to one of five categories drawn up on the basis of Buss's conceptualization of the two forms of shyness. Three categories reflected fearful shyness: (1) novel situations; (2) strangers; (3) fearful reactions. Two categories reflected self-conscious shyness: (1) feeling embarrassed (feeling foolish, turning red, being embarrassed); (2) being observed or conspicuous (speaking in front of a class or group).

Application of the content analysis to the interview protocols found support for age trends in children's conceptualizations of shyness. Responses by the youngest children were dominated by fearful shyness, and there was little mention of self-conscious shyness. The latter type increased across the age groups (see figure 2.1). However, this type did not replace the fearful type, and novel situations and meet-

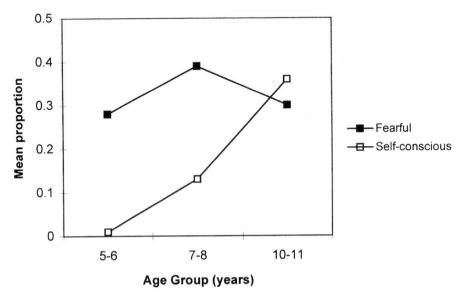

Figure 2.1. Age and mean proportion of responses in fearful and self-conscious categories.

ing new people remained sources of shyness for the 10- to 11-year-old children; this age group also associated shyness with feeling embarrassed and conspicuous.

The self-conscious type of shyness seemed to emerge at about 7 to 8 years. However, subsequent research by Yuill and Banerjee (1997) suggested that this estimate is too high, arguing that the interview task was too demanding for the youngest children. Their findings suggested an onset of self-conscious shyness between 4 and 6 years, in line with Buss's theory. They related this onset to the development of children's ability to understand emotional display rules involving others' evaluations of the self rather than to perspective-taking ability, as suggested by Crozier and Burnham (1990). Their study reinforces the utility of adopting these two categories of shyness and seems to confirm that fearful shyness is developmentally prior to the self-conscious type in children's conceptions of shyness.

Crozier (1995) reported a further attempt to investigate children's conceptions of fearful and self-conscious shyness. The task here was simpler. Children aged between 8 and 11 years were provided with a target word or phrase and were asked to write down the first things that came into their minds. The responses to "being shy" were entered into a database and sorted into alphabetical order, and the frequencies of words and phrases were tabulated. The most common responses, defined as those mentioned by 10 or more children, were as follows: scared (38 mentions), hide/hiding (34), cry/crying (24), new situations (people/class/school; 22), quiet (21), go red (19), frightened (19), sad (19), not talking/not speaking (17), unhappy/not happy (17), shy (16), blush/blushing (15), run away (14), nervous (13), embarrassed (11), smile (10). Responses were coded into fearful and self-conscious shyness categories using a coding schedule based on the words identified by Buss (1986) as descriptive of the two types of shyness.

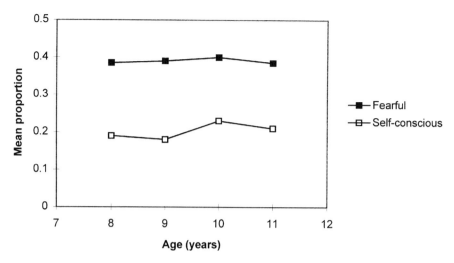

Figure 2.2. Age and mean proportion of fearful and self-conscious responses. (Crozier, 1995)

In order to test for age and gender differences in the use of words from the fearful and self-conscious categories, the proportions of fearful-category words to total words and of self-conscious-category words to total words were computed for each child. The mean proportion of "fearful" words (0.39) was found to be significantly higher than the mean proportion of "self-conscious" words (0.20). However, none of the remaining main effects or interaction terms was significant, showing that the target phrase referring to shyness elicited more responses of the fearful shyness type across all four age groups involved in the study (see figure 2.2).

Research has scarcely begun to investigate age changes in the nature of shyness. The study of children's conceptions of shyness does provide some support for the earlier emergence of fearful shyness. This research also suggests that there is no fading of the fearful form or displacement by self-conscious concerns. However, it is desirable to have other forms of empirical evidence, particularly about individual differences in the two forms—for example, through observational studies or the experimental manipulation of theoretically relevant variables. This development is hindered by difficulties in operationalizing the two forms of shyness.

A second issue concerns the reasons for the onset of self-conscious shyness. Although a certain level of maturity in processing information about the self might be a necessary condition for this form of shyness, it is not clear that it is a sufficient condition. If there are individual differences in self-conscious shyness, what predisposes individuals toward this? Is early inhibition a factor? Perhaps early inhibition predisposes individuals toward sensitivity to the opinions of others. The fears that are aroused by the strange come to be elicited by the prospect of being negatively evaluated by others. Perhaps inhibition leads to the development of strategies and styles of social behavior that also facilitate the emergence of the self-conscious form. Alternatively, the elaboration of the self-concept, in combination with those within-family and other experiences that influence self-esteem, might provide new recruits to the ranks of the shy. These new recruits would be missed by longitudinal studies that begin with samples of inhibited or fearfully shy infants. Little research has addressed these questions. We also have little knowledge of the role that the two forms of shyness play in adult conceptions. We next report findings from a study that applied the methodology of our studies of children's conceptions to the content analysis of material from interviews with a sample of adults.

## Fearful and Self-Conscious Shyness in Adults' Accounts of Shyness

This study is based on extended interviews with 21 adults, median age 40 years, age range 24–59 years, predominantly women and all studying at a British university. They were not selected for shyness but were interviewed with the primary goal of understanding the role, if any, that shyness had played in their adjustment, as mature adults, to student life. The interviews were tape-recorded and transcribed, and responses to specific questions were subjected to content analysis.

The first stage in the analysis was to identify all mentions of situations that elicited shyness and to categorize these in terms of the causes of fearful and self-conscious forms of shyness. These causes were identified on the basis of the account provided by Buss (1986). Fearful shyness is, in general, caused by new situations, intrusions into situations, being evaluated by others, and speaking in front of others. New situations were categorized into three groups: (1) novel situations, such as going to college for the first time; (2) meeting a single new person, such as going on a first date; and (3) meeting more than one new person, for example, interacting with strangers, going to an informal social gathering, or joining a new class. Speaking in front of others was divided into two categories: (1) making a presentation, as in public speaking or giving a paper in class; and (2) speaking in front of others, for example, expressing a point at a meeting. A further category dealt with being evaluated by others. There were no instances that fit the social intrusion category among the protocols.

Self-conscious shyness is caused by being looked at by others or being the focus of attention; being different from others; interacting with an authority figure or someone of different status; attending formal occasions; and being concerned with what other people think of oneself. These situations formed five categories for self-conscious shyness. A final category was formed for situations that did not fit into either category of fearful or self-conscious shyness.

Table 2.1 summarizes the frequencies of the various categories in these protocols. Eighty-eight situations could be classified as fearful and 48 as self-conscious. This tendency for there to be more fearful than self-conscious references was statistically reliable (fearful mean = 4.24, self-conscious mean = 2.24, $t = 4.90$, $df = 20$, $p < 0.01$). The single largest category related to meeting people for the first time and interacting with strangers; this accounts for more than one in four of all shyness-eliciting situations, and at least one instance of this category was mentioned by 16 out of the 21 respondents. There was a range of contexts for these social encounters: meeting people for the first time, meeting co-workers or friends of a spouse, conversing with people one doesn't know, introducing oneself to other parents at a child's school, joining a new class, going into a bar, or joining a group who are seated together in a restaurant.

Table 2.1  Analysis of interview protocols: Frequencies of situations coded into ·
fearful and self-conscious shy categories.

| Category | Frequency of mentions |
|---|---|
| Fearful | |
| New situations | 12 |
| Meeting one person for the first time | 10 |
| Meeting more than one person for the first time, strangers | 39 |
| Giving a public speech | 10 |
| Speaking up in front of a group | 14 |
| Being evaluated on appearance | 3 |
| Fearful Total | 88 |
| Self-Conscious | |
| Being looked at, being conspicuous, being object of attention | 15 |
| Concern with what others think | 1 |
| Interacting with authority figure or person of different status | 15 |
| Being aware of being different from others | 13 |
| Attending a formal occasion | 4 |
| Self-Conscious Total | 48 |
| Other | 8 |

Speaking in front of others accounts for 27 percent of fearful shy situations. Among this sample of student participants, presenting a paper to a group of other students was the most feared situation: for example, one man, aged 28, said: "seminar groups which are some of the most horrific social things you'll ever come across . . . terrified before and relieved afterwards but probably visibly shaking you know you can hear it in your own voice as you are delivering the thing and that doesn't help at all." Speaking up in front of others was not, however, restricted to public speaking and included answering questions in class and expressing a point of view at meetings.

The most common causes of self-conscious shyness were being looked at or being the focus of attention (arriving late at a lecture or crossing a room where others are seated); interacting with an authority figure (professor or boss) or a high-status person (e.g., someone with a "posh" accent); being aware that one is different from other people (e.g., feeling an outsider, being from a different social background, feeling older or less qualified than other students).

Finally, a small number of situations could not easily be categorized. These included attending an interview (without further elaboration), being assertive (returning an item of clothing to a department store), and using the telephone.

In the second stage of the analysis, the protocols were searched for words and short phrases that described responses to these situations. The categories were based on theoretical grounds, drawing on the characteristic responses of fearful and self-conscious shyness according to Buss (1986) and also reflecting common shyness responses as identified in previous shyness research (e.g., Zimbardo et al., 1974). The set of categories is listed in table 2.2, along with the frequencies of instances in each category for the two kinds of eliciting situations. The meanings of

Table 2.2 Interview protocols: Percentages of coded response categories in fearful and self-conscious shy situations.

| Response category | Fearful situation | Self-conscious situation |
|---|---|---|
| Shy | 18 | 17 |
| Inhibited | 18 | 2 |
| Tongue-tied | 9 | 9 |
| Quiet | 3 | 0 |
| Gabble | 0 | 3 |
| Averting gaze | 0 | 0 |
| Hiding | 0 | 3 |
| Anxious | 12 | 12 |
| Physiological symptoms | 7 | 0 |
| Fearing negative evaluation | 11 | 8 |
| Feeling awkward | 3 | 0 |
| Embarrassed | 0 | 5 |
| Blushing | 0 | 5 |
| Self-conscious | 10 | 14 |
| Feeling small or humiliated | 0 | 9 |
| Other | 5 | 9 |
| Number of coded phrases | 154 | 87 |

some categories require further elaboration. *Tongue-tied* refers to a group of responses in which articulation is impeded ("tongue-tied," "dry up," "mind goes blank," "can't think what to say"). *Inhibition* refers to feeling inhibited, fearful of saying the wrong thing, keeping in the background. *Gabbling* refers to gabbling, babbling, talking "rubbish." *Anxious* includes terms such as anxious, nervous, apprehensive, terrified, unnerved. *Physiological* responses include sympathetic nervous system reactions such as perspiring, sweating, or feeling a "knot in the stomach."

The aim of this analysis was to establish whether the two kinds of situations elicit different patterns of responses. Visual inspection of table 2.2 suggests both similarities and differences. The most conspicuous differences concern *inhibition,* which accounts for a substantial proportion of responses to fearful shy situations but is scarcely represented in self-conscious situations. We considered the possibility that inhibited responses only relate to specific fearful categories, for example, meeting groups or public speaking. However, further analysis of these responses showed that they are distributed across all the fearful shy categories in similar proportions (chi-square = 2.53, $df$ = 4, $p$ = 0.64). The next conspicuous difference concerns the categories *feeling small or humiliated, embarrassed,* and *blushing,* which, in line with Buss's predictions, are almost absent in fearful shy situations but more prevalent in self-conscious shy situations. A less conspicuous difference that is also compatible with the theory involves the category *self-conscious.* Other categories show considerable similarities between the two kinds of situations. The question posed to participants concerned situations in which they felt shy, and hence shyness was implicit in all their answers; nevertheless, a considerable number mentioned shyness explicitly, and the proportions are similar across the two types of situations.

Frequencies of references to anxiety are also similar across situations, although physiological reactions are mentioned in 6.5 percent of responses to fearful shy situations yet are absent in self-conscious situations.

In order to test for differences in the frequency of fearful and self-conscious reactions to the two kinds of situations, it was necessary to group categories because of the small number of responses in particular categories. Following Buss's characterization of the two forms of shyness, a fearful shyness response category was constructed from the *anxious, inhibited,* and *physiological symptoms* categories and a self-conscious category from the *blushing, embarrassed, self-conscious,* and *feeling small* categories. For each individual respondent, the numbers of fearful and self-conscious responses were computed for fearful and self-conscious situations. Significantly more fearful responses than self-conscious responses were elicited by fearful situations (sign test [one-tailed]; $p < 0.002$). Conversely, significantly more self-conscious than fearful responses were elicited by self-conscious situations (sign test [one-tailed]; $p < 0.046$).

A further possibility remains to be tested. It might be that either fearful responses or self-conscious responses are elicited by any particular situation; that is, there are two distinct response patterns. Alternatively, situations might elicit a mixture of fearful and self-conscious responses. Accordingly, we considered each fearful response to a situation as to whether (1) it appeared on its own; (2) it appeared only with another fearful response; (3) it appeared with at least one other fearful response and at least one self-conscious response; (4) it appeared with at least one self-conscious response; or (5) it appeared with a response other than these. Where there was more than one response in a category, the analysis was based on the first one that occurred in the sentence (that is, we did not double-count responses). A parallel analysis was undertaken for self-conscious responses. The results of these analyses are presented in table 2.3.

It does not seem to be the case that each form of shyness is expressed only on its own or only with another member of the same category. This pattern is found in approximately one in three responses, but for a substantial proportion of responses, any situation elicits a mixture of fearful and self-conscious reactions.

In conclusion, content analysis of the interview protocols of this sample of adults finds support for Buss's distinction between fearful and self-conscious forms of shyness. The situations that elicit shyness can be reliably categorized into these two forms. As was found in children's notions of shyness (Crozier, 1995), the fearful form is more common and is referred to in more accounts of the situations that produce shyness. There is evidence, too, that the two classes of situations elicit different patterns of responses. An index of fearful shyness, composed of mentions of inhibition, anxiety and nervousness, and physiological reactions, appears more frequently in the context of novel situations and speaking in front of others. Self-consciousness, embarrassment, blushing, and feeling small or humiliated are more frequent responses to being conspicuous and different and to interacting with authority figures.

Nevertheless, we must be careful not to exaggerate these differences. The two forms of shy reactions are not distinct reaction patterns, and any situation is likely to attract a mixture of the two kinds of reactions. Specifically, fearful situations do elicit self-conscious reactions, and self-conscious situations do elicit fearful reactions.

Table 2.3 Interview protocols: Co-occurrences of fearful and self-conscious responses.

| Fearful response co-occurs with | Percentage of fearful responses | Self-conscious response co-occurs with | Percentage of self-conscious responses |
|---|---|---|---|
| No other response | 19 | No other response | 22 |
| Only another fearful response | 19 | Only another self-conscious response | 8 |
| A fearful response and a self-conscious response | 6 | A self-conscious response and fearful response | 0 |
| A self-conscious response | 21 | A fearful response | 42 |
| Another kind of response | 34 | Another kind of response | 28 |

That references to the self-conscious form are to a form of shyness and are not evidence for a separate emotion, such as embarrassment, is supported by this mixture of reactions and also by the finding that explicit references to shyness are common in both kinds of situations. Further support is obtained from consideration of research that adopts a related approach—the study of prototypical elements of embarrassment and of people's accounts of the causes and consequences of embarrassment (e.g., Miller & Tangney, 1994; Parrott & Smith, 1991; Stonehouse & Miller, 1994, cited in Miller, 1996). In these studies, participants reported that embarrassment is elicited by specific social predicaments. Smiling is a characteristic reaction, and humor both as a reaction and as a means of escaping the predicament is conspicuous. These elements are absent in our protocols. Blushing is central to accounts of "typical" and actual embarrassment (Parrott & Smith, 1991), whereas it is rarely mentioned in the accounts of shyness in this study.

Our respondents do not talk about actual predicaments, but implicit in their accounts is concern about what might happen. Meeting new people or familiar people in novel circumstances, speaking in front of others, acting in front of others, being with authority figures, all carry risks of creating predicaments and giving rise to negative evaluation of the self by others. Nervousness about seminars was a common theme, but no one talked of any seminars that had actually produced the outcomes that they feared. It is this uncertainty that perhaps distinguishes shyness from embarrassment and that can serve to unify the two forms of shyness. As Asendorpf (1989) suggests, there are two routes to this uncertainty. Our research suggests that this uncertainty has a different flavor in the two routes.

## Conclusions and Implications for Future Research

Research into shyness has shown that it is a complex experience that is elicited by a range of social situations. It is not simply the province of shy individuals, and most people have personal experience of being shy. Theoretical approaches have consistently related shyness to fear and anxiety. Nevertheless, some theoretical approaches and a small amount of research have argued for the link between shyness and self-consciousness, conceptualizing it as closer to embarrassment and shame than to fear. We have drawn on studies of children's and adults' conceptions of shyness to suggest that there is some support for a distinction between two forms of shyness, fearful and self-conscious. Our studies also suggest that it is misleading to make too strong claims for the distinction, and the picture of self-conscious shyness that emerges is still very different from pictures of embarrassment (and of shame—see Parrott & Smith, 1991) that have emerged in other research.

The notion of self-conscious shyness is worthy of further research, drawing on a wider range of methods than has been discussed here. Such research will enhance our understanding of the complex experience of shyness. It will also contribute to the development of approaches to helping people overcome their shyness. At present, shyness interventions tend to be broad-based and to draw on a wide range of techniques, often within a single program, that are directed at cognitive, affective, and behavioral components of shyness. For example, the program developed in the Netherlands by van der Molen (1990) includes sessions devoted to clients' understanding of shyness, changes in cognitions, relaxation training, social skills training, and assertiveness training. The Shyness Clinic program training (Henderson & Zimbardo, 1998) also incorporates thought restructuring, exposure to feared stimuli, flooding, social skills training, and assertiveness. It is possible that more focused subsets of these techniques could be targeted at individuals with distinct profiles of shyness, resulting in more efficient programs. The distinction between fearful and self-conscious shyness offers a promising approach to developing such profiles.

The proposal that a focus on self-conscious shyness, in particular, is a promising line of research is reinforced by recent developments that emphasize shame-related cognitions in social anxiety (Henderson & Zimbardo, 1998; Lutwak & Ferrari, 1997). Henderson and Zimbardo summarize research that shows that shy individuals are higher in both state-shame and trait-shame and that they have patterns of self-blame and biased attributions for their social performance that are also identified in research into shame. Shyness, a self-blaming attribution style, and private self-consciousness are all correlated with measures of social anxiety. Lutwak and Ferrari (1997) report that shame-proneness is correlated with measures of social avoidance and distress, interaction anxiety, and fear of negative social evaluation.

The distinction between fearful and self-conscious shyness is also relevant to debates about the relationship between self-focused attention and social anxiety—for example, whether it is self-focus, in conjunction with self-doubts and low self-efficacy, that produces anxiety or whether worry-like cognitions and self-generated negative self-referent thinking are forms that anxiety takes in social situations. Interventions planned to change self-focused attention are associated with changes in the social functioning of shy and socially anxious individuals (Alden & Cappe, 1986; Woody, Chambless, & Glass, 1997). However, research has not considered whether individual differences in shyness are associated with different responses to these kinds of interventions. Research into the distinction between these forms of shyness and, in particular, into self-conscious shyness and its relationship to shame promises to contribute to our understanding of shyness and to efforts to help shy individuals overcome their social difficulties.

*Acknowledgments*   I am very grateful to Maria Burnham and Alison Garbert-Jones for their help with the empirical studies reported in this chapter.

## References

Alden, L. E., & Cappe, R. (1986). Interpersonal process training for shy clients. In W. H. Jones, J. M. Cheek, & S. R. Briggs (Eds.), *Shyness: Perspectives on research and treatment* (pp. 343–355). New York: Plenum Press.

Asendorpf, J. (1989). Shyness as a final common pathway for two different kinds of inhibition. *Journal of Personality and Social Psychology, 57,* 481–492.

Asendorpf, J. (1993). Beyond temperament: A two-factorial coping model of the development of inhibition during childhood. In K. H. Rubin & J. Asendorpf (Eds.), *Social withdrawal, inhibition, and shyness in childhood* (pp. 265–289). Hove, East Sussex, England: Erlbaum.

Briggs, S. R. (1988). Shyness: Introversion or neuroticism? *Journal of Research in Personality, 22,* 290–307.

Briggs, S. R., & Smith, T. G. (1986). The measurement of shyness. In W. H. Jones, J. M. Cheek, & S. R. Briggs (Eds.), *Shyness: Perspectives on research and treatment* (pp. 47–60). New York: Plenum Press.

Bruch, M. A., Giordano, S., & Pearl, L. (1986). Differences between fearful and self-conscious shy subtypes in background and current adjustment. *Journal of Research in Personality, 20,* 172–186.

Bruch, M. A., Hamer, R. J., & Heimberg, R. G. (1995). Shyness and public self-consciousness: Additive or interactive relation with social interaction? *Journal of Personality, 63,* 47–63.

Buck, R. W., & Parke, R. D. (1972). Behavioral and physiological response to the presence of a friendly or neutral person in two types of stressful situations. *Journal of Personality and Social Psychology, 24,* 143–153.

Buss, A. H. (1980). *Self-consciousness and social anxiety.* San Francisco: Freeman.

Buss, A. H. (1984). A conception of shyness. In J. A. Daly & J. C. McCroskey (Eds.), *Avoiding communication: Shyness, reticence and communication apprehension* (pp. 39–49). London: Sage.

Buss, A. H. (1986). A theory of shyness. In W. H. Jones, J. M. Cheek, & S. R. Briggs (Eds.), *Shyness: Perspectives on research and treatment* (pp. 39–46). New York: Plenum Press.

Cheek, J. M. , & Briggs, S. R. (1990). Shyness as a personality trait. In W. R. Crozier (Ed.), *Shyness and embarrassment: Perspectives from social psychology* (pp. 315–337). Cambridge: Cambridge University Press.

Cheek, J. M., & Buss, A. H. (1981). Shyness and sociability. *Journal of Personality and Social Psychology, 41,* 330–339.

Crozier, W. R. (1995). Shyness and self-esteem in middle childhood. *British Journal of Educational Psychology, 65,* 85–95.

Crozier, W. R. & Burnham, M. (1990). Age-related differences in children's understanding of shyness. *British Journal of Developmental Psychology, 8,* 179–185.

Drummond, P. D. (1989). Mechanism of emotional blushing. In N. W. Bond & D. A. T. Siddle (Eds.), *Psychobiology: Issues and applications* (pp. 363–370). Amsterdam: North-Holland.

Eysenck, H. J., & Eysenck, S. B. G. (1969). *Personality structure and measurement.* London: Routledge & Kegan Paul.

Henderson, L., & Zimbardo, P. G. (1998). Shyness. In H. S. Friedman (ed.), *The Encyclopedia of Mental Health, vol. 3* (pp. 497–509). San Diego: Academic Press.

Izard, C. E. (1971). *The face of emotion.* New York: Appleton-Century-Crofts.

Kagan, J. (1994). *Galen's prophecy: Temperament in human nature.* London: Free Association Books.

Keltner, D., & Buswell, B. N. (1997). Embarrassment: Its distinct form and appeasement functions. *Psychological Bulletin, 122,* 250–270.

Lewinsky, H. (1941). The nature of shyness. *British Journal of Psychology, 32,* 105–113.

Lutwak, N., & Ferrari, J. R. (1997). Shame-related social anxiety: Replicating a link with various social interaction measures. *Anxiety and Coping, 10,* 335–340.

Miller, R. S. (1995). On the nature of embarrassability: Shyness, social-evaluation, and social skill. *Journal of Personality, 63,* 315–339.

Miller, R. S. (1996). *Embarrassment: Poise and peril in everyday life.* New York: Guilford Press.

Miller, R. S., & Tangney, J. P. (1994). Differentiating embarrassment and shame. *Journal of Social and Clinical Psychology, 13,* 273–287.

Parrott, W. G., & Smith, S. F. (1991). Embarrassment: Actual vs. typical cases, classical vs. prototypical representations. *Cognition and Emotion, 5,* 467–488.

Schlenker, B. R., & Leary, M. (1982). Social anxiety and self-presentation: A conceptualization and a model. *Psychological Bulletin, 92,* 641–669.

Schmidt, L. A., & Robinson, T. N., Jr. (1992). Low self-esteem in differentiating fearful and self-conscious forms of shyness. *Psychological Reports, 70,* 255–257.

Tangney, J. P., & Fischer, K. W. (1995). *Self-conscious emotions: The psychology of shame, guilt, embarrassment, and pride.* New York: Guilford Press.

Tangney, J. P., Miller, R. S., Flicker, L., & Barlow, D. H. (1996). Are shame, guilt, and embarrassment distinct emotions? *Journal of Personality and Social Psychology, 70,* 1256–1264.

Taylor, G. (1985). *Pride, shame and guilt: Emotions of self-assessment.* Oxford: Clarendon Press.

Tomkins, S. S. (1963). *Affect, imagery, consciousness: Vol. 2. The negative affects.* New York: Springer.

van der Molen, H. T. (1990). A definition of shyness and its implications for clinical practice. In W. R. Crozier (Ed.), *Shyness and embarrassment: Perspectives from social psychology* (pp. 255–285). Cambridge: Cambridge University Press.

Woody, S. R., Chambless, D. L., & Glass, C. R. (1997). Self-focused attention in the treatment of social phobia. *Behaviour Research and Therapy, 35,* 117–129.

Yuill, N., & Banerjee, R. (1997, July). *Fear or self-consciousness? Children's developing conceptions of shyness.* Paper presented at the International Conference on Shyness and Self-Consciousness, Cardiff, Wales.

Zimbardo, P. G., Pilkonis, P. A., & Norwood, R. M. (1974). The silent prison of shyness. *Office of Naval Research Technical Report Z-17,* Stanford University.

# 3

## Attachment, Temperament, and Adrenocortical Function in Infancy

Kathy Stansbury

Bowlby (1969, 1973, 1979) defined attachment between infants and mothers as a warm, biologically motivated, selective bond, manifested in behavior by the infant such as maintaining physical contact and seeking proximity to the attachment figure (see figure 3.1), as well as in protest at separation from the attachment figure. He suggested that the predisposition to become attached is a survival mechanism. Behaviors indicative of attachment can be seen in most mammals but appear to be most highly specialized in primates. This may be a part of the success of our own primate species throughout evolution. Bowlby's belief in the biological pull of attachment and his elegantly expressed thoughts on attachment, separation, and loss have seduced many developmentalists into careers studying the "what," "how," and "when" of these relationships. Indeed, the idea that our studies of the first 3 years of life may show us the course of a child's future interactions is a mesmerizing one.

Although Bowlby's theory of attachment is clearly one of biobehavioral organization, based on evolutionary, ethological, and Freudian theory, research with humans that attempts to validate his model of attachment, separation, and loss has consisted primarily of efforts to measure behavioral rather than biological phenomena. The contributions of Ainsworth (Ainsworth, 1969; Ainsworth, Blehar, Waters, & Wall, 1978) and her students (e.g., Main & Goldwyn, 1984; Main, Tomasini, & Tolan, 1979; Main & Weston, 1981; Sroufe & Waters, 1977) to research on attachment relationships over the past 40 years have been dominated by efforts to empirically validate Bowlby's model through behavioral indices of attachment, and these efforts have been largely successful (e.g., De Wolff & van Ijzendoorn, 1997; Erickson, Sroufe, & Egeland, 1985). We now know a great deal about the "what," "how," and "when" of attachment in terms of individual differences in overt behaviors on the part of both the primary caregiver and the child. For example, we know that sensitive, responsive care by a primary caregiver in the 1st year of life leads to secure attachments and that rejecting or inconsistent care leads to avoidant or resistant attachments.[1] We can see this in organized patterns of overt behavior that present themselves when the attachment system is challenged by a stranger or a separation. And we know that attachment patterns in infancy are associated with personality characteristics in the toddler, preschool, and school-age periods, presumably based on the internal working model described by Bowlby. For example, secure attachment in infancy has been associated with characteristics such as independence, perseverance, and good peer relations in the preschool period and strong gender boundaries in middle childhood, all traits that are considered valuable in Western culture.

Research on nonhuman animals indicates that attachment behaviors performed by both mothers and infants appear to have a regulatory influence on the infants' developing physiology. A rich literature has accumulated regarding the relationship between attachment-type behaviors and physiological responses. One of the most broadly investigated of these physiological systems is the hypothalamic-pituitary-adrenocortical (HPA) system (Goldman, Coover, & Levine, 1973; Levine, Coe, Smotherman & Kaplan, 1978; Mason, 1968; Selye, 1936). The adrenocortical system is a key part of the body's stress-resistance response. Increased cortisol (the primary hormonal product of the HPA system in humans) in the bloodstream allows stored proteins to be released to supply the energy for the body's "flight or fight" response and has effects on the immune system and on learning and memory regarding the challenging context. These effects appear to be adaptive when cortisol is produced in moderate amounts (de Kloet, 1991; Gunnar, Tout, de Haan, Pierce, & Stansbury, 1997; Martinez, Villegas, & McEwen, 1993; McEwen, de Kloet, & Rostene, 1986; Stansbury & Gunnar, 1994; Stansbury & Harris, in press). For example, Gunnar and her colleagues (1997) found that the production of moderate elevations in cortisol during children's first semester in a new preschool environment was associated with bold temperament and higher competence ratings by teachers, indicating that, as Sapolsky and others have suggested, cortisol is not a "fear" or "stress" hormone but might be more accurately described as a "coping" hormone (figure 3.2; Gunnar, 1990; Sapolsky & Meaney, 1986; Stansbury, 1999; Stansbury & Gunnar, 1994).

Studying the adrenocortical system fits our interest in attachment in several ways. First, adrenocortical function is mediated by behaviors that occur in attachment contexts, reflecting the biobehavioral organization within the attachment relationship (Nachmias, Gunnar, Mangelsdorf, Hornik Parritz, & Buss, 1996; Spangler & Grossmann, 1993). Second, some individuals appear to be more physiologically reactive at birth (Higley & Suomi, 1989; Kagan, Reznick, & Snidman, 1988), producing higher adrenocortical responses to novel environments, pacifier withdrawal, inoculations, and other minor stressors early in life (Fox & Calkins, 1993; Gunnar, Hertsgaard, Larson, & Rigatuso, 1991; Lewis & Ramsay, 1995). Those who suggest that temperament provides the basis for individual differences in attachment classifications might find support for their argument in the examination of a physiological system that is already known to vary according to temperament (Higley & Suomi, 1989). Third, as we shall see, temperamental differences in reactivity interact with the development of attachment relationships in organizing developing physiological systems.

Figure 3.1. This securely attached infant exhibits contact maintenance by maximizing ventral–ventral body contact with her primary attachment figure.

## Attachment and Adrenocortical Function

### Research with Nonhuman Animals

Historically, Cannon (1927), Richter (1922, 1927), and others have made large contributions to our basic knowledge of adrenocortical functioning in emotionally stressful situations. Hofer's work on mother-offspring behavior and the cues that regulate a variety of physiological systems in the rat pup (Hofer, 1970, 1973a, 1973b, 1975; Hofer & Shair, 1978) provides the basis for our argument that the attachment relationship in humans serves to regulate biological function in infants. Hofer's studies showed indisputably that the mother-infant interaction, in at least

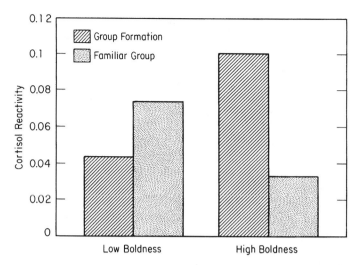

Figure 3.2. Bold, competent children were more likely than inhibited children to show moderate increases in cortisol during the group formation phase of a nursery school class. (Adapted from Gunnar et al., 1997.)

one species, functions as a system of regulation, and he argued persuasively that the behaviors seen in rat pups in response to separation are surprisingly similar to those seen in human infants. Hofer argues that the rat serves as an excellent model for studying what he now refers to as the "hidden regulators" in attachment relationships (Hofer, 1994, p. 192). For example, acute separation of the dam from her pups results in ultrasonic vocalizations, search behavior, and high levels of self-grooming by the pups (Hofer & Shair, 1978). Long-term separations also produce behaviors similar to those described by Bowlby in his essays on human infants and their responses to separation and loss. The hidden regulators embedded in the attachment relationship—the warmth, smell, and tactile stimulation of the pups by the dam—appear to disinhibit the mechanisms that regulate endocrine, autonomic, and behavioral systems. These systems appear well regulated when she is present but will deteriorate after several hours of separation. Studies of adrenocortical function in rats that complement this work were done by Stanton, Gutierrez, and Levine (1988). They reported that separation of young rats from their mothers resulted in increases in corticosterone[2] responses in the pups to a saline injection as well as to a novel environment while separated. In other words, reactivity to environmental stressors was greater when the "hidden regulators" of the mother were absent.

Levine and his colleagues found support for Hofer's ideas in studies of both rhesus and squirrel monkeys. For example, during a brief separation, both infant and mother were likely to show a strong adrenocortical response (Mendoza, Coe, Lowe, & Levine, 1978). Additionally, Levine's group (Coe, Mendoza, Smotherman, & Levine, 1978; Vogt & Levine, 1980) reported that infant squirrel monkeys separated from their mothers showed significant cortisol elevations, whereas others who were removed from their home cage along with their mothers did not. Levine and his colleagues also reported that infant vocalization during separation was positively related to the infant's cortisol response and that, although "aunting" behavior by other female monkeys reduced behavioral agitation in separated infants, "aunting" did not buffer the adrenocortical response; for this, the mother was necessary. Thus, the regulating effects of tactile, temperature, and olfactory cues appear to become specific to the mother or primary caregiver early in life.

In primates and in mammals in general, it appears that the behavioral mechanism that regulates this buffered adrenocortical response is proximity and contact facilitated by both the mother and the infant (Vogt & Levine, 1980). Infant monkeys show increased locomotion and increased vocalizations when conditions in the environment appear to be unstable or when the infant is exposed to some distressing experience. Similar to human infants, infant monkeys show a reduction in object manipulation, activity play, and social play as a result of involuntary separation from mother (Jones & Clark, 1973; Kaplan & Schusterman, 1972). The combination of these findings supports Hofer's view that contact with the mother regulates infant physiological reactivity. The mechanisms through which human mothers regulate physiology in children are likely to be similar to those observed in rats and monkeys: physical contact, perhaps visual or olfactory cues, and intense vocalizations by separated infants to prompt the retrieval.

Most recently, these findings have been replicated at a more molecular level by Meaney and his colleagues (Liu et al., 1997). They studied individual differences in rat dam behavior toward pups during the first 10 days of life. As adults, rats whose mothers had shown what might be termed stronger attachment behaviors (more licking and grooming of pups) showed lower adrenocortical responses to acute stress. These data suggest that rat pups may "internalize" the results of early maternal regulation, encoded as information about how easy or difficult it is to activate stress-sensitive systems in adulthood (see figure 3.3). Attachment behaviors in humans may similarly shape young children's physiological reactions to stress.

### Research with Human Infants

We know more about individual differences in attachment behaviors in children than we do about individual differences in rats and monkeys. Nevertheless, studies of these individual differences in conjunction with measures of adrenocortical functioning in humans are still relatively rare. Because we hypothesize that secure attachments foster better biobehavioral regulation, at first glance, researchers have expected that children with secure attachments should show lower cortisol responses to the Strange Situation than children with insecure attachments. In the four studies in which individual differences in both attachment and cortisol have been assessed, this hypothesis has not been supported (Gunnar, Mangelsdorf, Larson, & Hertsgaard, 1989; Hertsgaard, Gunnar, Erickson, & Nachmias, 1995; Nachmias et al., 1996; Spangler & Grossmann, 1993). These data appear to controvert the initial hypothesis that securely attached children would show lower adrenocortical reactivity, and it is possible that a different initial hypothesis is appropriate. Ainsworth (Ainsworth et al., 1978) and her students (e.g., Main, 1990) suggested that organized patterns of behavior exist in response to separation in all attached children, including those who showed avoidant or resistant attachments. If this is true, should we expect a difference in response to the Strange

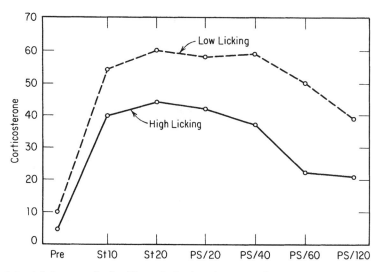

Figure 3.3. Adult rats who had been licked and groomed more as pups show lower levels of adrenocortical reactivity in response to stressors as adults. (Adapted from Liu et al., 1997.)

Situation among those groups that are equally organized, albeit in different ways? Perhaps not. Ainsworth and her colleagues (Ainsworth & Eichberg, 1991) have suggested that infants' use of the avoidant pattern as a defense strategy serves to reduce behavioral arousal. Additionally, Main and her colleagues (Main & Hesse, 1990) suggest that some type of biobehavioral organization, which would be the case for all three traditional attachment classifications (secure, avoidant, resistant), is better than none at all. Avoidant and resistant strategies, while "second best," are still, after all, strategies. On the basis of the limited data that exist so far, we can only conclude that the organized nature of the traditional classification (avoidant, resistant, secure), is enough to buffer a cortisol stress response to the Strange Situation even in insecure infants.

This conclusion is bolstered by results of two of the studies previously mentioned (Nachmias et al., 1996; Spangler & Grossmann, 1993). Those studies indicate that the lack of an organized attachment in human infants (i.e., children coded as having disorganized/disoriented attachments based on Main and Solomon's system; Main & Solomon, 1990) is associated with higher adrenocortical stress responses to the Strange Situation than traditionally attached infants, whether securely or insecurely attached. A complete lack of organized strategies for attachment-related stressors appears to create a significant vulnerability to stress reactivity. From a traditional attachment perspective, establishing contact after separation from mother "is the only adequate behavioral strategy for emotional reorganization" (Hertsgaard et al., 1995, p. 1448).

Furthermore, distress vocalizations in animals are considered normal in response to separation, and the same should be the case for those infants who cry in the Strange Situation. Since crying is likely to be associated with the mobilization of energy and resources in response to a stressor (Sapolsky, 1996), both the secure and insecure babies who cry are likely to show increases in adrenocortical output, obviating the possibility of significant differences between secure and insecure children on measures of cortisol in the Strange Situation. Data from my own laboratory support the notion that crying itself is positively associated with cortisol (see figure 3.4; e.g., Stansbury, Dugle Brainerd, & Goodson, 1998; Stansbury, Sethre-Hofstad, & Abeita, 1999). If some children are prone to becoming insecurely attached or to forming only disorganized attachments, it is likely that they are the children who have difficult-to-manage temperaments—and if we are interested in adrenocortical function, the interaction of inhibited temperaments and attachment, and in the effect of this interaction on adrenocortical activity, temperament must also be considered as an important variable.

## Temperament and Adrenocortical Function

Although Bowlby's theory of the biological drive to become attached is compelling, proponents of temperament theory such as Kagan and his colleagues (Kagan, Reznick, & Snidman, 1987, 1988, 1989) believe that attachment classifications are less important in the development of a child's personality than the constitutional mechanisms involved in temperament. This is a reasonable hypothesis. Although individual differences in attachment behaviors in nonhuman animals have not received much attention, it is probable that, like human children, there are some individuals for whom maternal cues are less effective.

Kagan's hypothesis that shy children are constitutionally more reactive, having a lower threshold for stress system activation than other individuals, has received support from a variety of studies. There appears to be great individual variability in autonomic nervous system and adrenocortical responses to challenging events, and although some events may be challenging enough to trigger an adrenocortical stress response in all individuals, most of the time whether or not an individual responds appears to depend partly on his or her temperament.

## Attachment, Temperament, and Adrenocortical Function

The idea that temperament influences the attachment behavior of mothers is supported by data from human mother-child interactions. For example, we know that human newborns who show high orientation, low irritability, and optimal behavior organization are more likely to be classified as securely attached than other babies (Crockenberg, 1981; Egeland & Farber, 1984; Grossmann, Grossmann, Spangler, Suess, & Unzner, 1985). Additionally, van den Boom (1989) has shown that infants with irritable or difficult temperaments are at greater risk for insecure attachments, but only if maternal attachment behavior (i.e., sensitivity) remains poor throughout the 1st year of life. One explanation for this finding is that individual differences in infant temperament, especially individual differences in thresholds for being soothed by maternal behaviors or cues, make a child more or less likely to show an adrenocortical response to stress after this parent-child interaction has been established. So, for example, by the age of 18 months, an infant who is innately difficult to soothe by typical maternal cues or behaviors, paired with a mother who does a poor job at providing the amount of consistency or persever-

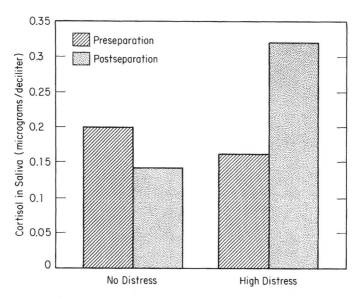

Figure 3.4. Cortisol response of child with lowest score on crying (left); cortisol of child with highest score on crying (right) in response to a 15-minute separation from mother. (Stansbury et al., 1999.)

ance that is needed to deal with such a reactive child, produces a low threshold for adrenocortical reactivity based on the history of these interactions.

At this writing, Nachmias, Gunnar, and their colleagues (Nachmias et al., 1996) have completed the only human study to date that was attempted to test this hypothesis. They studied 73 18-month-olds, examining pre- and post-stress cortisol levels in both the Strange Situation and in a challenging coping episode. They collected maternal reports of temperament and behavioral data on the toddlers' style of coping in the challenging coping episode. Children were classified into the three attachment groups: avoidant, resistant, and secure. The sample was not coded for disorganized/disoriented attachment. In both the Strange Situation and in the challenging coping episode, there was an interaction between attachment security and inhibited temperament (see figure 3.5). Children who were insecure and who had inhibited temperaments had greater cortisol response to both the Strange Situation and coping episode than securely attached toddlers, whether inhibited or not. Further, mothers' behavior in the coping episode was different for inhibited infants who were securely versus insecurely attached. Cortisol elevations in inhibited children were associated with maternal behaviors, including forcing the child into uninhibited coping strategies. It is possible that children who are insecurely attached and inhibited leave room for more attempts by mothers to get them to attend to novel stimuli—possibly intrusively—which resulted in higher cortisol responses. Whatever the specific mechanisms at work here, these data support the notion that our answers are to be found in interactions rather than main effects with respect to attachment, temperament, and adrenocortical functioning. Using recent pilot data from my own laboratory, we attempted to explore these interactions.

We addressed the hypothesis that attachment and temperament interact to produce the level of adrenocortical activity in a study similar to that of Nachmias et al. (1996). Our children ($n = 32$) ranged in age from 12 to 18 months. Mother-infant pairs participated in the traditional Strange Situation, and infants were classified in the three traditional groups by a trained attachment coder. Disorganized attachment coding was not done on this data set. Primary caregivers completed Goldsmith's Toddler Behavior Assessment Questionnaire (TBAQ; Goldsmith, 1987). Subscales that represented fear, anger, activity level, and sadness were used to index children's difficult temperament. Cortisol was measured in saliva.

Based on the brief review of the literature presented above, we predicted four results: (1) attachment behaviors such as contact-maintaining and proximity-seeking would be positively correlated with cortisol responses to the Strange Situation; (2) cortisol responses would be higher in children who cried than in those who did not; (3) attachment classification would be unrelated to cortisol response; and (4) negative temperament would not be associated with cortisol responses in this sample of normally developing children. All four hypotheses were supported in this pilot sample. First, a composite variable was created to represent positive attachment behaviors; it was computed as the sum of contact-maintaining and proximity-seeking, minus the sum of avoidance and resistance behavior in the Strange Situation. Higher scores meant more positive attachment behavior. This variable was positively correlated with cortisol responses (change scores) in the Strange Situation, $r(28) = .40$, $p < .05$, (see figure 3.6). Second, cortisol responses were significantly higher in children who cried than in children who did not, $t(28) = -2.42$, $p < .05$. Third, insecurely attached infants did not show higher cortisol responses than securely attached infants, $t(28) = -.23$, ns. Fourth, a composite variable representing negative temperament (comprised of the sum of the Fear, Anger, Activity Level, and Sadness subscale scores from the TBAQ) was unrelated to cortisol responses, $r(23) = .18$, ns. These results are consistent with existing literature on attachment behaviors and hormones in several animal species. Attachment behaviors such as maintaining contact, seeking proximity to the caregiver, and crying in response to separation appear to be marking the recruitment of physiological resources to deal with a separation stressor. Based on these results, infant temperament may be less important for normally developing infants.

## Discussion and Conclusions

The findings from our pilot data reported in this chapter, as well as those of the other studies of humans reviewed here, present an interesting picture. Although only a few studies on attachment and cortisol in humans have done, it is likely that thresholds for adrenocortical function are regulated by early mother-child interactions. The most consistent finding in this small body of literature is that infants with disorganized attachments show larger cortisol responses to the Strange Situation than do those with organized attachments. This supports Hofer's (1994) notion that the subtle cues given by mothers during attachment interactions, even if those interactions are not what Ainsworth (Ainsworth et al., 1978) and Main (1981) would call "optimal," serve to inhibit stress responses in young infants. It is not clear, however, whether analog "hidden regulators" such as those referred to

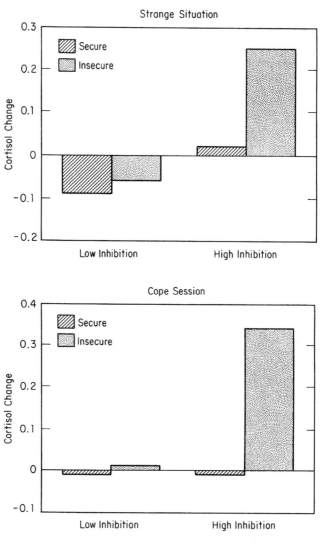

Figure 3.5. Only those children with difficult temperaments and insecure attachments showed an elevated cortisol response to the Strange Situation and to a challenging cope episode. (Adapted from Nachmias et al., 1996.)

by Hofer (1994) exist in humans. If so, they are likely to be found in behaviors that we currently consider as parts of sensitive and responsive care, e.g., body contact, vestibular stimulation, feeding, and so forth. If we think of cortisol as a "coping" hormone and expect differences in adrenocortical function between secure and insecure infants, it may be necessary for us to track infants' cortisol responses to stress for several hours after exposure to a stressor. Differences in cortisol levels between securely and insecurely attached infants may occur further along in the time frame of a stressful event, when regulation of the HPA axis functions homeo-

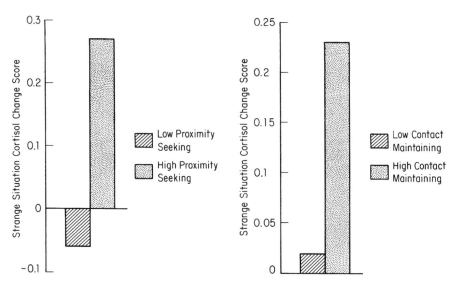

Figure 3.6. Attachment behaviors exhibited by children are positively related to cortisol responses. (Unpublished data from pilot study.)

statically. This is consistent with the view that cortisol is not a measure of fear but of the recruitment of resources. Successful recruitment of these resources should be associated with strong regulation of the HPA system, evidenced by fast returns to baseline levels after a stressor.

Further support for the existence of human examples of Hofer's "hidden regulators" within the attachment relationship is provided by a recent meta-analysis of studies on maternal sensitivity (De Wolff & van IJzendoorn, 1997). De Wolff and van IJzendoorn suggest that since the effect size of the relationship between maternal sensitivity and attachment security is only a moderate one, other factors must also play a role in the development of the attachment relationship. These factors may include mutuality, synchrony, stimulation, positive attitude, and emotional support. Their findings indicate that attachment security per se may not be the best predictor of adrenocortical organization but that a combination of behaviors involved in creating a secure attachment might be relevant.

It seems clear that the attachment system has evolutionary adaptive value. Support for this idea comes mostly from comparative studies. For example, Levine (1990) reported that in four studies, every squirrel and rhesus monkey mother showed a marked adrenocortical reaction to separation from her infant, no matter what the conditions of separation. Levine also reported that the magnitude of the reaction of these monkey mothers was as high as those in other highly noxious stressors, such as electric shock. Clearly, the relationship is an extremely important one for both mother and infant.

It is also important to keep in mind, not only with this study but with all studies of attachment security, that the data are correlational, and it is quite likely that inhibited temperaments will influence mothers' behavior, as well as maternal regulation of infant behavior. Nachmias and her colleagues (1996), for example, reported that inhibited children sought and received more comforting from mothers and were encouraged more frequently by mothers to approach the challenging stimulus during the coping episode. Findings from the same study indicated that securely attached children showed more competent coping and that their mothers encouraged their approach to the challenging stimulus less frequently than mothers of insecurely attached children. Inhibition in those toddlers was related to comfort seeking, mother encouragement to approach stimulus, and mother comforting. Those findings are consistent with the notion of a bidirectional relationship between child behavior and maternal support for coping. Other studies of children have suggested that those with difficult, irritable, or inhibited temperaments show stronger adrenocortical responses to challenging situations and may have higher than normal basal levels of cortisol (Goldsmith, 1989; Gunnar, 1990; Gunnar & Mangelsdorf, 1989; Kagan, Reznick, & Snidman, 1987, 1988, 1989). Suomi and his colleagues reported that increased adrenocortical activity was both heritable and able to be created by exposure to early stressors (Higley & Suomi, 1989).

Taking these findings as a whole, we may conclude that there are at least two pathways to hyperactivity of the adrenocortical system: (1) innate constitutional differences (referred to here as "temperament") and (2) less than optimal mother-infant interactions early in life. Moreover, it is likely that the majority of variance in these interactions would be captured by studies of the interaction between these two variables during early development. In other words, child temperament and parental attachment behaviors (i.e., the sensitive caregiving that leads to secure attachment as described by Ainsworth et al., 1978) are likely to interact in determining hyperreactivity of the adrenocortical system in human children. Children born with predispositions to hyperreactive adrenocortical function (usually marked by difficult, irritable, or extremely inhibited behavioral styles) may become well regulated in the context of optimal attachment behaviors on the part of the mother but will be at greater risk when combined with poor maternal behavior. Human newborns with high orientation, low irritability, and optimal behavior organization are significantly more likely to be classified as securely attached than other babies (Crockenberg, 1981; Egeland & Farber, 1984; Grossmann et al., 1985). Examining coping strategies in conjunction with adrenocortical functioning, as well as the functioning of other stress-related systems, may be the best way to demonstrate emerging regulatory abilities in human children.

Two kinds of studies might better delineate these issues. First, studies that compare cortisol responses across coping situations would allow us to confirm the finding by Nachmias et al. (1996) that the organization of the coping responses in the Strange Situation is part of a competent coping template that can be carried from situation to situation. Second, studies of cross-situational cortisol responses in older infants, previously classified as either secure or insecure, at an age when cognitive abilities would support the internalization of an internal working model should be done. This would help to address the hypothesis that the physiological relationship between attachment and cortisol seen in these studies is truly based on the infant's internalization of a secure versus insecure attachment structure.

The combination of results from the studies of maternal regulation of physiological responses in infants suggests to me the following rather radical possibility: Bowlby's internal working model may reside in the brain of the young child, created by the regulating effects of maternal behavior on gene expression in receptor sites in the hippocampus that regulate adrenocortical function (Liu et al., 1997), on the regulation of growth hormone in the infant brain (Kacsoh, Meyers, Crowley, & Grosvenor, 1990; Kuhn, Butler, & Schanberg, 1978), on central sympathetic activity (Alexander, Vasquez, Decuir, & Maronde, 1980), on brain catecholamine production (Hofer, 1980; Stone, Bonnet, & Hofer, 1976), on the action of adrenocortical hormones on vigilance mediated by the amygdala (LeDoux, 1993; Lee, Schulkin, & Davis, 1994), and probably on synaptogenesis in the frontal cortex. Processes such as these might be said to instantiate the internal working model Bowlby described.

*Notes*

1. The attachment classifications developed by Ainsworth are *secure, anxious-avoidant,* and *anxious-resistant;* the two latter classifications are considered insecure.
2. Corticosterone is the primary hormonal product of the adrenocortical system in rats.

*References*

Ainsworth, M. D. S. (1969). Object relationships, dependency and attachment. A theoretical review of infant-mother relationships. *Child Development, 40,* 969–1025.

Ainsworth, M. D. S., Blehar, M., Waters, E., & Wall, S. (1978). *Patterns of attachment: A psychological study of the Strange Situation.* Hillsdale, NJ: Erlbaum.

Ainsworth, M. D. S., & Eichberg, C. (1991). Effects on infant-mother attachment of mother's unresolved loss of an attachment figure or other traumatic experience. In C. M. Parkes, J. Stevenson-Hinde, & P. Harris (Eds.), *Attachment across the life span* (pp. 160–183). London: Tavistock/Routledge.

Alexander, N., Vasquez, M. T., Decuir, M., & Maronde, R. H. (1980). Indices of sympathetic activity in the sinoaortic denervated hypertensive rat. *American Journal of Physiology, 238,* H521–H526.

Bowlby, J. (1969). *Attachment and loss: Vol. 1. Attachment.* New York: Basic Books.

Bowlby, J. (1973). *Attachment and loss: Vol. 2. Separation, anxiety and anger.* New York: Basic Books.

Bowlby, J. (1979). *The making and breaking of affectional bonds.* London: Tavistock.

Cannon, W. B. (1927). The James-Lange theory of emotion: A critical examination and an alternative theory. *American Journal of Psychology, 39,* 106–124.

Coe, C. L., Mendoza, S. P., Smotherman, W. P., & Levine, S. (1978). Mother-infant attachment in the squirrel monkey: Adrenal response to separation. *Behavioral Biology, 22,* 256–263.

Crockenberg, S. B. (1981). Infant irritability, mother responsiveness and social support influences on the security of infant-mother attachment. *Child Development, 52,* 857–865.

de Kloet, E. R. (1991). Brain corticosteroid receptor balance and homeostatic control. *Frontiers in Neuroendocrinology, 12,* 95–164.

De Wolff, M. S., & van IJzendoorn, M. H. (1997). Sensitivity and attachment: A meta-analysis on parental antecedents of infant attachment. *Child Development, 68,* 571–591.

Egeland, B., & Farber, E. A. (1984). Infant-mother attachment: Factors related to its development and changes over time. *Child Development, 55,* 753–771.

Erickson, M. F., Sroufe, L. A., & Egeland, B. (1985). The relationship between quality of attachment and behavior problems in preschool in a high-risk sample. *Monographs of the Society for Research in Child Development, 50* (1–2), pp. 147–166.

Fox, N. A., & Calkins, S. D. (1993). Pathways to aggression and social withdrawal: Interaction among temperament, attachment, and regulation. In K. H. Rubin & J. Asendorpf (Eds.), *Social withdrawal, inhibition, and shyness in children* (pp. 80– 100). Hillsdale, NJ: Erlbaum.

Goldman, L., Coover, G. D., & Levine, S. (1973). Bidirectional effects of reinforcement shifts on pituitary adrenal activity. *Physiology and Behavior, 10,* 209–214.

Goldsmith, H. H. (1987). *The Toddler Behavior Assessment Questionnaire: A preliminary manual.* Eugene: University of Oregon, Department of Psychology.

Goldsmith, H. H. (1989). Behavior-genetic approaches to temperament. In G. A. Kohnstamm, J. E. Bates, and M. K. Rothbart (Eds.) *Temperament in childhood* (pp. 111–132). Chichester, UK: Wiley.

Grossmann, K., Grossmann, K. E., Spangler, G., Suess, G., & Unzner, L. (1985). Maternal sensitivity and newborns' orientation responses as related to quality of attachment in northern Germany. In I. Bretherton & E. Waters (Eds.), Growing points of attachment theory. *Monographs of the Society for Research in Child Development, 50,* (1–2, Serial No. 209), pp. 233–278.

Gunnar, M. R. (1990). The psychobiology of infant temperament. In J. Colombo, J. W. Fagen, et al., (Eds.), *Individual differences in infancy: Reliability, stability, prediction* (pp. 387–409). Hillsdale, NJ: Erlbaum.

Gunnar, M., Hertsgaard, L., Larson, M., & Rigatuso, J. (1991). Cortisol and behavioral responses to repeated stressor in the human newborn. *Developmental Psychobiology, 24,* 487–505.

Gunnar, M. R., & Mangelsdorf, S. (1989). The dynamics of temperament-physiology relations: A comment on biological processes in temperament. In G. A. Kohnstamm, J. E. Bates, and M. K. Rothbart (Eds.), *Temperament in childhood* (pp. 145–152). Chichester, UK: Wiley.

Gunnar, M. R., Mangelsdorf, S., Larson, M., & Hertsgaard, L. (1989). Attachment, temperament, and adrenocortical activity in infancy: A study of psychoendocrine regulation. *Developmental Psychology, 25,* 355–363.

Gunnar, M. R., Tout, K., de Haan, M., Pierce, S., & Stansbury, K. (1997). Temperament, social competence, and adrenocortical activity in preschoolers. *Developmental Psychobiology, 31,* 65–85.

Hertsgaard, L., Gunnar, M., Erickson, M., & Nachmias, M. (1995). Adrenocortical responses to the strange situation in infants with disorganized/disoriented attachment relationships. *Child Development, 66,* 1100–1106.

Higley, J. D., & Suomi, S. J. (1989). Temperamental reactivity in non-human primates. In G. A. Kohnstamm, J. E. Bates, and M. K. Rothbart (Eds.), *Temperament in childhood* (pp. 153–167). Chichester, UK: Wiley.

Hofer, M. A. (1970). Physiological responses of infant rats to separation from their mothers. *Science, 168,* 871–873.

Hofer, M. A. (1973a). The effects of brief maternal separations on behavior and heart rate of two week old rat pups. *Physiology and Behavior, 10,* 423–427.

Hofer, M. A. (1973b). Maternal separation affects infant rats' behavior. *Behavioral Biology, 9,* 629–633.

Hofer, M. A. (1975). Studies on how early maternal separation produces behavioral change in young rats. *Psychosomatic Medicine, 37,* 245–264.

Hofer, M. A. (1980). The effects of reserpine and amphetamine on the development of hyperactivity in maternally deprived rat pups. *Psychosomatic Medicine, 42,* 513–520.

Hofer, M. A. (1994). Hidden regulators in attachment, separation, and loss. In N. A. Fox (Ed.), The development of emotion regulation: Biological and behavioral considerations. *Monographs of the Society for Research in Child Development, 59,* (2–3, Serial No. 240), pp. 192–207.

Hofer, M. A., & Shair, H. N. (1978). Ultrasonic vocalization during social interaction and isolation in 2-week old rats. *Developmental Psychobiology, 11,* 495–504.

Jones, B. C., & Clark, D. L. (1973). Mother-infant separation in squirrel monkeys living in a group. *Developmental Psychobiology, 6,* 259–269.

Kacsoh, B., Meyers, J. S., Crowley, W. R., & Grosvenor, C. E. (1990). Maternal modulation of growth hormone secretion in the neonatal rat: Involvement of mother-offspring interactions. *Journal of Endocrinology, 124,* 233–240.

Kagan, J., Reznick, J. S. & Snidman, N. (1987). The physiology and psychology of behavioral inhibition. *Child Development, 58,* 1459–1473.

Kagan, J., Reznick, J. S., & Snidman, N. (1988). Biological bases of childhood shyness. *Science, 240,* 167–171.

Kagan, J., Reznick, J. S., & Snidman, N. (1989). The physiology and psychology of behavioral inhibition in children. In S. Chess, A. Thomas, et al. (Eds.), *Annual progress in child psychiatry and child development* (pp. 102–127). New York: Brunner/Mazel.

Kaplan, J., & Schusterman, R. J. (1972). Social preferences of mother and infant squirrel monkeys following different rearing experiences. *Developmental Psychobiology, 5,* 53–59.

Kuhn, C. M., Butler, S. R., & Schanberg, S. M. (1978). Selective depression of serum growth hormone during maternal deprivation in rat pups. *Science, 201,* 1034–1036.

LeDoux, J. E. (1993). Emotional memory systems in the brain. *Behaviourial Brain Research, 58,* 69–79.

Lee, Y., Schulkin, J., & Davis, M. (1994). Effect of corticosterone on the enhancement of the acoustic startle reflex by corticotropin releasing factor (CRF). *Brain Research, 666,* 93–98.

Levine, S. (1990). The hormonal consequences of mother-infant contact. Clinical infant reports. In *Clinical Infant Reports,* K. E. Barnard & T. B. Brazelton (eds.), *Touch: The foundation of experience: Full revised and expanded proceedings of Johnson & Johnson Pediatric Round Table X,* pp. 165–193.

Levine, S., Coe, C. L., Smotherman, W. P., & Kaplan, J. N. (1978). Prolonged cortisol elevation in the infant squirrel monkey after reunion with mother. *Physiological Behavior, 20,* 7.

Lewis, M., & Ramsay, D. S. (1995). Stability and change in cortisol and behavioral responses to stress during the first 18 months of life. *Developmental Psychobiology, 28,* 419–428.

Liu, D., Diorio, J., Tannenbaum, B., Caldji, C., Francis, D., Freedman, A., Sharma, S., Pearson, D., Plotsky, P. M., & Meaney, M. J. (1997). Maternal care, hippocampal glucocorticoid receptors, and hypothalamic-pituitary-adrenal responses to stress. *Science, 277,* 1659–1662.

Main, M. (1981). Avoidance in the service of attachment: A working paper. In K. Immelmann, G. Barlow, L. Petrinovich, & M. Main (Eds.), *Behavioral development: The Bielefeld Interdisciplinary Projects* (pp. 651–693). New York: Cambridge University Press.

Main, M. (1990). Cross-cultural studies of attachment organization: Recent studies, changing methodologies, and the concept of conditional strategies. *Human Development, 33,* 48–61.

Main, M., & Goldwyn, R. (1984). Predicting rejection of her infant from mother's representations of her own experience: Implications for the abused-abusing intergenerational cycle. *Child Abuse and Neglect, 8,* 205–217.

Main, M., & Hesse, E. (1990). Parents' unresolved traumatic experiences are related to infant disorganized attachment status: Is frightened and/or frightening parental behavior the linking mechanism? In M. T. Greenberg, D. Cicchetti, & E. M. Cummings (Eds.), *Attachment in the preschool years: Theory, research, and intervention* (pp. 161–182). Chicago: University of Chicago Press.

Main, M., & Solomon, J. (1990). Procedures for identifying infants as disorganized/disoriented during the Ainsworth Strange Situation. In M. T. Greenberg & D. Cicchetti (eds.), *Attachment in the preschool years: Theory, research, and intervention* (pp. 121–160). Chicago, IL: University of Chicago Press.

Main, M., Tomasini, & Tolan, W. (1979). Differences among mothers of infants judged to differ in security. *Developmental Psychology, 15*, 472–473.

Main, M., & Weston, D. (1981). The quality of the toddler's relationship to mother and father. *Child Development, 52*, 932–940.

Martinez, C. J., Villegas, M., & McEwen, B. S. (1993, November). *Moderate stress enhances acquisition of a spatial memory task in rats.* Poster presented at the meeting of the Society for Neuroscience, Washington, D.C.

Mason, J. W. (1968). A review of psychoendocrine research on the pituitary-adrenal cortical system. *Psychosomatic Medicine, 30*, 576.

McEwen, B. S., de Kloet, E. R., & Rostene, W. (1986). Adrenal steroid receptors and actions in the nervous system. *Physiological Review, 66*, 1121–1188.

Mendoza, S. P., Coe, C. L., Lowe, E. L., & Levine, S. (1978). The physiological response to group formation in adult male squirrel monkeys. *Psychoneuroendocrinology, 3*, 221–229.

Nachmias, M., Gunnar, M., Mangelsdorf, S., Hornik Parritz, R., & Buss, K. (1996). Behavioral inhibition and stress reactivity: The moderating role of attachment security. *Child Development, 67*, 508–522.

Richter, C. P. (1922). A behavioristic study of the activity of the rat. *Comparative Psychology Monographs, 1*, 1–55.

Richter, C. P. (1927). Animal behavior and internal drives. *Quarterly Review of Biology, 2*, 307–342.

Sapolsky, R. M. (1996). Why stress is bad for your brain. *Science, 273*, 749–750.

Sapolsky, R. M., & Meaney, M. J. (1986). Maturation of the adrenocortical stress response: Neuroendocrine control mechanisms and the stress hyporesponsive period. *Brain Research Reviews, 11*, 65–76.

Selye, H. (1936). A syndrome produced by diverse nocuous agent. *Nature, 138*, 32.

Spangler, S., & Grossmann, K. E. (1993). Biobehavioral organization in securely and insecurely attached infants. *Child Development, 64*, 1439–1450.

Sroufe, L. A., & Waters, E. (1977). Attachment as an organization construct. *Child Development, 48*, 1184–1119.

Stansbury, K. (1999). *A model of the role of cortisol in the development of emotion regulation.* Manuscript submitted for publication.

Stansbury, K., Dugle Brainerd, C., & Goodson, C. (1998, April). *Facilitative effects of stress and cortisol on memory for spatial location in children.* Poster presented at the conference of the Cognitive Neuroscience Society, San Francisco, CA.

Stansbury, K., & Gunnar, M. R. (1994). Adrenocortical function and emotion regulation. In N. A. Fox (Ed.), *Monographs of the Society for Research in Child Development, 59* (2–3, Serial No. 240), pp. 108–134.

Stansbury, K., & Harris, M. L. (in press). *Preschoolers' behavioral and adrenocortical responses in a peer entry situation: The role of uncertainty and engagement.* Journal of Experimental Child Psychology.

Stansbury, K., Sethre-Hofstad, L., & Abeita, L. (1998). *Relations between emotion regulation strategies, cortisol, and temperament in young children in response to four 'stress' paradigms.* Manuscript submitted for publication.

Stanton, M. E., Gutierrez, Y. A., & Levine, S. (1988). Maternal deprivation potentiates pituitary-adrenal stress responses in infant rats. *Behavioral Neuroscience, 102*, 692–700.

Stone, E. A., Bonnet, K. A., & Hofer, M. A. (1976). Survival and development of maternally deprived rats: Role of body temperature. *Psychosomatic Medicine, 38*, 242–249.

van den Boom, D. C. (1989). Neonatal irritability and the development of attachment. In G. A. Kohnstamm, J. E. Bates, & M. K. Rothbart (Eds.), *Temperament in childhood* (pp. 299–318). New York: Wiley.

Vogt, J. L., & Levine, S. (1980). Response of mother and infant squirrel monkeys to separation and disturbance. *Physiology & Behavior, 24,* 829–832.

# 4

# Conceptual, Biological, and Behavioral Distinctions Among Different Categories of Shy Children

Louis A. Schmidt & Nathan A. Fox

> It is [our] hope, as it presumably is that of all the
> students whose work is reported here, that from
> these studies there should arise a system of taxon-
> omy, or classification, or nosology, which may be
> regarded as firmly based on biological reality. . . .
>
> (Eysenck, 1953)

Over the last 2 decades, there has been an increasing amount of research directed toward the study of shyness. There are at least three important findings that have emerged from this corpus of work. One is that shyness is a ubiquitous phenomenon that over 90 percent of the population has reported experiencing at some point in their lives (Zimbardo, 1977). Second, a smaller percentage, around 15 percent of the general population, experience extreme shyness. Extreme shyness is characterized by an anxious preoccupation with the self in response to real or imagined social situations, by active avoidance of social contact, and by a host of psychophysiological correlates on static measures, including elevated basal stress hormones (Kagan, Reznick, & Snidman, 1987, 1988; Schmidt et al., 1997), heightened baseline heart rate (Kagan et al., 1987, 1988) and startle responses (Snidman & Kagan, 1994), and greater relative resting right frontal EEG activity (Fox et al., 1995). Extreme shyness is also characterized by increased risks for vascular diseases (Bell et al., 1993), low self-esteem (Schmidt & Fox, 1995), social withdrawal (see Rubin, Stewart, & Coplan, 1995), anxiety problems (Hirshfeld et al., 1992) and in some cases depression (Schmidt & Fox, 1995). A third finding is that there are different types of shyness (Buss, 1986), each of which has distinct behavioral (Bruch, Giordano, & Pearl, 1986; Cheek & Buss, 1981) and psychophysiological (Schmidt, 1999; Schmidt & Fox, 1994) correlates.

This chapter is divided into three sections. In the first section, we present a conceptualization of shyness in which we argue that individual differences emerge out of the underlying motivation tendencies of approach-avoidance (e.g., Asendorpf,

1990). We suggest that these motivational distinctions may be used as a framework to understand behavioral and physiological distinctions among different types of shyness. These different types may have distinct etiologies and most probably manifest themselves in alternate ways both behaviorally and physiologically. In the next section we review the evidence from studies of animals and humans that implicate the frontal cortex and the forebrain amygdala as a possible neuroanatomical circuit that underlies different types of shyness. We outline a diathesis-stress model that may account for different types of shyness, arguing that the individual differences in forebrain sensitivity may reflect a predisposition (i.e., diathesis) toward the dysregulation of fear responses. In the final section, we review evidence from a series of longitudinal studies that we have been conducting over the last decade with infants, preschoolers, school-aged children, and adults that corroborate this model. We conclude with a discussion of how knowledge of individual differences in shyness may inform theory and practice.

## Conceptualizing Different Types of Childhood Shyness

It has long been recognized that there are different reasons for shy or withdrawn behavior. Long before social scientists explored the behavioral patterns of the different types of shy people, their behavior was marked in literature and prose. William Wordsworth (cited in Williams, 1952) writes of an individual who is alone and without social interaction. In the poem, *The Solitary Reaper*, he writes:

Behold her, single in the field,
Reaping and singing by herself;
Alone she cuts and binds the grain;
And sings a melancholy strain;
A voice so thrilling never was heard

The poem exalts the ability of the individual to find solace in solitude and work rather than to be dependent on the company of others. However, Wordsworth notes, her song is melancholy and will never be heard. He notes then the sadness and loneliness associated with social isolation.

Another view of shyness may be seen in the description by the British physician H. Campbell (1896) before the British Medical Society:

His soul is full of love and longing, but the world knows it not;
the iron mask of shyness is riveted before his face, and beneath is never seen;
genial words and greetings are ever rising to his lips,
but they die away in unheard whispers before the steel clamps

Campbell describes an individual who wishes to affiliate with others but who cannot bring himself to do so.

The notion that there are different types of shy children is not new. Buss (1986) argued that there are at least two types of shyness: a fearful shyness and a self-conscious shyness. According to Buss (1986), fearful shyness is an early-developing form of shyness that emerges during the second half of the 1st year of life and coincides with the infant's fear of strangers. Self-conscious shyness, on the other hand, is a late-developing form of shyness which emerges around 5 to 6 years of age and coincides with the child's development of self and the ability to take on the perspective of others; Crozier (chapter 2, this volume) presents a more elaborate description of the distinction between these two types of shyness. The fearfully shy category shares many of the same features as Kagan's (chapter 1, this volume) description of temperamentally inhibited and shy children. Kagan and his colleagues (Kagan, 1994; Kagan & Snidman, 1991a,b) have identified a subset of temperamentally reactive infants who are fearful in the 2nd year of life and exhibit a bias toward shyness during the preschool years.

More recently, Asendorpf (1990; Asendorpf & Meier, 1993) has suggested that different types of shyness emerge as a result of differences in social approach and social avoidance motivational tendencies. According to Asendorpf (1990), social reticence (shyness) emerges from an approach-avoidance conflict. Socially reticent children wish to engage in play with their peers but cannot seem to enter the social play group successfully. This is contrasted with another type of shy child whom Asendorpf describes as avoidant. This type of child is high on avoidance and low on approach behavior. There appear to be different developmental outcomes associated with each of these types of children (see Rubin & Asendorpf, 1993). Children who experience an approach-avoidant conflict tend to be described as socially reticent and to experience a high degree of anxiety in socially evaluative situations (Fox et al., 1995). Children who are high avoidant/low approach are often described as socially withdrawn and, in some instances, depressed (see Rubin et al., 1995).

Although little empirical study has been directed toward either Buss's (1986) theory of shyness or Asendorpf's (1990) conceptualization, these two models are quite similar. Children who are fearfully shy are most likely those who are high in social avoidance and low in social approach motivations. Also, children who are self-consciously shy are most likely those who show high avoidance/high approach motivation. Interestingly, these two types of shyness share properties with two stereotypical fear responses seen conserved across mammals. One stereotypical fear response is to flee; this category is similar to fearful shyness or high avoidance/low approach. The other stereotypical fear response is to freeze; this category shares many of the features of the self-consciously shy and high approach/high avoidance category. Children in this latter shy category freeze in their behavioral responses during social encounters, possibly resulting from an approach-avoidance conflict.

Similar to Asendorpf (1990), we have used an approach-avoidance paradigm to account for at least two categories of shyness that form the basis of this chapter. As can be seen in figure 4.1, we find an example of self-consciously shy people (upper left quadrant), who were described earlier in Campbell's descriptive account. Such people are characterized by an approach-avoidance conflict. We will refer to this group as *conflicted* (see also Cheek & Krasnoperova, chapter 11, this volume). In the lower left quadrant, we find an example of fearfully shy people, who were described in Wordsworth's poem. Such people are characterized by high avoidance behavior and low approach behavior. We will refer to this group as *avoidant*. We believe that these two shy subtypes represent different temperamental categories, each of which is associated with distinct behavioral correlates and developmental outcomes.

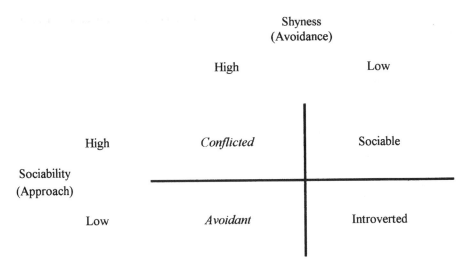

Figure 4.1. Approach-avoidance model in understanding different types of child-hood shyness. (After Asendorpf, 1990)

The behavioral properties which characterize the former category are distinguishable from the latter category. Children who fall into the category of fearfully shy become flooded with negative emotion during social situations. Rubin and his colleagues (Coplan, Rubin, Fox, Calkins, & Stewart, 1994) found that such children often avoid peers, try to escape from the playroom, and begin to cry and fret during play situations involving unfamiliar peers. This is contrasted with the self-consciously shy category, who typically display behavior which is indicative of an approach-avoidance conflict. They approach peers during the play group but have problems trying to enter the play group. Their attempts to enter the play group are often thwarted, and they exhibit overt signs of anxiety, such as circling the play group and increased frequencies of self-manipulations. Interestingly, Asendorpf (1990) suggests that children in the low approach/low avoidant group display behavior characterized by ignoring others (lower right quadrant). We believe that this category—which is often mistakenly labeled as another shyness category—comprises the early origins of introversion. That is, children in this group apparently are not bothered by having to interact with others; they just do not have a preference (or need) to do so.

There is an interesting parallel between the origins of subtypes of childhood shyness and those described in the adult personality literature. Cheek and Buss (1981) used a similar approach-avoidance model to describe different types of adults' shyness. Cheek and Buss (1981) argued that, contrary to lay people's understanding of shyness, shyness was not merely low sociability. Shyness and sociability were conceptually orthogonal dimensions of personality. Shyness reflects an anxious preoccupation with the self in response to real or imagined social interaction and is characterized by active avoidance of social interaction; sociability reflects a preference to be with others and an active approach of social situations. Cheek and Buss (1981) sought to empirically demonstrate that shyness was not merely low sociability by using scales they developed to measure these two broad-based personality dimensions. They found that the two dimensions were only modestly related. They then selected undergraduates who self-reported high and low shyness *and* sociability. Participants from each group were then unobtrusively observed while interacting in matched dyads. Cheek and Buss (1981) found a significant Shyness × Sociability interaction on behavioral measures indexed during the social interaction. High shy/high sociable participants exhibited more overt behavioral anxiety during the social interaction than participants in the other three groups. These data suggest that shyness and sociability are independent personality dimensions and that, within the intersection of these two dimensions, we see different types of shyness. Interestingly, Eysenck (1956), a quarter of a century earlier, examined the independence of extraversion and neuroticism dimensions of personality and found that the two were only modestly related. Extraversion and neuroticism are conceptually and empirically related to sociability and shyness, respectively.

The evidence reviewed here suggests that there are at least two types of shy behavior which are seen across development: an avoidant type and a conflicted type. We also believe that the individual differences in shyness can be conceptualized along differences in approach-avoidance tendencies. There have been a number of recent studies that have sought to understand the neurophysiological basis of emotions that are organized around approach-avoidance motivations. We now turn to a discussion of the neuroanatomical and neurophysiological substrates that may underlie emotions that are organized around approach-avoidance tendencies and how this knowledge may inform our understanding of the emergence of individual differences in shyness.

## Neurobiological Basis of Individual Differences in Shyness

### Frontal Lobe Functioning in Emotion Regulatory Processes

Current thinking suggests that individual differences in shy behavior may reflect dysregulation of the fear system (LeDoux, 1996; Nader & LeDoux, chapter 7, this volume). The frontal cortex is known to play a key role in the regulation of fear and other emotions. This region is involved in the motor facilitation of emotion expression, the organization and integration of cognitive processes underlying emotion, and the ability to regulate emotions (Fox, 1991, 1994).

The frontal region appears to modulate limbic sites involved in the expression of emotion. The amygdala (and central nucleus) is one such limbic site. There are demonstrated functional anatomical connections between the amygdala and the frontal region. The amygdala (and the central nucleus) receives input from neocortical sites, in particular the frontal cortex. There are also links between the amygdala (and the central nucleus) and lower brainstem nuclei used in the regulation of autonomic output. The central nucleus of the amygdala receives visceral projections from the solitary and parabrachial nuclei in the lower brainstem, projecting directly to these regions, in addition to other areas of the brainstem intimately involved in arousal (see Schulkin, McEwen, & Gold, 1994, for a review of the neuroanatomical connections of the amygdala).

The amygdala (and the central nucleus) is known to play an intimate role in the autonomic and behavioral aspects of conditioned fear (LeDoux, Iwata, Cicchetti, & Reis, 1988; see also Nader & LeDoux, chapter 7, this volume). Electrical stimulation of the central nucleus facilitates fear-potentiated startle responses (Rosen & Davis, 1988), whereas lesions to the amygdala and the central nucleus disrupt conditioned fear (Gallagher, Graham, & Holland, 1990; Hitchcock & Davis, 1986; Kapp, Frysinger, Gallagher, & Haselton, 1979; LeDoux, Sakaguchi, Iwata, & Reis, 1986). Still others have shown that electrically kindling the amygdala, but not the dorsal hippocampus, facilitates fear responses in rats (Rosen, Hamerman, Sitcoske, Glowa, & Schulkin, 1996). The amygdala is known to be more reactive in defensive rather than nondefensive cats (Adamec, 1991); it may play a role in the attentional aspects related to the recognition of changes in negatively valenced environmental stimuli (Gallagher & Holland, 1994); and it is known to be sensitive to the manipulation of glucocorticoids (see Schulkin et al., 1994, for a review; see also Schulkin & Rosen, chapter 8, this volume). Infusion of high doses of glucocorticoids to this area is known to potentiate the corticotrophin-releasing hormone (CRH) startle responses (Lee, Schulkin, & Davis, 1994) and freezing behaviors in rats (Takahashi & Rubin, 1994; see also Takahashi & Kalin, chapter 6, this volume). Interestingly, we recently found that administration of high doses of glucocorticoids affected self-reported mood and frontal, but not posterior, brain electrical activity in heathy adults (Schmidt, Fox, Goldberg, Smith, & Schulkin, 1999). Participants treated with high doses of glucocorticoids for 4 consecutive days exhibited a greater increase in self-reported negative emotion and right frontal EEG activity than adults treated with placebo. These data suggest that glucocorticoids may facilitate fear-related responses and that frontal brain activity is sensitive to synthetic steroid manipulation in humans.

Taken together, the anatomical and functional evidence reviewed here suggest that individual differences in the sensitivity of a frontal lobe–limbic circuit may contribute to an inability to regulate the experience of negative emotion in some individuals. We now turn to a discussion of how the pattern of frontal EEG activity may reflect individual differences in forebrain sensitivity in humans.

## Frontal EEG Activity as One Measure of Forebrain Sensitivity

Much of our knowledge regarding the role of the frontal cortex in emotion regulatory processes comes from studies that utilize measures of frontal brain electrical activity (EEG). Overall, these studies have yielded two important results. One is that the pattern of resting (or baseline) brain electrical activity (EEG) indexed off the anterior portion of the scalp may reflect a predisposition (i.e., trait marker) to experience positive and negative emotion and is predictive of individual differences in personality (see Davidson, 1993; Wheeler, Davidson, & Tomarken, 1993; see also Davidson & Rickman, chapter 5, this volume, and Fox, 1991, for reviews). In a series of studies with adults, Davidson and his colleagues have found that adults who exhibit greater relative resting right frontal EEG activity are known to be more depressed (Henriques & Davidson, 1990, 1991) and rate film clips more negatively than adults who exhibit greater relative left frontal EEG activity (Tomarken, Davidson, & Henriques, 1990). In a series of studies with infants, Fox and his colleagues (Davidson & Fox, 1989; Fox, Bell, & Jones, 1992) noted that the pattern of resting frontal EEG activity predicted infants' stress responses. Infants who exhibited greater relative right baseline frontal EEG activity were more likely to cry at stranger approach and maternal separation than infants who exhibited greater relative left frontal EEG activity. These data suggest that tonic differences in frontal EEG activity may underlie early personality differences.

A second finding from the EEG and emotion literature is that the pattern of frontal EEG recorded concurrently during the processing of emotion may serve as a state marker of emotion processes. In a series of studies with infants, Fox and his colleagues (Davidson & Fox, 1982; Fox & Davidson, 1986, 1987, 1988) found that infants exhibited greater relative right frontal EEG activity in response to the presentation of negative affective stimuli and greater relative left frontal EEG activity in response to the presentation of positive affective stimuli. As well, differences in asymmetry emerged during the overt expression of positive versus negative emotions.

## What Do Differences in Frontal EEG Asymmetry and Power Reflect?

We (Fox, 1991, 1994; Schmidt & Fox, 1998a) and others (Davidson, 1993; see also Davidson & Rickman, chapter 5, this volume) have speculated that the pattern of resting frontal brain electrical activity (EEG) may reflect a predisposition to experience positive and negative emotion and may directly index the degree of inhibition of limbic areas involved in emotion. Resting right frontal EEG activity has been routinely linked to negative emotion, withdrawal behaviors, and anxious behavioral profiles, whereas resting left frontal EEG activity has been consistently related to positive emotions, approach behaviors, and socially outgoing behavioral profiles. Dawson (1994) has also argued that frontal EEG asymmetry reflects the valence (or type) of emotion experienced, whereas EEG power reflects the intensity of the emotional experience.

It is also important to note that not only the relative frontal EEG activity but also the dynamic balance in frontal EEG power may be linked to individual differences in personality (see figure 4.2). Traditionally, frontal EEG asymmetry scores have been computed by subtracting left EEG power from right EEG power, with negative scores reflecting greater relative right activation. (EEG power is thought to be inversely related to activation, with lower power reflecting greater cortical activation; Lindsley & Wicke, 1974). Using this metric, there are at least two ways one can create a relative right frontal asymmetry score (relative to individuals who do not change), and at least two ways one can exhibit left frontal asymmetry. Right frontal EEG asymmetry could result from (1) a reduction in EEG power in the right lead with EEG power in the left lead remaining constant (an example of right EEG hyperactivation) or (2) EEG power in the right lead could remain constant with an increase in EEG power in the left lead (an example of left EEG hypoactivation). Left frontal EEG asymmetry could result from (1) a reduction in EEG power in the left lead with EEG power in the right remaining constant (an example of left EEG hyperactivation) or (2) EEG power in the left could remain constant with an increase in EEG power in the right lead (an example of right EEG hypoactivation).

The manner by which these varying patterns of frontal EEG asymmetry is derived may have different psychological meanings. For example, Henriques and Davidson (1991) found a pattern of right frontal EEG asymmetry in depressed

Left Frontal Hyperactivation

L    R

- heightened positive affect

-active social approach

Right Frontal Hyperactivation

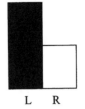

L    R

- heightened negative affect

-active social withdrawal

Left Frontal Hypoactivation

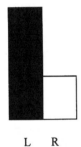

L    R

-reduced positive affect

-lack of social approach

Right Frontal Hypoactivation

L    R

-reduced negative affect

-lack of social withdrawal

Figure 4.2.  Four of a number of consequences of left or right frontal EEG activation or inhibition. Note that EEG power is inversely related to activation so lower values equal higher activation. (Adapted from Fox, 1994)

adults; right frontal asymmetry was a function of left hypoactivation (see figure 4.2, lower left quadrant). Henriques and Davidson (1991) speculated that left frontal EEG hypoactivation in depression may reflect lack of approach and an absence of positive affect rather than the presence of heightened negative affect. Schmidt and Fox (1996) recently found a pattern of left frontal EEG asymmetry in a sample of aggressive toddlers; left frontal EEG asymmetry was a function of right hypoactivation (see figure 4.2, lower right quadrant). Schmidt and Fox (1996) hypothesized that right frontal hypoactivation may reflect dysregulated approach and an inability to experience the consequences of negative emotion. Fox et al. (1995) found a pattern of right frontal EEG activity in extremely shy preschoolers; right frontal asymmetry was a function of right hyperactivity (see figure 4.2, upper right quadrant). Fox et al. (1995) suggested that right frontal hyperactivity may reflect active avoidance and an inability to regulate the experience of negative emotion. Thus the patterns of frontal EEG asymmetry and absolute EEG power may both be important metrics in understanding individual differences in affect style and personality and may reflect differences in frontal lobe–forebrain emotion regulatory processes.

## A Diathesis-stress Model of Individual Differences in Shyness

Utilizing the neuroanatomical evidence and behavioral studies described previously, we propose a diathesis-stress model to underlie different types of childhood shyness. As can be seen in figure 4.3, we view individual differences in the excitability of the central nucleus of the amygdala and the degree of frontal inhibition of the arousal as a diathesis that contributes to at least two types of shyness: social avoidance and conflicted approach. Children who display high social avoidance and low social approach exhibit a pattern of greater relative resting frontal EEG activity that is a function of less EEG power in the right versus left frontal lead (an example of right hyperactivation). They actively avoid social contact and may in fact ignore social bids for interaction. Children who show high social avoidance and high social approach exhibit a pattern of greater relative resting right frontal EEG activity that is a function of hyperactivity in both frontal leads, with slightly more activity in the right versus left frontal lead. They remain at the periphery of social situations, wanting to interact but being unable to do so. The dynamic balance of EEG activity recorded from the frontal hemispheres may reflect individual differences in the excitability of the central nucleus of the amygdala and the degree of inhibition of this arousal and predispose each category to different emotional regulatory strategies. We further believe that individual differences in the sensitivity of the central nucleus of the amygdala, given its projections to the hypothalamic-pituitary-adrenocortical (HPA) system and brainstem nuclei involved in the regulation of the autonomic output, are also responsible for the pattern of activity evidenced in peripheral measures such as elevated basal cortisol levels and high heart rate.

We speculate that when individuals who differ in specific types of limbic arousal are confronted with social stress, their responses are manifested in multiple behavioral and physiological levels. Both socially avoidant and socially conflicted individuals have similar patterns of limbic arousal. Thus, they will evidence similar patterns of heart rate and HPA axis activity. They will differ, however, in the manner in which cortical inhibition manifests itself in motor and cognitive responses. Children who avoid social situations are characterized by resting right frontal EEG hyperactivity. They are not able to regulate the experience of negative emotion during or in anticipation of such situations. When these children are confronted with social stress, this diathesis is manifested in avoidance behavior and an increase in right, but not left, frontal EEG activity, heart rate and adrenocortical activity.

These children in the avoidant group may be at risk for social withdrawal, social phobia, and depression. Exposure to social situations may be stressful, and they may avoid social interactions altogether. Engaging in social interactions,

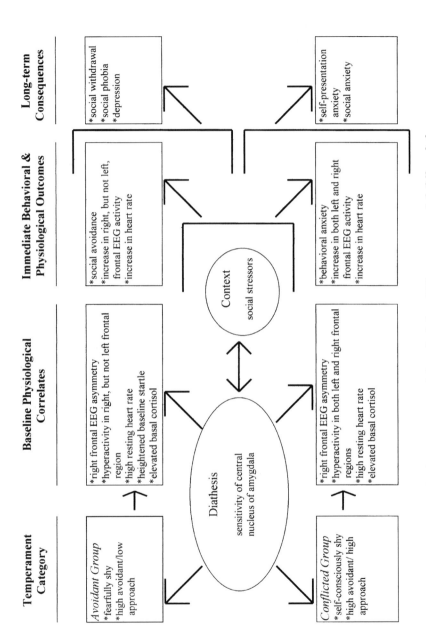

Figure 4.3. A diathesis-stress model underlying different types of childhood shyness.

however, is critical to the development of early social skills and social competence. Unfortunately, children in the avoidant group may adopt coping strategies that lead them down a path to isolation, precluding the development of positive social competence. Interestingly, children low in social competence exhibit greater adreno-cortical reactivity to self-presentation tasks compared with highly socially competent children (Schmidt, Fox, & Sternberg et al., 1999).

On the other hand, children who are characterized by resting right frontal EEG activity that is a function of hyperactivity in both frontal leads, with slightly more activity in the right than the left, may have a high need to affiliate with others but cannot bring themselves to successfully do so because they have problems regulating the competing experience of positive and negative emotions. Children in the conflicted group are anxious in social situations and exhibit an increase in both left and right frontal EEG activity and an increase in heart rate in response to social situations. Children in the conflicted group attempt to engage in social interactions but lack the requisite social skills that allow them to successfully join the social group. Their inability to successfully join the social group means that they may have fewer chances to develop and hone their social skills. The conflicted group may fail to develop a positive sense of social competence. Children in the conflicted group tend to be overly concerned about the self in anticipation of and during social encounters and to experience a high degree of self-presentation anxiety. It is highly possible that for some of the conflicted children, repeated unsuccessful attempts at being "social" may take its toll on them. Accordingly, they may start to question their abilities and social skills and start to develop feelings of low self-worth that are characteristic of children in the avoidant group. It is possible that persistent feelings of low self-worth may lead them in the direction of more severe emotional problems. In the next section, we consider findings from our series of longitudinal studies that provide evidence for these statements.

## The Development of Individual Differences in Shyness: Longitudinal Studies

The focus of our research program has been directed toward understanding the role of frontal lobe functioning in emotion regulatory processes in children. We have been using measures of regional brain electrical activity (EEG) to assess pre-frontal activity. We have found that a pattern of resting brain electrical activity indexed off the anterior portion of the scalp reflects a predisposition to experience positive and negative emotion and thus underlies individual differences in personality and affective style. Individuals who exhibit greater relative resting right frontal EEG activity appear to be shy, anxious, or depressed; individuals who exhibit greater relative resting left frontal EEG activity appear to be socially outgoing and extraverted. We have found that the pattern of frontal EEG activity predicts children's reactions to social stress. These findings have led us to consider whether there is a role for the frontal lobes in understanding the origins of different types of shyness in children. In this section, we review data from a series of studies we have been conducting with infants, preschoolers, early school-aged children, and young adults. The focus of these studies has been on the establishment of knowledge regarding the origins, developmental course, and outcomes of different types of shyness.

## Studies of Infants

Temperamental Antecedents of Shyness. Kagan and his colleagues (Kagan & Snidman, 1991a) have argued that the origins of extreme shyness in children may be found in individual differences in early infant reactivity. Infants who exhibit a high degree of motor activity and distress in response to the presentation of novel auditory and visual stimuli during the first half of the first year of life exhibit a high degree of behavioral inhibition and shyness during the preschool and early school-age years (Kagan, chapter 1, this volume).

Kagan (Kagan & Snidman, 1991b) and others (Rosen & Schulkin, 1998; Schmidt & Fox, 1998a) have speculated that the locus of this early temperament may be linked to hypersensitivity in forebrain limbic areas, particularly the amygdala. As reviewed herein, there are dense connections between the frontal cortex and limbic areas involved in the behavioral and autonomic regulation of emotion. Our working hypothesis is that the pattern of frontal EEG activity may reflect the degree to which cortex inhibits a limbic arousal specifically associated with the expression of fear. Our studies suggest the activity in the right prefrontal area is associated with a lack of regulation of negative effect. Conversely, activity in the left prefrontal area is associated with a dampening of distress, fear, and negative effect. As well, the balance of activity between these two areas provides a window into how modulation of affect will or will not occur.

We (Calkins, Fox, & Marshall, 1996) examined the behavioral and psychophysiological antecedents of shyness in a group of infants selected at 4 months of age for temperamental constellations thought to predict behavioral inhibition and shyness in early childhood. Eighty-one healthy (34 males, 47 females) infants were selected at 4 months of age from the larger sample of 207 using procedures similar to those reported by Kagan and Snidman (1991b). We observed the infants in their homes at 4 months of age and videotaped them as they responded to novel auditory and visual stimuli. The 81 infants were selected based on their frequency of motor activity and the degree of positive and negative affect displayed in response to these novel stimuli.

We formed three groups at 4 months of age: *Group 1: negative* ($n = 31$) comprised infants who displayed high amounts of both motor activity and negative affect and low amounts of positive affect. Kagan and Snidman (1991b) found that this temperamental group of infants was behaviorally inhibited at 14 months of age. *Group 2: positive* ($n = 19$) comprised infants who displayed high amounts of both motor activity and positive affect and low amounts of negative affect. *Group 3: low* ($n = 31$) comprised infants who displayed low amounts of motor activity and low amounts of both positive affect and negative affect.

The infants were seen in our laboratory at 9, 14, and 24 months, at which time EEG was recorded using a Lycra stretch cap from the left and right frontal, parietal, and occipital regions. EEG was recorded while the infant was seated, alert, and attending to a spinning bingo wheel. We predicted that infants who displayed a high frequency of motor activity and negative affect in response to novel stimuli at age 4 months would display greater relative right frontal EEG activation at 9, 14, and 24 months than infants in the other two 4-month temperament groups.

At 14 months each infant was unobtrusively observed interacting during a free play situation and with a series of unfamiliar stimuli designed to elicit his or her response to novelty. These stimuli comprised an unfamiliar adult, a toy robot, and a novel exploratory situation. Infants' responses to these stimuli were coded from videotapes. A single composite measure of behavioral inhibition was computed at 14 months using the sum of standardized scores that represented the following: latency to touch the first toy, latency to vocalize, and time spent in proximity to the mother during free play; latency to vocalize to and approach the stranger and robot and time spent in proximity to mother during the stranger, truck, and robot sequences; and frequency of displays of negative affect during all episodes. We predicted that the high motor–high negative infants would be more behaviorally inhibited at age 14 months than infants in the other two 4-month temperament groups.

We found that infants who were easily distressed by novelty at age 4 months exhibited greater relative right frontal EEG activation asymmetry at age 9 months, as well as at age 24 months, than infants in the other two groups. We have, most recently, found that this subset of infants exhibited greater fear-potentiated startle responses than infants in the other two temperamental groups (Schmidt & Fox, 1998b). In addition, infants who were easily distressed by novelty at age 4 months displayed a high proportion of behavioral inhibition in response to the unfamiliar at age 14 months compared with infants in the other two groups. The frontal EEG data and the startle response findings, taken together, corroborate the notion proposed earlier that the origins of some types of childhood shyness may be linked to the arousal of limbic areas that are involved in the expression of fear *and* the activity of frontal areas in the modulation of that fear.

Stability and Change in Frontal EEG and Temperamental Inhibition.    One logical question is: How stable is the frontal EEG metric in temperamental inhibition? We have found that the pattern of frontal EEG asymmetry exhibited over the first 2 years of life was stable in most temperamentally inhibited infants (Schmidt & Fox, 1999). Infants who displayed a pattern of stable right frontal EEG across the first 2 years tended to be more inhibited at both 14 and 24 months than infants who exhibited a pattern of stable left frontal EEG during this time (Fox, Calkins, & Bell, 1994).

We have also found evidence of change in some infants with a temperamental bias toward extreme shyness. Infants whose pattern of frontal EEG activity changed from right to left frontal EEG activity during the first 2 years were less likely to develop shyness than infants who exhibited a stable pattern of right frontal EEG activity in the first 2 years of life (Schmidt & Fox, 1999). These data suggest that environmental input during the first 2 years of life may affect brain re-organization and particular functions of the frontal lobe involved in the maintenance of fear in some human infants with a temperamental bias toward extreme shyness.

## Studies of Preschoolers

The experience of shyness is clearly present by age 4 because self-awareness and the ability to take on the perspective of others is in place. In a series of studies with preschoolers, we examined whether extremely shy children were distinguishable from their nonshy counterparts on baseline frontal EEG asymmetry (Fox et al., 1995; Fox, Schmidt, Calkins, Rubin, & Coplan, 1996) and basal morning salivary cortisol levels (Schmidt et al., 1997). We observed children at age 4 during a peer play session, and their behaviors were subsequently coded for measures of shyness (e.g., anxious and reticent behaviors) using the Play Observation Scale (POS) developed by Ken Rubin (Rubin, 1989).

We found that preschoolers who displayed a high proportion of anxious behavior and wariness in response to their peers (i.e., upper 30 percent) during the peer play session exhibited greater relative right frontal EEG activity and higher morning salivary cortisol levels than children who measured average (i.e., middle 40 percent) and low (i.e., bottom 30 percent) in shyness. These findings suggest that baseline measures of frontal EEG activity and basal adrenocortical activity may play a role in some types of shyness during the preschool years.

## Studies of Early-School-Aged-Children

We (Schmidt, Fox, & Schulkin, in press) next examined the convergence of multiple psychophysiological measures during a self-presentation task in a group of 7-year-olds, some of whom were extremely shy. We selected a self-presentation task because issues of self-evaluation are at the root of many social anxieties, shyness in particular. We chose to examine the relations among multiple psychophysiological measures at age 7 because this age is a particularly salient point in development, as it coincides with the child's transition into school and the development of social skills and peer relationships. The underlying rationale was that a multiple measure approach may index different levels and systems, and the association or disassociation among the measures may shed light on a possible biological mechanism that underlies extreme shyness.

We recorded behavior, brain electrical activity (EEG), and heart rate during a task designed to elicit self-presentation anxiety in middle childhood. We found that extremely shy children (i.e., upper 30 percent) displayed a greater decrease in EEG power (i.e., greater increase in activation), a greater increase in heart rate, and greater decrease in heart rate variability than children in the average-(i.e., middle 40 percent) and low-(i.e., bottom 30 percent) shy groups. EEG changes in frontal power were specific to the right lead only. The groups were not distinguishable on EEG power in the left frontal lead. These findings suggest that there are state changes in multiple psychophysiological measures that covary in some types of shy children during social stress.

## Studies of Young Adults

One of the goals of our research program on shyness has been to examine the developmental course and outcomes of different types of shyness beyond early childhood. In the main, the correlates and outcomes associated with childhood shyness are comparable to those seen in adults. For example, extremely shy adults are known to have more problems regulating negative emotion and are more likely to suffer from problems of poor self-concept (Crozier, 1981) and depression (Bell, et al., 1993; Schmidt & Fox, 1995) than their nonshy counterparts.

Using a design identical to that reported by Cheek and Buss (1981), we (Schmidt & Fox, 1994) recently examined whether we could distinguish different types of shyness on multiple psychophysiological measures. We (Schmidt & Fox, 1994) found a significant Shyness × Sociability interaction on two separate autonomic measures (mean heart rate and heart rate variability) just prior to an anticipated novel social encounter. High shy/high sociable participants exhibited a significantly faster and more stable heart rate than those in the other three groups.

There is also evidence to suggest that the pattern of resting frontal absolute EEG power distinguishes different types of adults' shyness. Schmidt (1999) recently found that adults who self-reported high shyness and high sociability (i.e., conflicted) and adults who self-reported high shyness and low sociability (i.e., avoidant) both exhibit greater relative right frontal EEG activity that was a function of less power in the right lead than in left frontal lead. The two shyness subtypes were distinguishable, however, based on the pattern of activity in the left frontal lead. As can be seen in figure 4.4, high shy/high sociable participants exhibited significantly less power (i.e., more activity) in the left frontal lead than participants in the high shy/low sociable group. These data suggest that shyness and sociability are distinguishable on a neurophysiological level and that each trait may be subserved by distinct neurophysiological systems. These data also suggest that there are different types of shyness, each of which is distinguishable on behavioral, central, and autonomic measures during resting and socially stressful conditions.

## Conclusions and Implications

A primary goal of most facets of scientific inquiry is to describe and classify phenomena. When classifying objects, we look for similarities and differences among features of the objects in question and then use this knowledge to distinguish the objects based on their shared and unshared properties. The ability to distinguish objects is applicable to all facets of scientific inquiry. A physician needs to be able distinguish the features associated with a benign intestinal virus from those of a terminal stomach cancer, although both may present with similar features. The civil engineer needs to know what distinguishes different types of soil sediments before building a bridge. Personality psychologists need to know what distinguishes one type of person from another in order to understand why people behave as they do. Regardless of the field of inquiry, the end goal is the same: to enhance prediction by reducing the amount of fuzziness around the boundaries and language we use in the description of the phenomenon we seek to understand.

Why should we be concerned with distinguishing different types of childhood shyness? It is easy to see how the language and concepts we use regarding complex human behavior can quickly become confusing. Such confusion limits how we study a phenomenon and leads often times to misclassification. For example, in the case of childhood shyness, two children may be described as shy because during peer play each child is engaged in solitary play, whereas other children are actively engaged in social play. On closer inspection, however, we notice that the quality of the play behavior for the two socially isolated children differs considerably. One child might be engaged in solitary constructive play and exhibit no overt signs of distress over the situation, whereas the other socially isolated child may

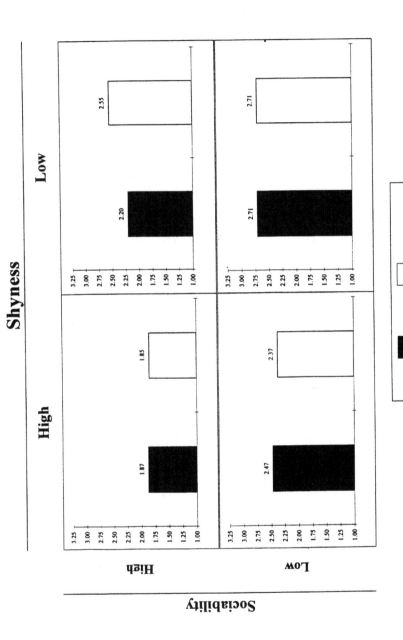

Figure 4.4. Frontal EEG power in shyness *and* sociability. Note that EEG power is inversely related to cortical activation, so lower power values equal greater activation. (Adapted from Schmidt, 1990)

be engaged in little to no play behavior and display overt signs of anxiety. The origins of these behaviors, their underlying causes, and their psychological meaning differ considerably between the two children. The former child may be displaying the earlier signs of introversion; this child will mostly likely not have problems affiliating with others but probably will not have a strong preference to do so. The latter child, on the other hand, may be exhibiting the early antecedents of extreme shyness. Both children are, however, often mistakenly labeled as shy by both teachers and parents. There are two major reasons for this: (1) laypersons make naive judgments based on their limited understanding of the phenomenon and (2) laypeople are limited by the number of properties at their disposal which they use to define shyness. We believe that an examination of the psychophysiological correlates of shyness may provide additional knowledge about properties of shyness which may not be inferred from behavioral measures. This knowledge not only may be useful in understanding the origins of childhood shyness, but also may facilitate our search to make finer distinctions among different categories of shy children, ultimately improving our ability to classify and predict with a greater degree of precision than before.

*Acknowledgments*   Much of the empirical work reported on in this chapter was supported by a grant from the National Institutes of Health (HD 17899) awarded to Nathan A. Fox. I (L.A.S.) also wish to acknowledge Thomas N. Robinson, who was influential in shaping my early thinking on issues related to the mind and brain/behavior relations, and Ariana Shahinfar for her support over the years.

## References

Adamec, R. E. (1991). Individual differences in temporal lobe sensory processing of threatening stimuli in the cat. *Physiology and Behavior, 49,* 445–464.

Asendorpf, J. B. (1990). Beyond social withdrawal: Shyness, unsociability and peer avoidance. *Human Development, 33,* 250–259.

Asendorpf, J. B., & Meier, G. H. (1993). Personality effects on children's speech in everyday life: Sociability-mediated exposure and shyness-mediated reactivity to social situations. *Journal of Personality and Social Psychology, 64,* 1072–1083.

Bell, I. R., Martino, G. M., Meredith, K. E., Schwartz, G. E., Siani, M. W., & Morrow, F. D. (1993). Vascular disease risk factors, urinary free cortisol, and health histories in older adults: Shyness and gender interactions. *Biological Psychology, 35,* 37–49.

Bruch, M. A., Giordano, S., & Pearl, L. (1986). Differences between fearful and self-conscious shy subtypes in background and current adjustment. *Journal of Research in Personality, 20,* 172–186.

Buss, A. H. (1986). A theory of shyness. In W. H. Jones, J. M. Cheek, & S. R. Briggs (Eds.), *Shyness: Perspectives on research and treatment* (pp. 39–46). New York: Plenum.

Calkins, S. D., Fox, N. A., & Marshall, T. R. (1996). Behavioral and physiological antecedents of inhibited and uninhibited behavior. *Child Development, 67,* 523–540.

Campbell, H. (1896). Morbid shyness. *British Medical Journal, 2,* 805–807.

Cheek, J. M., & Buss, A. H. (1981). Shyness and sociability. *Journal of Personality and Social Psychology, 41,* 330–339.

Coplan, R. J., Rubin, K. H., Fox, N. A., Calkins, S. D., & Stewart, S. (1994). Being alone, playing alone, and acting alone: Distinguishing among reticence and passive and active solitude in young children. *Child Development, 65,* 129–137.

Crozier, W. R. (1981). Shyness and self-esteem. *British Journal of Social Psychology, 20,* 220–222.

Davidson, R. J. (1993). The neuropsychology of emotion and affective style. In M. Lewis & J.M. Haviland (Eds.), *Handbook of emotion* (pp.143–154). New York: Guilford.

Davidson, R. J., & Fox, N. A. (1982). Asymmetrical brain activity discriminates between positive versus negative stimuli in human infants. *Science, 218,* 1235–1237.

Davidson, R. J., & Fox, N. A. (1989). The relation between tonic EEG asymmetry and ten-month-old emotional response to separation. *Journal of Abnormal Psychology, 98,* 127–131.

Dawson, G. (1994). Frontal electroencephalographic correlates of individual differences in emotional expression in infants. In N. A. Fox (Ed.), Emotion regulation: Behavioral and biological considerations. *Monographs of the Society for Research in Child Development, 59* (2–3, Serial No. 240), pp. 135–151.

Eysenck, H. J. (1953). *The structure of human personality.* London: Methuen.

Eysenck, H. J. (1956). The questionnaire measurement of neuroticism and extraversion. *Revista Psicologia, 50,* 113–140.

Fox, N. A. (1991). If it's not left, it's right: Electroencephalogram asymmetry and the development of emotion. *American Psychologist, 46,* 863–872.

Fox, N. A. (1994). Dynamic cerebral processes underlying emotion regulation. In N. A. Fox (Ed.), The development of emotion regulation: Behavioral and biological considerations. *Monographs of the Society for Research in Child Development, 59*(2–3, Serial No. 240), 152–166.

Fox, N. A., Bell, M. A., & Jones, N. A. (1992). Individual differences in response to stress and cerebral asymmetry. *Developmental Neuropsychology, 8,* 161–184.

Fox, N. A., Calkins, S. D., & Bell, M. A. (1994). Neural plasticity and development in the first two years of life: Evidence from cognitive and socioemotional domains of research. *Development and Psychopathology, 6,* 677–696.

Fox, N. A., & Davidson, R. J. (1986). Taste-elicited changes in facial signs of emotion and the asymmetry of brain electrical activity in human newborns. *Neuropsychologia, 24,* 417–422.

Fox, N. A., & Davidson, R. J. (1987). EEG asymmetry in ten-month-old infants in response to approach of a stranger and maternal separation. *Developmental Psychology, 23,* 233–240.

Fox, N. A. & Davidson, R. J. (1988). Patterns of brain electrical activity during the expression of discrete emotions in ten-month-old infants. *Developmental Psychology, 24,* 230–236.

Fox, N. A., Rubin, K. H., Calkins, S. D., Marshall, T. R., Coplan, R. J., Porges, S. W., Long, J. M., & Stewart, S. (1995). Frontal activation asymmetry and social competence at four years of age. *Child Development, 66,* 1770–1784.

Fox, N. A., Schmidt, L. A., Calkins, S. D., Rubin, K. H., & Coplan, R. J. (1996). The role of frontal activation in the regulation and dysregulation of social behavior during the preschool years. *Development and Psychopathology, 8,* 89–102.

Gallagher, M., Graham, P. W. A., & Holland, P. C. (1990). The amygdala central nucleus and appetitive Pavlovian conditioning: Lesions impair one class of conditioned behavior. *Journal of Neuroscience, 10,* 1906–1911.

Gallagher, M., & Holland, P. C. (1994). The amygdala complex: Multiple roles in associative learning and attention. *Proceedings of the National Academy of Sciences, 91,* 11771–11776.

Henriques, J. B., & Davidson, R. J. (1990). Regional brain electrical asymmetries discriminate between previously depressed subjects and healthy controls. *Journal of Abnormal Psychology, 99,* 22–31.

Henriques, J. B., & Davidson, R. J. (1991). Left frontal hypoactivation in depression. *Journal of Abnormal Psychology, 100,* 535–545.

Hirshfeld, D. R., Rosenbaum, J. F., Biederman, J., Bolduc, E. A., Faraone, S. V., Snidman, N., Reznick, J. S., & Kagan, J. (1992). Stable behavioral inhibition and its association with anxiety disorder. *Journal of the American Academy of Child and Adolescent Psychiatry, 31,* 103–111.

Hitchcock, J., & Davis, M. (1986). Lesion of the amygdala, but not the cerebellum or the red nucleus, block conditioned fear as measured with potentiated startle paradigm. *Behavioral Neuroscience, 100,* 11–22.

Kagan, J. (1994). On the nature of emotion. In N. A. Fox (Ed.), The development of emotion regulation: Behavioral and biological considerations. *Monographs of the Society for Research in Child Development, 59* (2–3, Serial No. 240), pp. 7–24.

Kagan, J., Reznick, J. S., & Snidman, N. (1987). The physiology and psychology of behavioral inhibition in children. *Child Development, 58,* 1459–1473.

Kagan, J., Reznick, J. S., & Snidman, N. (1988). Biological basis of childhood shyness. *Science, 240,* 167–171.

Kagan, J., & Snidman, N. (1991a). Temperamental factors in human development. *American Psychologist, 46,* 856–862.

Kagan, J., & Snidman, N. (1991b). Infant predictors of inhibited and uninhibited profiles. *Psychological Science, 2,* 40–44.

Kapp, B. S., Frysinger, R. C., Gallagher, M., & Haselton, J. R. (1979). Amygdala central nucleus lesions: Effects on heart rate conditioning in the rabbit. *Physiology and Behavior, 23,* 1109–1117.

LeDoux, J. E. (1996). *The emotional brain.* New York: Simon and Schuster.

LeDoux, J. E., Iwata, J., Cicchetti, P., & Reis, D. J. (1988). Different projections of the central amygdaloid nucleus mediate autonomic and behavioral correlates of conditioned fear. *Journal of Neuroscience, 8,* 2517–2519.

LeDoux, J. E., Sakaguchi, A., Iwata, J., & Reis, D. J. (1986). Interruption of projections from the medial geniculate body to an archi-neo-striatal field disrupts the classical conditioning of emotional responses to acoustic stimuli in the rat. *Neuroscience, 17,* 615–627.

Lee, Y., Schulkin, J., & Davis, M. (1994). Effect of corticosterone on the enhancement of the acoustic startle reflex by corticotropin releasing factor (CRF). *Brain Research, 666,* 93–98.

Lindsley, D. B., & Wicke, J. D. (1974). The EEG: Autonomous electrical activity in man and animals. In R. Thompson & M.N. Patterson (Eds.), *Bioelectrical recording techniques* (pp. 3–83). New York: Academic Press.

Rosen, J. B, & Davis, M. (1988). Enhancement of acoustic startle by electrical stimulation of the amygdala. *Behavioral Neuroscience, 102,* 195–202.

Rosen, J. B., Hamerman, E., Sitcoske, M., Glowa, J. R., & Schulkin, J. (1996). Hyperexcitability: Exaggerated fear-potentiated startle produced by partial amygdala kindling. *Behavioral Neuroscience, 110,* 43–50.

Rosen, J. B., & Schulkin, J. (1998). From normal fear to pathological anxiety. *Psychological Review, 105,* 325–350.

Rubin, K. H. (1989). The Play Observation Scale (POS). University of Waterloo.

Rubin, K. H., & Asendorpf, J. B. (1993). *Social withdrawal, inhibition, and shyness in childhood.* Hillsdale, NJ: Erlbaum.

Rubin, K. H., Stewart, S. L., Coplan, R. J. (1995). Social withdrawal in childhood: Conceptual and empirical perspectives. In T. Ollendick & R. Prinz (Eds.), *Advances in Clinical Child Psychology* (Vol. 17, pp. 157–196). New York: Plenum Press.

Schmidt, L. A. (1999). Frontal brain electrical activity (EEG) in shyness *and* sociability. *Psychological Science, 10,* 316–320.

Schmidt, L. A. (1999, August). Frontal brain electrical activity (EEG) in shyness subtypes. In L. A. Schmidt & J. M. Cheek (co-chairs), *Shyness: From temperament to self-concept.* Symposium conducted at the annual meeting of the American Psychological Association, Boston, MA.

Schmidt, L. A., & Fox, N. A. (1994). Patterns of cortical electrophysiology and autonomic activity in adults' shyness and sociability. *Biological Psychology, 38,* 183–198.

Schmidt, L. A., & Fox, N. A. (1995). Individual differences in young adults' shyness and sociability: Personality and health correlates. *Personality and Individual Differences, 19,* 455–462.

Schmidt, L. A., & Fox, N. A. (1996). Frontal EEG correlates of dysregulated social behavior in children [Abstract]. *Psychophysiology, 33,* S8.

Schmidt, L. A., & Fox, N. A. (1998a). The development and outcomes of childhood shyness: A multiple psychophysiological measure approach. In R. Vasta (Ed.), *Annals of Child Development* (Vol. 13, pp. 1–20). London: Kingsley.

Schmidt, L. A., & Fox, N. A. (1998b). Fear-potentiated startle responses in temperamentally different human infants. *Developmental Psychobiology, 32,* 113–120.

Schmidt, L. A., & Fox, N. A. (1999). *Cortical plasticity and temperamental inhibition in the first two years of life.* Manuscript submitted for publication.

Schmidt, L. A., Fox, N. A., Goldberg, M., Smith, C. C., & Schulkin, J. (1999). Effects of acute prednisone administration on memory, attention, and emotion in healthy adults. *Psychoneuroendocrinology, 24,* 461–483.

Schmidt, L. A., Fox, N. A., Rubin, K. H., Sternberg, E. M., Gold, P. W., Smith, C., & Schulkin, J. (1997). Behavioral and neuroendocrine responses in shy children. *Developmental Psychobiology, 30,* 127–140.

Schmidt, L. A., Fox, N. A., & Schulkin, J. (In press). Behavioral and psychophysiological correlates of self-presentation in temperamentally shy children. *Developmental Psychobiology.*

Schmidt, L. A., Fox, N. A., Sternberg, E. M., Gold, P. W., Smith, C., & Schulkin, J. (1999). Adrenocortical reactivity and social competence in seven-year-olds. *Personality and Individual Differences, 26,* 977–985.

Schulkin, J., McEwen, B. S., & Gold, P. W. (1994). Allostasis, amygdala, and anticipatory angst. *Neuroscience and Biobehavioral Reviews, 18,* 385–396.

Snidman, N., & Kagan, J. (1994). The contribution of infant temperamental differences to acoustic startle response [Abstract]. *Psychophysiology, 31,* S92.

Takahashi, L. K., & Rubin, W. W. (1994). Corticosteroid induction of threat-induced behavioral inhibition in preweanling rats. *Behavioral Neuroscience, 107,* 860–868.

Tomarken, A. J., Davidson, R. J., & Henriques, J. B. (1990). Resting frontal brain asymmetry predicts affective responses to films. *Journal of Personality and Social Psychology, 59,* 791–801.

Wheeler, R. W., Davidson, R. J., & Tomarken, A. J. (1993). Frontal brain asymmetry and emotional reactivity: A biological substrate of affective style. *Psychophysiology, 30,* 82–89.

Williams, O. (1952) (Ed.) *Immortal poems of the English language.* New York: Pocket Books.

Zimbardo, P. G. (1977). *Shyness: What is it and what to do about it.* New York: Symphony Press.

# 5

# Behavioral Inhibition and the Emotional Circuitry of the Brain

## Stability and Plasticity During the Early Childhood Years

Richard J. Davidson & Maureen Rickman

$A$mong the most striking features of human emotion is the variability that is apparent across individuals in the quality and intensity of dispositional mood and emotional reactions to similar incentives and challenges. For example, some people appear very reticent and wary, whereas others are outgoing and bold across a broad range of contexts. The myriad range of differences in these varied affective phenomena has been referred to as "affective style" (Davidson, 1992, 1998). Differences among people in affective style appear to be associated with temperament (Kagan, Reznick & Snidman, 1988), personality (Gross, Sutton & Ketelaar, 1998) and vulnerability to psychopathology (Meehl, 1975). Moreover, such differences are not a unique human attribute but appear to be present in a number of different species (e.g., Davidson, Kalin & Shelton, 1993; Kalin, 1993; Kalin, Larson, Shelton, & Davidson, 1998) and are apparent early in life (e.g., Kagan, Reznick, & Gibbons, 1989).

The next section presents a selective overview of the some of the key circuitry that underlies two major emotional and motivational systems—the approach and withdrawal systems. The third section considers individual differences in these basic systems, indicates how such differences might be studied, and discusses the behavioral consequences of such individual differences. In the fourth section, we specifically consider the problem of behavioral inhibition and present new findings on relations between prefrontal asymmetry and measures of behavioral inhibition in a longitudinal sample. The last section considers some of the implications of these data for understanding the mechanisms that underlie behavioral inhibition.

## The Functional Neuroanatomy of Approach and Withdrawal

Although the focus of our empirical research has been on measures of prefrontal brain activity, it must be emphasized at the outset that the circuitry that instantiates emotion in the human brain is complex and involves a number of interrelated structures. Preciously few empirical studies using modern neuroimaging procedures that afford a high degree of spatial resolution have yet been performed (see George et al., 1995, and Paradiso et al., 1997, for examples). Therefore, hypotheses about the set of structures that participate in the production of emotion must necessarily be speculative and based to a large extent on the information available from the animal literature (e.g., LeDoux, 1987) and from theoretical accounts of the processes involved in human emotion.

Based on the available strands of theory and evidence, numerous scientists have proposed two basic circuits, each mediating different forms of motivation and emotion (see e.g., Davidson, 1995; Gray, 1994; Lang, Bradley, & Cuthbert, 1990). The approach system facilitates appetitive behavior and generates certain types of positive affect that are approach-related, for example, enthusiasm, pride, and so forth. (see Depue & Collins, in press, for review). This form of positive affect is usually generated in the context of moving toward a desired goal (see Lazarus, 1991, and Stein & Trabasso, 1992, for theoretical accounts of emotion that place a premium on goal states). The representation of a goal state in working memory is hypothesized to be implemented in dorsolateral prefrontal cortex. The medial prefrontal cortex seems to play an important role in maintaining representations of behavioral-reinforcement contingencies in working memory (Thorpe, Rolls & Maddison, 1983). In addition, output from the medial prefrontal cortex to nucleus accumbens (NA) neurons modulates the transfer of motivationally relevant information through the NA (Kalivas, Churchill, & Klitenick, 1993). The basal ganglia are hypothesized to be involved in the expression of the abstract goal in action plans and in the anticipation of reward (Schultz, Apicella, Romo, & Scarnati, 1995; Schultz, Romo et al., 1995). The NA, particularly the caudomedial shell region of the NA, is a major convergence zone for motivationally relevant information from a myriad of limbic structures. Cells in this region of the NA increase their firing rate during reward expectation (see Schultz, Apicella, et al., 1995). There are likely other structures involved in this circuit which depend on a number of factors, including the nature of the stimuli that signal appetitive information, the extent to which the behavioral-reinforcement contingency is novel or overlearned, and the nature of the anticipated behavioral response.

In a very recent study using positron emission tomography (PET) with $^{18}$F-labeled deoxyglucose (FDG), we (Davidson et al., 1998) presented aversive or appetitive pictures during the FDG uptake procedure in separate sessions. We found significant left-sided metabolic increases during the appetitive condition in inferior prefrontal cortex, nucleus accumbens, and superior prefrontal, premotor, and motor regions. The significant left-sided focus of these metabolic increases was confirmed by formally testing the Condition $\times$ Hemisphere interactions for these regions. Similar findings have recently been reported by Thut et al. (1997) in response to monetary reward. These data imply that at least in humans, the circuitry for appetitive (and aversive) emotion is lateralized. Such a functional neuroanatomical arrangement may be advantageous in helping the brain to compute affective value (see Davidson et al., 1998, for additional discussion of this issue).

It should be noted that the activation of this approach system is hypothesized to be associated with one particular form of positive affect and not all forms of such emotion. It is specifically predicted to be associated with pregoal attainment positive affect, that form of positive affect that is elicited as an organism moves closer toward an appetitive goal. Postgoal attainment positive affect represents another form of positive emotion that is not expected to be associated with activation of this circuit (see Davidson, 1994, for a more extended discussion of this distinction). This latter type of positive affect may be phenomenologically experienced as contentment or joy (though conventional emotional terms appear inadequate in capturing these hypothesized differences) and is expected to occur when the prefrontal cortex goes off-line after a desired goal has been achieved. Cells in the NA have also been shown to decrease their firing rate during the postgoal consummatory phase (e.g., Henriksen & Giacchino, 1993).

Lawful individual differences can enter into many different stages of the approach system. For the moment, it is important to underscore two issues. One is that there are individual differences in the tonic level of activation of the approach system that alter an individual's propensity to experience approach-related positive affect. Second, there are likely to be individual differences in the capacity to shift between pre- and postgoal attainment positive affect and in the ratio between these two forms of positive affect. On reaching a desired goal, some individuals will immediately replace the just-achieved goal with a new desired goal and so will have little opportunity to experience postgoal attainment positive affect, or contentment. There may be an optimal balance between these two forms of positive affect, though this issue has never been studied.

There appears to be a second system concerned with the neural implementation of withdrawal. This system facilitates the withdrawal of an individual from sources of aversive stimulation and generates certain forms of negative affect that are withdrawal-related. Both fear and disgust are associated with increasing the distance between the organism and a source of aversive stimulation. From invasive animal studies and human neuroimaging studies, it appears that the amygdala is critically involved in this system (e.g., LeDoux, 1987). Using functional magnetic resonance imaging (fMRI), we have recently demonstrated for the first time activation in the human amygdala in response to aversive pictures compared with neutral control pictures (Irwin, et al., 1996; see figure 5.1). In addition, the temporal polar region also appears to be activated during withdrawal-related emotion (e.g., Reiman, Fusselman, Fox, & Raichle, 1989; but see Drevets, Videen, MacLeod, Haller, & Raichle, 1992). These effects, at least in humans, appear to be more pronounced on the right side of the brain (Davidson, 1992; see Davidson, 1993, for reviews). In the human PET and electrophysiological studies, the right frontal region is also activated during withdrawal-related negative affective states (e.g., Davidson, Ekman, Saron, Senulis & Friesen, 1990). In the recent FDG-PET study from our laboratory mentioned previously (Davidson et al., 1998), we observed increased glucose metabolism in response to aversive pictures (compared with appetitive pictures) in right prefrontal cortex (Brodmann's area 9) and amygdala. In addition to the prefrontal and temporal polar cortical regions and the amygdala, it is also likely that the basal ganglia and hypothalamus are involved in the motor and autonomic components, respectively, of withdrawal-related negative affect (see Smith, DeVita, & Astley, 1990).

The nature of the relation between these two hypothesized affect systems also remains to be delineated. The emotion literature is replete with different proposals regarding the inter-relations among different forms of positive and negative affect. Some theorists have proposed a single bivalent dimension that ranges from unpleasant to pleasant affect, with a second dimension that reflects arousal (e.g., Russell, 1980). Other theorists have suggested that affect space is best described by two orthogonal positive and negative dimensions (e.g., Cacioppo & Berntson, 1994; Watson & Tellegen, 1985). Still others have suggested that the degree of orthogonality between positive and negative affect depends on the temporal frame of analysis (Diener & Emmons, 1984). This formulation holds that, when assessed in the moment, positive and negative affect are reciprocally related, but when examined over a longer time frame, (e.g., dispositional affect), they are orthogonal. It must be emphasized that these analyses of the relation between positive and negative affect are all based exclusively on measures of self-report, and therefore their generalizability to other measures of affect are uncertain. However, based on new data from our lab that shows reciprocal relations between metabolic activity in the left prefrontal cortex and the amygdala (See Davidson, 1998, for a review of these findings), we believe that one function of positive affect is to inhibit concurrent negative affect. It seems likely that the presence of negative affect would interfere with the generation of pregoal attainment positive affect and with the production of approach behavior. It would therefore be adaptive for negative affect to be inhibited during the generation of positive affect. Of course, the time course of this hypothesized inhibition and the boundary conditions for its presence remain to be elucidated in future research.

## Individual Differences in Asymmetric Prefrontal Activation: What Do They Reflect?

This section presents a brief overview of recent work from our laboratory that was designed to examine individual differences in measures of prefrontal activation and their relation to different aspects of emotion, affective style, and related biological constructs. These findings will be used to address the question of what underlying constituents of affective style such individual differences in prefrontal activation actually reflect.

In both infants (Davidson & Fox, 1989) and adults (Davidson & Tomarken, 1989), we noticed that there were large individual differences in baseline electrophysiological measures of prefrontal activation and that such individual variation was associated with differences in aspects of affective reactivity. In infants, Davidson and Fox (1989) reported that 10-month-old babies who cried in response to maternal separation were more likely to have less left-sided and greater right-sided prefrontal activation during a preceding resting baseline than with those infants who did not cry in response to this challenge. In adults, we first noted that the phasic influence of positive and negative emotion elicitors (e.g., film clips) on measures of prefrontal activation asymmetry appeared to be superimposed on more tonic individual differences in the direction and absolute magnitude of asymmetry (Davidson & Tomarken, 1989).

During our initial explorations of this phenomenon, we needed to determine if baseline electrophysiological measures of prefrontal asymmetry were reliable and stable over time and could thus be used as a trait-like measure. Tomarken, Davidson, Wheeler, and Doss (1992) recorded baseline brain electrical activity from 90 normal participants on two occasions separated by approximately 3 weeks. At each testing session, brain activity was recorded during eight 1-minute trials, four with eyes open and four with eyes closed, presented in counterbalanced order. The data were visually scored to remove artifact and then Fourier-transformed. Our focus was on power in the alpha band (8–13 Hz), though we extracted power in all frequency bands (see Davidson, Chapman, Chapman, & Henriques, 1990, for a discussion of power in different frequency bands and their relation to activation). Using the asymmetry measures derived from each of the eight 1-minute trials as the data, we computed coefficient alpha, separately for each session, as a measure of internal consistency reliability. The coefficient alphas were quite high, with all values exceeding .85, indicating that the electrophysiological measures of asymmetric activation indeed showed excellent internal consistency reliability. The test-retest reliability was adequate, with intraclass correlations ranging from .65 to .75 depending on the specific sites and methods of analysis. The major finding of import from this study was the demonstration that measures of activation asymmetry based on power in the alpha band from prefrontal scalp electrodes showed both high internal consistency reliability and acceptable test-retest reliability to be considered a trait-like index.

The large sample size in the reliability study discussed here enabled us to select a small group of extreme left and extreme right frontally activated participants for MR scans to determine if there existed any gross morphometric differences in anatomical structure between these subgroups. None of our measures of regional volumetric asymmetry revealed any difference between the groups (Davidson, 1997, unpublished data). These findings suggest that whatever differences exist between participants with extreme left versus right prefrontal activation, such differences are likely functional and not structural.

On the basis of our prior data and theory, we reasoned that extreme left and extreme right frontally activated participants would show systematic differences in dispositional positive and negative affect. We administered the trait version of the Positive and Negative Affect Scales (PANAS; Watson, Clark & Tellegen, 1988) to examine this question and found that the left frontally activated participants reported more positive and less negative dispositional affect than their right frontally activated counterparts (Tomarken et al., 1992; see figure 5.2). More recently, with Sutton (Sutton & Davidson, 1997), we showed that scores on a self-report measure designed to operationalize Gray's concepts of behavioral inhibition and behavioral activation (the BIS/BAS scales; Carver & White, 1994) were even more strongly predicted by electrophysiological measures of prefrontal asymmetry than were scores on the PANAS scales (see figure 5.3). Participants with greater left-sided prefrontal activation reported more relative BAS to BIS activity than participants who exhibited more right-sided prefrontal activation. Importantly, in each of these studies, measures of asymmetry from posterior scalp regions derived from the identical points in time showed no relation with the affect variables. In the Sutton and Davidson (1997) study, in which we had a sufficiently large sample size, we tested the significance of the difference in the magnitude of correlation between measures of activation asymmetry in anterior and posterior regions and the BAS-BIS scores.

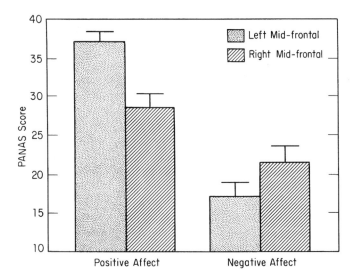

Figure 5.2. Dispositional positive affect (from scores on the PANAS-General Positive Affect Scale) in participants who were classified as extreme and stable left frontally active ($N = 14$) and extreme and stable right frontally active ($N = 13$) on the basis of electrophysiological measures of baseline activation asymmetries on two occasions separated by 3 weeks. From Tomarken, Davidson, Wheeler and Doss (1992). Copyright 1992 by American Psychological Association. Reprinted by permission.

We found that the prefrontal asymmetry measures were significantly more highly correlated with the affect measures than were the measures of posterior asymmetry from the identical periods, underscoring the specificity of this relation to the anterior scalp region.

   We also hypothesized that our measures of prefrontal asymmetry would predict reactivity to experimental elicitors of emotion. The model that we have developed over the past several years (see Davidson, 1992, 1994, 1995 for background) features individual differences in prefrontal activation asymmetry as a reflection of a diathesis which modulates reactivity to emotionally significant events. According to this model, individuals who differ in prefrontal asymmetry should respond differently to an elicitor of positive or negative emotion, even when baseline mood is partialled out. We (Wheeler, Davidson, & Tomarken, 1993) performed an experiment to examine this question. We presented short film clips designed to elicit positive or negative emotion. Brain electrical activity was recorded prior to the presentation of the film clips. Just after the clips were presented, participants were asked to rate their emotional experience during the preceding film clip. In addition, participants completed scales that were designed to reflect their mood at baseline. We found that individual differences in prefrontal asymmetry predicted the emotional response to the films even after measures of baseline mood were statistically removed. Those individuals with more left-sided prefrontal activation at baseline reported more positive affect to the positive film clips, and those with more right-sided prefrontal activation reported more negative affect to the negative film clips. These findings support the idea that individual differences in electrophysiological measures of prefrontal activation asymmetry mark some aspect of vulnerability to positive and negative emotion elicitors. The fact that such relations were obtained following the statistical removal of baseline mood indicates that any difference between left and right frontally activated individuals in baseline mood cannot account for the prediction of film-elicited emotion effects that was observed.

In a very recent study, we (Davidson, Dolski, Larson, & Sutton, 1998) examined relations between individual differences in prefrontal activation asymmetry and the emotion-modulated startle. In this study, we presented pictures from the International Affective Picture System (Lang, Bradley, & Cuthbert, 1995) while acoustic startle probes were presented and the EMG-measured blink response from the orbicularis oculi muscle region was recorded (see Sutton, Davidson, Donzella, Irwin, & Dottl, 1997, for basic methods). Startle probes were presented on separate trials both during the 6-second slide exposure as well as 500 ms following the offset of the pictures. We interpreted startle magnitude during picture exposure as providing an index related to the peak of emotional response, whereas startle magnitude following the offset of the pictures was taken to reflect the recovery from emotional challenge. Used in this way, startle probe methods can potentially provide new information on the time course of emotional responding. We expected that individual differences during actual picture presentation would be less pronounced than individual differences following picture presentation, because an acute emotional stimulus is likely to produce a normative response across participants, yet individuals are likely to differ dramatically in the time they take to recover. Similarly, we expected that individual differences in prefrontal asymmetry would account for more variance in predicting magnitude of recovery (i.e., post-stimulus startle magnitude) than in predicting startle magnitude during the stimulus. Our findings were consistent with our predictions and indicated that participants with greater left-sided prefrontal activation show a smaller blink magnitude following the offset of the negative stimuli after the variance in blink magnitude during the negative stimulus was partialled out. Measures of prefrontal asymmetry did not reliably predict startle magnitude during picture presentation. The findings from this study are consistent with our hypothesis and indicate that individual differences in prefrontal asymmetry are associated with the time course of affective responding, particularly the recovery following emotional challenge.

In addition to the studies described previously using self-report and psychophysiological measures of emotion, we have also examined relations between individual differences in electrophysiological measures of prefrontal asymmetry and other biological indices that in turn have been related to differential reactivity to stressful events. Two recent examples from our laboratory include measures of immune function and cortisol. In the case of the former, we examined differences between left and right prefrontally activated participants in natural killer (NK) cell activity, since declines in NK activity have been reported in response to stressful, negative events (Kiecolt-Glaser & Glaser, 1991). We predicted that participants with increased right prefrontal activation would exhibit lower NK activity than their left-activated counterparts because the former type of individual has been found to report more dispositional negative affect, to show higher relative BIS activity, and to respond more intensely to negative emotional stimuli. We found that right frontally activated participants indeed had lower levels of NK activity than their left frontally activated counterparts (Davidson, et al., in press; Kang et al., 1991).

In collaboration with Ned Kalin, our laboratory has been studying similar individual differences in scalp-recorded measures of prefrontal activation asymmetry in rhesus monkeys (Davidson, Kalin & Shelton, 1992, 1993). Recently, we (Kalin et al., 1998) acquired measures of brain electrical activity from a large sample of rhesus monkeys ($n = 50$). EEG measures were obtained during periods of manual restraint. A subsample of 15 of these monkeys was tested on two occasions 4 months apart. We found that the test-retest correlation for measures of prefrontal asymmetry was .62, suggesting similar stability of this metric in monkey and man. In the group of 50 animals, we also obtained measures of plasma cortisol during the early morning. We hypothesized that if individual differences in prefrontal asymmetry were associated with dispositional affective style, such differences should be correlated with cortisol, since individual differences in baseline cortisol have been related to various aspects of trait-related stressful behavior and psychopathology (see, e.g., Brown et al., 1996; Gold, Goodwin, & Chrousos, 1988). We found that animals with right-sided prefrontal activation had higher levels of baseline cortisol than their left frontally activated counterparts. Moreover, when blood samples were collected 2 years following our initial testing, animals classified as showing extreme right-sided prefrontal activation at age 1 year had significantly higher baseline cortisol levels when they were 3 years of age than animals who were classified at age 1 year as displaying extreme left-sided prefrontal activation. These findings indicate that individual differences in prefrontal asymmetry are present in nonhuman primates and that such differences predict biological measures that are related to affective style.

## Childhood Behavioral Inhibition and Prefrontal Activation Asymmetry

Research efforts to address the proximal causes of childhood behavioral inhibition have implicated a pattern of biological factors that appear to be associated with the development of this temperamental style (e.g., Kagan, Reznick, Clarke, Snidman, & Garcia-Coll, 1984; Kagan, Reznick, & Snidman, 1987, 1988). A previously reported electrophysiological study found increased relative right cortical activation in behaviorally inhibited 3-year-olds compared with uninhibited 3-year-olds (Finman, Davidson, Colton, Straus, & Kagan, 1989), a pattern of cortical asymmetry that has been interpreted as reflecting increased vulnerability to negative emotions (Davidson, 1992, 1998).

In the Finman et al. (1989) study, behavioral inhibition was measured at age 31 months in a laboratory play session, and electrophysiology was measured at age 37 months. For sake of simplicity, these will be referred to as age 3 data. In the play session, same-gender pairs of children who were unknown to each other were exposed to the mild stressors, including a talking robot and an adult stranger who tried to engage them in play. Measures of environmental engagement (latency to touch the first toy; latency to enter a toy tunnel; time within arms' reach of mother and not playing) and of social engagement (latency to approach talking robot; latency to speak first word; latency to approach the stranger) were used to determine level of behavioral inhibition. We tested 368 children. Twenty-four of the most inhibited children and 29 of the most uninhibited returned for an electrophysiological evaluation 6 months later. A control sample of 24 children who were intermediate in their level of behavioral inhibition was also tested (Finman et al., 1989).

The inhibited children had relatively more right than left frontal brain activity, whereas uninhibited children had relatively more left than right frontal brain activity. Middle children had brain activity patterns intermediate between the extreme groups.

### Behavioral Inhibition and Brain Asymmetry in Middle Childhood

This cohort of inhibited, middle, and uninhibited children returned to the laboratory at age 9 years for a follow-up evaluation (Rickman, 1997). An age-appropriate laboratory paradigm was designed to allow assessment of measures of environmental engagement and social engagement that were similar to the earlier assessment. On arrival, the child was escorted to a waiting room while the parent met with the experimenter in a separate room. The waiting room had numerous highly attractive toys on one side and chairs, end tables, and adult books and magazines on the other. A few minutes after being left alone, a female stranger entered the waiting room and over several minutes made increasingly more direct attempts to engage the child. A set of variables that had a face-valid relation to those included in the assessment at age 3 were coded from videotape: latency to touch first toy, latency to first spontaneous utterance to stranger, latency to approach within 3 feet of stranger, and total time inactive. A composite index of behavioral inhibition was calculated from these variables.

Approximately 1 year later, these children returned for an electrophysiological evaluation. EEG (electroencephalography) was recorded from 29 scalp locations with a Lycra cap fit with electrodes using the standard 10–20 system, referenced to the left ear, and placed using known anatomical landmarks. Mean power density from 7–11 Hz was used as the child equivalent of adult alpha (8–13 Hz). Asymmetry scores were calculated individually for each child as the difference in brain activity between homologous sites after correction for muscle artifact. A tercile split was done on behavioral inhibition (BI) scores extracted from the age 9 behavioral evaluation so that participants could be assigned to inhibited, middle, and uninhibited groups at age 9.

The relation between BI at age 9 and brain activity at age 10 was similar to the relation observed at age 3. Children who were inhibited at age 9 had relative right activation in frontal and lateral frontal regions measured approximately 1 year later, whereas children who were uninhibited at age 9 had relative left activation in the frontal and lateral frontal regions (vertex reference). Figure 5.4 shows that the inhibited group exhibited relative right frontal activation asymmetry, whereas the uninhibited group had a pattern of relative left frontal activation asymmetry. The middle group exhibited a pattern of activation asymmetry that was intermediate between the inhibited and uninhibited groups. The main effect of group at age 9 was statistically significant, $F(2,44) = 3.21$, $p < .05$.

A correlation was calculated between frontal asymmetry and the behavioral inhibition index (BI) to determine the extent to which extreme scores within groups contributed to the overall effect. As can be seen in figure 5.5, there is a monotonic relation between age 10 frontal asymmetry and BI score at age 9. Inhibited behav-

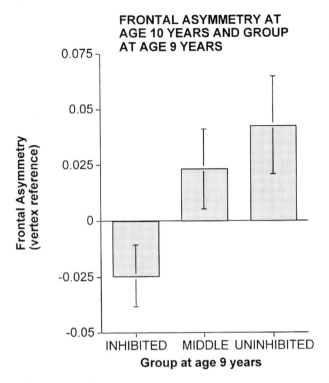

Figure 5.4. Children identified as inhibited at age 9 years had relative right frontal asymmetry at age 10 years. Uninhibited children had relative left frontal asymmetry, and middle children had intermediate asymmetry scores. (Adapted from Rickman, 1997).

ior is associated with increased relative right frontal activation. The magnitude of the correlation between frontal asymmetry and behavior at this age is comparable to that observed in early childhood.

This finding is consistent with predictions. Left frontal brain activity is associated with approach-oriented behavior, whereas right frontal brain activity appears to be associated with withdrawal. In both early childhood (age 3 years) and early school years (ages 9 and 10 years), we found the predicted relation between frontal asymmetry and behavioral inhibition.

### Stability of Behavioral Inhibition and Brain Asymmetry

In figure 5.5 we represent the group status at age 3 years of each of the participants who contributed to the analysis at ages 9 and 10 years. The impression of a lack of correlation between age 3 BI and age 9 BI is born out statistically. Chi-square analysis found that BI group at age 3 was unrelated to BI group at age 10. Using the continuous distribution of BI scores at each age, BI at age 3 was uncorrelated with BI at age 9, Spearman $r = .03$, $p > .8$.

At both ages, children were given time to engage themselves in play prior to be-

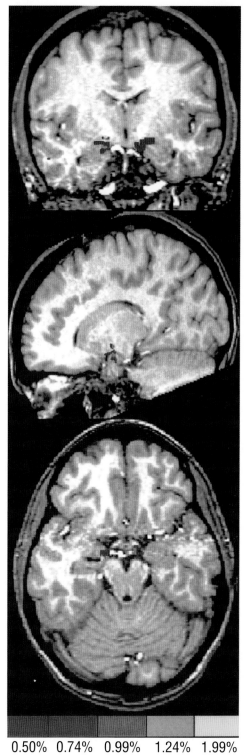

Figure 5.1 Group data showing bilateral activation in the amygdala detected with fMRI in response to aversive compared with neutral pictures. From Irwin et al. (1996).

0.50%  0.74%  0.99%  1.24%  1.99%

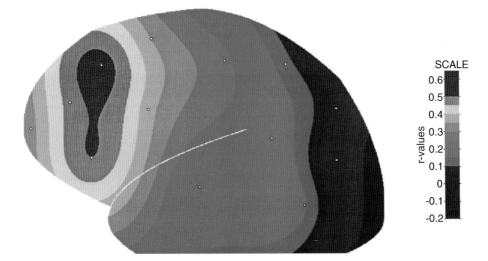

Figure 5.3 Relations between electrophysiological measures of asymmetry and the difference between the standardized score on the Behavioral Activation and Behavioral Inhibition Scales (BAS/BIS scales; Carver & White, 1994), $n = 46$. Electrophysiological data were recorded from each subject on two separate occasions at a 6-week interval. The BAS/BIS scales were also administered on these two occasions. Data were averaged across the two time periods prior to performing correlations. The topographic map displays the correlations between alpha power asymmetry (log right minus log left alpha power; higher values denote greater relative left-sided activation) and the difference score between the standardized BAS minus BIS scales. After correlations were performed for each homologous region, a spline-interpolated map was created. The yellow-orange end of the scale denotes positive correlations. The figure indicates that the correlation between the BAS-BIS difference score and the electrophysiology asymmetry score is highly positive in prefrontal scalp regions, denoting that subjects with greater relative left-sided activation report more relative behavioral activation compared with behavioral inhibition tendencies. The relation between asymmetric activation and the BAS-BIS difference is highly specific to the anterior scalp regions, as the correlation drops off rapidly more posteriorly. The correlation in the prefrontal region is significantly larger than the correlation in the parieto-occipital region. From Sutton & Davidson (1997).

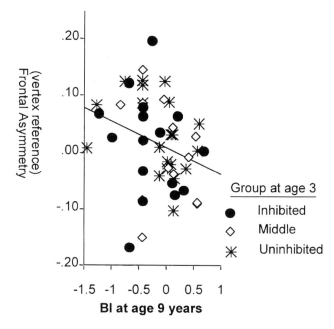

Figure 5.5. Frontal asymmetry (referenced to vertex) at age 10 years was significantly correlated with BI assessed at age 9 years, Spearman $r = -.37$, $p < .008$, $n = 50$. (Adapted from Rickman, 1997)

ing challenged. During the age 3 play session, the child was presented with two social challenges: first, a talking robot, and then an adult female stranger who brought in a tray of attractive toys. At age 9, the children were similarly given a free play "warm-up" period, followed by the introduction of a stranger. For both sessions, the stranger made increasingly more pointed attempts to engage the child. Despite the seeming similarities of the behavioral challenges at each session and of our efforts to replicate in an age-appropriate manner the manipulations at each assessment, BI at age 3 years was uncorrelated with BI at age 9 years. Table 5.1 illustrates the lack of correlation among these measures that compose the BI index at each age.

One possible explanation for the lack of stability of behavioral inhibition over time is that the scenarios in which behavior was observed were not genuinely analogous. An additional problem is that longitudinal assessment makes it difficult to be certain that the behaviors we observed were more powerfully related to individual differences in behavioral inhibition than to confounds associated with having been observed in similar situations. However, the lack of apparent stability in BI over time might be better explained as a consequence of the changing nature of the manifestations of BI.

Table 5.1  Correlations between age 3 = and age 9 = year variables used to calculate behavioral inhibition.

| Age 3 Variables | Age 9 Variables | | | |
| --- | --- | --- | --- | --- |
| | Latency to touch toy ($n = 60$) | Latency to speak word to stranger (n = 59) | Latency to approach within 3 feet of stranger ($n = 56$) | Time inactive (n = 59) |
| Proximity to mother | .07 | −.05 | .03 | .03 |
| Latency to approach robot | −.02 | .00 | −.04 | −.02 |
| Latency to speak | −.11 | −.09 | .12 | .02 |
| Latency to approach stranger | .06 | −.02 | .19 | .14 |
| Latency to touch first toy | .03 | −.14 | −.08 | −.05 |
| Latency to enter tunnel | −.03 | .01 | −.04 | −.01 |

*Note:* Values are Spearman correlations.

Early measures of behavioral inhibition, like other temperamental traits, may not be strongly predictive of later behavior. When predicting temperament from early infancy (age 8 months) to age 4 years, there are few participants who retain their classification, even when participants are selected from extremes (e.g., Maziade, Cote, Bernier, Boutin, & Thivierge, 1989). Even though there is a large body of literature that documents the sequelae of behavioral inhibition, a careful reading of the literature shows that only a limited sample of children show stability in their degree of behavioral inhibition over time. In one longitudinal study (Asendorpf, 1991), behavioral inhibition was assessed at 4 years, 6 years, and 8 years of age in an unselected sample of children. Only 13 of 87 children had behavioral inhibition scores in the upper quartile for all three assessment ages. In a different study, children from an unselected sample who were observed multiple times from 14 to 48 months of age did not show significant stability in laboratory observations of BI over time (Kagan et al., 1989). Similarly, social withdrawal in an unselected sample of kindergarten children was only modestly correlated with social withdrawal in Grade 2 and was not predictive of social withdrawal in Grade 4 (Rubin, 1993).

Apparent instability in BI may also be due, in part, to phasic changes in development. Numerous developmental psychologists from diverse areas of research have observed that the development process includes periods of stability, as well as periods of instability (Block, 1982; Haan, Millsap, & Hartka, 1986; Thelen, 1989). Some authors have suggested that the best time to measure long-standing traits is when the individual is under stress (Wright & Mischel, 1987). They suggest that in day-to-day functioning, influences such as coping mechanisms, social support, and the like sometimes overwhelm the behavioral expression of a trait. These authors found that children who were judged to be prototypically aggressive or withdrawn did not show predictable behaviors in low-demand situations but were characteristically aggressive or withdrawn in high-demand situations.

Our early childhood measures of BI were obtained at a key developmental period of differentiation and separation for children. Middle childhood can be characterized as a "settled" period, where developmental challenges are at a minimum. We may have found evidence of stability of behavioral inhibition had we assessed the children at a developmentally challenging time, such as during the transition to school or during puberty.

Implicit in this explanation is the presumption of an underlying temperamental "trait" or diathesis that is activated in response to stress. We tested the extent to which brain asymmetry indexed this hypothesized diathesis by comparing asymmetry scores at age 3 with those obtained at age 10 and by comparing age 3 asymmetry with age 9 BI. There was no correlation between brain asymmetry at age 3 and brain asymmetry at age 10. Further, age 3 asymmetry failed to predict age 9 BI. Given the finding of a correlation between BI and brain asymmetry within each age period, the lack of the longitudinal predictive relation between these variables is unlikely to be a function of a lack of validity of electrophysiological measures of prefrontal activation asymmetry in indexing affective style characteristics but rather may be a function of the fact that the period across which we sampled is one during which considerable plasticity is occurring.

It also may be that individual differences in brain asymmetry and BI are jointly influenced by plastic changes in the brain. There is a large body of data that shows that brain structures undergo significant development and reorganization from early to middle childhood. There are marked increases in synaptic density, dendritic branching, myelination, and overall brain mass during this period of development, with notable growth spurts around ages 2–4 years and age 7 (Fischer & Rose, 1994). Synaptic density in the frontal cortex peaks at ages 1 year and 7 years while neurons and synapses are continuously "pruned" and modified in a dynamic growth process. Neurons in the frontal lobes are among the last to myelinate, and they continue myelination into adulthood (Spreen, Tupper, Risser, Tuokko & Edgell, 1984).

Patterns of EEG also show notable changes during this period of development. EEG coherence is a measure which has been interpreted to reflect aspects of intracortical connectivity (Thatcher, 1994). The developmental trajectory of EEG coherence in the left hemisphere differs from that of the right hemisphere, and there appear to be growth spurts in the degree of EEG coherence at ages 5 to 7 years and 9 to 11 years, especially in the lateral frontal and frontal regions (Thatcher, 1992, 1994).

It may be that even if behavioral inhibition is not stable over time, brain asymmetry measures may predict a coherent pattern of affective style, and the relation between brain asymmetry and affective style may remain stable over time. This is a view that would hold that plastic changes in affective style occur over this developmental period, produced via a combination of heritable and experiential influences. These changes in affective style are associated with changes in prefrontal brain function, along with changes in behavioral signs of inhibition.

## Stability at the Extremes

Much of the published work on behavioral inhibition derives from the assumption that BI is an important temperamental trait that has long-term consequences for the individual. Shy children become shy adults and choose careers and lifestyles that are less adventuresome than those of their nonshy peers (Caspi, Bem, & Elder, 1989; Caspi, Elder, & Bem, 1988). Behaviorally inhibited children appear to be at increased risk of childhood psychiatric disorders (Rosenbaum et al., 1991). Behaviorally inhibited infants show persistence of phobic reactions to novel social situations from early childhood through adulthood (Kagan & Moss, 1962). These data and more suggest that at least for some individuals, behavioral inhibition remains stable and has long-lasting influences on personal development.

Given the large body of evidence that shows that individual differences in behavioral inhibition do have long-term consequences, we attempted to identify those children who were most likely to exhibit trait-like behavioral inhibition (Rickman, 1997). We predicted that although there was only limited evidence of stability in brain asymmetry and behavior from age 3 to age 10 overall, participants who showed stability in brain activity would also likely show stability in behavior. First, we selected individuals who showed stability in brain asymmetry from age 3 to age 10 years. A median split was done on frontal asymmetry scores at each age. Six children were categorized as stable left and nine children were categorized as stable right. Table 5.2 shows stable brain asymmetry classification by group at age 3. The distribution of stable frontal asymmetry category (stable left, stable right, unstable) to age 3 group status (inhibited, middle, uninhibited) differed marginally from chance ($p < .08$) and differed significantly from chance when the unstable group was excluded ($p < .03$). Fifty-five percent of children who showed stable right frontal asymmetry from age 3 to age 10 were inhibited at age 3 years; 83 percent of children who showed stable left frontal asymmetry from age 3 to age 10 were uninhibited at age 3 years. Three middle-group children showed stable right frontal asymmetry from age 3 to age 10 years.

We then tested the correlation between age 3 frontal asymmetry and age 9 BI in the subset of children who had stable frontal asymmetry scores. As seen in figure 5.6, frontal asymmetry referenced to vertex at age 3 was marginally significantly correlated in the predicted direction with BI at age 9, Spearman $r = -.50$, $p < .07$, $n = 14$. Among participants with stable frontal asymmetry, relative left frontal activation at age 3 was associated with uninhibited behavior at age 9, whereas relative right frontal activation at age 3 was associated with inhibited behavior at age 9.

These data suggest that when prefrontal brain asymmetry is stable, early childhood measures of these patterns predict later behavioral inhibition. This observation is similar to the findings from a recent study in which 7 of 30 infants who had

Table 5.2  Group distribution of stability of brain asymmetry from age 3 to age 10.

| Group at age 3 | Frontal asymmetry | | |
| --- | --- | --- | --- |
| | Stable Right | Stable Left | Unstable |
| Inhibited | 5 | 1 | 15 |
| Middle | 3 | 0 | 15 |
| Uninhibited | 1 | 5 | 19 |

This distribution differed marginally from chance, chi-square (4) = 8.66, Fisher's exact $p < .08$, and differed significantly from chance when the unstable group was excluded, chi-square (2) = 8.06, Fisher's exact $p < .03$.

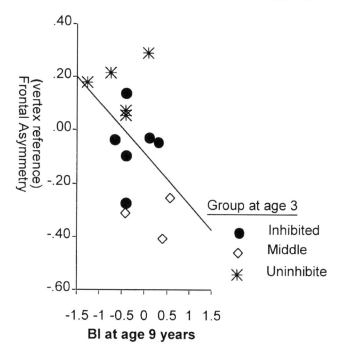

Figure 5.6. Frontal asymmetry at age 3 (referenced to vertex) was marginally correlated with BI at age 9 among children with stable frontal asymmetry scores, Spearman $r = -.50$, $p < .07$, $n = 14$. (Adapted from Rickman, 1997).

an inhibited profile at age 4 months had stable right asymmetry at ages 14 months and 24 months, but none of the infants with stable left asymmetry had an inhibited profile at 4 months (Fox, Calkins, & Bell, 1994).

We also did a separate analysis on children whose level of BI remained stable from age 3 to age 9 years (Rickman, 1997). Within this subset, there was no association between BI and frontal asymmetry at age 3. Stability in behavior does not appear to be related to early childhood brain asymmetry. However, among the behaviorally stable participants, we obtained the expected finding of a significant relation between BI at age 9 and brain asymmetry at age 10. Brain asymmetry at age 10 also significantly predicted BI at age 3.

## Summary and Conclusions

We began with a selective overview of some of the key circuitry that comprises two major emotional/motivational systems of the brain—the approach and withdrawal systems. The prefrontal cortex and amygdala were identified as two important structures within these circuits. We then considered a body of research on individual differences in prefrontal activation asymmetry and their relation to behavioral and biological indices of emotional reactivity. Individuals with greater relative left-sided prefrontal activation report more dispositional positive affect and greater relative behavioral activation than behavioral inhibition. Participants with greater right-sided prefrontal activation react more intensely to negative stimuli, show slower recovery of negative-emotion potentiated startle, and have lower levels of NK activity and higher levels of basal cortisol. We then considered the relation between individual differences in prefrontal activation asymmetry and childhood behavioral inhibition. Our new findings reveal that although concurrent measures of prefrontal activation asymmetry predict behavioral measures of inhibition, neither the measures of brain function nor the behavioral measures show stability from age 3 to 10 years. This is likely a period during which considerable plasticity is present and the impact of experiential events on brain function is greatest. In a very small subset of children who show stable asymmetry from age 3 to 10 years, measures of behavioral inhibition across this developmental period are also stable.

It is important to note that although in the second section we described a number of different structures that make up the circuitry of approach and withdrawal, our discussion of individual differences has focused on prefrontal activation asymmetry. In very recent work, we have developed procedures to examine individual differences in measures of basal activation level (Abercrombie et al., 1998), as well as reactivity (Irwin et al., 1997) of amygdala function, using PET and fMRI procedures. To date, these neuroimaging procedures have not been applied to the study of childhood behavioral inhibition, though fMRI is well suited for this purpose because it is completely noninvasive. In addition, individual differences in hippocampal function are likely to play an important role in the circuitry of withdrawal, since cortisol can have deleterious effects on hippocampal function and the hippocampus appears to play an important role in modulating emotional responses in a context-sensitive fashion (e.g., Maren & Fanselow, 1997). Thus future research on the proximal neural substrates of behavioral inhibition in childhood should take advantage of the corpus of knowledge in animals and use neuroimaging procedures to examine the subcortical contributions to this temperamental characteristic.

The data we presented in the fourth section indicate that although measures of prefrontal activation asymmetry predict concurrent measures of behavioral inhibition, neither the measures of brain function nor the behavioral measures of inhibition are stable from age 3 to 10 years. These findings have important implications for understanding the role of early plasticity in the shaping of brain circuitry critical to emotional responding. It is likely that early social and interpersonal events have profound influences on the brain's emotional circuitry. In the motor (e.g., Nudo, Wise, SiFuentes, & Milliken, 1996) and cognitive domains (e.g., Merzenich et al., 1996), substantial evidence has now accumulated that demonstrates the impact of training on neural plasticity, particularly if the training is accomplished early in life. When we consider the possible impact of the emotional environment on brain function, it is clear that many individuals are saturated with a particular "emotional climate" or interpersonal context from very early in life.

Given the prolonged period of parental care in early human infancy, the capacity for experiential shaping of the emotional circuitry in the brain is profound. We believe that the lack of stability in behavioral and biological measures that reflect temperamental inhibition from ages 3 to 10 years is likely a function of plastic changes that occur during early childhood, a period during which the developing child is typically exposed to prolonged interaction with his or her mother and other caregivers. The identification of the relevant environmental factors that shape these characteristics and the documentation that such experiential exposure is associated with consistent changes in brain function should be on the agenda in the next phase of research on this topic.

Having emphasized early plasticity, it is important not to lose sight of the fact that there were a small number of children who remained stable in their patterns of prefrontal activation asymmetry from age 3 to 10 years. Note that our sample was selected at age 3 years from a group of 368 children who fell into one of three groups—extremely inhibited, extremely uninhibited, and middle. Thus our sample was extreme to begin with. Of the 64 children who were available for electrophysiology follow-up at age 10 years, 23 percent remained stable in their patterns of prefrontal asymmetry. Stability in this case was defined based on a median split at each of the two ages. Thus, to be classified as stable, a child simply had to retain his or her position in the top or bottom half of the distribution on each occasion. Of course, a more stringent criterion would result in even fewer individuals earning a classification as stable. However, those children identified as stable even with the rather coarse definition we used did show evidence of behavioral stability. These findings indicate that when these measures of prefrontal activation asymmetry exhibit stability over several years of early childhood, they do have predictive validity, and they therefore may be useful in identifying individuals early in life who may be potentially at risk for psychopathology. Longitudinal follow-up of these stable individuals will be critical in determining the utility of these measures of prefrontal brain function in the prediction of subsequent affective and anxiety disorders.

*References*

Abercrombie, H. C., Schaefer, S. M., Larson, C. L., Oakes, T. R., Lindgren, K. A., Holden, J. E., Perlman, S. E., Turski, P. A., Krahn, D. D., Benca, R. M., & Davidson, R. J. (1998). Metabolic rate in the right amygdala predicts negative affect in depressed patients. *NeuroReport, 9,* 3301–3307.

Asendorpf, J. B. (1991). Development of inhibited children's coping with unfamiliarity. *Child Development, 62,* 1460–1474.

Block, J. (1982). Assimilation, accommodation, and the dynamics of personality development. *Child Development, 53,* 281–295.

Brown, L. L., Tomarken, A. J., Orth, D. N., Loosen, P. T., Kalin, N. H., & Davidson, R. J. (1996). Individual differences in repressive-defensiveness predict basal salivary cortisol levels. *Journal of Personality and Social Psychology, 70,* 362–371.

Cacioppo, J. T., & Berntson, G. G. (1994). Relationship between attitudes and evaluative space: A critical review, with emphasis on the separability of positive and negative substrates. *Psychological Bulletin, 115,* 401–423.

Carver, C. S., & White, T. L. (1994). Behavioral inhibition, behavioral activation and affective responses to impending reward and punishment: The BIS/BAS scales. *Journal of Personality and Social Psychology, 67,* 319–333.

Caspi, A., Bem, D. J., & Elder, G. H. (1989). Continuities and consequences of interactional styles across the life course. *Journal of Personality, 57,* 375–406.

Caspi, A., Elder, G. H., & Bem, D. J. (1988). Moving away from the world: Life-course patterns of shy children. *Developmental Psychology, 24,* 824–831.

Davidson, R. J. (1992). Emotion and affective style: Hemispheric substrates. *Psychological Science, 3,* 39–43.

Davidson, R. J. (1993). Cerebral asymmetry and emotion: Conceptual and methodological conundrums. *Cognition and Emotion, 7,* 115–138.

Davidson, R. J. (1994). Asymmetric brain function, affective style and psychopathology: The role of early experience and plasticity. *Development and Psychopathology, 6,* 741–758.

Davidson, R. J. (1995). Cerebral asymmetry, emotion and affective style. In R.J. Davidson and K. Hugdahl (Eds.), *Brain asymmetry* (pp. 361–387). Cambridge, MA: MIT Press.

Davidson, R. J. (1997). Unpublished data.

Davidson, R. J. (1998). Affective style and affective disorders: Perspectives from affective neuroscience. *Cognition and Emotion, 12,* 307–330.

Davidson, R. J., Chapman, J. P., Chapman, L. P., & Henriques, J. B. (1990). Asymmetrical brain electrical activity discriminates between psychometrically-matched verbal and spatial cognitive tasks. *Psychophysiology, 27,* 528–543.

Davidson, R. J., Coe, C. C., Dolski, I., & Donzella, B. (in press.) Individual differences in prefrontal activation asymmetry predict natural killer cell activity at rest and in response to challenge. *Brain, Behavior, and Immunity.*

Davidson, R. J., Dolski, I., Larson, C., & Sutton, S. K. (1998). *Electrophysiological measures of prefrontal asymmetry predict recovery of emotion-modulated startle.* Manuscript in preparation.

Davidson, R. J., Ekman, P., Saron, C., Senulis, J., & Friesen, W. V. (1990). Approach/withdrawal and cerebral asymmetry: Emotional expression and brain physiology. I. *Journal of Personality and Social Psychology, 58,* 330–341.

Davidson, R. J., & Fox, N. A. (1989). Frontal brain asymmetry predicts infants' response to maternal separation. *Journal of Abnormal Psychology, 98,* 127–131.

Davidson, R. J., Kalin, N. H., & Shelton, S. E. (1992). Lateralized effects of diazepam on frontal brain electrical asymmetries in rhesus monkeys. *Biological Psychiatry, 32,* 438–451.

Davidson, R. J., Kalin, N. H., & Shelton, S. E. (1993). Lateralized response to diazepam predicts temperamental style in rhesus monkeys. *Behavioral Neuroscience, 107,* 1106–1110

Davidson, R. J., Sutton, S. K., Schaefer, S. M., Ward, R. T., Larson, C. L., Abercrombie, H. C., Holden, J. E., Perlman, S. B., & Turski, P. A. (1998). *Lateralized circuitry for appetitive and aversive emotion in the human brain.* Manuscript in preparation.

Davidson, R. J., & Tomarken, A. J. (1989). Laterality and emotion: An electrophysiological approach. In F. Boller and J. Grafman (Eds.), *Handbook of Neuropsychology,* pp. 419–441. Amsterdam: Elsevier.

Depue, R. A., & Collins, P. F. (In press). Neurobiology of the structure of personality: Dopamine, incentive motivation and extroversion. *Behavioral and Brain Sciences.*

Diener, V. E., & Emmons, R. A. (1984). The independence of positive and negative affect. *Journal of Personality and Social Psychology, 47,* 1105–1117.

Drevets, W. C., Videen, T. O., MacLeod, A. K., Haller, J. W., & Raichle, M. E. (1992). PET images of blood changes during anxiety: Correction. *Science, 256,* 1696.

Finman, R., Davidson, R. J., Colton, M. B., Straus, A. M., & Kagan, J. (1989). Psychophysiological correlates of inhibition to the unfamiliar in children. *Psychophysiology, 26,* S24.

Fischer, K. W., & Rose, S. P. (1994). Dynamic development of coordination of components in brain and behavior. In G. Dawson & K.W. Fischer (Eds.), *Human Behavior and the Developing Brain* (pp. 3–66). New York: Guilford Press.

Fox, N., Calkins, S., & Bell, M. A. (1994). Neural plasticity and development in the first two years of life: Evidence from cognitive and socioemotional domains of research. *Development and Psychopathology, 6,* 677–696.

George, M. S., Ketter, T. A., Parekh, P. I., Horwitz, B., Herscovitch, P., & Post, R. M. (1995). Brain activity during transient sadness and happiness in healthy women. *American Journal of Psychiatry, 152,* 341–351.

Gold, P. W., Goodwin, F. K., & Chrousos, G. P. (1988). Clinical and biochemical manifestations of depression: Relation to the neurobiology of stress. *New England Journal of Medicine, 314,* 348–353.

Gray, J. A. (1994). Three fundamental emotion systems. In P. Ekman & R. J. Davidson (Eds.), *The Nature of Emotion: Fundamental Questions* (pp. 243–247). New York: Oxford University Press.

Gross, J. J., Sutton, S. K., & Ketelaar, T. V. (1998). Relations between affect and personality: Support for the affect-level and affective-reactivity views. *Personality and Social Psychology Bulletin, 24,* 279–288.

Haan, N., Millsap, R., & Hartka, E. (1986). As time goes by: Change and stability in personality over 50 years. *Psychology and Aging, 1,* 220–232.

Henriksen, S. J., & Giacchino, J. (1993). Functional characteristics of nucleus accumbens neurons: Evidence obtained from *in vivo* electrophysiological recordings. In P. W. Kalivas & C. D. Barnes, (Eds.), *Limbic motor circuits and neuropsychiatry* (pp. 101–124). Boca Raton, FL: CRC Press.

Irwin, W., Davidson, R. J., Lowe, M. J., Mock, B. J., Sorenson, J. A., & Turski, P. A. (1996). Human amygdala activation detected with echo-planar functional magnetic resonance imaging. *NeuroReport, 7,* 1765–1769.

Irwin, W., Mock, B. J., Sutton, S. K., Orendi, J. L., Sorenson, J. A., Turski, P. A., Kalin, N. H., & Davidson, R. J. (1997). Positive and negative affective responses: Neural circuitry revealed using functional magnetic resonance imaging. *Society for Neuroscience, 23,* 1318.

Kagan, J., & Moss, H. A. (1962). *Birth to maturity: A study in psychological development.* New York and London: Wiley.

Kagan, J., Reznick, J. S., Clarke, C., Snidman, N., & Garcia-Coll, C. (1984). Behavioral inhibition to the unfamiliar. *Child Development, 55,* 2212–2225.

Kagan, J., Reznick, J. S., & Gibbons, J. (1989). Inhibited and uninhibited types of children. *Child Development, 60,* 838–845.

Kagan, J., Reznick, J. S., & Snidman, N. (1987). The physiology and psychology of behavioral inhibition in children. *Child Development, 58,* 1459–1473.

Kagan, J., Reznick, J. S., & Snidman, N. (1988). Biological bases of childhood shyness. *Science, 240,* 167–171.

Kalin, N. H. (1993). The neurobiology of fear. *Scientific American, 268,* 94–107.

Kalin, N. H., Larson, C., Shelton, S. E., & Davidson, R. J. (1998). Asymmetric frontal brain activity, cortisol, and behavior associated with fearful temperament in Rhesus monkeys. *Behavioral Neuroscience, 112,* 286–292.

Kalivas, P. W., Churchill, L., & Klitenick, M. A. (1993). The circuitry mediating the translation of motivational stimuli into adaptive motor responses. In P. W. Kalivas & C. D. Barnes, (Eds.), *Limbic motor circuits and neuropsychiatry* (pp. 237–287). Boca Raton, FL: CRC Press.

Kang, D. H., Davidson, R. J., Coe, C. L., Wheeler, R. W., Tomarken, A. J., & Ershler, W. B. (1991). Frontal brain asymmetry and immune function. *Behavioral Neuroscience, 105,* 860–869.

Kiecolt-Glaser, J. K., & Glaser, R. (1991). Stress and immune function in humans. In R. Ader, D. L. Felten, and N. Cohen (Eds.), *Psychoneuroimmunology* (2nd ed., pp. 849–867). San Diego, CA: Academic Press.

Lang, P. J., Bradley, M. M., & Cuthbert, B. N. (1990). Emotion, attention and the startle reflex. *Psychological Review, 97,* 377–398.

Lang, P. J., Bradley, M. M., & Cuthbert, B. N. (1995). *International affective picture system (IAPS): Technical manual and affective ratings*. Gainsville, FL: Center for Research in Psychophysiology, University of Florida.

Lazarus, R. S. (1991). *Emotion and adaptation*. Oxford University Press.

LeDoux, J. E. (1987). Emotion. In F. Plum (Ed.), *Handbook of Physiology. Section I: The Nervous System: Higher Functions of the Brain* (Vol. 5, pp. 419–460). Bethesda, MD: American Physiological Society.

Maren, S., & Fanselow, M. S. (1997). Electrolytic lesions of the fibria/fornix, dorsal hippocampus, or entorhinal cortex produce anterograde deficits in contextual fear conditioning in rats. *Neurobiology of Learning and Memory, 67*, 142–149.

Maziade, M., Cote, R., Bernier, H., Boutin, P., & Thivierge, J. (1989). Significance of extreme temperament in infancy for clinical status in pre-school years. I: Value of extreme temperament at 4–8 months for predicting diagnosis at 4.7 years. *British Journal of Psychiatry, 154*, 535–543.

Meehl, P. E. (1975). Hedonic capacity: Some conjectures. *Bulletin of the Menninger Clinic, 39*, 295–307.

Merzenich, M. M., Jenkins, W. M., Johnston, P., Schreiner, C., Miller, S. L., & Tallal, P. (1996). Temporal processing deficits of language-learning impaired children ameliorated by training. *Science, 271*, 77–81.

Nudo, R. J., Wise, B. M., SiFuentes, F., & Milliken, G. W. (1996). Neural substrates for the effects of rehabilitative training on motor recovery after ischemic infarct. *Science, 272*, 1791–1794.

Paradiso, S., Robinson, R. G., Andreasen, N. C., Downhill, J. E., Davidson, R. J., Kirchner, P. T., Watkins, G. L., Boles, L. L., & Hichwa, R. D. (1997). Emotional activation of limbic circuitry in elderly and normal subjects in a PET study. *American Journal of Psychiatry, 154*, 382–389.

Reiman, E. M., Fusselman M. J. L., Fox B. J., & Raichle, M. E. (1989). Neuroanatomical correlates of anticipatory anxiety. *Science, 243*, 1071–1074.

Rickman, M. D. (1997). *Behavioral inhibition, emotional vulnerability and brain asymmetry: A biobehavioral study of inhibited, middle and uninhibited children from age 30 months to age 10 years*. Unpublished doctoral dissertation, University of Wisconsin, Madison.

Rosenbaum, J. F., Biederman, J., Hirshfeld, D. R., Bolduc, E. A., Faraone, S. V., Kagan, J., Snidman, N., & Reznick, J. S. (1991). Further evidence of an association between behavioral inhibition and anxiety disorders: Results from a family study of children from a non-clinical sample. *Journal of Psychiatry Research, 25*, 49–65.

Rubin, K. H. (1993). The Waterloo longitudinal project: Correlates and consequences of social withdrawal from childhood to adolescence. In K. H. Rubin & J. B. Asendorpf (Eds.), *Social withdrawal, inhibition, and shyness in childhood* (pp. 291–314). Hillsdale, NJ: Erlbaum.

Russell, J. A. (1980 ). A circumplex model of emotion. *Journal of Personality and Social Psychology, 39*, 1161–1178.

Schultz, W., Apicella, P., Romo, R., & Scarnati, E. (1995). Context-dependent activity in primate striatum reflecting past and future behavioral events. In J. C. Houk, J. L. Davis, & D. G. Beiser (Eds.), *Models of information processing in the basal ganglia* (pp. 11–28). Cambridge, MA: MIT Press.

Schultz, W., Romo, R., Ljungberg, T., Mirenowicz, J., Hollerman, J. R., & Dickinson, A. (1995). Reward-related signals carried by dopamine neurons. In J.C. Houk, J. L. Davis, & D. G. Beiser (Eds.), *Models of information processing in the basal ganglia* (pp. 233–248). Cambridge, MA: MIT Press.

Smith, O. A., DeVita, J. L., & Astley, C. A. (1990). Neurons controlling cardiovascular responses to emotion are located in lateral hypothalamus-perifornical region. *American Journal of Physiology, 259*, R943–R954.

Spreen, O., Tupper, D., Risser, A., Tuokko, H., & Edgell, D. (1984). *Human Developmental Neuropsychology*. New York: Oxford University Press.

Stein, N. L., & Trabasso, T. (1992). The organization of emotional experience: Creating links among emotion, thinking, language and intentional action. *Cognition and Emotion, 6,* 225–244.

Sutton, S. K., & Davidson, R. J. (1997). Prefrontal brain asymmetry: A biological substrate of the behavioral approach and inhibition systems. *Psychological Science, 8,* 204–210.

Sutton, S. K., Davidson, R. J., Donzella, B., Irwin, W., & Dottl, D. A. (1997). Manipulating affective state using extended picture presentation. *Psychophysiology, 34,* 217–226.

Thatcher, R. W. (1992). Cyclic cortical reorganization during early childhood. *Brain and Cognition, 20,* 24–50.

Thatcher, R. W. (1994). Cyclic cortical reorganization: Origins of human cognitive development. In G. Dawson & K. F. Fischer (Eds.), *Human behavior and the developing brain* (pp. 232–268). New York: Guilford Press.

Thelen, E. (1989). Self-organization in developmental processes: Can systems approaches work? In M. R. Gunnar & E. Thelen (Eds.), *Systems and Development* (pp. 77–117). Hillsdale, NJ: Erlbaum.

Thorpe, S., Rolls, E., & Maddison, S. (1983). The orbitofrontal cortex: Neuronal activity in the behaving monkey. *Experimental Brain Research, 49,* 93–113.

Thut, G., Schultz, W., Roelcke, U., Nienhusmeier, M., Missimer. J., Maguire, R. P., & Leenders, K. L. (1997). Activation of the human brain by monetary reward. *Neuroreport, 8,* 1225–1228.

Tomarken, A. J., Davidson, R. J., Wheeler, R. E., & Doss, R. C. (1992). Individual differences in anterior brain asymmetry and fundamental dimensions of emotion. *Journal of Personality and Social Psychology, 62,* 676–687.

Watson, D., Clark, L. A., & Tellegen, A. (1988). Developmental and validation of brief measures of positive and negative affect: The PANAS scales. *Journal of Personality and Social Psychology, 54,* 1063–1070.

Watson, D., & Tellegen, A. (1985). Toward a consensual structure of mood. *Psychological Bulletin, 98,* 219–235.

Wheeler, R. E., Davidson, R. J., & Tomarken, A. J. (1993). Frontal brain asymmetry and emotional reactivity: A biological substrate of affective style. *Psychophysiology, 30,* 82–89.

Wright, J. C., & Mischel, W. (1987). A conditional approach to dispositional constructs: The local predictability of social behavior. *Journal of Personality and Social Psychology, 53,* 1159–1177.

# Temperament, Fear, and Shyness

## Mary K. Rothbart

This important volume treats the origins, mechanisms, and outcomes of extreme fear, shyness, and social phobia. Its first major section, the subject of this commentary, specifically addresses the origins of and biological mechanisms in the study of childhood shyness and fear, including the contributions of individual differences in temperament. Since the early contributions of Thomas and Chess and colleagues (Thomas, Chess, Birch, Hertzig, & Korn, 1963), individual differences in temperament have been used to predict and to understand later personality and psychopathology (see Rothbart & Bates, 1998, for a recent review), and each of the five chapters in this section considers important contributions of early temperament to later development. Four of the chapters discuss possible direct linkages between temperament and later outcomes (Kagan, chapter 1; Crozier, chapter 2; Schmidt & Fox, chapter 4; and Davidson & Rickman, chapter 5), and two chapters deal with additional systems related to fear, shyness, and stress responses, including attachment (Stansbury, chapter 3) and self-consciousness (Crozier, chapter 2).

## Temperament Terminology

Because each of the chapters addresses the role of temperament in the development of fear and shyness, a good deal of integration might be expected in these chapters. The reader must be cautioned, however, that in these chapters, there is considerable variability in the terms used to describe fear-related temperament. In fact, the five chapters of this section use five different basic terms, although some introduce additional terminology within a given chapter. The terms used are: behavioral inhibition (chapter 1), fearful shyness (chapter 2), difficult temperament (chapter 3), withdrawal (chapter 4), and avoidance (chapter 5). Unfortunately, applying different terms to what appear to be similar temperament dimensions can lead others to view the temperament area as a site of dissension and confusion. For example, one anthropologist looking at the temperament field today writes, "psychologists think of temperament as a rather amorphous cluster of behaviors with biological underpinnings. . . . But no two researchers agree on exactly which behaviors should be included under the label 'temperament'" (Small, 1998, p. 161). I would argue that there is actually much more agreement in the area than is apparent in the vocabulary used. Acknowledging agreement on subject mater when it exists can lead to real advances in a field, as in the agreement among personality researchers on the "Big Five" as a subject of study (Wiggins, 1996).

We have attempted to pull together several widely used temperament terms in a review of temperament in childhood (Rothbart & Bates, 1998). We found in this work that constructs of temperament referred to by a variety of names were frequently associated with a single basic affective-motivational system. These basic systems, including fear, frustration, and approach, are evolutionarily conserved, shared with other species, and influenced by experience, and they can be understood at multiple levels of analysis (Rothbart, Derryberry, & Posner, 1994). Probably the most widely studied of these systems is frequently called fear, and fear seems to share major characteristics with each of the terms used by authors in this section. Conditioned and unconditioned *fear,* to novel and intense and other evolutionarily prepared stimuli, including social fear or *shyness,* can be reflected in *behavioral inhibition* or freezing (arrest of ongoing behavior), vigilance, and distinctive facial expression. It is also evidenced in potentiated startle and is related to changes in heart rate, blood pressure, and respiration that can support *avoidance* or *withdrawal* (Davis, Hitchcock, & Rosen, 1987). Measures at different levels of analysis can thus be taken as indicators of fear, and important links to amygdala functioning in animals (Davis, 1992; LeDoux, 1987) and humans (reviewed by Davidson & Rickman, chapter 5, this volume) support the existence of brain sites for central processing of fear.

Arguing that we are studying individual differences in a basic affective motivational system does not mean, however, that the individual terms used to label it are unimportant. Research is needed to allow us to better understand relationships among fear indicators such as behavioral arrest (inhibition), withdrawal from novel and/or intense stimulation, and learned avoidance. For example, recent research on conditioned fear in developing rats indicates that freezing, heart rate, and potentiated startle are manifestations of fear that emerge at different times in development (Hunt & Campbell, 1997). It will be important to learn in detail about the development of indicators of fear in humans, and initial advances have been made in this area (Bronson, 1966; Kagan, chapter 1, this volume; Rothbart, 1988). However, the point of general agreement about the basic temperamental system is equally important.

The term I find most problematic in this section, however, is the term *difficult temperament* used by Stansbury. Such a designation stresses others' reactions to a set of behaviors or processes rather than the basic processes themselves, and the term can be and has been attached to a wide variety of temperament dimensions and situations (see discussion in Rothbart & Bates, 1998). This can result in confusion from study to study as to exactly what is being measured, although in Stansbury's research, the dimensions used are clearly specified.

### Hemispheric Asymmetry

Having identified a temperamental dimension of inhibition, avoidance or withdrawal, Kagan (chapter 1), Schmidt and Fox (chapter 4), and Davidson and Rickman (chapter 5) note its relation to a measure of hemispheric asymmetry, that is, to higher relative EEG activation of right than of left frontal areas. This measure has been related to measures of negative affect and to behavioral signs of fear (behavioral inhibition) at varying ages. The hemispheric asymmetry measure is intriguing with respect to localizing brain sources of individual differences. It is nevertheless still a gross localization, and as Schmidt and Fox point out, differences in asymmetry scores can result from a number of underlying conditions. Both the Schmidt and Fox chapter and the Davidson and Rickman chapter report progress in developing more differentiated measures, and Schmidt and Fox introduce an approach construct related to left hemisphere functioning, positing two kinds of shyness that are high or low in approach tendencies. Davidson and Rickman also report links between human fear and amygdala activation, as well as to a recovery phase of fear-potentiated startle.

### Stability

Issues of stability of individual differences in hemispheric asymmetry arise, however, in the Davidson and Rickman chapter. In their research, a lack of stability was found in behavioral measures of inhibition and in measures of hemispheric asymmetry between the ages of 3 and 9–10 years. They also were unable to predict later behavioral inhibition directly from earlier hemispheric asymmetry. This is surprising, given that behavioral stability has been reported as early as Wanda Bronson's (1966) review, with relatively stable individual differences in active, spontaneous, or extraverted behavior versus shyness and reserve. In our laboratory studies of infant temperament, 13-month-old infants' fear (distress and withdrawal to novel and unpredictable stimuli in the laboratory) predicted parents' reports of both shyness (distress and latency to approach unfamiliar people) and fear (general distress and latency to approach novelty) at age 7 years (Rothbart, Derryberry, & Hershey, in press). As a "trait" measure, and unlike most shyness measures, the hemispheric asymmetry assay may show trait-like characteristics only within specific developmental time periods.

### Shyness and Self-Consciousness

Kagan importantly differentiates shyness from fear by describing shyness as a kind of behavioral inhibition seen in the social domain; other inhibition or fear is shown toward nonsocial objects. His analysis predicts a positive relation between shyness and fear. In both childhood and adulthood, shyness and fear are positively related (see review by Rothbart & Mauro, 1990), and in factor analytic studies of parent-reported temperament in both toddlers and children aged 3–7 years, shyness shows a primary loading on a broad negative affectivity factor, with a substantial secondary negative loading on a broad approach, surgency, or extraversion factor (Rothbart, Ahadi, Hershey, & Fisher, 1997; Rothbart & Jones, 1998).

Both Kagan and Crozier also note that other aspects of development than temperamental fear contribute to shy behavior. Crozier provides evidence for self-consciousness as one of these variables. The approach of relating shyness to other aspects of social development is a helpful one, and has been followed by others in the literature. Asendorpf (1990), for example, has reported that some children demonstrate an apparently temperamental or early developing shyness at the beginning of school, whereas other children show increasing shyness over time. Inhibition in class, over time, is also increasingly related to being ignored or rejected by peers. Asendorpf (1990) suggests that this later-appearing shyness may result from punishment by the children's peers, related to their social evaluation of a child's behavior. In his studies in Germany, Asendorpf (1994) predicted later low social self-esteem from the later-appearing, but not from early-appearing, temperamental shyness.

## Fear and Approach: Effortful Control and Affiliative Tendencies

Schmidt and Fox and Davidson and Rickman raise the importance of the temperamental dimension of approach. In measures of hemispheric asymmetry, higher relative left activation has been associated with positive affect and approach. Schmidt and Fox suggest that children who are high in both approach and avoidance as reflected in high absolute levels of activation of both hemispheres are likely to be socially anxious, whereas children high in avoidance and low in approach are likely to be socially avoidant. This analysis stresses that different combinations or patterns of temperamental characteristics may lead to different social outcomes.

The terms used in this analysis raise questions, however, about the degree to which approach might be related to active avoidance. In our laboratory observations of infants' self-regulatory strategies in distress-related situations, we found that infants who were more likely to approach intense and unpredictable stimuli were also more likely to actively avoid them (Rothbart, Ziaie, & O'Boyle, 1992). This could be because approaching infants experienced the stimuli at higher intensity levels due to their closer proximity. It may also be the case, however, that infants who are more active in approach are also more active in avoidance/withdrawal, as suggested in Gray's (1971, 1982) descriptions of the Behavioral Activation System (BAS). Gray distinguishes between passive inhibition of action in the Behavioral Inhibition System (BIS) and active avoidance, as seen as part of the BAS or approach system. In his model, high approach might be more related to avoidance than to anxiety.

The idea that behaviors reflect a balance between multiple temperamental tendencies is nevertheless important. In this regard, at least two other temperamental dimensions might be expected to interact with fear and shyness. One of these is effortful control by attention (see discussions by Rothbart & Bates, 1998, and Rothbart, Derryberry, & Posner, 1994). One aspect of effortful control is the ability to inhibit a dominant response in order to perform a subdominant response. Just as fear can inhibit approach, so effortful attention can control either approach or fear, although these affective-motivational systems can also "catch hold" of attention (Derryberry & Rothbart, 1997). Effortful control may also be operating when participants are required to look at pictures that might elicit withdrawal, as in the fear-potentiated startle research described by Davidson and Rickman.

Another possible temperament variable is one we have called affiliativeness (Rothbart & Bates, 1998). Affiliativeness appears to be related to functioning of the opioid systems and oxytocin (see review by Rothbart, et al., 1994). We would expect affiliativeness to be related to the personality dimension of agreeableness and that it might be assessed through aspects of a social orientation of a quieter sort than an extravert's appreciation of parties and social excitement. Affiliative tendencies might also be related to the kind of approaching shyness described in Schmidt and Fox's discussion of social anxiety and to attachment, as discussed in Stansbury's excellent contribution to this volume.

## Temperament and Attachment

Stansbury develops an approach to interactions between temperamental dispositions and treatment by parents that is very promising. The chapter introduces the construct of children's internal representations or models of others from the attachment literature. Children's models of others can be added to the self-consciousness variable discussed by Crozier to illuminate our understanding of shyness. Stansbury also reports relations between cortisol and measures of temperament and attachment that link multiple levels of analysis.

## Summary

In addition to reviewing strong individual research programs, these chapters provide important insights on childhood shyness, with the general message that temperamental shyness or fear is only one of many contributors to shyness as it develops over the life span. The chapters also describe biological assays of individuality that may prove useful in the future localization and study of brain systems of temperament. Ideas put forward in these chapters regarding the balance of temperamental tendencies and interactions between temperament and social environment in producing outcomes will be very helpful for future research.

### Acknowledgments

This research and commentary have been supported by grants MH43361 and MH01471 from the National Institutes of Health. Thanks to Michael Posner for his comments on a previous version of the commentary.

### References

Asendorpf, J. B. (1990). Development of inhibition during childhood: Evidence for situational specificity and a two-factor model. *Developmental Psychology, 26,* 721–730.

Asendorpf, J. B. (1994). The malleability of behavioral inhibition: A study of individual developmental functions. *Developmental Psychology, 30,* 912–919.

Bronson, W. C. (1966). Central orientations: A study of behavior organization from childhood to adolescence. *Child Development, 37,* 125–155.

Davis, M. (1992). The role of the amygdala in fear and anxiety. *Annual Review of Neuroscience, 15,* 353–375.

Davis, M., Hitchcock, J. M., & Rosen, J. B. (1987). Anxiety and the amygdala: Pharmacological and anatomical analysis of the fear-potentiated startle paradigm. In G. Bower (Ed.), *The psychology of learning and motivation* (Vol. 21, pp. 263–305). San Diego, CA: Academic Press.

Derryberry, D., & Rothbart, M. K. (1997). Reactive and effortful processes in the organization of temperament. *Development and Psychopathology, 9,* 631–650.

Gray, J. A. (1971). *The psychology of fear and stress.* New York: McGraw-Hill.

Gray, J. A. (1982). *The neuropsychology of anxiety.* Oxford: Oxford University Press.

Hunt, P. S., & Campbell, B. A. (1997). Developmental dissociation of the components of conditioned fear. In M. E. Bouton & M. S. Fanselow (Eds.), *Learning, motivation, and cognition* (pp. 53–74). Washington, DC: American Psychological Association.

LeDoux, J. E. (1987). Emotion. In F. Plum (Ed.), *Handbook of physiology. Section I: The nervous system: Higher functions of the brain* (Vol. 5. pp. 419–460). Bethesda, MD: American Psychological Society.

Rothbart, M. K. (1988). Temperament and the development of inhibited approach. *Child Development, 59,* 1241–1250.

Rothbart, M. K., Ahadi, S., Hershey, K., & Fisher, P. (1997). *Investigations of temperament at 3–7 years: The Children's Behavior Questionnaire.* Manuscript submitted for publication.

Rothbart, M. K., & Bates, J. E. (1998). Temperament. In N. Eisenberg (Ed.), *Handbook of child psychology: Social, emotional, and personality development* (Vol. 3. pp. 105–176). New York: Wiley.

Rothbart, M. K., Derryberry, D., & Hershey, K. (in press). Stability of temperament in childhood: Laboratory infant assessment to parent report at seven years. In V. J. Molfese & D. L. Molfese (Eds.), *Temperament and personality development across the life span.* New Jersey: Erlbaum.

Rothbart, M. K., Derryberry, D., & Posner, M. I. (1994). A psychobiological approach to the development of temperament. In J. E. Bates & T. D. Wachs (Eds.), *Temperament: Individual differences at the interface of biology and behavior* (pp. 83–116). Washington, DC: American Psychological Association.

Rothbart, M. K., & Jones, L. B. (1998). Temperament, self regulation, and education. *School Psychology Review, 27,* 479–491.

Rothbart, M. K., & Mauro, J. A. (1990). Temperament, behavioral inhibition and shyness in childhood. In H. Leitenberg (Ed.), *Handbook of social and evaluation anxiety* (pp. 139–160). New York: Plenum.

Rothbart, M. K., Ziaie, H., & O'Boyle, C. G. (1992). Self-regulation and emotion in infancy. In N. Eisenberg & R. A. Fabes (Eds.), *Emotion and its regulation in early development: New directions for child development, 55,* 7–24.

Small, M. F. (1998). *Our babies, ourselves.* New York: Anchor Books.

Thomas, A., Chess, S., Birch, H. G., Hertzig, M. E., & Korn, S. (1963). *Behavioral individuality in early childhood.* New York: New York University Press.

Wiggins, J. S. (1996). *The five-factor model of personality.* New York: Guilford Press.

# PART II

## ENDOCRINE AND NEURAL
## BASES OF FEAR

Implications for Understanding Extreme Shyness
and Developmental Outcome

# 6

## Neural Mechanisms and the Development of Individual Differences in Behavioral Inhibition

Lorey K. Takahashi & Ned H. Kalin

Vertebrates have evolved defensive behavioral responses that facilitate survival from threatening stimuli such as predators. When alarmed or threatened, these defensive responses take immediate precedent over ongoing activities such as vocalizations, feeding, and reproduction (Ficken & Witkin, 1977; Magurran & Girling, 1986; Schaller, 1972). One defensive response pattern expressed by many species is to inhibit all body movements and assume an immobile or freezing posture. This behavioral inhibitory response is effective in preventing detection and attack by predators (Palmer, 1909; Ratner, 1967).

Although selection processes have led to the development of behavioral responses that facilitate survival from threats, optimal expression of defensive behavior is equally important (Lima & Dill, 1990). That is, when behavioral inhibition is continually expressed at inappropriate levels or out of context it may interfere with other significant activities. Excessive displays of defensive acts may reflect uncontrolled levels of fear and anxiety induced by a dysregulated neural system, and the consequences may have significant clinical implications (Kalin & Shelton, in press). In humans, some defensive reactions that are inappropriately expressed, such as behavioral inhibition, are linked to the development of psychopathology. Importantly, individuals at risk to develop anxiety disorders and depression can be identified in early childhood on the basis of their behavioral inhibition profile (Biederman et al., 1993; Kagan, Reznick, & Snidman, 1988).

Very little information currently exists on the neural development of behavioral inhibition. In an effort to fill this knowledge gap, we have developed animal models of behavioral inhibition with the aim of providing unique insights into processes involved in the development of the neural circuitry that underlies the regulation of this response. Identifying and characterizing the neural developmental

97

processes involved in the expression of behavioral inhibition have broad implications for understanding factors responsible for individual differences. This chapter examines the neurodevelopment of behavioral inhibition with emphasis on the body of work derived from our studies on the laboratory rat and rhesus monkey. In these studies, the behavioral inhibition response that is described is akin to an emotional predisposition. That is, the behavioral inhibition or freezing response represents the individual's characteristic or developmental reaction to threat.

## Development and Variability in Behavioral Inhibition

Although adults are capable of freezing, the developmental appearance of behavioral inhibition varies across species. In species with precocial young that have relatively mature sensory and motor systems at birth, vocalizations and motor activity are rapidly inhibited when animals are alarmed (Greig-Smith, 1980; Miller, 1980). In laboratory-reared chicks and quails, exposure to unfamiliar situations results in a reduction in behavioral movements accompanied by quiet lying postures with eye closure (Jones, Mills, & Faure, 1991; Montevecchi, Gallup, & Dunlap, 1973; Murphy & Wood-Gush, 1978).

In contrast, nonprecocial or altricial young that exhibit immature sensory and motor abilities and require considerable maternal care during the immediate postnatal period do not display behavioral inhibition immediately after birth. For example, rat pups do not exhibit behavioral inhibition or freezing until the end of the 2nd postnatal week (Collier & Bolles, 1980; Takahashi, 1992b). Prior to this time, infant rats emit high levels of ultrasonic vocalizations in response to unfamiliar environmental and social stimuli (Noirot, 1972; Takahashi, 1992a). These ultrasounds may serve to elicit and direct maternal attention to the pup (Hofer, 1996; Noirot, 1972). However, at approximately 2 weeks of age, rat pups exposed to an unfamiliar anesthetized adult male rat placed on the opposite side of a wire mesh barrier exhibit a robust freezing response accompanied by a reduction in ultrasounds (Takahashi, 1992b). At this age, the attenuation in vocalizations and concurrent display of freezing may facilitate survival when encountering an unfamiliar and potentially infanticidal male rat (Paul & Kupferschmidt, 1975; Takahashi & Lore, 1982) or predator during excursions from the nest. In these studies, unfamiliarity of the adult male rat is a critical factor in the elicitation of behavioral inhibition. When rat pups are tested in the presence of a familiar adult male rat, high levels of freezing do not occur (Takahashi, 1994b).

In some species, the ability to exhibit behavioral inhibition may be present at an early age; however, rapid modulation of its expression in response to varying threatening situations occurs only after a period of further development (figure 6.1). For example, 9- to 12-week-old rhesus monkeys respond to varying threats with a set of specific defensive responses (Kalin, Shelton, & Takahashi, 1991). As with the neonatal rat, when the infant monkey is separated from its mother and placed in social isolation, vocalizations referred to as coos are emitted that serve to signal the infant's location and facilitate maternal retrieval (Newman, 1985). However, when a human enters the test situation and avoids eye contact, vocalizations cease, and the monkey immediately freezes. If the human then stares at the monkey, aggressive barking is rapidly elicited. This ability to change from one behavior pattern to an-

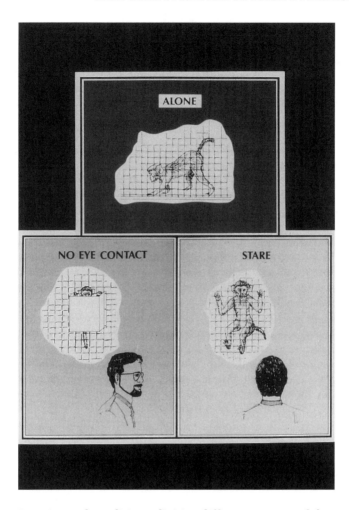

Figure 6.1. Experimental conditions eliciting different patterns of rhesus monkey defensive behavior. Infant rhesus monkeys isolated in a cage (top panel) are usually behaviorally active and frequently emit coo vocalizations to solicit maternal behavior. However, when a human intruder enters the test room and avoids eye contact with the monkey (lower left panel), the monkey rapidly seeks cover behind the food bin and freezes. In contrast, if the human intruder turns to stare at the monkey, hostile behavior such as barking is immediately elicited (lower right panel).

other in response to varying features of the human threat is not present in monkeys less than 2 weeks of age (Kalin et al., 1991). These results suggest that although the mechanisms responsible for the induction of behavioral inhibition are present in early life, the neural systems that coordinate this response with other defensive reactions still require an extended postnatal period of maturation.

In addition to interspecific differences in the development of behavioral inhibition, individuals within a species vary in their freezing response (reviewed by

Boissy, 1995; Gray, 1987). For example, different strains of rats differ in the magnitude of threat-induced freezing (Pare, 1989; Sakaguchi, LeDoux, Sved, & Reis, 1984) suggesting that genetic factors contribute to the expression of behavioral inhibition. Similarly, studies in humans support the view that behavioral inhibition is, in part, genetically determined (Matheny, 1989). The early environment may also contribute to the development of individual differences in behavioral inhibition. Rat pups exposed to a handling procedure, in which they are removed daily from the nest and placed in social isolation for a brief period of time, exhibit a subsequent reduction in emotionality (Denenberg, 1967; Levine, Haltmeyer, Karas, & Denenberg, 1967). For instance, when placed in an unfamiliar environment, handled rodents engage in greater levels of locomotor exploration than nonhandled animals. In contrast, rat pups exposed to longer periods of isolation during the early postnatal period exhibit increased levels of emotionality as evidenced by a suppression of feeding in an unfamiliar environment (Caldji, Sharma, Plotsky, & Meaney, 1996).

Studies in animals and humans further indicate that the propensity to display behavioral inhibition and other defensive responses appears, in general, to be a stable characteristic of individuals (e.g., Brim & Kagan, 1980; MacDonald, 1993; Stevenson-Hinde, 1983). In rhesus monkeys, freezing duration scores measured at 5 to 7 months of age and again at later ages show a strong positive relation (Kalin & Shelton, 1989). In humans, some infants who are confronted with a stranger become extremely agitated and engage in high levels of crying and motor activity that involves flexing and extending of the arms and legs. These infants who exhibit high levels of motor activity and crying at 4 months of age are more likely to become behaviorally inhibited at 9 and 14 months of age than infants who showed a lower intensity of these responses (Kagan & Snidman, 1991).

## Hypothalamic-Pituitary-Adrenal Hormones and Behavioral Inhibition

The physiological response to a threat or stressor often involves the activation of the hypothalamic-pituitary-adrenal (HPA) system. The secretion of glucocorticoids from the adrenal gland is the final step in a series of complex events initiated by the perception of threat leading to the release of hypothalamic secretagogues such as corticotropin-releasing hormone (CRH) that facilitates adrenocorticotropin secretion from the pituitary. Glucocorticoids are noted especially for their varied peripheral physiological effects, such as changes in carbohydrate metabolism and alterations in immune and inflammatory processes (Munck, Guyre, & Holbrook, 1984). The effects of glucocorticoids are mediated by intracellular receptors that bind glucocorticoids, resulting in transformation of the hormone-receptor complex into a DNA-binding protein that is translocated to the nucleus (Beato, Herrlich, & Schultz, 1995; Walters, 1985). The binding of the steroid-receptor complex to DNA sequences results in transcriptional effects capable of either stimulating or repressing gene activity.

Glucocorticoids and extrahypothalamic CRH systems also have prominent effects on brain function and behavior. For example, glucocorticoids may influence cognitive processes such as learning and memory (Bohus, De Kloet, & Veldhuis,

1982; De Kloet, 1991). In adult animals, extrahypothalamic CRH systems are implicated in stress-induced behavioral responses. Activation of CRH systems by central administration of CRH plays a key role in potentiating stress-induced behavior, whereas opposite behavioral effects are produced after administration of CRH receptor antagonists (Koob et al., 1993; Takahashi & Kalin, 1989). These extrahypothalamic CRH cell bodies, fibers, and receptors are widely distributed throughout the brain (Palkovits, Brownstein, & Vale, 1985; Sawchenko & Swanson, 1990), where, in addition to its behavioral effects, CRH may modulate stress-induced autonomic activation (Brown & Fisher, 1990).

During development, glucocorticoids facilitate the maturation of peripheral tissues (Ballard, 1979; Fowden, 1995; Henning, 1981) and regulate cellular processes in the central nervous system (Doupe & Patterson, 1982; Meyer, 1985). Some of these glucocorticoid-induced effects have major implications for the development of the neural system that underlies behavioral inhibition (see the subsequent section on glucocorticoid influence on hippocampal development).

Although less is known about the development of brain CRH systems, available data indicate that CRH immunoreactivity and mRNA are first detected in the rat hypothalamic paraventricular nucleus during the last week of gestation (Bugnon, Fellmann, Gouget, & Cardot, 1982; Grino, Young, & Burgunder, 1989). In this nucleus, CRH mRNA levels increase several days before birth, then decrease during the early postnatal period before increasing again on postnatal day 7. Cortical CRH receptors emerge during the last week of gestation and attain the adult laminar distribution by postnatal day 14 (Insel, Bataglia, Fairbanks, & De Souza, 1988). In addition, brain CRH receptors are functionally linked to second messenger systems as early as postnatal day 3 (Insel et al., 1988). In situ hybridization studies further reveal that brain CRH receptor mRNA is clearly detectable on postnatal day 2 (Avishai-Eliner, Yi, & Baram, 1996). At this time, CRH receptor mRNA in cortex is maximal and decreases to adult levels by day 12. Other brain regions such as the amygdala and hippocampus (HC) first exhibit a gradual increase in CRH receptor mRNA before declining to adult levels around the 2nd to 3rd postnatal week.

### Evidence for an Early Developmental Relationship Between Glucocorticoids and Behavioral Inhibition

Studies suggest a developmental linkage between endogenous glucocorticoid levels and behavioral inhibition. In a study using 7-month-old infant rhesus monkeys, a positive relationship occurs between baseline levels of the glucocorticoid cortisol and the monkey's propensity to freeze (Kalin, Shelton, Rickman, & Davidson, 1998; see figure 6.2). In that study, the hormone-behavior relationship was also observed in adult monkeys, which indicates that the glucocorticoid–behavioral inhibition relationship is present in infancy and adulthood. In humans, 4-year-old children who are extremely wary of social interactions have elevated levels of salivary cortisol (Schmidt et al., 1997). In addition, salivary cortisol measured in early childhood correlates with indices of behavioral inhibition measured earlier in infancy (Kagan et al., 1988; Schmidt et al., 1997).

Studies also demonstrate associations among glucocorticoid levels, behavioral inhibition, and frontal cortical electroencephalogram (EEG) activity. In monkeys

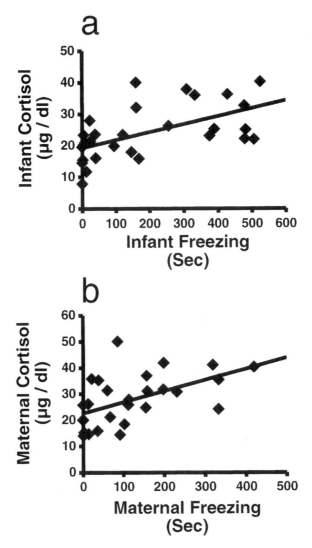

Figure 6.2. Relationship between glucocorticoid and freezing in infant (panel a, $r_s$ = 0.62, $P < 0.001$) and mother rhesus monkeys (panel b, $r_s$ = 0.53, $P < 0.01$). Mother (mean age = 11.0 years) and infants (mean age = 7.5 months) were scored for freezing in a 10-min no-eye-contact condition (see figure 6.1). Infant and mother blood samples were obtained for cortisol determination approximately 2.5 months after behavioral testing. From Kalin et al. (1998). Copyright 1998 by American Psychological Association. Reprinted by permission.

and humans, asymmetric EEG activation of right prefrontal brain regions is associated with negative affect (Davidson, Kalin, & Shelton, 1993; Tomarken, Davidson, Wheeler, & Kinney, 1992). Furthermore, children with extreme behavioral inhibition traits generally exhibit relatively pronounced right prefrontal asymmetrical activation (Davidson, 1992; see also Davidson & Rickman, chapter 5, this volume).

In rhesus monkeys, basal cortisol levels are significantly correlated with right asymmetrical frontal activity. Monkeys with increased right asymmetrical frontal activity have greater cortisol levels and more intense defensive behavioral responses, including freezing, than animals with high left frontal activation (Kalin, Larson, Shelton, & Davidson, 1998).

Further support for the positive relationship between early endogenous glucocorticoid levels and a developmental predisposition to exhibit behavioral inhibition is obtained from prenatal stress studies. A stressful pregnancy is capable of elevating maternal levels of glucocorticoids, which enter the fetal circulation. In adulthood, prenatally stressed offspring exposed to unfamiliar or stressful situations exhibit behavioral patterns indicative of heightened fear and anxiety. For example, adult prenatally stressed rats are less active in the open field (Fride, Dan, Feldon, Halevy, & Weinstock, 1986; Wakshlak & Weinstock, 1990) and prefer the closed safe arms of the elevated plus maze (Fride & Weinstock, 1988). In addition, prenatally stressed rats display high levels of shock-induced freezing (Takahashi, Turner, & Kalin, 1992). As juveniles, prenatally stressed rats appear wary of unfamiliar situations, as indicated by long latencies to engage in appetitive social play behavior (Takahashi, Haglin, & Kalin, 1992). Similar to these latter observations, prenatally stressed juvenile rhesus monkeys show less social contact and proximity than control animals (Clarke & Schneider, 1993).

## Developmental Influence of Glucocorticoids on Behavioral Inhibition

Studies that manipulate the early hormonal milieu reveal a major role of glucocorticoids in the developmental expression of behavioral inhibition. This developmental influence of glucocorticoids was demonstrated in a study in which rat pups were adrenalectomized at 10 days of age and tested for behavioral inhibition at 14 days of age, when the response normally appears (Takahashi & Rubin, 1993). In rats, plasma glucocorticoid concentrations are reduced to very low levels shortly after birth and begin to increase only toward the end of the 2nd postnatal week (Henning, 1978; Sapolsky & Meaney, 1986). Hence, removal of adrenal glands at 10 days of age effectively blocks the normal increase in plasma glucocorticoid levels and their potential developmental effects on the brain. Behavioral results indicated that adrenalectomized rat pups failed to exhibit freezing in response to an unfamiliar adult male rat. Importantly, this adrenalectomy-induced freezing deficit was reversed by daily administration of exogenous corticosterone (Takahashi & Rubin, 1993).

Additional studies indicated that after freezing developed, endogenous glucocorticoids no longer have a major effect on the expression of behavioral inhibition. For example, when adrenalectomy is performed at 14 days of age, freezing levels measured after a 4-day period were comparable to sham-operated rats (Takahashi, 1994a). Similar results were reported in adult rats, and in some cases adrenalectomized adult rats may exhibit higher levels of freezing than intact control animals (Sakaguchi et al., 1984; Weiss, McEwen, Silva, & Kalkut, 1970).

That the developing behavioral inhibition neural system is especially sensitive to glucocorticoids and vulnerable to its absence is demonstrated in a study in

Table 6.1 Description of 4-group experimental design used to isolate the developmental period when CORT plays an essential role in facilitating the expression of behavioral inhibition. Immediately after ADX on day 10 and at 24 h intervals, rat pups were injected with either vehicle or CORT (3 mg/kg, ip). On day 18, 24 h after the last treatment, all rats were tested for behavioral inhibition.

| Group | ADX | Daily Treatment | Behavioral Inhibition Test |
|---|---|---|---|
| VEH | Day 10 - - - - - - - - - - - - - - -Vehicle- - - - - - - - - - - - - - - - - - | | Day 18 |
| VEH/CORT | Day 10 - - - Vehicle - - - - - - -Day 14 - - - - - - - CORT - - - - - - - | | Day 18 |
| CORT/VEH | Day 10 - - - CORT - - - - - - - -Day 14 - - - - - - - Vehicle - - - - - - | | Day 18 |
| CORT | Day 10 - - - - - - - - - - - - - - -CORT- - - - - - - - - - - - - - - - - - | | Day 18 |

Derived from Takahashi (1994a).

which the timing of glucocorticoid exposure was varied (Takahashi, 1994a). In this study, 10-day-old rats were adrenalectomized and daily exogenous corticosterone (CORT) treatments began either immediately for 4 days or after a 4-day delay period (see table 6.1). When tested for behavioral inhibition at 18 days of age, rats that received glucocorticoid treatments immediately after adrenalectomy exhibited higher levels of freezing than animals in the delayed glucocorticoid treatment group (figure 6.3).

To summarize, these results suggest that: (1) the increase in endogenous corticosterone at the end of the 2nd postnatal week facilitates the development of behavioral inhibition; (2) the absence of glucocorticoids during this developmental period results in an altered behavioral inhibition neural system that fails to respond to subsequent glucocorticoid treatment; and (3) after a period of further development the behavioral inhibition neural system is no longer acutely sensitive to circulating glucocorticoids.

These data parallel some of the work demonstrating sensitive periods for the effects of gonadal steroids on sexual differentiation of the brain and behavior (reviewed by Breedlove, 1992; Dörner, 1980; Gorski, 1971; Goy & McEwen, 1980). Both androgens and glucocorticoids appear to be necessary during an early developmental period for the subsequent expression of adaptive behavior. Disrupting the actions of hormones in early life dramatically alters the course of development of neural systems that regulate behavioral expression.

## Glucocorticoid Influence on Hippocampal Development: Functional Implications for the Expression of Behavioral Inhibition

The developing neural system sensitive to the behavioral inhibitory effects of endogenous glucocorticoids remains to be fully elucidated. However, recent work implicates the hippocampus (HC) as a major component of the neural circuitry involved in the development of behavioral inhibition (reviewed by Takahashi, 1996). Traditionally, the HC is known for playing an important role in physiological and cognitive functions, and alterations in HC structure and function are implicated in

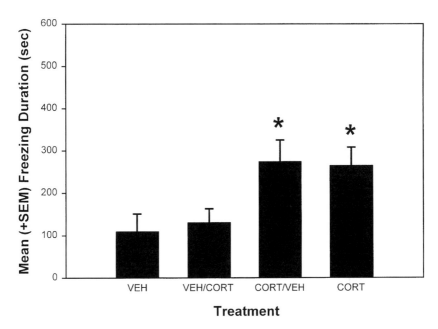

Figure 6.3. Mean duration of freezing by 18-day-old rats ($n = 9$–12 per group) during a 10-min exposure period to an anesthetized unfamiliar adult male rat. (*$P < 0.05$, significantly different from VEH and VEH/CORT groups. From Takahashi (1994a). Copyright 1994 by Elsevier Science. Reprinted by permission.

various pathological conditions (Chan-Palay & Kohler, 1989; O'Keefe & Nadel, 1978; Ribak, Gall, & Moody, 1992; Squire, 1992). The HC is also a prominent target site of adrenal steroids (see McEwen, chapter 9, this volume). Studies reveal that the HC contains high densities of both mineralocorticoid and glucocorticoid receptors (De Kloet, 1991; McEwen, De Kloet, & Rastene, 1986). These receptors are present in the dentate gyrus and pyramidal neurons of Ammon's horn from the 1st postnatal week (Rosenfeld, van Eckalen, Levine, & De Kloet, 1993). One physiological function of HC corticosteroid receptors is to facilitate glucocorticoid negative feedback (Jacobson & Sapolsky, 1991; McEwen et al., 1986).

In addition to containing high densities of corticosteroid receptors, the HC is one of the few brain structures that undergoes an extended period of postnatal development. Whereas rat HC pyramidal neurons in cornus ammonis or CA fields develop between embryonic days 16 through 20 (Bayer, 1980a), over 80 percent of dentate granule cells are formed during the 1st postnatal week (Bayer, 1980b). These newly formed cells migrate from the hilus to the granule cell layer of the dentate gyrus (Rickmann, Amaral, & Cowan, 1987; Schlessinger, Cowan, & Gottlieb, 1975). After postnatal day 18, neurogenesis of granule cells declines to 5–10 percent. This extended postnatal period of HC dentate gyrus development also occurs in other species, including the mouse, guinea pig, rabbit, cat, and rhesus monkey (Altman & Das, 1967; Angevine, 1965; Gueneau, Privat, Drouet, & Court, 1982; Rakic & Nowakowski, 1981; Wyss & Sripanidkulchai, 1985).

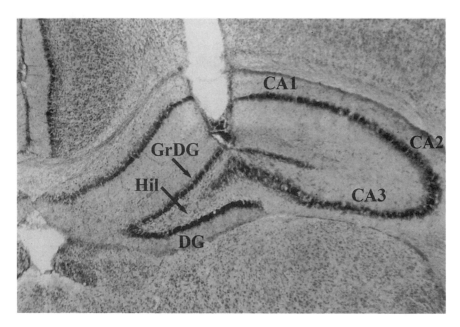

Figure 6.4. Location of 30-gauge cannula tip in the dorsal hippocampal dentate gyrus. Rat pups were implanted bilaterally with cannulae at 9 days of age and adrenalectomized. When tested for behavioral inhibition at 14 days of age, rats with corticosterone-filled cannulae exhibited higher levels of freezing than rats with cholesterol-filled cannulae. DG = dentate gyrus; GrDG = granular layer of dentate gyrus; Hil = hilus; CA1, CA2, CA3 = pyramidal cell subfields. (From Takahashi, 1995).

Studies indicate that the hormonal milieu has a significant impact on HC neural development and function. When plasma corticosterone concentrations are normally low, as in the 1st postnatal week, administration of exogenous corticosteroids produces increased levels of pyknotic cells in the HC dentate gyrus (Gould & Cameron, 1996). However, as development proceeds and corticosterone levels begin to increase at the end of the 2nd postnatal week, HC dentate gyrus cell survival becomes dependent on the actions of glucocorticoids, as indicated by adrenalectomy-induced increases in pyknotic cell density (Gould, Woolley, & McEwen, 1991).

Two lines of evidence link the developmental actions of glucocorticoids in the HC to the expression of behavioral inhibition (Takahashi, 1995). One line of evidence demonstrates that corticosterone-filled cannula placed into the dorsal HC dentate gyrus of rat pups effectively reverses the adrenalectomy-induced deficits in freezing (figure 6.4). The second line of evidence shows that, when rat pups are infused with neurotoxins selective for HC dentate granule cells, freezing duration is markedly reduced in the behavioral inhibition test. Together, these results extend previous work that demonstrated the importance of glucocorticoids in the development of behavioral inhibition. Importantly, these studies identify a neural structure whose maturation is dependent, in part, on endogenous glucocorticoids

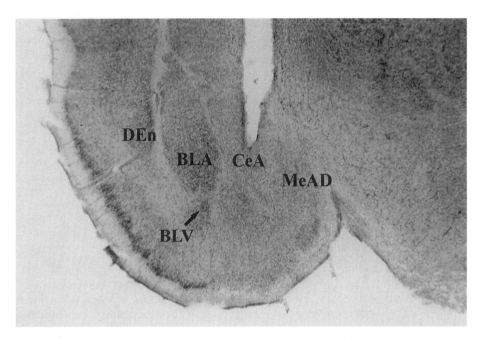

Figure 6.5. Location of 30-gauge cannula tip in the CeA. Adrenalectomized rat pups were implanted bilaterally in the CeA with cholesterol- or corticosterone-filled cannula on postnatal day 9 and tested on day 14 in the presence of an anesthetized adult male rat for behavioral inhibition. Results indicated that freezing scores of corticosterone-implanted rats ($N = 10$, mean $\pm$ SE, 148.3 $\pm$ 33.5 sec) did not differ significantly, $t(17) = 1.15$, $P > 0.05$, from cholesterol-implanted animals ($N = 9$, 96.4 $\pm$ 29.3 sec). BLA = basolateral amygdala nucleus, anterior; BLV = basolateral amygdala nucleus, ventral; CeA = central amygdala nucleus; DEn = dorsal endopiriform nucleus; MeAD = medial amygdala, anterodorsal.

and that plays a critical role in the expression of behavioral inhibition. An implication of these investigations is that alterations in glucocorticoid-induced effects on the developing HC may contribute importantly to the production of individual differences in behavioral inhibition.

The developmental actions of glucocorticoids in other brain regions may also influence the display of behavioral inhibition. To begin evaluating this issue, studies were conducted to examine the effects of corticosterone implants in the central nucleus of the amygdala (CeA), which is implicated in mediating a broad range of emotionally charged autonomic and behavioral responses, especially those associated with learning or conditioned fear and freezing (Davis, 1992; Kapp, Whalen, Supple, & Pascoe, 1992; see also Nader & LeDoux, chapter 7, this volume). Within the amygdaloid complex, the CeA, as well as the cortical amygdala nucleus, contains the highest densities of mineralocorticoid and glucocorticoid receptors (Reul & De Kloet, 1985). These corticosteroid receptor concentrations in the amygdala are low during the early postnatal period and gradually increase over the next 2 weeks (Meaney, Sapolsky, & McEwen, 1985; Rosenfeld et al., 1993).

In the corticosterone implant study, behavioral results showed that corticosterone implants in the CeA, failed to reverse freezing deficits produced by adrenalectomy (figure 6.5; Takahashi & Goh, 1997, unpublished observations). These data suggest that glucocorticoid actions in the CeA, in contrast to the HC, do not appear to be critically involved in the development of behavioral inhibition. These results, however, do not exclude the possibility that glucocorticoid actions in the CeA mediate other aspects of defensive behavioral expression, such as those involved in the conditioning process. In our behavioral tests, the level of behavioral inhibition shown by the animal represents its defensive predisposition to unfamiliar and potentially harmful stimuli. Under these test conditions, the underlying neural pathways that are activated to elicit behavioral inhibition may depend critically on a functional HC system.

## Hippocampal CRH Receptors and the Developmental Modulation of Behavioral Inhibition

In addition to the developmental effects of glucocorticoids on HC development and behavioral inhibition, CRH systems in the HC may play a role in the developmental modulation of behavioral inhibition. Potential support for a developmental influence of brain CRH receptors on behavioral inhibition is obtained from studies in the rhesus monkey (Grigoriadis et al., 1995). In this study, CRH receptor densities in the majority of brain regions examined did not change significantly from the first 2 weeks after birth. However, some regions, such as the lateral and medial geniculate, insular cortex, and claustrum, showed a decline in CRH receptor levels between the first 2 postnatal weeks and weeks 11 to 12. Another striking finding was the observation that only HC CRH receptor densities, which are low at 1–2 weeks of age, increased twofold by 11 to 12 weeks. Within the HC, CRH receptors were located prominently in dentate granule cell layers. Other HC regions, including the pyramidal cell fields, showed no age-dependent change in CRH receptor density.

This increase in CRH receptor densities in the HC dentate gyrus may have important implications for behavioral inhibition in view of the observation indicated earlier that at 9–12 weeks of age, rhesus monkeys begin to effectively modulate their behavioral responses to varying threatening stimuli (Kalin et al., 1991). That is, CRH receptor activation in the HC dentate gyrus may facilitate or coordinate rapid modulatory changes in defensive patterns of behavior in response to altering features of the threat.

Another implication is that alterations in HC CRH receptors may contribute to varied stress-induced physiological and behavioral alterations. In tree shrews, chronic exposure to psychosocial stress disrupts the regulation of feeding and sleeping and produces behavioral depression in subordinate animals (von Holst, 1972). Furthermore, these subordinate tree shrews have decreased CRH receptor binding densities in the anterior pituitary, regions of the superior colliculus, and HC dentate gyrus and pyramidal fields (Fuchs & Flügge, 1995). In rats, infusion of a CRH receptor antisense oligonucleotide into the HC that induced a knockdown of CRH receptor mRNA produced elevated exploratory behavior in an unfamiliar activity chamber (Wu, Chen, Lee, & Lee, 1997). Rat behavioral activity is usually

inhibited in an unfamiliar environment, and exogenous CRH administration potentiates this behavioral suppression (Takahashi, Kalin, Vanden Burgt, & Sherman,
1989). This latter finding is similar to that reported in the rhesus monkey. In 4- to
9-month-old infant rhesus monkeys, intracerebral injections of CRH results in less
behavioral activity during maternal separation (Kalin, Shelton, & Barksdale, 1989).
At higher doses, CRH-treated monkeys appear to show a prolonged withdrawn inhibited pattern of behavior typical of despair (Kalin, Shelton, Kraemer, &
McKinney, 1983). Whether these behavioral patterns are induced by CRH receptor
activation in the HC deserves further examination.

Presently, it is not clear whether CRH receptor actions have neurotrophic effects
(Strand et al., 1991) capable of producing alterations in brain circuits that underlie behavioral inhibition. Developmental alterations in brain CRH systems may
also result, in part, from glucocorticoid-induced actions. As demonstrated in adult
rodents, chronic exposure to high levels of exogenous corticosteroids is associated
with alterations in CRH mRNA levels in the paraventricular nucleus of the hypothalamus and CeA (Makino, Gold, & Schulkin, 1994; Swanson & Simmons, 1989;
see also Schulkin & Rosen, chapter 8, this volume).

## Early Environmental Influences on the Behavioral
## Inhibition Neural System

### Prenatal Stress, Glucocorticoids, and the Hippocampus

Animal studies demonstrate that exposure to specific environmental conditions in
early life may produce long-term alterations in the expression of behavioral inhibition. As previously indicated, exposure to prenatal stress appears to increase animals' sensitivity to stressors, as revealed by their propensity to exhibit enhanced
levels of stress-induced behavior, including behavioral inhibition. Furthermore,
in many cases, exposure to a stressful situation produced an increase in HPA
hormones (Fride et al., 1986; Henry, Kabaj, Simon, Le Moal, & Maccari, 1994;
Takahashi, Kalin, Barksdale, Vanden Burgt, & Brownfield, 1988).

Recent studies suggest that these heightened levels of behavioral and hormonal
responsiveness may result, in part, from early stress-induced glucocorticoid effects
on the developing HC. For example, prenatally stressed rats have significant reductions in HC corticosteroid receptors (Henry et al., 1994). HC mineralocorticoid
receptor densities are reduced by 70 percent, along with a 30 percent reduction in
glucocorticoid receptors. That stress-induced maternal glucocorticoid levels contribute to these HC receptor changes is suggested by work that shows that suppression of stress-induced corticosterone secretion during pregnancy prevents the
reduction in offspring HC corticosteroid receptor densities (Barbazanges, Piazza,
Le Moal, & Maccari, 1996). In addition, adrenalectomized pregnant dams that were
administered stress-like doses of exogenous corticosterone and exposed to stress
produced offspring with reduced levels of HC corticosteroid receptors. These alterations in HC corticosteroid receptors, which are involved in glucocorticoid negative feedback regulation, may then contribute to the elevated HPA hormone levels noted in prenatally stressed young.

## Early Handling and Maternal Factors: Glucocorticoids, Hippocampus, and CRH Systems

Whether the prenatal stress-induced reduction in HC corticosteroid receptor densities is also a factor that contributes to an enhanced expression of behavioral inhibition is not known. However, research that examines the effects of early handling procedures may offer insight into the behavioral changes induced by prenatal stress. These studies demonstrate that in addition to a reduction in emotionality, handled rats exhibit lower stress-induced HPA hormone secretion than nonhandled control rats (Haltmeyer, Denenberg, & Zarrow, 1967; Levine et al., 1967; Meaney et al., 1991). This handling-induced decrease in HPA hormones appears to be linked to increased glucocorticoid negative feedback effects produced by elevated levels of hippocampal glucocorticoid receptor density and binding (Meaney, Aitken, Bhatnagar, Van Berkel, & Sapolsky, 1988; Meaney et al., 1991). These effects of early postnatal handling procedures—increased HC corticosteroid receptor binding, decreased HPA responses, decreased levels of emotionality—appear to be opposite to those induced by prenatal stress.

Furthermore, studies indicate that rats handled in infancy develop increased densities of cells in the HC dentate gyrus and neocortex (Altman, Das, & Anderson, 1968). This handling-induced alteration in the HC dentate gyrus is particularly notable because strong evidence links the development of this brain region with behavioral inhibition. The potential relevance of this finding for prenatal stress studies is that increased expression of behavioral inhibition in offspring may also be associated with developmental alterations occurring in the HC dentate gyrus.

Another notable finding is that exposure to early postnatal handling is effective in reversing the enhanced behavioral emotionality induced by prenatal stress (Wakshlak & Weinstock, 1990). This result suggests that neural circuits that modulate behavioral inhibition are not altered and fixed at birth by exposure to prenatal stress but appear malleable and responsive to further early environmental influence.

Variations in rat maternal behavior may also contribute to offspring HPA development and responsiveness to stress (Liu et al., 1997). In this study, rats were divided into two groups on the basis of the amount of maternal care received during infancy. In adulthood, offspring that received high levels of maternal licking and grooming and arched-back nursing showed less stress-induced HPA hormone secretion, less hypothalamic CRH mRNA, and increased HC glucocorticoid receptor mRNA relative to offspring that received less maternal care. These neuroendocrine alterations are similar to those that occur after exposure to early handling procedures. Indeed, handled pups that are returned to the nest box after separation appear to induce higher levels of maternal care and arch-back nursing postures than nonhandled pups (Liu et al., 1997).

Other studies conducted on rhesus monkeys also point to a potential maternal influence on neuroendocrine responses of the infant. In these studies, a negative relationship was found between maternal parity and infant cortisol levels (Kalin, Shelton, et al., 1998). Furthermore, although maternal age and parity were positively correlated, maternal age did not correlate significantly with infant cortisol levels. Together, the mother's past reproductive experiences appear to be a significant factor that influences infant cortisol values.

Finally, recent studies reported that rat pups exposed to long-term maternal separation procedures during the first 2 weeks of life subsequently exhibited increased fearfulness and HPA responses to stress (Caldji et al., 1996; Pearson, Sharma, Plotsky, Pfaus, & Meaney, 1997). In this case, maternal separation-induced changes in brain CRH may contribute to these behavioral and hormonal changes. Consistent with this hypothesis, maternal separation produced long-term alterations in brain CRH systems, including increased CRH mRNA expression in the paraventricular nucleus of the hypothalamus, the amygdala, and bed nucleus (Heim, Owens, Plotsky, & Nemeroff, 1997). In addition, after 24-h of maternal deprivation, 12-day-old rats showed increased CRH receptor densities in frontal cortex, HC, amygdala, and cerebellum, suggesting that long-term maternal deprivation sensitizes brain CRH receptors.

## Conclusions

This chapter provides a developmental neurobiological view that may account for individual differences in threat-induced behavioral inhibition. Unlike the wealth of data concerning the neurobiology of adult defensive behavior, knowledge of the developmental neural basis of behavioral inhibition is scarce. However, the data suggest that developmental actions of glucocorticoids have an influential role in the production of differences in the intensity of behavioral inhibition. More specifically, early exposure to elevated levels of endogenous glucocorticoids is associated with an enhanced occurrence of behavioral inhibition. Furthermore, as shown in the rat, the behavioral inhibitory effects of glucocorticoids appear to occur during a limited period of development. This result underscores the existence of developmental periods when the underlying neural system responsible for behavioral inhibition expression is most sensitive to the actions of glucocorticoids.

A major component of the behavioral inhibitory neural system is the HC, which is notable for its late-developing features in comparison with other neural structures. The HC is a prominent neural target site for endogenous glucocorticoids, as indicated by high densities of corticosteroid receptors. Normal development of the HC dentate gyrus is dependent, in part, on the changing pattern of glucocorticoid levels that occurs during the early postnatal period. In the rat, this glucocorticoid-induced facilitation of HC dentate gyrus development appears to be a critical event that facilitates the age-dependent appearance of behavioral inhibition.

In addition to corticosteroid receptors, the HC contains CRH receptors. In the monkey, the developmental appearance of CRH receptors in the HC dentate gyrus may be involved in the modulation of defensive patterns of behavior, including behavioral inhibition. Because brain CRH systems are involved in modulating stress-induced autonomic and behavioral responses, developmental alterations in CRH systems may contribute to the production of individual differences in behavioral inhibition.

Results of studies discussed in the chapter further indicate that the responsiveness of the behavioral inhibition system may be modified by early environmental events. Exposure to prenatal stress and resultant elevations in glucocorticoid levels appear to increase the sensitivity of behavioral and neuroendocrine systems involved in the stress response. In contrast, postnatal handling procedures and some forms of maternal care produce a decreased sensitivity or more rapid recovery in stress-induced behavioral and hormonal responses. In both cases, the HC is again implicated in some of the more predominant behavioral and hormonal alterations induced by early environmental events. The sensitivity of the HC to environmental perturbations is reflected by alterations in corticosteroid receptor densities and possibly dentate gyrus cell development. The former is associated with altered HPA regulation, whereas the latter may be linked to changes in behavioral inhibition expression. We believe that continued investigations into the developmental actions of glucocorticoids on the HC and HC developmental influences on other neural systems and regions will yield a more comprehensive understanding, which may have important clinical implications, of the neural processes that underlie adaptive, as well as extreme or uncontrolled, displays of behavioral inhibition.

*Acknowledgements*  Our research described herein was supported by grants MH43986, MH46792, MH5234, and NIMH P50-MH523554 to the Wisconsin Center for Affective Science, the Graduate School, the Health Emotions Research Institute, and Meriter Hospital.

*References*

Altman, J., & Das, G. D. (1967). Postnatal neurogenesis in the guinea-pig. *Nature 214,* 1098–1101.

Altman, J., Das, G. D., & Anderson, W. J. (1968) Effects of infantile handling on morphological development of the rat brain: An exploratory study. *Developmental Psychobiology, 1,* 10–20.

Angevine, J. B. (1965). Time of neuron origin in the hippocampal region: An autoradiographic study in the mouse. *Experimental Neurology 2,* 1–17.

Avishai-Eliner, S., Yi, S. J., & Baram, T. Z. (1996). Developmental profile of messenger RNA for the corticotropin-releasing hormone receptor in the rat limbic brain. *Developmental Brain Research, 91,* 159–163.

Ballard, P. L. (1979). Glucocorticoids and differentiation. In J. D. Baxter & G. G. Rousseau (Eds.), *Monographs in endocrinology* (pp. 493–515). New York: Springer-Verlag.

Barbazanges, A., Piazza, P. V., Le Moal, M., & Maccari, S. (1996). Maternal glucocorticoid secretion mediates long-term effects of prenatal stress. *Journal of Neuroscience, 16,* 3943–3949.

Bayer, S. A. (1980a). Development of the hippocampal region in the rat: I. Neurogenesis examined with $^3$H-thymidine autoradiography. *Journal of Comparative Neurology, 87,* 87–114.

Bayer, S. A. (1980b). Development of the hippocampal region in the rat: II. Morphogenesis during embryonic and early postnatal life. *Journal of Comparative Neurology, 87,* 115–134.

Beato, M., Herrlich, P., & Schutz, G. (1995). Steroid hormone receptors: Many actors in search of a plot. *Cell, 83,* 851–857.

Biederman, J., Rosenbaum, J. F., Bolduc-Murphy, E. A., Faraone, S. V., Chaloff, J., Hirshfeld, D. R., & Kagan, J. (1993). A 3-year follow-up of children with and without behavioral inhibition. *Journal of American Academy of Child and Adolescent Psychiatry, 32,* 814–821.

Bohus, B., De Kloet, E. R., & Veldhuis, H. D. (1982). Adrenal steroids and behavioral adaptation: Relationship to brain corticoid receptors. In D. Ganten and D. Pfaff (Eds.), *Adrenal actions on brain* (pp. 107–148). New York: Springer-Verlag.

Boissy, A. (1995). Fear and fearfulness in animals. *Quarterly Review of Biology, 70,* 165–191.

Breedlove, S. M. (1992). Sexual dimorphism in the vertebrate nervous system. *Journal of Neuroscience, 11,* 4133–4142.

Brim, O. G., Jr., & Kagan J., (Eds.). (1980). *Constancy and change in human development.* Cambridge: Harvard University Press.

Brown, M. R., & Fisher, L. A. (1990). Regulation of the autonomic nervous system by corticotropin-releasing factor. In E. B. DeSouza and C. B. Nemeroff (Eds.), *Corticotropin-releasing factor: Basic and clinical studies of a neuropeptide* (pp. 291–298). Boca Raton, FL: CRC Press.

Bugnon, C. D., Fellmann, D., Gouget, A., & Cardot, J. (1982). Ontogeny of the cortico-liberin neuroglandular system in rat brain. *Nature, 298,* 159–161.

Caldji, C., Sharma, S., Plotsky, P. M., & Meaney, M. J. (1996). Postnatal handling/maternal separation alters responses to novelty stress, open field exploration and central benzodiazepine receptor levels in adult rats. *Society for Neuroscience Abstracts, 22,* 1341.

Chan-Palay, V., & Kohler, C. (1989). *The hippocampus: New vistas.* New York: Liss.

Clarke, A. S., & Schneider, M. L. (1993). Prenatal stress has long-term effects on behavioral responses to stress in juvenile rhesus monkeys. *Developmental Psychobiology, 26,* 293–304.

Collier, A. C., & Bolles, R. C. (1980). The ontogenesis of defensive reactions to shock in preweanling rats. *Developmental Psychobiology, 13,* 141–150.

Davidson, R. J. (1992). Anterior cerebral asymmetry and the nature of emotion. *Brain and Cognition, 20,* 125–151.

Davidson, R. J., Kalin, N. H., & Shelton, S. E. (1993). Lateralized response to diazepam predicts temperamental style in rhesus monkeys. *Behavioral Neuroscience, 107,* 1106–1110.

Davis, M. (1992). The role of the amygdala in fear and anxiety. *Annual Review of Neuroscience, 15,* 353–375.

De Kloet, E. R. (1991). Brain corticosteroid receptor balance and homeostatic control. *Frontiers in Neuroendocrinology, 12,* 95–164.

Denenberg, V. H. (1967). Stimulation in infancy, emotional reactivity, and exploratory behavior. In D. C. Glass (Ed.), *Neurophysiology and emotion* (pp. 161–222). New York: Rockefeller University Press.

Dörner, G. (1980). Sexual differentiation in the brain. *Vitamins and Hormones, 38,* 325–381.

Doupe, A. J., & Patterson, P. H. (1982). Glucocorticoids and the developing nervous system. In D. Ganten and D. Pfaff (Eds.), *Adrenal actions on brain* (pp. 23–43). New York: Springer-Verlag.

Ficken, M. S., & Witkin, S. R. (1977). Responses of black-capped chickadees to predators. *Auk, 94* 156–157.

Fowden, A. (1995). Endocrine regulation of fetal growth. *Reproduction, Fertility and Development, 7,* 351–363.

Fride, E., Dan, Y., Feldon, J., Halevy, G., & Weinstock, M. (1986). Effects of prenatal stress on vulnerability to stress in prepubertal and adult rats. *Physiology and Behavior, 37,* 681–687.

Fride, E., & Weinstock, M. (1988). Prenatal stress increases anxiety-related behavior and alters cerebral lateralization of dopamine activity. *Life Sciences, 42,* 1059–1065.

Fuchs, E., & Flügge, G. (1995). Modulation of binding sites for corticotropin-releasing hormone by chronic psychological stress. *Psychoneuroendocrinology, 20,* 33–51.

Gorski, R. A. (1971). Gonadal hormones and the perinatal development of neuroendocrine function. In W. F. Ganong & L. Martini (Eds.), *Frontiers in Neuroendocrinology* (pp. 237–290). New York: Oxford University Press.

Gould, E., & Cameron, H. A. (1996). Regulation of neuronal birth, migration and death in the rat dentate gyrus. *Developmental Neuroscience, 18,* 22–35.

Gould, E., Woolley, C. S., & McEwen, B. S. (1991). Adrenal steroids regulate postnatal development of the rat dentate gyrus: I. Effects of glucocorticoids on cell death. *Journal of Comparative Neurology, 313,* 479–485.

Goy, R. W., & McEwen, B. S. (1980). *Sexual differentiation of the brain.* Cambridge, MA: MIT Press.

Gray, J. A. (1987). *The psychology of fear and stress.* Cambridge: Cambridge University Press.

Greig-Smith, P. W. (1980). Parental investment in nest defence by stonechats (*Saxicola torquata*). *Animal Behavior, 28,* 604–619.

Grigoriadis, D. E., Dent, G. W., Turner, J. G., Uno, H., Shelton, S. E., De Souza, E. B., & Kalin, N. H. (1995). Corticotropin-releasing factor (CRF) receptors in infant rhesus monkey brain and pituitary gland: Biochemical characterization and autoradiographic localization. *Developmental Neuroscience, 17,* 357–367.

Grino, M., Young, W. S., III, & Burgunder, J. M. (1989). Ontogeny of expression of the corticotropin-releasing factor gene in the hypothalamic paraventricular nucleus and of the proopiomelanocortin gene in rat pituitary. *Endocrinology, 124,* 60–68.

Gueneau, G., Privat, A., Drouet, J., & Court, L. (1982). Subgranular zone of the dentate gyrus of young rabbits as a secondary matrix. *Developmental Neuroscience, 5,* 345–358.

Haltmeyer, G. C., Denenberg, V. H., & Zarrow, M. X. (1967). Modification of the plasma corticosterone response as a function of infantile stimulation and electric shock parameters. *Physiology and Behavior, 2,* 61–63.

Heim, C., Owens, M. J., Plotsky, P. M., & Nemeroff, C. B. (1997). The role of early adverse life events in the etiology of depression and posttraumatic stress disorder. Focus on corticotropin-releasing factor. *Annals of the New York Academy of Science, 821,* 194–207.

Henning, S. J. (1978). Plasma concentrations of total and free corticosterone during development in the rat. *American Journal of Physiology, 235,* E451–E456.

Henning, S. J. (1981). Postnatal development: coordination of feeding, digestion, and metabolism. *American Journal of Physiology, 241,* G199–G214.

Henry, C., Kabaj, M., Simon, H., Le Moal, M., & Maccari, S. (1994). Prenatal stress increases the hypothalamo-pituitary-adrenal axis response in young and adult rats. *Journal of Neuroendocrinology, 6,* 341–345.

Hofer, M. A. (1996). Multiple regulators of ultasonic vocalizations in the infant rat. *Psychoneuroendocrinology, 21,* 203–217.

Insel, T. R., Bataglia, G., Fairbanks, D. W., & De Souza, E. B. (1988). The ontogeny of brain receptors for corticotropin-releasing factor and the development of their functional association with adenylate cyclase. *Journal of Neuroscience, 8,* 4151–4158.

Jacobson, L., & Sapolsky, R. (1991). The role of the hippocampus in feedback regulation of the hypothalamic-pituitary-adrenal axis. *Endocrine Reviews, 12,* 118–134.

Jones, R. B., Mills, A. D., & Faure, J. M. (1991). Genetic and experiential manipulation of fear-related behavior in Japanese quail chicks (*Coturniz coturnix japonica*). *Journal of Comparative Psychology, 105,* 15–24.

Kagan, J., Reznick, J. S., & Snidman, N. (1988). Biological bases of childhood shyness. *Science, 240,* 167–171.

Kagan, J., & Snidman, N. (1991). Infant predictors of inhibited and uninhibited profiles. *Psychological Science, 2,* 40–44.

Kalin, N. H., Larson, C., Shelton, S. E., & Davidson, R. J. (1998). Asymmetric frontal brain activity, cortisol, and behavior associated with fearful temperaments in rhesus monkeys. *Behavioral Neuroscience, 112,* 286–292.

Kalin, N. H., & Shelton, S. E. (1989). Defensive behaviors in infant rhesus monkeys: Environmental cues and neurochemical regulation. *Science, 240,* 167–171.

Kalin, N. H., & Shelton, S. E. (in press) The regulation of defensive behaviors in rhesus monkeys: Implications for understanding anxiety disorders. In R. J. Davidson (Ed.), *Wisconsin Symposium on Emotions. Vol. 1.*

Kalin, N. H., Shelton, S. E., & Barksdale, C. M. (1989). Behavioral and physiological effects of CRH administered to infant primates undergoing maternal separation. *Neuropsychopharmacology, 2,* 97–104.

Kalin, N. H., Shelton, S. E., Kraemer, G. W., & McKinney, W. T. (1983). Corticotropin-releasing factor administered intraventricularly to rhesus monkeys. *Peptides, 4,* 217–220.

Kalin, N. H., Shelton, S. E., Rickman, M., & Davidson, R. J. (1998). Individual differences in freezing and cortisol in infant and mother rhesus monkeys. *Behavioral Neuroscience, 112,* 251–254.

Kalin, N. H., Shelton, S. E., & Takahashi, L. K. (1991). Defensive behaviors in infant rhesus monkeys: Ontogeny and context-dependent selective expression. *Child Development, 62,* 1175–1183.

Kapp, B. S., Whalen, P. J., Supple, W. F., & Pascoe, J. P. (1992). Amygdaloid contributions to conditioned arousal and sensory information processing. In J. P. Aggleton (Ed.), *The amygdala: neurobiological aspects of emotion, memory, and mental dysfunction* (pp. 229–254). New York: Wiley-Liss.

Koob, G. F., Heinrichs, S. C., Pich, E. M., Menzaghi, F., Baldwin, H., Miczek, K., & Britton, K. T. (1993). The role of corticotropin-releasing factor in behavioural responses to stress. *Ciba Foundation Symposium, 172,* 277–289.

Levine, S., Haltmeyer, G. C., Karas, G. G., & Denenberg, V. H. (1967). Physiological and behavioral effects of infantile stimulation. *Physiology and Behavior, 2,* 55–59.

Lima S. L., & Dill L. M. (1990). Behavioral decisions made under the risk of predation: A review and prospectus. *Canadian Journal of Zoology, 68,* 619–640.

Liu, D., Diorio, J., Tannenbaum, B., Caldji, C., Francis, D., Freedman, A., Sharma, S., Pearson, D., Plotsky, P. M., & Meaney, M. J. (1997). Maternal care, hippocampal glucocorticoid receptors, and hypothalamic-pituitary-adrenal responses to stress. *Science, 277,* 1659–1662.

MacDonald, K. (1993). Stability of individual differences in behavior in a litter of wolf cubs *(Canis lupus)*. *Journal of Comparative Psychology, 97,* 99–106.

Magurran, A.E., & Girling, S. L. (1986). Predator model recognition and response habituation in shoaling minnows. *Animal Behavior, 34,* 510–518.

Makino, S., Gold, P. W., & Schulkin, J. (1994). Corticosterone effects on corticotropin-releasing hormone mRNA in the central nucleus of the amygdala and the parvocellular region of the paraventricular nucleus of the hypothalamus, *Brain Research, 640,* 105–112.

Matheny, A. P., Jr. (1989). Children's behavioral inhibition over age and across situations: Genetic similarity for a trait during change. *Journal of Personality, 57,* 215–35.

McEwen, B. S., De Kloet, E. R., & Rastene, W. (1986). Adrenal steroid receptors and actions in the nervous system. *Physiological Reviews, 66,* 1121–1188.

Meaney, M. J., Aitken, D. H., Bhatnagar, S., Van Berkel, C. H., & Sapolsky, R. M. (1988). Postnatal handling attenuates neuroendocrine, anatomical, and cognitive impairments related to the aged hippocampus. *Science, 238,* 766–768.

Meaney, M. J., Mitchell, J. B., Aitken, D. H., Bhatnagar, S., Bodnoff, S. R., Iny, L. J., & Sarrieau, A. (1991). The effects of neonatal handling on the development of the adrenocortical response to stress: Implications for neuropathology and cognitive deficits in later life. *Psychoneuroendocrinology, 16,* 85–103.

Meaney, M. J., Sapolsky, R. M., & McEwen, B. S. (1985). The development of the glucocorticoid receptor system in the rat limbic brain. I. Ontogeny and autoregulation. *Developmental Brain Research, 18,* 159–164.

Meyer, J. S. (1985). Biochemical effects of corticosteroids on neural tissue. *Physiological Review, 65,* 946–1020.

Miller, D. B. (1980). Maternal vocal control of behavioral inhibition in mallard ducklings *(Anas platyrhynchos)*. *Journal of Comparative Physiological Psychology, 94,* 606–623.

Montevecchi, W. A.; Gallup, G. G., Jr., & Dunlap, W. A. (1973). The peep vocalization in group reared chicks (*Gallus domesticus*): Its relation to fear. *Animal Behavior, 21,* 116–123.

Munck, A., Guyre, P. M., & Holbrook, N. J. (1984). Physiological functions of glucocorticoids in stress and their relations to pharmacological actions. *Endocrine Reviews, 5,* 25–44.

Murphy, L. B., & Wood-Gush, D. G. M. (1978). The interpretation of the behaviour of domestic fowl in strange environments. *Biology of Behavior, 3,* 39–61.

Newman, J. D. (1985). The infant cry of primates: An evolutionary perspective. In B. M. Lester & C. F. Zachariah Boukydis (Eds.), *Infant crying* New York: Plenum Press.

Noirot, E. (1972). Ultrasounds and maternal behavior in small rodents. *Developmental Psychobiology, 5,* 371–387.

O'Keefe, J., & Nadel, L. (1978) *The hippocampus as a cognitive map.* New York: Oxford University Press.

Palkovits, M., Brownstein, M. J., & Vale, W. (1985). Distribution of corticotropin-releasing factor in rat brain. *Federation Proceedings, 44,* 215–219.

Palmer, W. (1909). Instinctive stillness in birds. *Auk, 26,* 23–36.

Pare, W. P. (1989). Stress ulcer susceptibility and depression in Wistar Kyoto (WKY) rats. *Physiology & Behavior, 46,* 993–998.

Paul, L., & Kupferschmidt, J. (1975). Killing of conspecific and mouse young by male rats. *Journal of Comparative and Physiological Psychology, 88,* 755–763.

Pearson, D., Sharma, S., Plotsky, P. M., Pfaus, J. G., & Meaney, M. J. (1997). The effect of the postnatal environment on stress-induced changes in hippocampal Fos-like immunoreactivity in adult rats. *Society of Neuroscience Abstracts, 23,* 1849.

Rakic, P., & Nowakowski, R. S. (1981). The time of origin of neurons in the hippocampal region of the rhesus monkey. *Journal of Comparative Neurology, 196,* 99–128.

Ratner, S. C. (1967). Comparative aspects of hypnosis. In J. E. Gordon (Ed.), *Handbook of clinical and experimental hypnosis* (pp. 550–587). New York: Macmillian.

Reul, J. M. H. M., & De Kloet, E. R. (1985). Two receptor systems for corticosterone in rat brain: microdistribution and differential occupation. *Endocrinology, 117,* 2505–2511.

Ribak, C. E., Gall, C. M., & Moody, I. (1992). *The dentate gyrus and its role in seizures.* Amsterdam: Elsevier.

Rickmann, M., Amaral, D. G., & Cowan, W. M. (1987). Organization of radial glial cells during development of the rat dentate gyrus. *Journal of Comparative Neurology, 264,* 449–479.

Rosenfeld, P., van Eckalen, J. A. M., Levine, S., & De Kloet, E. R. (1993). Ontogeny of corticosteroid receptors in the brain. *Cellular and Molecular Neurobiology, 13,* 295–319.

Sakaguchi, A., LeDoux, J. E., Sved, A. F., & Reis D. J. (1984). Strain difference in fear between spontaneously hypertensive and normotensive rats is mediated by adrenal cortical hormones. *Neuroscience Letters, 46,* 59–64.

Sapolsky, R. M., & Meaney, M. J. (1986). Maturation of the adrenocortical stress response: neuroendocrine control mechanisms and the stress hyporesponsive period. *Brain Research Reviews, 11,* 65–76.

Sawchenko, P. E., & Swanson, L. S. (1990). Organization of CRF immunoreactive cells and fibers in the rat brain: Immunohistochemical studies . In E. B. DeSouza & C. B. Nemeroff (Eds.), *Corticotropin-releasing factor: Basic and clinical studies of a neuropeptide* (pp. 29–51). Boca Raton: CRC Press.

Schaller, G. B. (1972). *The Serengeti lion.* Chicago: University of Chicago Press.

Schlessinger, A. R., Cowan, W. W., & Gottlieb, D. I. (1975). An autoradiographic study of the time of origin and the pattern of granule cell migration in the dentate gyrus of the rat. *Journal of Comparative Neurology, 159,* 149–176.

Schmidt, L. A., Fox, N. A., Rubin, K. H., Sternberg, E. M., Gold, P. W., Smith, C. C., &

Schulkin, J. (1997). Behavioral and neuroendocrine responses in shy children. *Developmental Psychobiology, 30,* 127–140.

Squire, L. R. (1992). Memory and hippocampus: A synthesis from findings with rats, monkeys, and humans. *Psychological Review, 99,* 195–231.

Stevenson-Hinde, J. (1983). Individual characteristics: A statement of the problem. Consistency over time. Predictability across situations. In R. A. Hinde (Ed.), *Primate social relationships: An integrated approach* (pp. 28–34). Oxford: Blackwell Scientific Publications.

Strand, F. L., Rose, K. J., Zuccarelli, L. A., Kume, J., Alves, S. E., Antonawich, F. J., & Garrett, L. Y. (1991). Neuropeptide hormones as neurotrophic factors. *Physiological Reviews, 71,* 1017–1046.

Swanson, L. W., & Simmons, D. M. (1989). Differential steroid hormone and neural influences on peptide mRNA levels in CRH cells of the paraventricular nucleus: An hybridization histochemical study in the rat. *Journal of Comparative Neurology, 285,* 413–435.

Takahashi, L. K. (1992a). Developmental expression of defensive responses during exposure to conspecific adults in preweanling rats (*Rattus norvegicus*). *Journal of Comparative Psychology, 106,* 69–77.

Takahashi, L. K. (1992b). Ontogeny of behavioral inhibition induced by unfamiliar adult male conspecifics in preweanling rats. *Physiology and Behavior, 52,* 493–498.

Takahashi, L. K. (1994a). Organizing action of corticosterone on the development of behavioral inhibition in the preweanling rat. *Developmental Brain Research, 81,* 121–127.

Takahashi, L. K. (1994b). Stimulus control of behavioral inhibition in the preweanling rat. *Physiology & Behavior, 55,* 717–721.

Takahashi, L. K. (1995). Glucocorticoids, the hippocampus, and behavioral inhibition in the preweanling rat. *Journal of Neuroscience, 15,* 6023–6034.

Takahashi, L. K. (1996). Glucocorticoids and the hippocampus: Developmental interactions facilitating the expression of behavioral inhibition. *Molecular Neurobiology, 13,* 213–226.

Takahashi, L. K., Goh, C.-S. (1997). Role of the amygdala in the development of behavioral inhibition. Unpublished observations.

Takahashi, L. K., Haglin, C., & Kalin, N. H. (1992). Prenatal stress potentiates stress-induced behavior and reduces the propensity to play in juvenile rats. *Physiology & Behavior, 51,* 319–323.

Takahashi, L. K., & Kalin, N. H. (1989). Role of corticotropin-releasing factor in mediating the expression of defensive behavior. In R. J. Blanchard, P. F. Brain, D. C. Blanchard, & S. Parmigiani (Eds.), *Ethoexperimental approaches to the study of behavior* (pp. 580–594). Norwell: Kluwer Academic Publishers.

Takahashi, L. K., Kalin, N. H., Barksdale, C. M., Vanden Burgt, J. A., & Brownfield, M. S. (1988). Stressor controllability during pregnancy influences pituitary-adrenal hormone concentrations and analgesic responsiveness in offspring. *Physiology & Behavior, 42,* 323–329.

Takahashi, L. K., Kalin, N. H., Vanden Burgt, J. A., & Sherman, J. E. (1989). Corticotropin-releasing factor modulates defensive-withdrawal and exploratory behavior in rats. *Behavioral Neuroscience, 103,* 648–654.

Takahashi, L. K., & Lore, R. K. (1982). Intermale and maternal aggression in adult rats tested at different ages. *Physiology & Behavior, 29,* 1013–1018.

Takahashi, L. K., & Rubin, W. W. (1993). Corticosteroid induction of threat-induced behavioral inhibition in preweanling rats. *Behavioral Neuroscience, 107,* 860–866.

Takahashi, L. K., Turner, J. G., & Kalin, N. H. (1992). Prenatal stress alters brain catecholaminergic activity and potentiates stress-induced behavior in adult rats. *Brain Research, 574,* 131–137.

Tomarken, A. J., Davidson, R. J., Wheeler, R. E., & Kinney, L. (1992). Psychometric properties of resting anterior EEG asymmetry: Temporal stability and internal consistency. *Psychophysiology, 29,* 576–592.

von Holst, D. (1972). Social stress in the tree-shrew: Its causes and physiological and ethological consequences. In R. D. Martin, G. A. Doyle, and A. C. Walker (Eds.), *Prosimian biology* (pp. 389–411). Pittsburgh, PA: University of Pittsburgh.

Wakshlak, A., & Weinstock, M. (1990). Neonatal handling reverses behavioral abnormalities induced in rats by prenatal stress. *Physiology & Behavior, 48,* 289–292.

Walters, M. (1985). Steroid hormone receptors and the nucleus. *Endocrine Reviews, 6,* 512–543.

Weiss, J. M., McEwen, B. S., Silva, T., & Kalkut, M. (1970). Pituitary-adrenal alterations and fear responding. *American Journal of Physiology, 218,* 864–868.

Wu, H. C., Chen, K. Y., Lee, W. Y., & Lee, E. H. Y. (1997). Antisense oligonucleotides to corticotropin-releasing factor impair memory retention and increase exploration in rats. *Neuroscience, 78,* 147–153.

Wyss, J. M., & Sripanidkulchai, B. (1985). The development of Ammon's horn and the fascia dentata in the cat: A [$^3$H]thymidine analysis. *Brain Research, 350,* 185–198.

# 7

# The Neural Circuits That Underlie Fear

Karim Nader & Joseph LeDoux

## Why Fear?

It is likely that the fear system of the brain is involved in extreme shyness. The reasons for thinking this are twofold. First, the behavioral and physiological indices that are used to categorize children as extremely shy are similar to the spectrum of responses that fearful objects elicit in humans and animals (Kagan, Reznick, & Snidman, 1988). Included are such factors as time to approach a new object (behavioral inhibition), changes in autonomic nervous system activity, and increased levels of stress hormones (such as cortisol). Second, in both animal models and humans, these responses are known to be mediated by the amygdala, the centerpiece of the brain's fear system (see Davis, 1992; Kapp, Wilson, Pascoe, Supple, & Whalen, 1990; LeDoux, 1996b; Maren & Fanselow, 1996). The hypothesis that extreme shyness involves dysfunctions in the fear system provides us with a heuristic model that can guide research into the underlying mechanisms. This chapter outlines much of what we know about the fear system.

## Fear Conditioning

One of the most commonly used procedures for measuring the fearful properties of a stimulus is called fear conditioning (Brown, Kalish, & Farber, 1951; Kamin, 1965). In this Pavlovian conditioning paradigm, an initially neutral stimulus (the conditioned stimulus; CS) is paired with a noxious event (the unconditioned stimulus; US), typically a foot shock (figure 7.1A). Even after a single pairing of these two stimuli, presentation of the CS alone elicits a spectrum of stereotyped re-

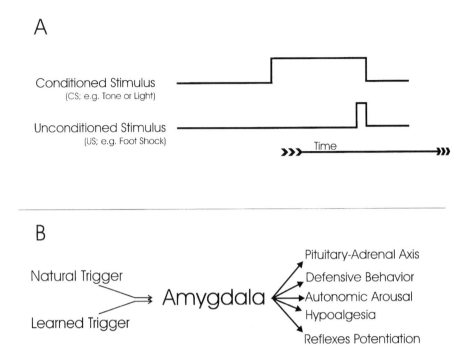

Figure 7.1. (A) The fear-conditioning paradigm used to confer fear-eliciting properties onto initially neutral CSs. A CS is presented which coterminates with the presentation of a noxious US. In most experiments, the US employed is a foot shock.
(B) After fear conditioning, presentation of the CS (learned trigger) elicits the same
spectrum of responses as does presentation of a natural predator (natural trigger).
Furthermore, both learned and natural triggers require the integrity of the amygdala for fear responses to be expressed.

sponses (Fanselow & Bolles, 1979). Some of these include freezing (immobility;
Blanchard & Blanchard, 1969; Bouton & Bolles, 1980), the cessation of ongoing behavior (instrumental behavior; Brady, 1956; Estes & Skinner, 1941; Hunt, 1956),
and autonomic and endocrine responses (Cohen & Randall, 1984; Kapp, Gallagher,
Frysinger, & Applegate, 1981; LeDoux, Sakaguchi, & Reis, 1984; Mason, 1968;
Smith, Astley, Devito, Stein, & Walsh, 1980; van de Kar, Piechowski, Rittenhouse,
& Gray, 1991; see figure 7.1B). Furthermore, cues that have been paired with shock
can potentiate the magnitude of an animal's startle response to a brief auditory
stimulus (Brown et al., 1951). If the CS and US are presented in a random relationship to each other, the CS does not acquire fear-eliciting properties (Rescorla,
1968). In an informational sense, these fear responses are elicited by stimuli in the
environment that predict or create an expectation of a threatening event
(Dickinson, 1980; Rescorla & Wagner, 1972). Implicit in this conceptualization is
that fear occurs not only when we directly encounter a dangerous event but also
when we detect cues that predict danger.

Of particular relevance is the fact that the response profile mentioned here is
similar to that seen when animals are presented with a natural threat. When en-

closed with an anesthetized cat, rats tend to freeze extensively, even if never exposed to a cat before (Blanchard & Blanchard, 1971). The finding that cues that predict foot shock elicit the same behavioral and physiological responses as the presence of a natural predator suggests that the brain treats the stimuli in the same way. Specifically, both predict danger and the animal then responds to each by expressing fear responses. Furthermore, the fact that freezing is elicited the very first time a rat is exposed to a cat suggests that this response has been hard-wired into the brain by evolution (Blanchard & Blanchard, 1971; Bolles, 1972).

An early clue to the neural basis of fear came from the classic studies of Kluver and Bucy (Kluver & Bucy, 1937, 1939). They found that lesions of the temporal lobe, which included the amygdala, transformed aggressive monkeys into tame animals. Not only was their aggression circumscribed but also their fears of both novel items and natural enemies, such as snakes, were abolished. This was a powerful demonstration of a particular brain region's involvement in emotional reactions. Subsequent research that attempted to pinpoint the neuroanatomical locus of critical importance in this syndrome identified the amygdala as a critical structure for mediating many of the emotional reactions (Horel, Keating, & Misantone, 1975; Pribram, Douglas, & Pribram, 1969; Schreiner & Kling, 1953; Weiskrantz, 1956). Consistent with the putative involvement of the amygdala in defensive reactions, subsequent studies showed that lesions restricted to the amygdala eliminated freezing behavior in rats when presented with either an anesthetized cat or a CS that had been paired previously with foot shock (Blanchard & Blanchard, 1972). Whereas sham-lesioned rats never made contact with the cat and spent most of their time freezing, lesioned animals made multiple contacts with the cat and even climbed on top of it! The cat no longer represented a threat. The similarity in both the behavioral responses and the neuroanatomical systems that mediate these responses to a natural threat and a CS paired with foot shock is validation of fear conditioning as a model of natural fear.

## From Sensation to Emotional Response:
## The Reactive Fear System

Over the past 20 or so years, many studies have examined the pathways that underlie the acquisition and expression of emotional memories induced by fear conditioning. Some of the questions that have been asked include: (1) What systems transmit information about the CS and US? (2) Where in the brain does information about the CS and US converge? (3) What computations are performed to endow the once-neutral CS with the ability to elicit defensive reactions? and (4) What are the output pathways that mediate the conditioned responses themselves?

Not surprisingly, given the observations described previously, the amygdala turns out to be a key part of the neural system that underlies fear conditioning. It is required for the acquisition and expression of fear responses to conditioned stimuli (see Blanchard & Blanchard, 1972; Davis, 1992; Kapp, Whalen, Supple, & Pascoe, 1992; LeDoux, 1996a). Through the process of Pavlovian conditioning, the CS acquires the capacity to access and trigger a hardwired fear response network organized in the amygdala and its output connections to the brainstem, producing a cascade of innate defensive reactions. It is thus important to understand how in-

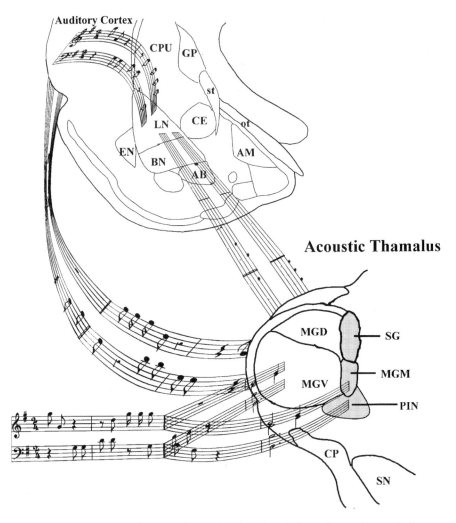

Figure 7.2. Emotional auditory information is relayed from the auditory thalamus to the amygdala via either a direct or indirect pathway. In this case, the emotional auditory information is an opera by Verdi. Auditory information arriving in the dorsal and ventral divisions of the medial geniculate body (MGD and MGV, respectively) is relayed to the auditory cortex and then the lateral nucleus of the amygdala. This is the indirect thalamo-cortico-amygdala pathway. The direct thalamo-amygdala pathway transmits auditory information arriving at the medial division of the medial geniculate body (MGM) and the posterior intralaminar nucleus (PIN) to the lateral nucleus of the amygdala. Note that the characteristics of the auditory information are preserved by the indirect pathway. In contrast to this, the direct pathway only supports crude representations of auditory stimuli. Abbreviations: AB-accessory basal amygdala nucleus; AM-medial amygdala nucleus; BN-basal amygdala nucleus; CE-central nucleus of the amygdala; CP-cerebral peduncle; CPU-caudate putamen; EN-endopiriform nucleus; GP-globus pallidus; LN-lateral amygdala nucleus; MGD/MGM/MGV-dorsal/medial/ventral divisions of the medial geniculate body, respectively; ot-optic tract; PIN-posterior intralaminar nucleus; SG-suprageniculate nucleus; SN-substantia nigra; st-stria terminalis.

formation about the CS is transmitted to, and processed by, the amygdala, and to determine the cellular mechanisms in the amygdala that underlie the changes in processing during learning.

Auditory CS information is transmitted from the ear through auditory pathways of the brainstem to the auditory relay nucleus in the thalamus, the medial geniculate body (MGB; LeDoux et al., 1984). The signal is then relayed to the amygdala by way of two parallel pathways. A direct monosynaptic projection originates in a particular subset of nuclei of the auditory thalamus (LeDoux, Farb, & Ruggiero, 1990). A second, indirect pathway conveys information from all areas of the auditory thalamus to the auditory cortex. Several cortico-cortical pathways then transmit auditory information to the amygdala (Mascagni, McDonald, & Coleman, 1993; Romanski & LeDoux, 1993). Both the direct and indirect pathways terminate in the lateral nucleus of the amygdala (LA; LeDoux, Cicchetti, Xagoraris, & Romanski, 1990; Mascagni et al., 1993; Romanski & LeDoux, 1993; Turner & Herkenham, 1991), often converging onto single neurons (Li, Stutzmann, & LeDoux, 1996; figure 7.2).

Although the auditory cortex is not required for the acquisition of conditioned fear to a simple auditory stimulus (Armony, Servan-Schreiber, Romanski, Cohen, & LeDoux, 1997; Romanski & LeDoux, 1992), processing of the CS by cells in the auditory cortex is modified as a result of its pairing with the US (see Quirk, Armony, Repa, Li, & LeDoux, 1997; Weinberger, 1995). In situations that involve more complex stimuli that must be discriminated, recognized, and/or categorized, the auditory cortex is required (e.g. Cranford & Igarashi, 1977; Whitfield, 1980) and may be an essential link to the amygdala.

What are the advantages of the parallel processing capabilities of this system? First, the existence of a subcortical pathway allows the amygdala to detect threatening stimuli in the environment quickly, in the absence of a complete and time-consuming analysis of the stimulus. This quick-and-dirty processing route may confer an evolutionary advantage to the species. Second, the rapid subcortical pathway may function to "prime" the amygdala to evaluate subsequent information received along the cortical pathway (LeDoux, 1986; Li et al., 1996). For example, a loud noise may be sufficient to alert the amygdala, at the cellular level, to prepare it to respond to a dangerous predator lurking nearby, but defensive reactions may not be fully mobilized until the auditory cortex analyzes the location, frequency, and intensity of the noise to determine specifically the nature and extent of this potentially threatening auditory signal. The convergence of the subcortical and cortical pathways onto single neurons in the lateral nucleus (Li et al., 1996) provides a means by which the integration could take place. Third, recent computational modeling studies show that the subcortical pathway can function as an interrupt device (Simon, 1967) that enables the cortex, by way of amygdalo-cortical projections, to shift attention to dangerous stimuli that occur outside the focus of attention (see Armony, Quirk, & LeDoux, 1998).

Information from the two sensory pathways converges onto cells in the lateral nucleus of the amygdala (LeDoux et al., 1990; Mascagni et al., 1993; Romanski & LeDoux, 1993; Turner & Herkenham, 1991). This is the point at which it is thought that computations are performed on the auditory stimuli to transform them from meaningless sensory events to potent elicitors of fear reactions (for reviews of the cellular plasticity that takes place in this system, see Quirk et al., 1997; Weinberger,

1995). Although the pathways that mediate US information are not known, physiological experiments have revealed that individual cells in the lateral amygdala respond to both auditory and noxious somatosensory stimulation (Romanski, LeDoux, Clugnet, & Bordi, 1993). This convergence of CS and US information has been proposed as a necessary criteria for learning since Pavlov (Pavlov, 1927; see Gallistel, 1989, for a critique of this approach). Lesions of the lateral nucleus block the acquisition of conditioned freezing, increases in blood pressure, and fear potentiated startle in response to presentation of a tone that has been paired previously with foot shock (LeDoux et al., 1990; Sananes & Davis, 1992). These findings confirm the physiological data in showing that the lateral nucleus is critical for fear conditioning to occur.

Although lesions allow us to identify a structure as participating in a process, in this case Pavlovian conditioning, they do not allow us to determine the exact component of the process that is being interfered with. For example, it is possible that the lateral nucleus has no role in the acquisition of emotional memories; rather, it may be involved in the recall of a stored emotional memory. Because the lesions are present during both training and testing, it is impossible to delineate its role. One way of overcoming this problem is to use what is called a reversible lesion. In this case, a structure is turned off or inactivated only during one particular phase of the paradigm. This can be accomplished by injecting a drug called muscimol that activates inhibitory gamma-amino butyric acid (GABA) receptors, in turn shutting off neurons in a region of interest. When muscimol is infused directly into the lateral and basal nuclei only during acquisition and the animals are tested for expression of fear responses without any muscimol injections, no freezing to the CS is seen (Helmstetter & Bellgowan, 1994; Muller, Corodimas, Fridel, & LeDoux, 1997). Similarly, when muscimol is infused into the lateral and basal nuclei prior only to test and not prior to acquisition, rats again fail to show any fear reactions (Muller et al., 1997). These findings, in conjunction with the recent data that demonstrates that lesions of the basal nucleus do not interfere with auditory fear conditioning, argue that the lateral nucleus is a critical site for both the acquisition and expression of emotional memories.

In contrast to the lateral nucleus, which seems to be involved in forming an association between a neutral CS and a noxious stimulus, the central nucleus is critical for the expression of conditioned fear responses (Davis, 1992; Kapp, Wilson, Pascoe, Supple, & Whalen, 1990; LeDoux, 1996b; Maren & Fanselow, 1996). There are both direct projections and indirect projections from the lateral nucleus to the central nucleus (Pitkanen, Savander, & LeDoux, 1997; Pitkanen et al., 1995; Stefanacci et al., 1992). The indirect pathway goes via the basal and accessory basal nuclei.

The projections from the lateral nucleus to the central and basal–accessory basal nuclei may contribute to two different kinds of fear conditioning. The first is the paradigm we have been discussing in which the CS is a discrete tone. This kind of conditioning is called auditory fear conditioning. However, another association animals can learn is one between the cues that define its environment and the foot shock US. This second kind of fear conditioning is called contextual fear conditioning. In the case of contextual conditioning, a structure called the hippocampus is necessary for first creating a representation of the environment, which is then sent to the amygdala, where that representation is associated with shock (Phillips

& LeDoux, 1992; Rudy & Pugh, 1996; Young, Bohenek, & Fanselow, 1994). Lesions of the hippocampus block conditioning to the context but spare freezing to an auditory CS (Kim & Fanselow, 1992; Phillips & LeDoux, 1992; Selden, Everitt, Jarrard, & Robbins, 1991). Regardless, however, of whether the nature of the CS is a punctate or complex cue, the same fear responses are observed.

Recent evidence suggests that contextual and punctate auditory stimuli use different intra-amygdala pathways to access the central nucleus. Lesions of the basal–accessory basal nuclei attenuate freezing to a context but have no effect on freezing to an auditory stimulus (Majidishad, Pelli, & LeDoux, 1996). This suggests that auditory information is relayed directly from the lateral nucleus to the central nucleus for the expression of fear responses. Conversely, if the CS is a diffuse context, information goes from the hippocampus to the basal–accessory basal nuclei and then to the central nucleus.

Once the representation of an association between a CS and a noxious US arrives at the central nucleus, it is transformed into a spectrum of fear responses of appropriate magnitude. Lesions of the central nucleus block all measures of conditioned fear. For example, such lesions have been shown to block conditioned freezing, changes in heart rate, potentiation of startle, release of ACTH and corticosterone, increases in blood pressure, and so forth (see Davis, 1992; Kapp et al., 1990; LeDoux, 1996b; Maren & Fanselow, 1996). In fact, stimulation of the central nucleus produces many of the behavioral responses that are observed after fear conditioning, suggesting that these responses are innately hardwired (see Davis, 1992). It is still unclear, however, whether the central nucleus is involved in storing some aspect of the memory of a learned CS-US representation itself or rather is simply the motor interface between the recall and expression of an emotional memory which is stored elsewhere in the brain.

Although the central nucleus acts as a common output for the various conditioned responses elicited by fearful stimuli, the anatomical sites that mediate the distinctive conditioned responses themselves are distributed throughout the brain. Divergent projections from the central nucleus to these various sites activates the individual fear responses. For example, lesions of the periaqueductal gray block freezing behavior but not changes in blood pressure. Conversely, lesions of the lateral hypothalamus block conditioned increases in blood pressure but not freezing behavior (LeDoux, Iwata, Cicchetti, & Reis, 1988). This pattern of findings is consistent with the view that the sites that mediate plasticity are upstream or afferent to these structures.

## Stress and the Fear System

One of the variables proposed to contribute to the development of an inhibited behavioral phenotype in humans is increased cortisol levels (e.g., Kagan & Snidman, 1991; Schmidt et al., 1997). This steroid is thought to be released in response to stressful events in the environment (for an alternate description of the process that results in cortisol release, see Gunnar, Narvinny, Isensee, & Fisch, 1989). Stress and manipulations of corticosterone (the rat homologue of cortisol) are intimately related to the fear system. Presentation of a fearful stimulus leads to increases in corticosterone and corticosterone directly impacts the functioning of the fear system (Gray,

1982; Thach, 1975; van de Kar et al., 1991). Stress can influence distinct components of the fear system. It can influence the amygdala directly to change its sensitivity to discrete cues in the environment that predict danger, or it can influence the hippocampus to interfere with its ability to create a representation of the environment.

Manipulations that induce stress in adult rats, such as social isolation, cause deficits in auditory fear conditioning (Rudy & Pugh, 1996). This deficit is manifested as an increase in the generalization of fear responses to other tones. In other words, stress impoverishes the representation of the characteristics of the tone such that tones of different frequencies elicited the same degree of freezing as the training frequency. Similarly, directly manipulating levels of corticosterone itself also produces significant effects on both the development and function of the fear system. Removal of the adrenal glands that produce and release corticosterone retards the development of behavioral inhibition as defined by freezing (Takahashi & Rubin, 1993). Injecting adrenalectomized rats with replacement corticosterone causes recovery of behavioral inhibition, demonstrating that corticosterone levels can have a direct impact on the development of the fear system. In contrast to these studies, increasing corticosterone only on test day to levels that mimic those seen in stressful situations results in a potentiation of freezing behavior to an auditory CS (Corodimas, LeDoux, Gold, & Schulkin, 1994). This demonstrates that elevated corticosterone can increase the sensitivity or output of the amygdala. Thus consistently increased levels of stress/cortisol could cause a number of psychological dysfunctions that could result in a hyperactive amygdala, the putative etiology of extreme shyness. First, cues which normally would not be capable of engaging the fear system can now elicit fear responses due to stress-induced increases in generalization to a discrete fear-eliciting stimulus. Second, increased levels of cortisol would increase the sensitivity/output of the amygdala such that supranormal responses to discrete fear-eliciting stimuli will be produced. It is easy to see how these two factors contribute to creating a hyperactive amygdala.

Many of these same manipulations also affect the functioning of the hippocampus system. Interestingly, however, the psychological nature of the deficits is different. Whereas social isolation had no effect on the magnitude of auditory fear conditioning, this same manipulation decreases contextually elicited freezing (Rudy, 1996; Rudy & Pugh, 1996). The nature of this deficit seems to be that stress is interfering with the ability of the animal to create a representation of the context that has to be constructed prior to forming an association with shock. In adults, adrenalectomizing rats causes a reduction in contextual fear conditioning but not in auditory fear conditioning. Replacement therapy with corticosterone rescued this deficit (Pugh, Tremblay, Fleshner, & Rudy, 1997). Again this deficit was in the animal's ability to form a representation of the environment. Although removal of the adrenal glands had no effect on auditory fear conditioning, it is possible that adrenalectomized rats will show enhanced generalization to other frequencies aside from the training frequency.

At first glance it may seem that a dysfunctional hippocampus that results in a decrease in contextual fear conditioning would not contribute to pathological hyperactivity of the amygdala fear system. How could making one component of the fear system nonfunctional contribute to heightened functioning in that same system? In order to understand how a dysfunctional hippocampus can contribute to a supersensitive fear system, we need to introduce some new learning concepts.

So far we have only referred to simple Pavlovian conditioning in the ability of stimuli to either elicit or not elicit conditioned responses. However, every simple association that is acquired is learned within a particular environment or context. Furthermore, depending on the environment, a simple association may or may not be expressed. In fact, it is thought that the context within which simple associations are acquired is a critical component of what is learned (Bouton, 1993). Take the example of a person who was mugged by someone wearing a bright red jacket. It would be evolutionarily disadvantageous if every time the victim saw a red jacket the fear system was engaged. This would render him or her nonfunctional. However, because the context in which the mugging occurred is also learned, the sight of a red jacket only predicts fear in certain contexts. One name for this kind of learning is *occasion setting* (e.g. Holland, 1983). Explicitly stated, the learning takes the form of two logical statements: (1) in the presence of stimulus A, CSx will be followed by the US; and (2) in the presence of stimulus B, CSx is not followed by the US. Thus an impairment due to stress or "stress" steroids in the ability to form representations of the environment could have very drastic consequences. Instead of responding to a discrete cue such as a red jacket as being dangerous only when that cue occurs within a certain context, now each experience of that cue will engage the fear system. This lack of differential contextual control over discrete fear conditioning, in conjunction with both the supranormal fear responses and increased generalization to discrete cues mentioned previously, could potently drive the fear system in ways that lead to pathological conditions.

## The Nature of Behavioral Inhibition

The use of terms such as *behavioral inhibition* invokes more questions than it explains. For example, is there only one behavioral inhibition system in the brain, or are there many? Kagan, Snidman, and Reznick (1989) have suggested that there may be two qualitatively distinct behavioral inhibition processes that could contribute to extreme shyness—one that functions in social settings and a second that functions in response to novelty (Kagan et al., 1989). If there is more than one, then is the qualitative nature of the inhibition the same across systems, or do different behavioral inhibition systems use different strategies to inhibit behavior? If the concept of behavioral inhibition is to be something more than a simple restatement of the phenomena, then we need to know the answers to these questions. We would then be in a better position to understand and address severe shyness in individuals. The intent of this section is not to argue in support of one mechanism of behavioral inhibition over another in inhibited children. Rather, it is to stimulate discussion with regard to what behavioral inhibition means and whether behavioral inhibition is best conceptualized as a single process or as multiple processes.

Work in our laboratory has addressed the issue of behavioral inhibition by testing whether the same neural manipulation affects different operationally defined kinds of behavioral inhibition. For example, animals placed in an environment explore their environment. When a tone that has been paired previously with shock is presented, exploration of that environment is replaced by freezing behavior (Blanchard & Blanchard, 1969). This is an example of response competition in which one response, such as freezing, competes with and overpowers a second response, exploration. Freezing inhibits behavior by acting as a brake on exploratory behavior. As previously mentioned, we know the precise mechanisms by which this behavior is produced. If we remove the central nucleus, the output nucleus for all fear responses, or the periaqueductal gray that mediates this particular conditioned response, freezing will be lost.

Now compare the inhibition defined by freezing with the behavioral inhibition defined by suppression in a conditioned emotional response (CER) paradigm (Estes & Skinner, 1941). A typical CER paradigm has animals performing some instrumental behavior, such as pressing a bar for food. Presentation of a tone that has been paired previously with shock causes an immediate decrease in the rate at which animals perform the operant response. Is this behavioral inhibition mediated by the same mechanisms that mediate freezing? One theory of the nature of suppression answers yes (Kamin, 1965; Miller, 1951). Suppression of bar pressing is highly correlated with freezing (Bouton & Bolles, 1980; Mast, Blanchard, & Blanchard, 1982) but not with other responses such as conditioned autonomic responses (De Toledo & Black, 1966). Thus it is postulated that the suppression seen in the CER was due to competition between the responses of freezing and bar pressing. Although this interpretation is parsimonious with regard to positing a single process that mediates behavioral inhibition, recent findings indicate that it is unlikely to be accurate.

A simple study was recently undertaken in our laboratory to directly examine this issue. We predicted that if the behavioral inhibition defined by freezing and suppression represented the function of a single process, then the same manipulations should affect both behaviors. In order to test this directly, we examined what effect lesions of the periaqueductal gray, which block freezing, would have on suppression behavior in a CER paradigm. We found that lesions of the periaqueductal gray which blocked freezing had no effect on suppression (Amorapanth, Nader, & LeDoux, 1998), suggesting the presence of multiple behavioral inhibition systems.

For some reason the brain has evolved such that, when an animal is simply exploring an environment and detects danger, a freezing strategy is used to inhibit ongoing behavior. Conversely, when an animal is engaged in goal-directed behavior and detects danger, the brain no longer uses a freezing strategy to produce inhibition but rather makes recourse to some other process. What this process is remains unclear. One theory proposes that the process that mediates the behavioral inhibition defined by suppression is motivational in nature (Estes, 1969; Millenson & de Villiers, 1972; Rescorla & Solomon, 1967). The reason animals stop pressing the bar is that, once a fear-conditioned tone is presented, it turns down the rewarding properties of food and cues associated with food. Therefore, pressing a bar for food is no longer a high priority for the animals. This would remove any competing desire to press the bar and leave the animal free to attend to potential dangers in the environment. If this interpretation of suppression is correct, then it would demonstrate that not only are there different inhibitory mechanisms in the brain but also that the qualitative nature of the inhibition can differ across systems. In the case of freezing, the nature of behavioral inhibition seems to be response competition, whereas the mechanisms that mediate suppression may be motivational in nature. Interestingly, both the mechanisms that mediate freezing and suppression are the product of a single fear system.

Gray's (1982) theory of anxiety proposed that the hippocampus was key to behavioral inhibition, with freezing behavior being a prototypical example of inhibition. However, as we have seen, freezing elicited by threats is controlled more by the amygdala than the hippocampus. Contextual threats are an exception, since the hippocampus is required to process the context. However, even in these instances, the amygdala is crucial as the link between the hippocampus and the motor control systems in the brainstem. Interestingly, much of the data base Gray used can be thought of as involving contextually elicited inhibition. In the end, the hippocampal and amygdala theories of inhibition may not be so different.

## The Active Fear System

An important aspect of fear has been left out of the discussion so far. This is the role of the reinforcing properties of fear. Pavlovian conditioning not only endows the CS with the ability to elicit defensive behaviors but also endows it with conditioned aversive properties that can reinforce the acquisition of a new response (Miller, 1951; Mowrer & Lamoreaux, 1942, 1946). Whereas the hardwired defensive responses of the fear system bring a person fast and efficient strategies with which to cope with cues that predict immediate danger, the aversive properties of fear allow for flexibility in responses. This is because the aversive properties do not dictate behavior but merely influence it. For example, if you were mugged at a particular corner store, the subsequent sight of the store probably would not produce massive freezing behavior. It is likely, however, that you will avoid that store. Furthermore, there are innumerable ways in which you can avoid it. You could simply cross the street, turn down the next street, or stop and retrace your steps, to mention a few possibilities. The specific way in which you avoid the store is up to you. The one common denominator that links all of these responses together is that they result in moving you away from the store. Thus aversion is not a behavior we can observe, but rather is a construct we invoke in order to explain systematic variations in behavior.

In contrast to the enormous amount of work done on delineating the neuroanatomical mechanisms that mediate defensive responses such as freezing behavior, hardly any studies have addressed the neural mechanisms that mediate the conditioned aversive properties of fear. Part of the reason for this is the difficulty involved in measuring something that is not directly observable, such as freezing. Furthermore, in the avoidance literature, there seems to have been a bias away from invoking constructs in order to explain behavior (see Levis, 1989). Therefore, in order to get a clue as to what structures in the brain are involved in conferring reinforcing value onto a CS, we need to look elsewhere—for instance, to work done on conditioned reward.

A large body of work has implicated the amygdala in mediating the conditioned rewarding properties of CSs that have been paired with rewarding USs (Cador, Robbins, & Everitt, 1989; Hiroi & White, 1991; McDonald & White, 1993; Murray, Gaffan, & Mishkin, 1993; Murray & Mishkin, 1985). Much of the evidence for this proposition comes from studies that utilized an acquisition of a new response paradigm. The first phase of this paradigm entailed giving rats classical conditioning sessions in which a CS was paired with an appetitive US, such as water. Animals were then placed in operant chambers that had two levers. Depressing one lever resulted in the delivery of the CS alone, whereas depressing the second lever had no programmed consequences. Rats learned to press much more on the lever that resulted in CS presentation as opposed to the second lever. Furthermore, if the CS and US were explicitly unpaired during the Pavlovian component of this task, then the CS was impotent to support the acquisition of a new response (e.g., Beninger & Phillips, 1980). This demonstrates that the reinforcing property acquired by the CS was contingent on an association between the CS and US. Lesions of the basolateral amygdala (BLA, defined as basal and lateral nuclei) have consistently been shown to block the acquisition of a new response, regardless of whether the US used in the Pavlovian component was food, fluid, or drugs of abuse, a finding that suggests that this structure mediates the conditioned rewarding properties regardless of the nature of the original rewarding US (Everitt & Robbins, 1992; Robbins, Cador, Taylor, & Everitt, 1989).

An alternative approach that tests the BLA's role in conditioned reward without requiring animals to learn an operant task is to make use of a second-order conditioning paradigm. The initial phase of the experiment entails first-order CS-US pairings. In the second phase, rats are presented with a second distinctive CS (CS2) prior to presentation of the first-order CS (CS1). Again, it is the reinforcing properties that CS1 has acquired during first-order conditioning that will reinforce the acquisition of second-order conditioning (Mackintosh, 1983). Using this paradigm, Hatfield, Han, Conley, Gallagher, and Holland (1996) demonstrated that lesions of the BLA blocked second-order, but not first-order, conditioning using food as the US. Given that BLA-lesioned animals acquired normally the first-order association, then the deficit could not be due to an impairment in CS or US processing or in the ability to form and express an association. Rather, the deficit is the result of the loss of the conditioned rewarding properties elicited by CS1 after first-order conditioning. Thus the findings from multiple paradigms are consistent in identifying the BLA as a site that mediates conditioned reward.

Using the work done with rewarding US as guideposts, work by numerous researchers (Killcross, Robbins, & Everitt, 1997) has started to examine how lesions of different nuclei of the amygdala affect both freezing behavior and the aversive properties of fear. In order to measure the aversive properties of fear, we used an acquisition of a new response paradigm called the *escape-from-fear* paradigm (McAllister & McAllister, 1971). Our version of this paradigm entails giving animals fear conditioning in one distinctive environment using a tone as the CS. The following day, rats are put into one chamber of a two-chamber avoidance box. Ten seconds after they are placed in the box, a guillotine door is opened, and 10 seconds later the CS is presented. Moving to the other identical environment causes the CS to terminate. The reinforcing event in this paradigm is the termination of the aversion elicited by the CS.

Using this paradigm in conjunction with anatomical manipulations, we are in a position to test whether the neural mechanisms that mediate the aversive properties of fear and the behavioral responses to fear are equivalent or not. Given that the lateral nucleus is thought to be the site that mediates the association between the CS and the US, we could not create a lesion in this structure. Instead, we constrained our lesions to the basal nuclei which spare the acquisition of auditory fear conditioning. Lesions of the basal nuclei blocked the acquisition of the escape-

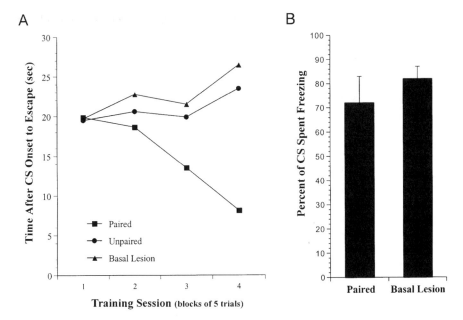

Figure 7.3. The effects of lesions of the basal amygdala nuclei on the acquisition of the escape from fear task and conditioned freezing behavior. (A) The escape-from-fear paradigm is used as a measure of the aversive properties that a CS has come to acquire through Pavlovian conditioning with a noxious US. This is shown by the fact that only control animals that received paired but not unpaired presentations of the CS (a tone) and US (foot shock) escaped to the alternate compartment with increasing shorter latencies after CS onset. Rats with lesions of the basal nuclei did not acquire the escape-from-fear task. This demonstrates that these lesions blocked the conditioned aversive properties normally elicited by CSs that have been paired previously with a noxious US. (B) Freezing scores from the control and basal lesion animals that had paired CS/US presentations. In contrast to the findings from the escape-from-fear task, there is no difference in the amount of freezing demonstrated by these two groups. Thus the neural mechanisms that mediate the conditioned aversive and defensive behaviors of fear are distinct from each other.

from-fear task but had no effect on the normal expression of freezing to the CS (figure 7.3). Given that these lesions had no effect on the acquisition or expression of freezing, the impairment cannot be due to either the ability to acquire an association between the CS and US or in sensory processing. These data provide strong evidence that the mechanisms that mediate the conditioned defensive behaviors and conditioned aversion of fear are distinct.

The most parsimonious model of the neuroanatomical systems that mediate the fear-eliciting properties of a tone posits that the formation of the association between the CS and US occurs in the lateral nucleus of the amygdala. Information is then directly relayed to the CN to engage the reactive defensive conditioned response. Conversely, information from the lateral nucleus traverses to the basal nuclei, possibly projecting to the basal ganglia, to mediate the conditioned aversive properties

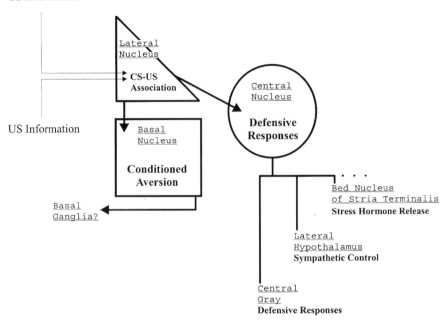

Figure 7.4. Schematic of the flow of information through various intra-amygdala nuclei and the respective psychological function attributed to those nuclei. Underlined words refer to the names of the neuroanatomical site. Words in bold refer to the function of that site with regard to auditory fear conditioning. Information about the CS and US arrives at the lateral nucleus, where an association is formed. Subsequent presentation of the CS elicits two qualitatively distinct conditioned processes. Projections to the basal nucleus mediate the conditioned aversive properties elicited by the CS, which then outputs putatively to the basal ganglia (the active system). Alternatively, projections from the lateral nucleus to the central nucleus mediate the classical defensive responses (the reactive system). From the central nucleus, information is transmitted to the various brain nuclei that mediate the various specific defensive responses, of which three are listed. The bed nucleus of the stria terminalis is thought to control release of stress hormones, the lateral hypothalamus controls sympathetic changes, and the central gray controls defensive responses such as freezing.

of fear and its ability to influence ongoing behavior. This distinction between the mechanisms that mediate the conditioned aversive properties of fear and the defensive behaviors elicited by fear introduces another hierarchical level of organization in the conditioned responses brought forth by fear-eliciting stimuli (figure 7.4).

## Interactions Between the Reactive and Active Systems

Fear-eliciting stimuli will activate two different systems that could influence our behavior. Activation of the reactive system, which includes information going to the central nucleus, will cause the generation of defensive reactions. The active fear system, on the other hand, requires information to reach the basal nuclei, and the subsequent elicitation of aversion will cause an individual to avoid that stimulus in a flexible manner. The outputs of these two systems are not always compatible. Freezing is incompatible with moving away. One of the issues that needs to be addressed is what the variables are that dictate which of the two output systems will dominate in any given situation. Because the basal nucleus output system has only recently been identified, studies have not begun to directly address this issue using neurobiological manipulations. However, data from behavioral studies suggest a number of possibilities.

One variable seems to be whether the response required to avoid an aversive stimulus is similar to any of an animal's species-specific defensive responses, such as running away or jumping. CS termination and the subsequent decrease in conditioned aversion make almost no contribution to the acquisition of avoidance behavior when the response the animal is required to perform is part of its defensive repertoire (Bolles & Grosen, 1969; Bolles, Stokes, & Younger, 1966). As the difference between the avoidance response and the rat's species-specific defensive behaviors increases, the contribution of CS termination to the acquisition of avoidance also increases. Therefore, the nature of the response that the animal is required to perform will influence which of the two output systems will dominate (Bolles, 1972). If the response is similar to the hardwired defensive responses, then the reactive system is engaged. Conversely, if the response required of the animal is not preprogrammed, but rather the animal must construct a novel motor solution for the task, then the output of the basal nucleus will likely be necessary to reinforce the acquisition of this novel response.

Alternately, the degree of fear may be the critical factor which will determine what strategy the amygdala adopts in a given situation. It has been proposed that defensive behaviors change along the dimension of degree of fear (Fanselow, 1994). Situations that elicit a small amount of fear cause a reorganization of feeding behavior (Fanselow, Lester, & Helmstetter, 1988). As fear continues to increase, freezing behavior, and then "circa strike" attack behavior, are elicited. It is possible that the mechanisms that mediate the conditioned aversion predominate in situations that have low levels of fear and cause the reorganization of feeding behavior. Conversely, when there are cues in the environment that elicit significant amounts of fear, the reactive system dominates, even though the active system is still functioning.

These two variables, similarity of a response to an animal's species-typical defensive behavior and degree of fear, represent two dimensions along which the reactive and active systems may interact. There are likely to be others, such as whether an animal has a successful coping strategy for dealing with dangerous situations or not. Because we have a manipulation that can block the active system, specifically lesions of the basal nucleus, we are in a position to test the parameters that define whether the output of the active or the reactive system dominates. Behaviors that are the product of the active system should be sensitive to lesions of the basal nucleus. Conversely, behaviors that are the product of the reactive system should be insensitive to lesions of the basal nucleus but should be blocked by lesions of the central nucleus.

## Summary

We know a tremendous amount about how the brain systems that have evolved to warn us of danger are organized, what the mechanisms are that underlie the transformation of a sensory representation into an emotional cue, and the subsequent systems involved in mediating the defensive responses to that cue. The amygdala plays a central role in all of these functions. It seems to be the place where both learning and expression of fear responses occur.

Although there are numerous questions that still need to be resolved, we are at a point where we can postulate testable models of how psychological processes such as stress can affect the neural mechanisms that mediate fear and vice versa. These models can both inform and direct our research into questions such as the etiology of extreme shyness, as well as other psychopathological conditions such as posttraumatic stress disorder.

*References*

Amorapanth, P., Nader, K., & LeDoux, J. (1998). *Lesions of the periaqueductal gray block freezing, but not conditioned suppression behavior.* Manuscript submitted for publication.

Armony, J. L., Quirk, G. J., & LeDoux, J. E. (1998). Differential effects of amygdala lesions on early and late plastic components of auditory cortex spike trains during fear conditioning. *Journal of Neuroscience, 18,* 2592–2601.

Armony, J. L., Servan-Schreiber, D., Romanski, L. M., Cohen, J. D., & LeDoux, J. E. (1997). Stimulus generalization of fear responses: Effects of auditory cortex lesions in a computational model and in rats. *Cerebral Cortex, 7,* 157–165.

Beninger, R. J., & Phillips, A. G. (1980). The effect of pimozide on the establishment of conditioned reinforcement. *Psychopharmacology, 68,* 147–153.

Blanchard, C. D., & Blanchard, R. J. (1972). Innate and conditioned reactions to threat in rats with amygdaloid lesions. *Journal of Comparative Physiological Psychology, 81,* 281–290.

Blanchard, R. J., & Blanchard, D. C. (1969). Crouching as an index of fear. *Journal of Comparative Physiological Psychology, 67,* 370–375.

Blanchard, R. J., & Blanchard, D. C. (1971). Defensive reactions in the albino rat. *Learning and Motivation, 2,* 351–362.

Bolles, R. C. (1972). Reinforcement, expectancy, and learning. *Psychological Review, 79,* 394–409.

Bolles, R. C., & Grosen, N. E. (1969). The non-operant nature of the bar-press escape response. *Psychonomic Science, 11,* 261–262.

Bolles, R. C., Stokes, L. W., & Younger, M. S. (1966). Does CS termination reinforce avoidance behavior? *Journal of Comparative and Physiological Psychology, 62,* 201–207.

Bouton, M. E. (1993). Context, time, and memory retrieval in the interference paradigms of Pavlovian learning. *Psychological Bulletin, 114,* 80–99.

Bouton, M. E., & Bolles, R. C. (1980). Conditioned fear assessed by freezing and by the suppression of three different baselines. *Animal Learning and Behavior, 8,* 429–434.

Brady, J. V. (1956). Assessment of drug effects on emotional behavior. *Science, 123,* 1033–1034.

Brown, J. S., Kalish, H. I., & Farber, I. E. (1951). Conditioned fear as revealed by magnitude of startle response to an auditory stimulus. *Journal of Experimental Psychology, 41,* 317–328.

Cador, M., Robbins, T. W., & Everitt, B. J. (1989). Involvement of the amygdala in stim-ulus-reward associations: Interaction with the ventral striatum. *Neuroscience, 30,* 77–86.

Cohen, D. H., & Randall, D. C. (1984). Classical conditioning of cardiovascular re-sponses. *Annual Review of Physiology, 46,* 187–197.

Corodimas, K. P., LeDoux, J. E., Gold, P. W., & Schulkin, J. (1994). Corticosterone po-tentiation of learned fear. *Annals of the New York Academy of Sciences, 746,* 392–393.

Cranford, J. L., & Igarashi, M. (1977). Effects of auditory cortex lesions on temporal sum-mation in cats. *Brain Research, 136,* 559–564.

Davis, M. (1992). The role of the amygdala in conditioned fear. In J. P. Aggleton (Ed.), *The amygdala: Neurobiological aspects of emotion, memory, and mental dysfunc-tion* (pp. 255–306). New York: Wiley-Liss.

De Toledo, L., & Black, A. H. (1966). Heart rate: Changes during conditioned suppres-sion in rats. *Science, 152,* 1404–1406.

Dickinson, A. (1980). *Contemporary animal learning theory.* Cambridge: Cambridge University Press.

Estes, W. K. (1969). Outline of a theory of punishment. In B. A. Campbell & R. M. Church (Eds.), *Punishment and aversive behavior* (pp. 57–82). New York: Appleton-Century-Crofts.

Estes, W. K., & Skinner, B. F. (1941). Some quantitative properties of anxiety. *Journal of Experimental Psychology, 29,* 390–400.

Everitt, B. J., & Robbins, T. W. (1992). Amygdala-ventral striatal interactions and reward-related processes. In J. P. Aggleton (Ed.), *The amygdala: Neurobiological aspects of emotion, memory, and mental dysfunction* (pp. 401–429). New York: Wiley-Liss.

Fanselow, M. S. (1994). Neural organization of the defensive behavior system responsi-ble for fear. *Psychonomic Bulletin and Review, 1,* 429–438.

Fanselow, M. S., & Bolles, R. C. (1979). Naloxone and shock-elicited freezing in the rat. *Journal of Comparative Physiological Psychology, 93,* 736–744.

Fanselow, M. S., Lester, L. S., & Helmstetter, F. J. (1988). Changes in feeding and forag-ing patterns as an antipredator defensive strategy: A laboratory simulation using aversive stimulation in a closed economy. *Journal of the Experimental Analysis of Behavior, 50,* 361–374.

Gallistel, C. R. (1989). *The organization of learning.* Cambridge, MA: MIT Press.

Gray, J. A. (1982). *The neuropsychology of anxiety.* New York: Oxford University Press.

Gunnar, M., Narvinny, D., Isensee, J., & Fisch, R. O. (1989). Coping with uncertainty: New models of the relations between hormonal, behavioral, and cognitive pro-cesses. In D. S. Palermo (Ed.), *Coping with uncertainty* (pp. 101–131). Hillsdale, NJ: Erlbaum.

Hatfield, T., Han, J.-S., Conley, M., Gallagher, M., & Holland, P. (1996). Neurotoxic le-sions of basolateral, but not central, amygdala interfere with pavlovian second-order conditioning and reinforcer devaluation effects. *Journal of Neuroscience, 16(16),* 5256–5265.

Helmstetter, F. J., & Bellgowan, P. S. (1994). Effects of muscimol applied to the basolat-eral amygdala on acquisition and expression of contextual fear conditioning in rats. *Behavioral Neuroscience, 108,* 1005–1009.

Hiroi, N., & White, N. M. (1991). The lateral nucleus of the amygdala mediates expres-sion of the amphetamine-produced conditioned place preference. *Journal of Neu-roscience, 11,* 2107–2116.

Holland, P. C. (1983). "Occasion-setting" in conditional discriminations. In M. L. Commons, R. J. Herrnstein, & A. R. Wagner (Eds.), *Quantitative analyses of behav-ior: Discrimination processes* (Vol. 4, pp. 183–206). New York: Ballinger.

Horel, J. A., Keating, E. G., & Misantone, L. J. (1975). Partial Kluver-Bucy syndrome pro-duced by destroying temporal neocortex or amygdala. *Brain Research, 94,* 347–359.

Hunt, H. F. (1956). Some effects of drugs on classical conditioning. *Annals of the New York Academy of Science, 65,* 258–267.

Kagan, J., Reznick, J. S., & Snidman, N. (1988). Biological bases of childhood shyness. *Science, 240,* 167–171.

Kagan, J., & Snidman, N. (1991). Infant predictors of inhibited and uninhibited profiles. *Psychological Science, 2,* 40–43.

Kagan, J., Snidman, N., & Reznick, J. S. (1989). The constructs of inhibition and lack of inhibition to unfamiliarity. In D. S. Palermo (Ed.), *Coping with uncertainty* (pp. 131–149). Hillsdale, NJ: Erlbaum.

Kamin, L. J. (1965). Temporal and intensity characteristics of the conditioned stimulus. In W. F. Prokasy (Ed.), *Classical Conditioning* (pp. 119–148). New York: Appleton-Century-Crofts.

Kapp, B. S., Gallagher, M., Frysinger, R. C., & Applegate, C. D. (1981). The amygdala, emotion and cardiovascular conditioning. In Y. Ben-Ari (Ed.), *The amygdaloid complex* (pp. 355–366). New York: Elsevier/North-Holland Biomedical Press.

Kapp, B. S., Whalen, P. J., Supple, W. F., & Pascoe, J. P. (1992). Amygdaloid contributions to conditioned arousal and sensory information processing. In J. P. Aggleton (Ed.), *The amygdala: Neurobiological aspects of emotion, memory, and mental dysfunction* (pp. 229–254). New York: Wiley-Liss.

Kapp, B. S., Wilson, A., Pascoe, J., Supple, W., & Whalen, P. J. (1990). A neuroanatomical systems analysis of conditioned bradycardia in the rabbit. In M. Gabriel & J. Moore (Eds.), *Learning and computational neuroscience: Foundations of adaptive networks* (Vol. 1, pp. 53–90). Cambridge, MA: MIT Press.

Killcross, S., Robbins, T. W., & Everitt, B. J. (1997). Different types of fear-conditioned behavior mediated by separate nuclei within amygdala. *Nature, 388,* 377–380.

Kim, J. J., & Fanselow, M. S. (1992). Modality-specific retrograde amnesia of fear. *Science, 256,* 675–677.

Kluver, H., & Bucy, P. C. (1937). "Psychic blindness" and other symptoms following bilateral temporal lobectomy in rhesus monkeys. *American Journal of Physiology, 119,* 352–353.

Kluver, H., & Bucy, P. C. (1939). Preliminary analysis of functions of the temporal lobes in monkeys. *Archives of Neurology and Psychiatry, 42,* 979–1000.

LeDoux, J. E. (1986). Sensory systems and emotion. *Integrative Psychiatry, 4,* 237–248.

LeDoux, J. E. (1996a). The emotional brain: Clues from fear conditioning. In T. Ono, B. L. McNaughton, S. Molotchnikoff, E. T. Rolls, & H. Nishijo (Eds.), *Perception, memory and emotion: Frontiers in neuroscience* (pp. 513–524). Cambridge: Cambridge University Press.

LeDoux, J. E. (1996b). *The emotional brain.* New York: Simon and Schuster.

LeDoux, J. E., Cicchetti, P., Xagoraris, A., & Romanski, L. M. (1990). The lateral amygdaloid nucleus: Sensory interface of the amygdala in fear conditioning. *Journal of Neuroscience, 10,* 1062–1069.

LeDoux, J. E., Farb, C. F., & Ruggiero, D. A. (1990). Topographic organization of neurons in the acoustic thalamus that project to the amygdala. *Journal of Neuroscience, 10,* 1043–1054.

LeDoux, J. E., Iwata, J., Cicchetti, P., & Reis, D. J. (1988). Different projections of the central amygdaloid nucleus mediate autonomic and behavioral correlates of conditioned fear. *Journal of Neuroscience, 8,* 2517–2529.

LeDoux, J. E., Sakaguchi, A., & Reis, D. J. (1984). Subcortical efferent projections of the medial geniculate nucleus mediate emotional responses conditioned by acoustic stimuli. *Journal of Neuroscience, 4,* 683–698.

Levis, D. J. (1989). The case for a return to a two-factor theory of avoidance: The failure of non-fear interpretations. In S. B. Klein & R. R. Mowrer (Eds.), *Contemporary learning theories: Pavlovian conditioning and the status of traditional learning theory* (pp. 227–277). Hillsdale, NJ: Erlbaum.

Li, X. F., Stutzmann, G. E., & LeDoux, J. L. (1996). Convergent but temporally separated inputs to lateral amygdala neurons from the auditory thalamus and auditory cortex use different postsynaptic receptors: *In vivo* intracellular and extracellular recordings in fear conditioning pathways. *Learning and Memory, 3*, 229–242.

Mackintosh, N. J. (1983). *Conditioning and associative learning*. New York: Oxford University Press.

Majidishad, P., Pelli, D. G., & LeDoux, J. E. (1996). Disruption of fear conditioning to contextual stimuli but not to a tone by lesions of the accessory basal nucleus of the amygdala. *Society for Neuroscience Abstracts, 22*, 1116.

Maren, S., & Fanselow, M. S. (1996). The amygdala and fear conditioning: Has the nut been cracked? *Neuron, 16*, 237–240.

Mascagni, F., McDonald, A. J., & Coleman, J. R. (1993). Corticoamygdaloid and cortico-cortical projections of the rat temporal cortex: A phaseolus vulgaris leucoagglutinin study. *Neuroscience, 57*, 697–715.

Mason, J. W. (1968). A review of psychoendocrine research on the sympathetic-adrenal medullary system. *Psychosomatic Medicine, 30*, 631–653.

Mast, M., Blanchard, R. J., & Blanchard, C. (1982). The relationship of freezing and response suppression in a CER situation. *Psychological Record, 32*, 151–167.

McAllister, W. R., & McAllister, D. E. (1971). Behavioral measurement of conditioned fear. In F. R. Brush (Ed.), *Aversive conditioning and learning* (pp. 105–179). New York: Academic Press.

McDonald, R. J., & White, N. M. (1993). A triple dissociation of memory systems: Hippocampus, amygdala, and dorsal striatum. *Behavioral Neuroscience, 107*, 3–22.

Millenson, J. R., & de Villiers, P. A. (1972). Motivational properties of conditioned anxiety. In R. M. Gilbert & J. R. Millenson (Eds.), *Reinforcement: Behavioral analyses* (pp. 125–157). New York: Academic Press.

Miller, N. E. (1951). Learnable drives and rewards. In S. S. Stevens (Ed.), *Handbook of experimental psychology* (pp. 435–472). New York: Wiley.

Mowrer, O. H., & Lamoreaux, R. R. (1942). Avoidance conditioning and signal duration: A study of secondary motivation and reward. *Psychological Monographs, 54.*

Mowrer, O. H., & Lamoreaux, R. R. (1946). Fear as an intervening variable in avoidance conditioning. *Journal of Comparative Psychology, 39*, 29–50.

Muller, J., Corodimas, K. P., Fridel, Z., & LeDoux, J. E. (1997). Functional inactivation of the lateral and basal nuclei of the amygdala by muscimol infusion prevents fear conditioning to an explicit CS and to contextual stimuli. *Behavioral Neuroscience, 111*, 683–691.

Murray, E. A., Gaffan, D., & Mishkin, M. (1993). Neural substrates of visual stimulus-stimulus association in Rhesus monkeys. *Journal of Neuroscience, 13*, 4549–4561.

Murray, E. A., & Mishkin, M. (1985). Amygdalectomy impairs cross modal association in monkeys. *Science, 228*, 604–606.

Pavlov, I. P. (1927). *Conditioned reflexes*. New York: Dover.

Phillips, R. G., & LeDoux, J. E. (1992). Differential contribution of amygdala and hippocampus to cued and contextual fear conditioning. *Behavioral Neuroscience, 106*, 274–285.

Pitkanen, A., Savander, V., & LeDoux, J. L. (1997). Organization of intra-amygdaloid circuitries: An emerging framework for understanding functions of the amygdala. *Trends in Neurosciences, 20*, 517–523.

Pitkanen, A., Stefanacci, L., Farb, C. R., Go, C.-G., LeDoux, J. E., & Amaral, D. G. (1995). Intrinsic connections of the rat amygdaloid complex: Projections originating in the lateral nucleus. *Journal of Comparative Neurology, 356*, 288–310.

Pribram, K. H., Douglas, R. J., & Pribram, B. J. (1969). The nature of nonlimbic learning. *Journal of Comparative Physiological Psychology, 69*, 765–772.

Pugh, C. R., Tremblay, D., Fleshner, M., & Rudy, J. W. (1997). A selective role or corticosterone in contextual-fear conditioning. *Behavioral Neuroscience, 111*, 503–511.

Quirk, G. J., Armony, J. L., Repa, J. C., Li, X.-F., & LeDoux, J. E. (1997). Emotional memory: A search for sites of plasticity. *Cold Spring Harbor Symposia on Biology, 61,* 247–257.

Rescorla, R. A. (1968). Probability of shock in the presence and absence of CS in fear conditioning. *Journal of Comparative Physiological Psychology, 66,* 1–5.

Rescorla, R. A., & Solomon, R. L. (1967). Two process learning theory: Relationships between Pavlovian conditioning and instrumental learning. *Psychological Review, 74,* 151–182.

Rescorla, R. A., & Wagner, A. R. (1972). A theory of Pavlovian conditioning: Variations in the effectiveness of reinforcement and nonreinforcement. In A. A. Black & W. F. Prokasy (Eds.), *Classical conditioning: II. Current research and theory* (pp. 64–99). New York: Appleton-Centry-Crofts.

Robbins, T. W., Cador, M., Taylor, J. R., & Everitt, B. J. (1989). Limbic-striatal interactions in reward-related processes. *Neuroscience Biobehavioral Reviews, 13,* 155–162.

Romanski, L. M., & LeDoux, J. E. (1992). Equipotentiality of thalamo-amygdala and thalamo-cortico-amygdala projections as auditory conditioned stimulus pathways. *Journal of Neuroscience, 12,* 4501–4509.

Romanski, L. M., & LeDoux, J. E. (1993). Information cascade from primary auditory cortex to the amygdala: Corticocortical and corticoamygdaloid projections of temporal cortex in the rat. *Cerebral Cortex, 3,* 515–532.

Romanski, L. M., LeDoux, J. E., Clugnet, M. C., & Bordi, F. (1993). Somatosensory and auditory convergence in the lateral nucleus of the amygdala. *Behavioral Neuroscience, 107,* 444–450.

Rudy, J. W. (1996). Postconditioning isolation disrupts contextual conditioning: An experimental analysis. *Behavioral Neuroscience, 110,* 238–246.

Rudy, J. W., & Pugh, C. R. (1996). A comparison of contextual and generalized auditory-cue fear conditioning: Evidence for similar memory processes. *Behavioral Neuroscience, 110,* 1299–1308.

Sananes, C. B., & Davis, M. (1992). N-methyl-D-aspartate lesions of the lateral and basolateral nuclei of the amygdala block fear-potentiated startle and shock sensitization of startle. *Behavioral Neuroscience, 106,* 72–80.

Schmidt, L. A., Fox, N. A., Rubin, K. H., Sternberg, E. M., Gold, P. W., Smith, C. C., & Schulkin, J. (1997). Behavioral and neuroendocrine responses in shy children. *Developmental Psychobiology, 30,* 127–140.

Schreiner, L. H., & Kling, A. (1953). Behavioral changes following rhinencephalic injury in cat. *Journal of Neurophysiology, 16,* 643–659.

Selden, N. R. W., Everitt, B. J., Jarrard, L. E., & Robbins, T. W. (1991). Complementary roles for the amygdala and hippocampus in aversive conditioning to explicit and contextual cues. *Neuroscience, 42(2),* 335–350.

Simon, H. A. (1967). Motivational and emotional controls of cognition. *Psychological Review, 74,* 29–39.

Smith, O. A., Astley, C. A., Devito, J. L., Stein, J. M., & Walsh, R. E. (1980). Functional analysis of hypothalamic control of the cardiovascular responses accompanying emotional behavior. *Federation Proceedings, 39,* 2487–2494.

Stefanacci, L., Farb, C. R., Pitkanen, A., Go, G., LeDoux, J. E., & Amaral, D. G. (1992). Projections from the lateral nucleus to the basal nucleus of the amygdala: A light and electron microscopic PHA-L study in the rat. *Journal of Comparative Neurology, 323,* 586–601.

Takahashi, L. K., & Rubin, W. W. (1993). Corticosteroid induction of threat-induced behavioral inhibition in preweanling rats. *Behavioral Neuroscience, 107,* 860–868.

Thach, W. T. (1975). Timing of activity in cerebellar dentate nucleus and cerebral motor cortex during prompt volitional movement. *Brain Research, 88,* 233–241.

Turner, B., & Herkenham, M. (1991). Thalamoamygdaloid projections in the rat: A test of the amygdala's role in sensory processing. *Journal of Comparative Neurology, 313,* 295–325.

van de Kar, L. D., Piechowski, R. A., Rittenhouse, P. A., & Gray, T. S. (1991). Amygdaloid lesions: Differential effect on conditioned stress and immobilization-induced increases in corticosterone and renin secretion. *Neuroendocrinology, 54,* 89–95.

Weinberger, N. M. (1995). Retuning the brain by fear conditioning. In M. S. Gazzaniga (Ed.), *The cognitive neurosciences* (pp. 1071–1090). Cambridge, MA: MIT Press.

Weiskrantz, L. (1956). Behavioral changes associated with ablation of the amygdaloid complex in monkeys. *Journal of Comparative Physiological Psychology, 49,* 381–391.

Whitfield, I. C. (1980). Auditory cortex and the pitch of complex tones. *Journal of the Acoustical Society of America, 67,* 644–647.

Young, S. L., Bohenek, D. L., & Fanselow, M. S. (1994). NMDA processes mediate anterograde amnesia of contextual fear conditioning induced by hippocampal damage: Immunization against amnesia by context preexposure. *Behavioral Neuroscience, 108,* 19–29.

# 8

# Neuroendocrine Regulation
# of Fear and Anxiety

Jay Schulkin & Jeffrey B. Rosen

This chapter discusses fear and its neuroendocrine regulation. Fear is a motivational/emotional state that serves animals in adapting to danger. The neural circuits that mediate the emotion of fear subserve the appraisal/perception of danger and behavioral and autonomic fear-related responses. The neural fear circuits and the functions of these systems are regulated by neuroendocrine substances, particularly those of the adrenal gland (i.e., glucocorticoids). A brain region that is critical for fear is the amygdala or extended amygdala (i.e., the bed nucleus of the stria terminalis).

We suggest that one function of glucocorticoid hormones is to facilitate the synthesis of the neuropeptide corticotropin-releasing hormone (CRH) in the amygdala in maintaining and coping with events that are perceived as frightening. The neuroendocrine hypothesis is that elevated levels of glucocorticoids, secreted by the adrenal gland, act on the amygdala or extended amygdala (bed nucleus of the stria terminalis) to facilitate CRH gene expression and the central motive state of fear. In addition, epinephrine and norepinephrine secreted by the adrenal medulla also modulate amygdala function, possibly through neurons containing GABA (gamma-amino butyric acid) and acetylcholine.

We begin with a discussion of the central motive state of fear and its biological basis. We then discuss the neural circuitry that underlies the perception of fearful events and fear-related behaviors. We then move to a description of the neuroendocrine basis of fear and a discussion of glucocorticoids and CRH in sustaining fear-related behaviors. We also discuss the role of norepinephrine and epinephrine in facilitating responses to and memory of aversive events.

## Central Motive State of Fear

The concept of central motive states historically emerged with those psychologists or biologists who investigated the central nervous system and the organization of behavior. A central motive state is a functional state of the brain that organizes and motivates a particular behavioral outcome. The term *central motive state* was coined by Lashley (1938) and quickly embraced by Beach (1942); Beach used the term *central excitatory states*. It was taken up by a number of ethologists (e.g., Tinbergen, 1951), psychobiologists (e.g., Hebb, 1949) and physiological psychologists (e.g., Morgan & Stellar, 1950).

The concept of central motive states anchored to basic biological systems found a clear use in neuroscience and in understanding behavior, measuring, for example, the performance of animals when they are hungry, thirsty, sexually aroused, or fearful (see Gallistel, 1980; Pfaff, 1980). The classic paper by Eliot Stellar (1954), "The Physiology of Motivation," along with the elegant experimental designs of Neal Miller (1957), legitimated the use of the term in modern scientific vernacular. Central motive states, such as fear, were placed in functional biological contexts.

Fear is a prototypical example of a central state—a state of the brain (LeDoux, 1987). Although systemic physiological changes influence the state of fear (James, 1884, 1890), peripheral responses are not sufficient for the emotional expression of motivated behaviors such as fear (Bard, 1939; Cannon, 1915/1929). It is functional neural activity in the brain that is linked to the state of fear. Bodily events nevertheless influence and reinforce the state (Damasio, 1994; James, 1890).

The central state of fear is knotted to attention and learning (Mackintosh, 1975) and the assessment of relevant information (Dickinson, 1980) that are important in predicting future outcomes (Miller, 1959; Rescorla & Wagner, 1972). The central fear state would occur if something unpredictable happens, particularly if there is a possibility of danger. The central state of fear is tied to attention (Lang, 1995), appraisal of environmental stimuli (LeDoux, 1996) and a tendency to act or behave in defensive ways (Arnold, 1960; Frijda, 1986).

## Biological Basis of Fear

Fear is an adaptive perceptual/behavioral response to danger, and it is fundamental to problem solving. In fact, fear as an emotion is thought to have evolved as part of problem solving (Darwin, 1872/1965). Emotions prepare the animal to respond in appropriate ways to environmental stimuli. For example, amusement in an activity increases excitement and motivates a person to perform the activity again. In contrast, fear prepares an animal to respond to danger by heightening vigilant attention (Gallagher & Holland, 1994; Lang, 1995) and motivating behavior (Bindra, 1978; Mowrer, 1947) that includes defensive behaviors (Bolles & Fanselow, 1980). The state of fear is one in which there is a readiness to perceive events as dangerous or alarming (LeDoux, 1987, 1996; Rosen, Hamerman, Sitcoske, Glowa, & Schulkin, 1996). The state is knotted to learning about what is safe and what is not (Miller, 1959) and the informational value of stimuli that have predictive value to the animal (Dickinson, 1980; Rescorla & Wagner, 1972).

Physiological and behavioral emotional responses are rooted in our evolutionary past. They are adaptive (Lazarus, 1991). However, fearful emotional responses are rooted in fast, possibly automatic, appraisals and judgments about stimuli and responses that facilitate survival (Arnold, 1960; Frijda, 1986). Fear organizes perceptual and behavioral systems to function quickly, and the appropriate behavior may be freezing or immobilization in response to danger (Bolles & Fanselow, 1980).

However, fear certainly does not always seem adaptive in our everyday life. In fact, the traditional view of negative emotions, such as fear, characterizes them as dysfunctional (e.g., Freud, 1926/1959; Goldstein, 1939/1995; Sabini & Silver, 1996; Spinoza, 1677/1955; see figure 8.1), disorganizing (Hebb, 1949) or as magical thinking (Sartre, 1948). And, in fact, chronic, exaggerated and/or inappropriate fear responses to threat are typically manifested in the anxiety disorders. Under these conditions the adaptiveness of fear has reached its limit; pathology now sets in (Rosen & Schulkin, 1998).

Once one characterizes emotions, such as fear, as part of an active and fast response to danger, they appear to be quite rational and adaptive and to function to organize behavior to avoid harm. Moreover, the emotions are cognitive; appraisals of danger are cognitive. An assessment can be fast and still cognitive (Chomsky, 1972); after all, language is fast and exemplifies what we mean by cognition (Fodor, 1981, 1983). Moreover, cognitive processing of language is biologically prewired, and therefore "prepared," but a specific language is not; similarly, the cognitive processes of fear are also prepared, but the idea of what a fearful stimulus is is not necessarily prewired. For example, monkeys are prepared to make the association between fear and snakes, but they must observe another monkey responding in a fearful way to a snake before snakes evoke fear (Mineka, 1985; Mineka & Zinberg, 1996). Emotions are cognitive because learning and appraisal processes are involved (e.g., Arnold, 1960). This does not mean that the cognitive processes of emotions are necessarily conscious. Evolution selected an unconscious "affective computational" system that underlies states such as fear (Parrott & Schulkin, 1993).

The computational fear system also has constraints similar to other perceptual/appraisal systems. The allocation of perceptual attention in any system of this type (Pashler, 1998) is limited and finite. The perception of fearful events may be constrained by neuronal processing of information and have a finite amount of neural substrate. The vigilance that is required during fear would limit the attention to particular stimuli that might normally be used elsewhere. Interference with attention to already known dangers occurs when an unknown stimulus enters the environment (Davis, Falls, Campeau, & Kim, 1993).

In addition to perception/appraisal, judgments, and computations, emotions such as fear are linked to action tendencies (Frijda, 1986). Fear motivates behavior in response to danger (Ohman, 1993) in very characteristic ways (Blanchard & Blanchard, 1972; Bolles & Fanselow, 1980). In many species, freezing with high muscle tension is the initial and prototypical fear response. Because of increased arousal and muscle tension, startle is more easily elicited or potentiated during a state of fear. Freezing behaviors and startle responses are expressions of fear across many species.

Although fear is linked to defensive behaviors (e.g., fight or flight), the two are not the same (Rosen & Schulkin, 1998). Fear functions to alert the animal to danger. The motivated animal seeks relief from this state, and with the elimination of fear there is the sense of relief (Miller, 1959; Mowrer, 1947). In other words, fear

Figure 8.1. Depiction of a man in terror. From Darwin (1872/1965). Copyright 1965 by University of Chicago Press. Reprinted by permission.

functions as a central motive state in threatening contexts, resulting in defensive behaviors that are adaptive in reducing or warding off harm.

Fear is also a communicative device to others in an elaborate social orchestration (Ekman & Davidson, 1994; Marler & Hamilton, 1966; Smith, 1977). Submissive behaviors, facial displays, and acoustic signals are part of the central state of fear (Hauser, 1996). The central state of fear embodies an elaborate and complex organization of behavior that includes social signals that reduce fighting and maintain alliances (Hauser, 1996; Marler & Hamilton, 1966).

Moreover, there is more than one kind of fear (Hebb, 1946; Kagan & Schulkin, 1995); fear of unfamiliar events is not the same as conditioned fear. For example, Hebb in his early studies emphasized fear of unfamiliar objects or familiar objects that are perceptually altered (Hebb, 1946, 1949); discrepant events not only elicit fear-related learning but also other forms of learning (Dewey, 1894, 1895; Dickinson, 1980; Rescorla & Wagner, 1972). We now turn to one critical brain region that underlies some aspects of fear.

## Fear and the Amygdala

The amygdala has been known to be important to fear for some time (Kluver & Bucy, 1939). It is centered in the temporal region of mammals (Herrick, 1905) and derived its name from its almond shape ("amygdala" in Greek means "almond"). It was originally called the "smell brain"; however, it has long been considered part of the limbic system in the organization of emotional responses (e.g., Bard, 1939; Papez, 1937).

Regions of the amygdala have been characterized as a "sensory gateway" (Aggleton & Mishkin, 1986; LeDoux, Cicchetti, Xagoraris, & Romanski, 1990; Turner & Herkenham, 1992) because they receive information from both cortical and subcortical regions (Amaral, Price, Pitkanen, & Carmichael, 1992; Krettek & Price, 1978). Specifically, the lateral and basal lateral regions are richly innervated from neocortical and subcortical sites, which then relay information to the central nucleus (e.g., Krettek & Price, 1978; Pitkanen et al., 1995; Turner & Herkenham, 1992). The central nucleus also receives visceral information from brainstem sites that include the solitary and parabrachial nuclei (Ricardo & Koh, 1978; Norgren, 1978) and projects to these brainstem regions (e.g., Schwaber, Kapp, Higgins, & Rapp, 1982). The amygdala's direct link to the nucleus acumbens led Nauta (1961; Nauta & Domesick, 1982) to suggest an anatomical route by which motivation and motor control action are linked in the organization of behavior (see also Mogenson, 1987).

Damage to the amygdala interferes with fear-related behavioral responses (e.g., Fonberg, 1972; Kling 1981). In the past 20 years, evidence has converged to show that the central nucleus within the amygdala orchestrates the behavioral autonomic fear responses (Davis, 1992; Kapp et al., 1992; LeDoux, 1995, 1996). Lesions, or stimulation, of the central nucleus are known to influence behaviors associated with fear (Hitchcock & Davis, 1986; Kapp, Frysinger, Gallagher, & Haselton, 1979; Iwata, Chida, & LeDoux, 1987; Kapp, Gallagher, Underwood, McNall, & Whitehorn, 1982; LeDoux, Iwata, Cicchetti, & Reis, 1988; Rosen & Davis, 1988). Stimulation of the central nucleus of the amygdala, for example, activates the neural circuitry that underlies startle responses and amplifies the startle response (Rosen & Davis, 1988; figure 8.2). Stimulation of the amygdala heightens attention toward events that are perceived as fearful (Gallagher & Holland, 1994; Rosen et al., 1996). Or, put differently, amygdala activation increases the likelihood that an event will be perceived as fearful. Amygdala activation has been linked to attention to uncertain and aversive events (Gallagher & Holland, 1994) and to anticipatory angst (Schulkin, McEwen, & Gold, 1994). Infusions into the basolateral nucleus of N-methyl-D-aspartate (NMDA) antagonists interferes with fear-related conditioning (Davis et al., 1993; Fanselow, 1994). Neurons within the amygdala are reactive to fearful signals (Rogan & LeDoux, 1996). Thus data from many avenues strongly suggest that the amygdala and its associated neural circuitry appraise fearful signals and orchestrate behavioral and autonomic responses to these events.

Within the last 2 decades, several groups of researchers have delineated anatomical circuits that underlie conditioned fear behaviors in rats, rabbits, and pigeons For example, Kapp and his colleagues (1979) were the first to demonstrate that the central nucleus of the amygdala, through its pathway to the nucleus of the solitary trace, dorsal motor nucleus of the vagus, and nucleus ambiguous, was necessary for fear-conditioned bradycardia to occur in a mammal.

In great detail, LeDoux and his colleagues (e.g., LeDoux, 1995, 1996; LeDoux et al., 1988), have outlined an anatomical circuit that underlies conditioned freezing in rats to an auditory cue. In part, it consists of pathways from the medial geniculate nucleus en route to the lateral and central nuclei of the amygdala. The central

# Enhancement of Acoustic Startle by Stimulation
## of the Central Nucleus of the Amygdala

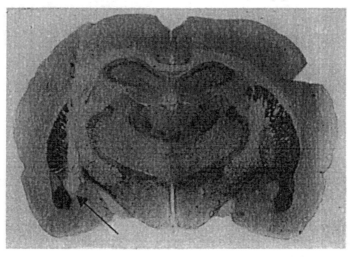

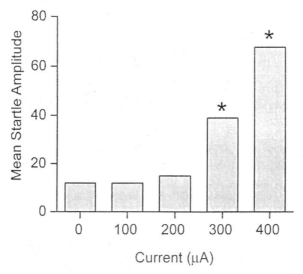

Figure 8.2. Enhancement of acoustic startle by central nucleus of the amygdala stimulation in naive rats. Top: Location of the stimulating electrode in the central nucleus of the amygdala (arrow). Bottom: Effects of different levels of electrical stimulation (25 msec train of 0.1 msec pulses) of the amygdala on the acoustic startle response in rats. Amygdala stimulation onset was 25 msec before the presentation of a 40 msec acoustic startle stimulus. No or low levels of amygdala stimulation current did not affect acoustic startle. Only current above a particular threshold enhanced the acoustic startle response. (Adapted from Rosen & Davis, 1988)

nucleus, through its projections to the periaqueductal gray, regulates freezing and escape behaviors (LeDoux, 1987, 1996). In addition, projections from the auditory and perirhinal regions of the neocortex through the lateral nucleus en route to the central nucleus of the amygdala convey information about acoustic and visual conditioning (Burwell, Witter, & Amaral, 1995). Interruption of this input from the perirhinal cortex to the lateral and central nucleus of the amygdala impairs the expression of already conditioned fear but does not block new fear learning (Corodimas, LeDoux, Gold, & Schulkin, 1994; Rosen et al., 1992).

Davis and his colleagues have delineated a similar circuit for fear-potentiated startle using a light or tone as a conditioned stimulus. The perirhinal cortex conveys both light and tone information to the lateral nucleus of the amygdala, which then projects to the basolateral and central nucleus. From the central nucleus there are direct and indirect pathways to the startle circuit (Frankland & Yeomans, 1995; Rosen, Hitchcock, Sananes, Miserendino, & Davis, 1991). The neural circuitry for both conditioned freezing and fear-potentiated startle (Blanchard & Blanchard, 1972; Davis, Walker, & Lee, 1997; Rosen et al., 1991) requires the same nuclei in the amygdala; the lateral and basolateral nuclei integrate sensory information, and the central nucleus orchestrates the behavioral and autonomic responses. Other regions in the forebrain that participate to organize fear include the prefrontal cortex (Morgan & LeDoux, 1995), the perirhinal cortex (Rosen et al., 1992), the hippocampus (Kim, Rison, & Fanselow, 1993; Phillips & LeDoux, 1992), and the bed nucleus of the stria terminalis (Davis et al. 1997; Gray et al, 1993), which, as we will describe below, may be linked to the neuroendocrine regulation of fear.

There is also a good deal of evidence in humans that the amygdala is linked to fear (see LeDoux, 1996). For example, recently it has been observed that lesions of the amygdala impair fear-related behavior and autonomic responses to conditioned stimuli (e.g., Angrilli et al., 1996; Bechara et al., 1993; LaBar, LeDoux, Spencer, & Phelps, 1995). Several studies have found that lesions of the amygdala interfere with the recognition of fearful facial expression (Adolphs, Tranel, Damasio, & Damasio, 1995; Allman et al., 1994) and vocalizations (Scott et al., 1997).

Positron emission tomography (PET) imaging studies have shown greater activation of the amygdala during fear- and anxiety-provoking stimuli (Ketter et al., 1994). Such PET studies have revealed that the amygdala is activated when presented with fearful as opposed to happy faces (Morris et al., 1996; figure 8.3). With the use of functional magnetic resonance imaging (MRI), it has further been shown that the amygdala is first activated and then habituates when shown fearful in contrast to neutral or happy faces. Activation of the amygdala also occurs during precipitated posttraumatic anxiety episodes and periods of obsessive-compulsive imagery in anxiety disorder patients (e.g., Rauch et al., 1996).

Clinically, some forms of depression (melancholic) are associated with fear (Gold, Goodwin, & Chrousos, 1988). Changes in blood flow to the amygdala have been observed using PET in patients who are fearful and depressed (Drevets et al., 1992). The metabolic rate of the amygdala, in humans, has also been used to predict both depression and the condition of negative affect (Abercrombie et al., 1998; Ketter et al., 1994).

Clinical data suggest that amygdala activity is increased in people with anxiety and unipolar depression (Drevets et al., 1992). They also suggest that hyperexcitability or sensitivity in the amygdala produces exaggerated fear responses. To

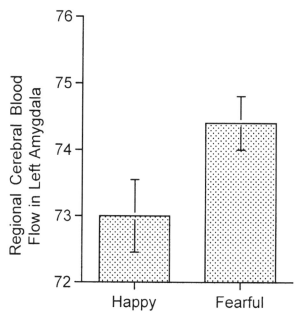

Figure 8.3. Differences in regional cerebral blood flow in the human left amygdala while viewing happy or fearful faces. Blood flow was significantly increased during the presentation of fearful faces and decreased during happy face presentations. Data are unweighted means of blood flow 2 SEM. (Adapted from Morris et al., 1996)

experimentally produce hyperexcitability in the amygdala, we stimulated the amygdala at levels that elicited electrographic seizure activity (Rosen et al., 1996). This stimulation, which is called partial kindling, is a way to excite the brain through electrodes targeted to an anatomical site and through electrical current delivered to the brain region (e.g., Adamec, 1990). In other words, the result of partial kindling of the amygdala is a putative hyperexcitable site in the brain which would be reflected in exaggerated fear responses. As a comparison, partial kindling in the dorsal hippocampus should not produce exaggerated fear-potentiated startle, because it is not critical for fear responses to a visual fear stimulus. The idea was that partial amygdala kindling would potentiate fear-related behavioral responses but that dorsal hippocampal kindling would not (Rosen et al, 1996).

We tested that idea in the following way: Rats were conditioned to be fearful of a light paired with foot shock. Over the next several days they received partial kindling of the amygdala or the dorsal hippocampus. Rats were then presented with an auditory startle stimulus in the presence or absence of the light to measure their startle responses to the fear stimulus (Rosen et al., 1996). The group that underwent amygdala kindling displayed elevated startle amplitude in the presence of the light compared with a control group, whereas the hippocampal-kindled rats did not. Interestingly, startle responses in the absence of the light were not exaggerated in the amygdala- or hippocampal-kindled rats. This is important because

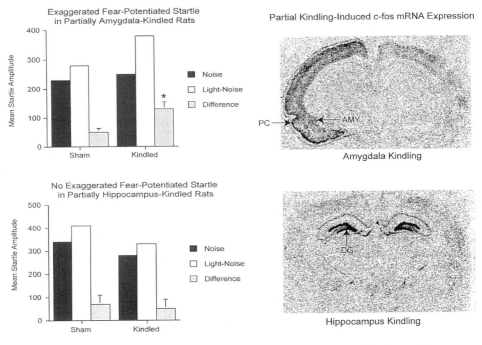

Figure 8.4. Top left: Exaggerated fear-potentiated startle as a result of partial amygdala kindling. Rats were conditioned to be fearful of a light (light–foot-shock pairing). Rats received two amygdala-kindling stimulations or sham stimulations over the next 2 days. Fear-potentiated startle tested 24 hours after partial amygdala kindling was significantly increased compared to sham-kindled rats (*, $p < 0.03$). There were no differences between the groups when baseline startle was elicited in the absence of the fear-conditioned stimulus (noise alone). Differences between the groups were found only when fear was induced (i.e., acoustic startle stimulus was presented while the fear conditioned stimulus was on light-noise). Bottom left: Exaggeration of fear-potentiated startle was not produced by partial kindling of the hippocampus. Although both groups displayed fear-potentiated startle, the hippocampus-kindled group was no different from the sham-kindled group. Right: Neuronal activation by partial unilateral amygdala (top) and hippocampus (bottom) kindling as visualized by 35S in situ hybridization of c-fos mRNA expression 15 minutes after kindling stimulation. Amygdala kindling induced widespread ipsilateral cortical c-fos mRNA expression, including parts of the fear circuit—amygdal (am) and perirhinal (pr) cortex. Hippocampus kindling induced bilateral c-fos mRNA expression that was confined to the hippocampus and dentate gyrus (dg). (Adapted from Rosen et al., 1996)

it demonstrates that the hyperexcitability induced by partial amygdala kindling did not merely result in a hyperresponsive animal but that the exaggerated responses were specific to being in the presence of the fear stimulus (figure 8.4). A marker of neuronal activity, c-fos mRNA expression, also indicated that different structures were activated by partial kindling in the amygdala and hippocampus: c-fos mRNA expression was seen in the amygdala, perirhinal cortex (structures of the fear circuit), and other cortical structures following amygdala partial kindling, whereas partial hippocampus kindling resulted in c-fos mRNA expression in the hippocampus and dentate gyrus only (figure 8.4). These data, in conjunction with the exaggerated fear responses after partial amygdala but not hippocampus kindling suggest that hyperexcitability in the amygdala and the related fear circuit results in increased responsivity that is specific to fearful stimuli.

## The Extended Amygdala: A Role for the Bed Nucleus of the Stria Terminalis

In addition to the amygdala, the bed nucleus of the stria terminalis is important for unconditioned fear and perhaps may underlie pathological anxiety (Davis, et al., 1997). Embryologically, the bed nucleus of the stria terminalis can be considered the rostral extension of the amygdala (Alheid, deOlmos, & Beltramino, 1996; Alheid & Heimer, 1988; Canteras, Simerly, & Swanson, 1995; Petrovich & Swanson, 1997). Both the bed nucleus of the stria terminalis and the central nucleus of the amygdala contain a number of neuropeptide-producing cells, including CRH (Gray, 1990). The lateral part of the bed nucleus of the stria terminalis is considered the rostral part of the central nucleus of the amygdala, whereas the medial portion is the rostral part of the medial nucleus. Additionally, the brainstem projections of the bed nucleus of the stria terminalis innervate many of the same structures as the central nucleus of the amygdala (Alheid et al., 1996). The role of the bed nucleus of the stria terminalis in controlling physiological activity of the hypothalamic-pituitary-adrenal (HPA) axis in response to stress (Herman & Cullinan, 1997) also suggests that it may have an important influence on fear and pathological anxiety.

Interesting data by Davis and his colleagues suggest that the bed nucleus of the stria terminalis may play a role in nonspecific fear as opposed to cue-specific fear. Rats are innately fearful of brightly lit environments and startle more in such environments than in dimly lit chambers (Davis et al., 1997). Lesions of the bed nucleus of the stria terminalis reduce startle levels in the bright light to levels found in a dimly lit chamber. Lesions of the central nucleus of the amygdala have no effect on the increased startle. Conversely, amygdala lesions block cue-specific fear-potentiated startle, whereas bed nucleus lesions do not (Hitchcock & Davis, 1991). Thus the central nucleus of the amygdala may be important for cue-specific fear and the bed nucleus of the stria terminalis for unconditioned fear (Lee & Davis, 1997). In any event, there is more than one kind of fear, and different parts of the central nervous systems underlie them.

### Neuroendocrine Regulation of Fear

Fear is sustained by neuroendocrine events. Under duress, the HPA axis is activated (e.g., Cannon, 1915/1929; Selye, 1956/1976), as are sites in the brain that participate in the regulation of fear. We discuss the glucocorticoids first.

The secretion of glucocorticoids helps sustain a number of behavioral responses, including fear-related behaviors (Richter, 1949). Without glucocorticoids, as Richter (1949) noted, animals die under duress (see also Selye, 1956/1976). Adrenalectomized animals are unable to tolerate fear, duress, or chronic stress and suffer fatality. Glucocorticoids prepare the animal to cope with emergency and taxing environmental contexts (Cannon, 1915/1929; Richter, 1949).

Glucocorticoids are also essential in the development of fear (Takahashi, 1995; Takahashi & Kim, 1994). Removal of corticosterone in rats before but not after 14 days of age impairs fear of unfamiliar objects (Takahashi & Rubin, 1993). In other words, there is a critical period in neonatal development in which glucocorticoids facilitate the normal expression of fear of unfamiliar objects (Takahashi & Kim, 1994).

Glucocorticoids are secreted under a number of experimental conditions in which fear, anxiety, novelty, and uncertainty are manipulated (Brier, 1989; Mason, 1975; Mason, Brady, & Sidman, 1957). In contexts in which there is loss of control or the perception of it and in which worry is associated with the loss of control, glucocorticoids are secreted. This holds across a number of species, including humans (e.g., Brier, Albus, Pickar, Zahn, & Wolkowitz, 1987). Perceived control reduces the levels of glucocorticoids that circulate. In rats, for example, predicting the onset of an aversive signal reduces the level of circulating glucocorticoids (Kant, Bauman, Anderson, & Moughey, 1992).

From a biological view, the chronic activation of glucocorticoid hormones is costly. The subordinate male macaque, for example, has elevated cortisol levels but lower levels of testosterone than the dominant one (Sapolsky, 1992). The lower level of testosterone decreases its reproductive fitness. The cost of chronic subordination is perhaps more fearfulness and uncertainty of attack and decreased likelihood of successful reproduction. This phenomenon of high corticosterone and low testosterone has been demonstrated in a number of species (e.g., Lance & Elsey, 1986).

Fear is also a metabolically costly event. Although glucocorticoids are essential in the development of neuronal tissue and in adapting to duress, when this response is sustained over time, tissue begins to deteriorate (Sapolsky, 1992). Chronic glucocorticoid activation, for example, increases the likelihood of neurotoxicity and neural endangerment through the loss of glucocorticoid receptors.

Perhaps to avoid this deterioration, negative regulation of the HPA axis evolved to restrain the stress response. In other words, glucocorticoids restrain the output of the paraventricular nucleus of the hypothalamus (PVN) and pituitary gland, decreasing CRH and adrenocorticotrophic hormone (ACTH) and thereby limiting their own production (Munck, Guyre, & Holbrook, 1984; Sawchenko, 1987). This is classic negative feedback. Negative feedback is one mechanism to restrain the activation of the HPA (Munck et al., 1984; see figure 8.5). The restraint of CRH at the level of the PVN is profound and sustained over time. The restraint of HPA function appears to be regulated in part through glucocorticoid activation of the hippocampus and bed nucleus of the stria terminalis (Beaulieu, DiPaolo, Cote, & Barden, 1987; Cullinan, Herman, & Watson, 1993; Sapolsky, Zola-Morgan, & Squire, 1991). This occurs in part through efferent control of the PVN by GABA-mediated inhibitory neurons (Herman & Cullinan, 1997). The amygdala also coordinates behavioral and neuroendocrine responses of fear and stress.

With regard to cortisol, on the clinical side, one of the most consistent findings in depressed fearful patients is elevated levels of cortisol and an enlarged adrenal cortex (Carroll et al., 1976; Nemeroff et al., 1992; Sachar, Hellman, Fukushima, & Gallagher, 1970). These findings are congruent with those of Richter (1949), who

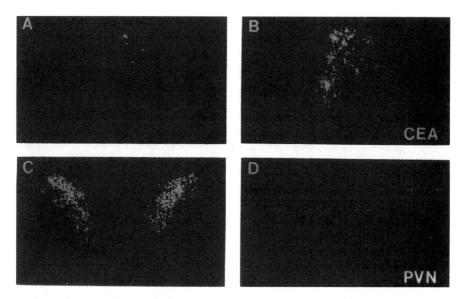

Figure 8.5. The effects of corticosterone (CORT) injection on CRH mRNA levels of the central nucleus of the amygdala (CEA; a is control and b is CORT-treated) and the paraventricular nucleus of the hypothalamus (PVN; c is control and d is CORT-treated). Silver grains mark the location of hybridized probe and accumulation of grains are seen in the CEA and PVN. (Adapted from Makino, Gold, & Schulkin, 1994a)

observed an enlarged adrenal gland in stressed, fearful wild rats when compared with unstressed laboratory rats.

Consider now CRH. Corticotropin-releasing hormone is a peptide hormone initially characterized in the PVN. It is a 41-amino-acid peptide hormone that facilitates the secretion of ACTH (Vale, Speiss, Rivier, & Rivier, 1981). But CRH is also synthesized in a number of sites outside the PVN. They include the central nucleus of the amygdala and the lateral bed nucleus of the stria terminalis (Gray, 1990; Ju, Swanson, & Simerly, 1989; Swanson, Sawcheako, Rivier, & Vale, 1983). Corticotropin-releasing hormone is also synthesized in the prefrontal cortex and in cells around the locus ceruleus in Barrington's nucleus, parabrachial region, and solitary nucleus. Moreover, fiber pathways connect many of these regions with one another (Gray, 1990; Swanson et al., 1983). Also, many of these CRH-producing cells are co-localized with glucocorticoid receptors (e.g., Honkaniemi et al., 1992; Kainu, Honkaniemi, Gustafsson, Rechardt, & Markku, 1993).

A recently cloned CRH receptor contains a 451-amino-acid protein. It is linked to a G protein and to increased intracellular cAMP and calcium levels and activates adenylate cyclase cascade (Owens & Nemeroff, 1991). Studies have revealed that there are several different CRH receptor subtypes, one of which is dominant in limbic regions and one of which is more widespread (Potter et al., 1994).

It is well known that central infusions, and not peripheral infusions, of CRH potentiate fear of unfamiliar events, startle, or freezing behaviors (e.g., Britton, Lee, Vale, Rivier, & Koob, 1986; Koob et al., 1993; Swerdlow, Britton, & Koob, 1989).

This has been demonstrated in a number of species and across a number of fear-related behaviors (see Kalin, 1985; Koob & Bloom, 1985).

One clear result from CRH infusions is a set of coordinated behavioral and physiological responses that includes enhanced fear and inhibition of ingestion and sexual behavior (e.g., Gold et al., 1988; Koob & Bloom, 1985). Corticotropin-releasing hormone injections directly into the central nucleus of the amygdala increase fear-related responses to unfamiliar environments and increase freezing in anticipation of aversive events (Wiersma, Baauw, Bohus, & Koolhaas, 1995). Importantly, lesions of the PVN do not impair CRH-induced effects on startle responses (Liang et al., 1992). Interference of CRH expression by pharmacological antagonists within the central nucleus of the amygdala disrupts fear-related behavioral responses (Koob et al., 1993).

Pathophysiologically, one of the first outstanding observations about CRH was that it was elevated in the cerebrospinal fluid of melancholic depressed patients (Gold et al., 1984; Holsboer et al., 1984; Nemeroff, 1992). Among such patients, the appetites for food and sex are reduced, and their sleep and immune response can be compromised (Gold et al., 1988).

Clinicians interpreted this situation of elevated systemic levels of cortisol and high central CRH as an aberration and a reflection of the pathology, because high cortisol should be associated with low central CRH. However, an alternative interpretation was that the high cortisol was activating CRH gene expression within specific regions of the brain, resulting in greater fear (Schulkin, 1994; see the next section).

Corticotropin-releasing hormone in the cerebrospinal fluid has been reported to be elevated in patients with posttraumatic stress disorder (Darnell et al., 1994). Interestingly, such patients have low basal levels of cortisol but hypersecrete cortisol when the HPA axis is normally provoked (Yehuda, 1997). This also holds for rape victims and Holocaust survivors (e.g. Yehuda et al., 1995; Yehuda, 1997). The major point is that such people may have elevated central CRH in the cerebrospinal fluid, and it is the elevation of central CRH that underlies the states of fear.

## Glucocorticoid Effects on Corticotropin-Releasing Hormone Gene Expression in the Brain

One hypothesis is that the regulation of hypothalamic CRH gene expression and its restraint by glucocorticoids was one system linked to systemic regulation and that a second CRH system in extrahypothalamic sites, such as the central nucleus of the amygdala and lateral bed nucleus of the stria terminalis, was regulated quite differently and linked to the central state of fear.

In one experiment, adrenally intact rats were treated with high systemic levels of corticosterone over either a 4-day, 1-week or 2-week period (Makino, Gold, & Schulkin, 1994a). The results from one study are shown in figure 8.5. They demonstrated that high levels of corticosterone can result in elevated levels of CRH mRNA in the central nucleus of the amygdala, particularly in the centro-medial region of the central nucleus. This is very much in contrast to the reduction of CRH mRNA in the PVN in the same animals.

In experiments with adrenalectomized rats, Swanson and Simmons (1989) and then Watts and Sanchez-Watts (1995) found something similar in differentiating the effects of corticosterone on CRH gene expression in the central nucleus of the amygdala from that of the PVN, that is, an experimental context in which CRH mRNA is decreased in the PVN while it is increased simultaneously in the central nucleus of the amygdala (Watts, 1996; Watts & Sanchez-Watts, 1995). Thus there is differential regulation of CRH gene expression at the level of the PVN and the central nucleus of the amygdala (see also Albeck et al., 1997).

In addition, other evidence has demonstrated that CRH is elevated in the central nucleus of the amygdala during restraint stress—a condition of adversity and presumably fear. Under these conditions corticosterone is also elevated. One study using microdialysis found that CRH was elevated during restraint stress in the central nucleus of the amygdala, in addition to the medial basal hypothalamus (Pich et al., 1993; Pich et al., 1995). And in another study with similar experimental conditions, the experimenters found increased CRH mRNA levels in the central nucleus of amygdala in addition to the PVN (Kalin, Takahashi, & Chen, 1994). Chronic restraint stress results in the loss of normal inhibition of CRH in the PVN and concurrent induction of CRH in the amygdala (Takahashi & Kim, 1994).

Similar results were also obtained in the bed nucleus of the stria terminalis. The lateral region of the bed nucleus corresponds with that of the central nucleus, and it is this region that is rich in CRH-producing cells, particularly the dorsal lateral region (Gray, 1990; Ju et al., 1989; Makino, Gold, & Schulkin, 1994b; Watts & Sanchez-Watts, 1995; figure 8.6). Again the results demonstrated that CRH mRNA was increased following corticosterone pretreatment in this region (Makino et al., 1994b). Similar effects were also observed in adrenalectomized rats treated with corticosterone on CRH mRNA in the dorsal lateral bed nucleus (Watts & Sanchez-Watts, 1995).

The receptors for CRH are located primarily outside the central nucleus of the amygdala or the lateral bed nucleus of the stria terminalis. They are present in the lateral nucleus and the medial nucleus of the amygdala (e.g., Makino et al., 1995). Lesions of the lateral nucleus region block both context- and cue-specific fear conditioning (LeDoux, 1996); glucocorticoid infusions into this region facilitate aversive conditioning (Roozendaal & McGaugh, 1997; Roozendaal, Quirarte, & McGaugh, 1997). In addition, neuronal markers of gene expression indicate that there is elevated activity in the lateral region during context-fear conditioning (Rosen, unpublished observations).

Thus there is differential regulation of CRH-producing cells in the brain by glucocorticoid hormones (Makino et al., 1994a; Makino et al., 1994b; Swanson & Simmons, 1989; Watts & Sanchez-Watts, 1995; see also Imaki, Nahan, Rivier, & Vale, 1991). While one important role of glucocorticoids is to restrain their own production by the inhibition of hypothalamic-pituitary activation, another is perhaps to sustain the central state of fear. One would want to minimize and restrain one system (bodily functions) while maintaining vigilance and cautiousness.

## Functional Relationships Between Glucocorticoids and Central CRH

One hypothesis is that pretreatment with glucocorticoids, which raise CRH levels in the amygdala, would facilitate fear-related conditioned freezing responses (Corodimas et al., 1994; Jones, Beuving & Blokhuis, 1988). Rats were first taught to

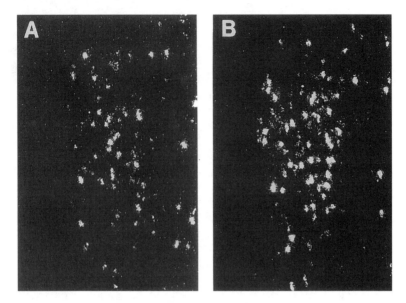

Figure 8.6. Effects of corticosterone (CORT) on CRH mRNA levels in the bed nucleus of the stria terminalis (BNST). Dark-field photomicrographs show the autoradiographic distribution of CRH mRNA in the BNST of control (a) and CORT-treated rats (b). Autoradiographic silver grains appear white. (Adapted from Makino, Gold, & Schulkin, 1994b)

associate shock with an auditory cue. Conditioned freezing is the typical response. Several days after the last conditioning trial, rats were treated for 5 days with corticosterone or a vehicle only. When tested again, the rats treated with corticosterone demonstrated elevated freezing responses compared with controls when placed in the conditioning chamber (figure 8.7).

Freezing can be one expression of conditioned fear; startle can be another. Therefore, rats were tested to determine whether pretreatment with glucocorticoids would facilitate CRH-induced startle responses (Lee, Schulkin, & Davis, 1994). Rats were pretreated for several days with corticosterone and then infused centrally with CRH. A dose of CRH that would not normally elicit startle was used. Once again, it did elicit startle in those rats pretreated with corticosterone, and that response was specific to corticosterone and not aldosterone (Lee, Davis, & Schulkin, unpublished observations).

---

Figure 8.7. The potentiating effects of glucocorticoids on fear-related behaviors and seizures. Top: Glucocorticoids (5 days of 7.5 mg/kg corticosterone, s.c.) facilitate conditioned fear-induced freezing. Adapted from Corodimas et al., (1994). Middle: Glucocorticoids (5 days of 7.5 mg/kg corticosterone, s.c.) facilitate corticotropin-releasing hormone (CRH) (0.25 g, i.c.v.)-enhanced acoustic startle. Adapted from Lee et al., (1994). Bottom: Glucocorticoids (3 days of 100 g/kg dexamethasone, s.c.) facilitate CRH (3 g, i.c.v.)-induced seizures. (Adapted from Rosen et al., 1994)

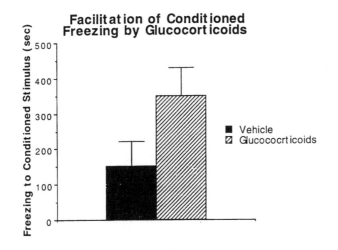

**Facilitation of Conditioned Freezing by Glucocorticoids**

Freezing to Conditioned Stimulus (sec)

■ Vehicle
▨ Glucocorticoids

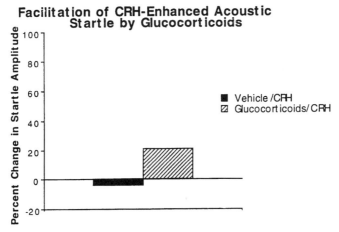

**Facilitation of CRH-Enhanced Acoustic Startle by Glucocorticoids**

Percent Change in Startle Amplitude

■ Vehicle /CRH
▨ Glucocorticoids/CRH

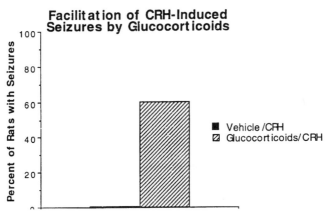

**Facilitation of CRH-Induced Seizures by Glucocorticoids**

Percent of Rats with Seizures

■ Vehicle /CRH
▨ Glucocorticoids/CRH

Finally, high doses of CRH can facilitate seizures that reflect amygdala activation (Weiss et al., 1986). Low doses of centrally infused CRH, which by itself does not induce seizures, did so when rats were pretreated with glucocorticoids (at doses which also did not induce seizures). In other words, instead of reducing the seizures, as predicted by negative restraint, the glucocorticoids actually potentiated the seizures. That is, the glucocorticoids, by increasing central CRH, lowered the threshold for seizures that is linked to amygdala activation (Rosen et al., 1994). This is a very different outcome from what many in the field would have predicted based on glucocorticoid regulation of CRH gene expression at the level of the PVN.

Thus, in addition to restraining physiological events, glucocorticoids facilitate a number of behavioral responses, particularly those associated with fear and seizures that are mediated by the amygdala-centered fear circuit. Glucocorticoids may influence behavioral responses by facilitatory regulation of neuropeptide gene expression, such as CRH, in the amygdala and extended amygdala. In other words, cortisol influences the expression of central CRH in the brain, thereby facilitating behaviors associated with the central motive state of fear. The vigilance associated with sustained fear is linked to the elevation of both glucocorticoids and central CRH.

Importantly, there are also instances in which all three CRH-producing sites are increased. In other words, there are several experimental contexts in which both hypothalamic (PVN; e.g., Raadsheer, Hoogendijk, Stam, Tilders, & Swaab, 1994) and extrahypothalamic (central nucleus of the amygdala and bed nucleus of the stria terminalis) CRH can be elevated at the same time, typically under extreme duress (Kalin et al., 1994; Koob et al., 1993; Plotsky & Meaney, unpublished observations). It is conceivable that in patients with clinical depression in whom there is extreme fearfulness there is at the same time a compromised restraint on CRH production in the hypothalamic PVN and a simultaneous sustained increase of CRH in the two extrahypothalamic CRH-producing sites.

Finally, note that corticosterone is essential not only in the normal development of fear (Takahashi, 1995) but also for context-related fear learning (Fleshner, Pugh, Tremblay, & Rudy, 1997; Pugh, Tremblay, Fleshner, Fleshner, & Rudy, 1997). These effects on context fear may be mediated by central CRH, since infusions of CRH directly into the bed nucleus of the stria terminalis facilitate fear- and anxiety-related behavioral responses; antagonists of CRH into this region do the converse (Lee & Davis, 1997). It has been suggested that the activation of CRH in the amygdala is linked to fear, whereas the activation of CRH in the bed nucleus of the stria terminalis is linked to anxiety (Davis et al., 1997).

## Early Developmental Effects on Central CRH

Trauma at an early age, particularly separation of an infant from its mother, has a detrimental effect on emotional development (Bowlby, 1973). Numerous animal studies have demonstrated that maternal separation or deprivation can have prolonged effects on behavior and physiology. Short, repeated separations may actually be immunizing or protective against later stress, whereas longer periods of maternal deprivation can increase later responses to stress (e.g., Levine, 1993; Meaney

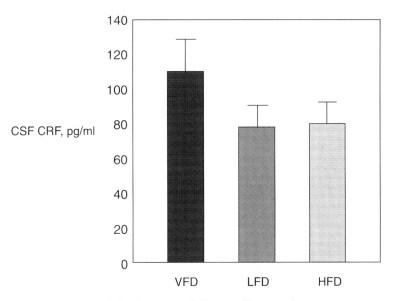

Figure 8.8. Cerebrospinal fluid CRH in differentially reared macaques exposed to low (LFD), high (HFD), and variable (VFD) foraging demands as infants. (Adapted from Coplan et al., 1996)

et al., 1993). Interestingly, studies throughout several decades demonstrate that maternal behavior can ameliorate the effects of early stress on later behavioral and physiological responses to stress (Levine, 1967; Liu et al., 1997).

Biological stress responses, whether as a result of trauma, early stressful experience, or a genetic predisposition, may be important for the development of hyperexcitability. It is well known that endocrine events during critical stages in development have long-term consequences for both brain organization and behavioral expression (Goy & McEwen, 1980). A recent study found that infant monkeys reared by mothers who experienced unpredictable foraging conditions had higher CRH in cerebrospinal fluid in adulthood than infant monkeys reared by mothers that had either a predictable overabundance or a scarcity of food (Coplan et al., 1996). The study showed that unpredictability in early life, and not just chronic hardship, led to persistently higher hormone levels in adulthood (figure 8.8).

Corticosterone levels during critical stages of development have profound effects on the organization of the brain and the expression of fear-related behaviors (Takahashi & Kim, 1994). Early life events, such as maternal deprivation or maternal contact that increases corticosterone levels and CRH levels (Habib et al., 1999), have long-term consequences for both brain and behavior (e.g., Levine, 1993; Liu et al., 1997; Meaney et al., 1993). For example, rats deprived of maternal closeness for 3 hours a day for a 2-week period as pups were found to have higher levels of CRH mRNA expression in the hypothalamus and central nucleus of the amygdala as adults than rats separated only 15 minutes a day (Plotsky & Meaney, unpublished observations). These maternally deprived rats were also more likely to develop helpless behavior in uncontrollable aversive contexts, suggesting that these rats were excessively stressed or fearful. Interestingly, their systemic levels of corticosterone as adults were not different from those of normal rats, but the central state of exaggerated fear induced by the early experience was long lasting.

The long-lasting effects of increased glucocorticoids and CRH indicate that the brain, and particularly fear circuits, become sensitized. In each of the conditions described, whether it is early stress or normal and abnormal fear in adults, cortisol facilitates the expression of the CRH, resulting in the central state of fearfulness. We suggest that this is due to facilitation of CRH expression in the amygdala and bed nucleus of the stria terminalis. In addition, these endocrine events can occur months or years before they have deleterious effects on behavior. Thus these stress- and fear-induced endocrine events can have long-lasting effects on brain and behavioral organization. In this regard, this is not dissimilar to organizational effects that occur as a result of gonadal steroid hormones (e.g., Goy & McEwen, 1980).

## Effects of Norepinephrine and Epinephrine on Aversive Conditioning

In addition to the release of glucocorticoids from the adrenal cortices during stress and fear, norepinephrine and epinephrine are released from the adrenal medulla. Much work over the years, performed primarily by McGaugh (McGaugh et al., 1993), has shown that in various learning tasks (particularly aversive tasks), posttrial peripheral administration of epinephrine and norepinephrine can potentiate memory and increase the resistance to extinction of conditioned responses. Conversely, adrenergic antagonists interfere with the memory of the learned behavior (McGaugh et al., 1993). Because the potentiating and inhibiting properties of these manipulations are done subsequent to training but well before the testing sessions, it has been hypothesized that they facilitate or interfere with memory-consolidation processes (McGaugh et al., 1993).

In human subjects, the noradrenergic beta blocker propranolol was shown to impair the memory of an aversive story more than the memory of an emotionally neutral story, suggesting that noradrenergic activation preferentially enhances emotional experiences (Cahill, Prins, Weber, & McGaugh, 1994). These findings have led to the notion that the pathogenesis of posttraumatic stress disorder may be due to overstimulation of endogenous stress systems during traumatic events that potentiate overconsolidation of the memory of the trauma and thus lead to intrusive recall and emotional responses, which are hallmarks of posttraumatic stress disorder (Pitman, 1997).

Perhaps elevated cortisol, epinephrine, and norepinephrine induce greater activation of the amygdala through the memory-enhancing mechanisms similar to those just described and thereby increase the level of vigilance and the expectation of adversity. Lesions of the central nucleus of the amygdala have been shown to block the integration of behavioral, neurochemical, and neuroendocrine responses to a conditioned fear stimulus (Goldstein, Rasmusson, Bunney, & Roth, 1996). The amygdala plays an important role in central nervous system mediation of the potentiating effects of peripheral stress-responsive factors (McGaugh et al., 1993; Roozendaal et al., 1997). Injection of noradrenergic antagonists into the amygdala block the memory-potentiating effects of peripherally administered epinephrine and other compounds. Gamma-amino butyric acid and acetylcholine are also included with norepinephrine in a neuromodulator pathway in the amygdala that is important for the memory-enhancing effects of peripheral stress hormones (McGaugh et al., 1993).

## Neuroendocrine Basis of Excessive Shyness and Fear in Children

From 10 to 15 percent of young children are shy and fearful (Kagan, Reznick, & Snidman, 1988). Shyness appears to be a heritable trait—a temperamental characteristic (Hebb, 1949; Kagan et al., 1988). These traits have been noted in the first few months of life and remain stable over time. Shy children are typically quiet, vigilant, and withdrawn in social contexts. For example, these children are behaviorally inhibited in novel situations and socially wary. In fact, social anxiety (e.g., public performance) is a primary feature of shy children and adults. Shy fearful children remain close to their mothers when presented with novel situations, and they show exaggerated startle responses (Gunnar, Mangelsdorf, Larson, & Hertsgaard, 1989; Schmidt et al., 1997).

These young children have high levels of cortisol and elevated catecholamines (Gunnar et al., 1989; Kagan et al., 1988; Schmidt et al., 1997). Cortisol remains elevated until at least 7 years of age and is correlated with maternal rating of children's fearfulness and behavioral inhibition in novel contexts (Schmidt et al., 1999). In other words, heightened levels of arousal and fear responses to strangers and novel situations found in shy human infants also persist at least into later childhood, and these children may have exaggerated cortisol and autonomic physiological responses (Gunnar et al., 1989; Kagan et al., 1988; Schmidt et al., 1997). Indeed, excessively shy children display both exaggerated startle (though this effect is modest) and high salivary cortisol levels (Schmidt et al., 1997).

Interestingly, a subset of macaque monkeys resembles these shy children; they are excessively fearful and behaviorally inhibited or shy. Cortisol is elevated in these animals, and they demonstrate longer periods of freezing behavior than other monkeys when placed in novel contexts (e.g., Champoux, Coe, Schanberg, King, & Suomi, 1989). Moreover, the macaque mothers whose offspring freeze for longer periods also respond in the same manner (Kalin, Shelton, Rickman, & Davidson, 1998). Something similar appears to be the case in a subset of human mothers and their children; that is, the mothers of fearful, inhibited, shy children demonstrated greater shyness and greater avoidance behaviors (Rickman & Davidson, 1994).

Excessively shy, fearful children may be vulnerable to anxiety disorders as adults (Hirshfeld et al., 1992; Windle, 1994). One hypothesis is that high cortisol kindles exaggerated CRH production in the amygdala and/or the extended amygdala, resulting in preparedness to see events as fearful. An inability to reduce these levels may contribute to allostatic load and deterioration of tissue (e.g., vulnerability to immune disorders; Bell, Jasnoski, Kagan, & King, 1990).

In children, one important adaptation to excessive behavioral inhibition or fear is through the sense of attachment (Nachmias, Gunnar, Mangelsdorf, Parritz, & Buss, 1996). A secure attachment to a parent or caregiver is fundamental (Bowlby, 1973) and part of behavioral homeostasis (Hofer, 1994). The desire to secure object

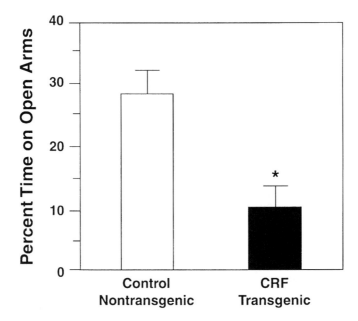

Figure 8.9. Time spent on the open arms of control or CRF transgenic mice over a 5-minute period on the elevated plus maze. (Adapted from Stenzel-Poore et al., 1994)

constancy may be an exaggerated trait in these children. Interestingly, one adaptation to reduce cortisol levels is children's attachment to their parents; the greater the degree of estrangement, the greater the degree of circulating cortisol (Nachmias et al., 1996; see also Levine & Wiener, 1988, for a similar phenomenon in monkeys).

Genetic determinants of CRH expression may be fundamentally important in individuals who are vulnerable to excessive fearfulness—excessively shy, fearful children. In this regard, engineered transgenic mice models in which CRH is overproduced in the brain along with greater levels of systemic corticosterone suffer greater fear (in this experiment, fear of unfamiliar settings; Stenzel-Poore, Heinrichs, Rivest, Koob, & Vale, 1994; figure 8.9). One would predict that excessively shy, fearful children would have greater CRH if one could measure it in their cerebrospinal fluid, as experimenters have done with fearful, depressed patients and posttraumatic patients. One would predict that the extreme version of shyness linked to fear would reveal something similar with regard to hypersecretion of CRH (Kalin, Shelton, & Davidson, unpublished observations; Habib et al., unpublished observations).

### Hyperactive Fear Circuits: From Normal Fear to Pathological Anxiety

Kagan suggested that "inhibited children possess a more excitable circuit from the amygdala" (Kagan,1989, p. 172). We have suggested elsewhere (Rosen & Schulkin, 1998) that hyperexcitability in fear circuits, particularly in the amygdala and extended amygdala, may not only produce exaggerated fear behavior but also states of hypervigilance. This would include exaggerated conditioned and some innate types of fear but perhaps not all states of fear (Kagan & Schulkin, 1995; Treit, Pesold, & Rotzinger, 1993). The same circuitry that mediates normal attention, perception and behavior to detect and respond to danger or in times of uncertainty (Gallagher & Holland, 1994; Schulkin et al., 1994) would also mediate these processes during pathological conditions of hypervigilance. With overstimulation of the fear circuits, thresholds for activation are lowered; fearful behavior and worry are accentuated. In this context, individuals with hyperexcitable fear circuits are more likely to freeze, withdraw, and interpret their world as dangerous and fearful.

Our hypothesis suggests that the amygdala and/or bed nucleus of the stria terminalis would be hyperactive in socially fearful shy children while they are in the midst of an anxious episode but not necessarily hyperactive during basal conditions. Hyperexcitability in fear circuits may be a common core abnormality in all anxiety disorders, including excessive shyness in children. Exaggerated responses to specific cues, such as selective interoceptive cues in panic disorders or external cues in specific phobias, may develop from associative conditioning with sensitized, hyperexcitable fear circuits.

The idea of a hyperexcitable amygdala and extended amygdala as a biological substrate for pathological anxiety leads to interesting notions about accessibility to fear circuits and the organization, development, and formation of connectivity in the fear circuits with pathological fear and anxiety. Through experience, or experimentally through kindling, the amygdala becomes hyperexcitable, suggesting that the synaptic connections in fear circuits have lowered thresholds for activation and thus that the connectivity within these circuits is stronger. With repeated strong activation, these hyperexcitable connections may become relatively permanent. In other words, repetitive activation of the amygdala by repeated episodes of excessive fear may produce chronic hyperexcitability in the amygdala that eventually becomes functionally autonomous. Fear-related responses may eventually become independent of a triggering stimulus. Thus anxious feelings and behavior and the associated hypervigilance develop lives of their own. The mechanisms responsible for hypervigilance and the attentional bias toward interpretation of the environment as threatening are inappropriately regulated. Although there may be an awareness of the anxious state, there is a feeling of a loss of control.

This type of inaccessibility can be seen in excessively shy, socially anxious children. The chronic state of hyperexcitability of excitatory mechanisms within fear circuits is not dampened properly by normal inhibitory processes. This constant, uncontrollable worry would expend large amounts of energy with costly psychological and biological consequences (e.g., McEwen, 1998; Schulkin, Gold, & McEwen, 1998). Finding out what these excitatory and inhibitory mechanisms for developing and sustaining hyperexcitability are and how they change the characteristics of normal, adaptive, fear-related behaviors into exaggerated responses has promise for developing a better understanding of the etiology and pathology of clinical anxiety disorders.

## Conclusion

From an evolutionary point of view, motivational states such as fear prepare one for action in the face of uncertainty (Dewey, 1894, 1895) that functionally serves to avoid harm. The mechanisms that orchestrate fear are those linked to a readiness to be active (e.g., to perceive an event) and to generate the requisite motor behavior. All of this is under the rubric of functional relationships between mental and physical events. Thus two facts about functionalism stand out and have relevance to the concept of central motive state of fear: The first is biological adaptation; the second is the internal workings of the central state.

The concept of fear, therefore, is a hybrid term: It includes reference to both brain and psychological events. The key for behavioral neuroscientists is to link them. The concept of central motive states forces one to retain this linkage. Our focus in this chapter was for the most part to link them in a very specific way through steroid/neuropeptide interactions.

In conclusion, a set of neural structures underlies the perception of and the behavioral response to frightening events. We suggest that neuropeptides such as CRH chemically code the sense of fear that is sustained by elevated cortisol and that may underlie the excessively shy, fearful child's hyperexcitable central state. When driven to excess, overproduction of CRH within hyperexcitable fear circuits lends itself to pathological anxiety and chronic anticipatory angst. Without the behavioral adaptation that is seen in some shy children with excess cortisol and presumably elevated central CRH, these children may be living under chronic fear and anxiety and increased vulnerability to disease states.

*References*

Abercrombie, H. C., Schaefer, S. M., Larson, C. L., Oakes, T. R., Lindgren, K. A., Holden, J. E., Perlman, S. E., Turski, P. A., Krahn, D. D., Benca, R. M., & Davidson, R. J. (1998). Metabolic rate in the amygdala predicts negative affect and depression severity in depressed patients: An FDG-PET study. *Neuro Report, 9,* 3301–3307.

Adamec, R. E. (1990). Amygdala kindling and anxiety in the rat. *Neuro Report, 1,* 255–258.

Adolphs, R., Tranel, D., Damasio, H., & Damasio, A. R. (1995). Fear and the human amygdala. *Journal of Neuroscience, 15,* 5879–5891.

Aggleton, J. P., & Mishkin, M. (1986). The amygdala: Sensory gateway to the emotions. In R. Plutchik & H. Kellerman (Eds.), *Emotion: Theory, research and experience* (pp. 981–999). Orlando, FL.: Academic Press.

Albeck, D. S., McKittnick, C. R., Blanchard, D. C., & Blanchard, R. J. (1997). Chronic social stress alters levels of corticotropin-releasing hormone and arginine vasopressin mRNA in rat brain. *Journal of Neuroscience, 17,* 4895–4903.

Alheid, G. F., deOlmos, J., & Beltramino, C. A. (1996). Amygdala and extended amygdala. In G. Paxinos (Ed.), *The rat nervous system* (2nd ed., pp. 495–578). San Diego: Academic Press.

Alheid, G. F., & Heimer, L. (1988). New perspectives in basal forebrain organization and special relevance for neuropsychiatric disorders: The striatopallidal, amygdaloid, and corticipetal components of substantia innominate. *Journal of Neuroscience, 22,* 1–39.

Allman, J., & Brothers, L. (1994). Faces, fear and the amygdala. *Nature, 372,* 613–614.

Amaral, D. G., Price, J. L., Pitkanen, A., & Carmichael, S. T. (1992). Anatomical organization of the primate amygdaloid complex. In J. P. Aggleton (Ed.), *The amygdala: Neurobiological aspects of emotion, memory and mental dysfunction* (pp. 1–66). New York: Wiley-Liss.

Angrilli, A., Mauri, A., Palomba, D., Flor, H., Birbaumer, N., Sartori, G., & di Paola, F. (1996). Startle reflex and emotion modulation impairment after a right amygdala lesion. *Brain, 119,* 1991–2000.

Arnold, M. B. (1960). Emotion and anxiety: Structural, biological and psychological determinants. In A. O. Rorty (Ed.), *Explaining emotions.* Berkeley: University of California Press.

Bard, P. (1939). Central nervous mechanisms for emotional behavior patterns in animals. *Research in Nervous and Mental Disease, 29,* 190–216.

Beach, F. A. (1942). Central nervous mechanisms involved in the reproductive behaviors of vertebrates. *Psychological Bulletin, 26,* 200–225.

Beaulieu, S., DiPaolo, T., Cote, T., & Barden, N. (1987). Participation of the central amygdaloid nucleus in the response to ACTH secretion to immobilization stress: Opposing roles of the noradrenergic and dopaminergic systems. *Neuroendocrinology, 45,* 37–46.

Bechara, A., Tranel, D., Damasio, H., Adolphs, R., Rockland, C., & Damasio, A. R. (1993). Double dissociation of conditioning and declarative knowledge relative to the amygdala and hippocampus in humans. *Science, 269,* 1115–1118.

Bell, I. R., Jasnoski, M. L., Kagan, J., & King, D. S. (1990). Is allergic rhinitis more frequent in young adults with extreme shyness? A preliminary survey. *Psychosomatic Medicine, 52,* 517–525.

Bindra, D. (1978). How adaptive behavior is produced: A perceptual-motivational alternative to response-reinforcement. *Behavioral Brain Science, 1,* 41–91.

Blanchard, D. C., & Blanchard, R. J. (1972). Innate and conditioned reactions to threat in rats with amygdaloid lesions. *Journal of Comparative Physiology and Psychology, 81,* 281–290.

Bolles, R. C., & Fanselow, M. S. (1980). A perceptual-defensive-recuperative model of fear and pain. *Behavioral Brain Sciences, 3,* 291–323.

Bowlby, J. (1973). *Attachment and Loss: Vol. 2. Separation.* New York: Basic Books.

Brier, A. A. E. (1989). Experimental approaches to human stress research: Assessment of neurobiological mechanisms of stress in volunteers and psychiatric patients. *Biological Psychiatry, 26,* 438–462.

Brier, A., Albus, M., Pickar, D., Zahn, T. P., & Wolkowitz, O. M. (1987). Controllable and uncontrollable stress in humans: Alterations in mood and neuroendocrine and psychophysiological function. *American Journal of Psychiatry, 144,* 1419–1425.

Britton, K. T., Lee, G., Vale, W., Rivier, J., & Koob, G. F. (1986). CRF receptor antagonist blocks activating and anxiogenic action of CRF in the rat. *Brain Research, 369,* 303–306.

Burwell, R. D., Witter, M. P., & Amaral, D. G. (1995). Perirhinal and postrhinal cortices of the rat: A review of the neuroanatomical literature and comparison with findings from the monkey brain. *Hippocampus, 5,* 390–408.

Cahill, L., Prins, B., Weber, M., & McGaugh, J. L. (1994). Beta-adrenergic activation and memory for emotional events. *Nature, 371,* 702–704.

Cannon, W. B. (1929). *Bodily changes in pain, hunger, fear and rage.* New York: Harper & Row. (original work published 1915)

Canteras, N. S., Simerly, R. B., & Swanson, L. W. (1995). Organization of projections from the medial nucleus of the amygdala: A PHAL study in the rat. *Journal of Comparative Neurology, 360,* 213–245.

Carroll, B. J., Curtis, C. G., Davies, B. M., Mendels, J., & Sugarman, A. A. (1976). Urinal free cortisol excretion in depression. *Psychological Medicine, 6,* 43–50.

Champoux, M., Coe, C. L., Schanberg, S. M., King, C. M., & Suomi, S. (1989). Hormonal effects of early rearing conditions in infant rhesus monkeys. *American Journal of Primatology, 19,* 111–118.

Chomsky, N. (1972). *Language and Mind.* New York: Harcourt, Brace & Jovanovich.

Coplan, J. D., Andrews, M. W., Rosenblum, L. A., Owens, M. J., Friedman, S., Gorman, J. M., & Nemeroff, C. B. (1996). Persistent elevations of cerebrospinal fluid concentrations of corticotropin-releasing hormone in adult nonhuman primates exposed to early life stressors. *Proceedings of the National Academy of Sciences, 93,* 1619–1623.

Corodimas, K. J., LeDoux, J. E., Gold, P. W., & Schulkin, J. (1994). Corticosterone potentiation of learned fear. In R. DeKloet, E. C. Azmita, & P. W. Longfield (Eds.), *Brain
   corticosteroid receptor* (pp. 392–393). New York: New York Academy of Sciences.
Cullinan, W. E., Herman, J. P., & Watson, S. J. (1993). Ventral subicular interaction with
   the hypothalamic paraventricular nucleus: Evidence for a relay in the bed nucleus
   of the stria terminalis. *Journal of Comparative Neurology, 332,* 1–20.
Damasio, A. (1994). *Descartes' error: Emotion, reason and the human brain.* New York:
   Grosset/Putnam.
Darnell, A., Bremner, J. D., Licinio, J., et al. (1994). Cerebrospinal fluid levels of corti-
   cotropin releasing factor in chronic post-traumatic stress disorder. *Neuroscience
   Abstracts, 20,* 15.
Darwin, C. (1965). *The expression of emotions in man and animals.* Chicago: University
   of Chicago Press. (original work published 1872)
Davis, M. (1992). The role of the amygdala in conditioned fear. In J. P. Aggleton (Ed.),
   *The amygdala: Neurobiological aspects of emotion, memory and mental dysfunc-
   tion* (pp. 255–306). New York: Wiley-Liss.
Davis, M., Falls, W. A., Campeau, S., & Kim, M. (1993). Fear-potentiated startle: A neural
   and pharmacological analysis. *Behavior Brain Research, 58,* 175–98.
Davis, M., Walker, D. L., & Lee, Y. (1997). Amygdala and bed nucleus of the stria termi-
   nalis: Differential roles in fear and anxiety measured with the acoustic startle re-
   flex. *Annals of the New York Academy of Sciences, 821,* 305–331.
Dewey, J. (1894). The theory of emotions: I. The theory of the emotions. Emotional atti-
   tudes. *Psychological Review, 1,* 553–569.
Dewey, J. (1895). The theory of emotions: II. The significance of emotions. *Psychological
   Review, 2,* 13–32.
Dickinson, A. (1980). *Contemporary animal learning theory.* Cambridge: Cambridge
   University Press.
Drevets, W. C., Videen, T. O., Price, J. L., Preskorn, S. H., Carmichael, S. T., & Raichle,
   M. E. (1992). A functional anatomical study of unipolar depression. *Journal of
   Neuroscience, 12,* 3628–3641.
Ekman, P., & Davidson, R. J. (1994). *The nature of emotions: Fundamental questions.*
   New York: Oxford University Press.
Fanselow, M. S. (1994). Neural organization of the defensive behavior system responsi-
   ble for fear. *Psychonomic Bulletin Review, 1,* 429–438.
Fleshner, M., Pugh, C. R., Tremblay, D., & Rudy, J. W. (1997). DHEA-S selectively im-
   pairs contextual-fear conditioning: Support for the antiglucocorticoid hypothesis.
   *Behavioral Neuroscience, 111,* 512–517.
Fodor, J. (1981). *Representations. Philosophical essays on the foundations of cognitive
   science.* Cambridge, MA: MIT Press.
Fodor, J. (1983). *The modularity of the mind.* Cambridge, MA: MIT Press.
Fonberg, E. (1972). Control of emotional behavior through the hypothalamus and amyg-
   daloid complex. In D. Hill (Ed.), *Physiology, emotion, and psychosomatic illness.*
   Amsterdam: Elsevier.
Frankland, P. W., & Yeomans, J. S. (1995). Fear-potentiated startle and electrically
   evoked startle mediated by synapses in rostrolateral midbrain. *Behavioral Neu-
   roscience, 109,* 669–680.
Freud, S. (1959). Inhibition, symptom and anxiety. In J. Strachey (Ed. and Trans.), *The
   standard edition of the complete psychological works of Sigmund Freud* (Vol. 20).
   London: Hogarth Press. (original work published 1926)
Frijda, N. H. (1986). *The Emotions.* New York: Cambridge University Press.
Gallagher, M., & Holland, P. C. (1994). The amygdala complex: Multiple roles in asso-
   ciative learning and attention. *Proceedings of the National Academy of Science,
   91,* 11771–11776.
Gallistel, C. R. (1980). *The organization of action.* Hillsdale, NJ: Erlbaum.
Gold, P. W., Chrousos, G., Kellner, C., Post, R., Roy, A., Augerinas, P., Schulte, H.,
   Oldfield, E., & Loriaux, D. L. (1984). Psychiatric implications of basic and clinical

studies with corticotropin releasing hormone. *American Journal of Psychiatry, 141,* 619–627.

Gold, P. W., Goodwin, F. K., & Chrousos, G. P. (1988). Clinical and biochemical manifestation of depression: Relation to the neurobiology of stress. *New England Journal of Medicine, 319,* 348–353.

Goldstein, K. (1995). *The organism.* New York: American Book Co. (original work published 1939)

Goldstein, L. E., Rasmusson, A. M., Bunney, B. S., & Roth, R. H. (1996) Role of the amygdala in the coordination of behavioral, neuralendocrine and prefrontal cortical monomaine responses to psychological stress. *Journal of Neuroscience, 16,* 4787–4798.

Goy, R. W., & McEwen, B. S. (1980). *Sexual differentiation of the brain.* Cambridge, MA: MIT Press.

Gray, T. S. (1990). The organization and possible function of amygdaloid corticotropin releasing hormone pathways. In E. B. De Souza & C. B. Nemeroff (Eds.), *Corticotropin releasing hormone: Basic and clinical studies of a neuropeptide.* New York: CRC Press.

Gray, T. S., Piechowski, R. A., Yracheta, J. M., Rittenhouse, P. A., Bethea, C. L., & Van de Kar, L. D. (1993). Ibotenic acid lesions in the bed nucleus of the stria terminalis attenuate conditioned stress induced increases in prolactin, ACTH and corticosterone. *Neuroendocrinology, 57,* 571–524.

Gunnar, M. R., Mangelsdorf, S., Larson, M., & Hertsgaard, L. (1989). Attachment, temperament, and adrenocortical activity in infancy: A study of psychoendocrine regulation. *Developmental Psychology, 25,* 355–363.

Habib, K. E., Weld, K. P., Schulkin, J., Pushkas, S., Listwak, S., Champaux, M., Shannon, C., Chrousos, G. P., Gold, P. W., & Higley, J. D. (1999). Cerebrospinal fluid levels of corticotropine-releasing hormone correlate positively with acute and chronic social stress in non-human primates. *Society for Neuroscience Abstracts.*

Hauser, M. D. (1996). *The evolution of communication.* Cambridge, MA: MIT Press.

Hebb, D. O. (1946). On the nature of fear. *Psychological Review, 53,* 259–276.

Hebb, D. O. (1949). *The organization of behavior: A neuropsychological theory.* New York: Wiley.

Herman, J. P., & Cullinan, W. E. (1997). Neurocircuitry of stress: Central control of the hypothalamic-pituitary-adrenocortical axis. *Trends in Neuroscience, 20,* 78–84.

Herrick, C. J. (1905). The central gustatory pathway in the brain of bony fishes. *Journal of Comparative Neurology, 15,* 375–456.

Hirshfeld, D. R., Rosenbaum, J. F., Biederman, J., Bolduc, E. A., Faraone, S. V. Snidman, N., Reznick, J. S., & Kagan, J. (1992). Stable behavioral inhibition and its association with anxiety disorder. *Journal of the American Academy of Child and Adolescent Psychiatry, 31,* 103–111.

Hitchcock, J. M., & Davis, M. (1986). Lesions of the amygdala, but not of the cerebellum or red nucleus, block conditioned fear as measured with the potentiated startle paradigm. *Behavioral Neuroscience, 100,* 11–22.

Hitchcock, J. M., & Davis, M. (1991). Efferent pathway of the amygdala involved in conditioned fear as measured with the fear-potentiated startle paradigm. *Behavioral Neuroscience, 105,* 826–842.

Hofer, M. A. (1994). Early relationships as regulators of infant physiology and behavior. *Acta Paediatric Supplements, 397,* 1–9.

Holsboer, F., Muller, O. A., Doerr, H. G., Sippell, W. G., Stalla, G. K., Gerken, A., Steiger, A., Boll, E., & Benkert, O. (1984). ACTH and multisteroid responses to corticotropin-releasing factor in depressive illness: Relationship to multisteroid responses after ACTH stimulation and dexamethasone suppression. *Psychoneuroendocrinology, 9,* 147–160.

Honkaniemi, J., Pelto-Huikko, M., Rechardt, L., Isola, J., Lammi, A., Fuxe, K., Gustafsson, J. A., Wikstrom, A. C., & Hokfelt, T. (1992). Colocalization of peptide and glucocorticoid receptor immunoreactivities in rat central amygdaloid nucleus. *Neuroendocrinology, 55,* 451.

Imaki, T., Nahan, J. L., Rivier, C., & Vale, W. (1991). Differential regulation of corti-cotropin-releasing hormone mRNA in rat brain regions by glucocorticoids and stress. *Journal of Neuroscience, 11*, 585–599.

Iwata, J., Chida, K., & LeDoux, J. E. (1987). Cardiovascular response elicited by stimu-lation of neurons in the central amygdaloid nucleus in awake but not anesthetized rats resemble conditioned emotional responses. *Brain Research, 418*, 183–188.

James, W. (1884). What is an emotion? *Mind, 9*, 188–205.

James, W. (1890). *The principles of psychology.* New York: Dover.

Jones, R. B., Beuving, G., & Blokhuis, H. J. (1988). Tonic immobility and heterophil/lym-phocyte responses of the domestic fowl to corticosterone infusion. *Physiology and Behavior, 42*, 249–253.

Ju, G., Swanson, L. W., & Simerly, R. B. (1989). Studies on the cellular architecture of the bed nuclei of the stria terminalis in the rat: II. Chemoarchitecture. *Journal of Comparative Neurology, 280*, 603–621.

Kagan, J. (1989). *Unstable ideas, temperament, cognition, and self.* Cambridge, MA: Harvard University Press.

Kagan, J., Reznick, J. S., & Snidman, N. (1988). Biological bases of childhood shyness. *Science, 240*, 167–171.

Kagan, J., & Schulkin, J. (1995). On the concepts of fear. *Harvard Review of Psychiatry, 3*, 231–234.

Kainu, T., Honkaniemi, J., Gustafsson, J. A., Rechardt, L., & Markku, P. H. (1993). Colocalization of peptide-like immunoreactivities with glucocorticoid receptor- and fos-like immunoreactivities in the rat parabrachial nucleus. *Brain Research, 615*, 245–251.

Kalin, N. H. (1985). Behavioral effects of corticotropin releasing factor administered to rhesus monkeys. *Federation Proceedings, 44*, 249–253.

Kalin, N. H., Shelton, S. E., Rickman, M., & Davidson, R. J. (1998). Individual differ-ences in freezing and cortisol in infant and mother rhesus monkeys. *Behavioral Neuroscience, 112*, 251–254.

Kalin, N. H., Takahashi, L. K., & Chen, F. L. (1994). Restraint stress increases corti-cotropin releasing hormone mRNA content the amygdala and the paraventricular nucleus. *Brain Research, 656*, 182–186.

Kant, G. J., Bauman, R. B., Anderson, S. M., & Moughey, E. H. (1992). Effects of con-trollable vs. uncontrollable chronic stress on stress-responsive plasma hormones. *Physiology and Behavior, 51*, 1285–1288.

Kapp, B. S., Frysinger R. C., Gallagher, M., & Haselton, J. R. (1979). Amygdala central nucleus lesions: Effects on heart rate conditioning in the rabbit. *Physiology and Behavior, 23*, 1109–1117.

Kapp, B. S., Gallagher, M., Underwood, M. D., McNall, C. L., & Whitehorn, D. (1982). Cardiovascular responses elicited by electrical stimulation of the amygdala central nucleus in the rabbit. *Brain Research, 234*, 251–264.

Kapp, B. S., Whalen, P. J., Supple, W. F., & Pascoe, J. P. (1992). Amygdaloid contribu-tions to conditioned arousal and sensory information processing. In J. P. Aggleton (Ed.), *The amygdala: Neurobiological aspects of emotion, memory, and mental dys-function* (pp. 229–254). New York: Wiley-Liss.

Ketter, T. A., George, M. S., Ring, H. A., & Pazzaglia, P. (1994). Primary mood disorders: Structural and resting functional studies. *Psychiatric Annals, 24*, 637–642.

Kim, J. J., Rison, R. A., & Fanselow, M. S. (1993). Effects of amygdala, hippocampus, and periaqueductal gray lesions on short and long-term contextual fear. *Behavioral Neuroscience, 107*, 1093–1098.

Kling, A. (1981). Influence of temporal lobe lesions on radio-telemetered electrical ac-tivity of amygdala of social stimuli in monkey. In Y. Ben-Ari (Ed.), *The amygdaloid complex.* New York: Elsevier.

Kluver, H., & Bucy, C. P. (1939). Preliminary analysis of functions of the temporal lobes in monkeys. *Archives of Neurology and Psychology, 42*, 979–1000.

Koob, G. F., & Bloom, F. E. (1985). Corticotropin-releasing factor and behavior. *Federation Proceedings, 44,* 259–263.

Koob, G. F., et al. (1993). The role of corticotropin releasing hormone in behavioral responses to stress. In K. Chadwick, J. Marsh, & K. Ackrill (Eds.), *Corticotrophin releasing factor.* New York: Wiley.

Krettek, J. E., & Price, J. L. (1978). Amygdaloid projections to subcortical structures within the basal forebrain and brainstem in the rat and cat. *Journal of Comparative Neurology, 78,* 225–254.

LaBar, K. S., LeDoux, J. E., Spencer, D. D., & Phelps, E. A. (1995). Impaired fear conditioning following unilateral temporal lobectomy in humans. *Journal of Neuroscience, 15,* 6846–6855.

Lance, V. A., & Elsey, R. M. (1986). Stress-induced suppression of testosterone secretion in alligators. *Journal of Experimental Zoology, 239,* 241–246.

Lang, P. J. (1995). The emotion probe: Studies of motivation and attention. *American Psychologist, 50,* 272–285.

Lashley, K. S. (1938). An experimental analysis of instinctive behavior. *Psychological Review, 45,* 445–471.

Lazarus, R. S. (1991). *Emotion and adaptation.* New York: Oxford University Press.

LeDoux, J. E. (1987). Emotion. In F. Plum (Ed.), *Handbook of physiology: The nervous system* (pp. 419–60). Bethesda, MD: American Physiological Society.

LeDoux, J.E. (1995). Emotion: Clues from the brain. *Annual Review of Psychology, 46,* 209–235.

LeDoux, J. E. (1996). *The emotional brain.* New York: Simon & Schuster.

LeDoux, J. E., Cicchetti, P., Xagoraris, A., & Romanski, L. M. (1990). The lateral amygdaloid nucleus: sensory interface of the amygdala in fear conditioning. *Journal of Neuroscience, 10,* 1062–1069.

LeDoux, J. E., Iwata, J., Cicchetti, P., & Reis, D. (1988). Different projections of the central amygdaloid nucleus mediate autonomic and behavioral correlates of conditioned fear. *Journal of Neuroscience, 8,* 2517–2529.

Lee, Y., & Davis, M. (1997). Role of the hippocampus, the bed nucleus of the stria terminalis, and the amygdala in the excitatory effect of corticotropin releasing hormone on the acoustic startle reflex. *Journal of Neuroscience, 17,* 6434–6446.

Lee, Y., Schulkin, J., & Davis, M. (1994). Effect of corticosterone on the enhancement of the acoustic startle reflex by corticotropin releasing hormone. *Brain Research, 666,* 93–98.

Levine, S. (1967). Maternal and environmental influences on adrenal cortical response to stress in weanling rats. *Science, 156,* 258–260.

Levine, S. (1993). The influence of social factors on the response to stress. *Psychotherapy and Psychosomatics, 60,* 33–38.

Levine, S., & Weiner, S. G. (1988). Psychoneuroendocrine aspects of mother-infant relationships in non-human primates. *Psychoneuroendocrinology, 13,* 143–154.

Liang, K. C., Melia, K. R., Campeau, S., Falls, W. A., Miserendino, M. J., & Davis, M. (1992). Lesions of the central nucleus of the amygdala, but not the paraventricular nucleus of the hypothalamus, block the excitatory effects of CRF on the acoustic startle response. *Journal of Neuroscience, 12,* 2313–2320.

Liu, D., Diorio, J., Tannenbaum, B., Caldji, C., Francis, D., Freedman, A., Sharma, S., Pearson, D., Plotsky, P. M., & Meaney, M. J. (1997). Maternal care, hippocampal glucocorticoid receptors, and hypothalamic-pituitary-adrenal responses to stress. *Science, 277,* 1659–1662.

Mackintosh, N. J. (1975). A theory of attention: Variations in the associability of stimulus and reinforcement. *Psychological Review, 82,* 276–298.

Makino, S., Gold, P. W., & Schulkin, J. (1994a). Corticosterone effects on corticotropin-releasing hormone mRNA in the central nucleus of the amygdala and the parvocellular region of the paraventricular nucleus of the hypothalamus. *Brain Research, 640,* 105–112.

Makino, S., Gold, P. W., & Schulkin, J. (1994b). Effects of corticosterone on CRH mRNA and content in the bed nucleus of the stria terminalis; comparison with the effects in the central nucleus of the amygdala and the paraventricular nucleus of the hypothalamus. *Brain Research, 657,* 141–149.

Makino, S., Schulkin, J., Smith, M. A., Pacak, K., Palkovits, M., & Gold, P. W. (1995). Regulation of corticotropin-releasing hormone receptor messenger ribonucleic acid in the rat brain and pituitary by glucocorticoids and stress. *Endocrinology, 136,* 4517–4525.

Marler, P., & Hamilton, W. J. III (1966). *Mechanism of animal behavior.* New York: Wiley.

Mason, J. W. (1975). Emotions as reflected as patterns of endocrine integration. In L. Levi (Ed.), *Emotions: Their parameters and measurements.* New York: Raven Press.

Mason, J. W., Brady, J. V., & Sidman, M. (1957). Plasma 17-hydroxycorticosteroid levels and conditioned behavior in rhesus monkeys. *Endocrinology, 60,* 741–752.

McEwen, B. S. (1998). Protective and damaging effects of stress mediators: Allostasis and allostatic load. *New England Journal of Medicine, 338,* 171–179.

McGaugh, J. L., Introini-Collison, I. B., Cahill, L. F., Castellano, C., Dalmaz, C., Parent, M. B., & Williams, C. L. (1993). Neuromodulatory systems and memory storage: Role of the amygdala. *Behavior and Brain Research, 58,* 81–90.

Meaney, M. J., Bhathagar, S., Larocque, S., McCormick, C., Shanks, S, Sharma, S., Smyth, J., Viau, V., & Plotsky, P. M. (1993). Individual differences in the hypothalamic pituitary adrenal stress response and the hypothalamic CRF system. *Annals of the New York Academy of Sciences, 697,* 70–85.

Miller, N. E. (1957). Experiments on motivation: Studies using psychological, physiological and pharmacological techniques. *Science, 126,* 1271–1278.

Miller, N. E. (1959). Liberalization of basic S-R concepts: Extensions to conflict behavior, motivation and social learning. In S. Koch (Ed.), *Psychology: A study of a science.* Vol. 2. New York: McGraw Hill.

Mineka, S. (1985). Animal models of anxiety-based disorders: Their usefulness and limitations. In A. H. Tuma & J. D. Masur (Eds.), *Anxiety and the anxiety disorders* (pp. 199–244). Hillsdale, NJ: Erlbaum.

Mineka, S., & Zinberg, R. (1996). Conditioning and ethological models of anxiety disorders: Stress-in-dynamic-context anxiety models. In D. A. Hope (Ed.), *Nebraska Symposium on Motivation: Vol. 43. Perspectives on anxiety, panic and fear* (pp. 135–210). Lincoln: University of Nebraska Press.

Mogenson, G. J. (1987). Limbic-motor integration. In A. N. Epstein & J. M. Sprague (Eds.), *Progress in psychobiology and physiological psychology.* New York: Academic Press.

Morgan, M. A., & LeDoux, J. E. (1995). Differential contribution of dorsal and ventral medial prefrontal cortex to the acquisition and extinction of conditioned fear in rats. *Behavioral Neuroscience, 109,* 681–688.

Morgan, C., & Stellar, J. (1950). *Physiological psychology* (2nd ed.). New York: McGraw-Hill.

Morris, J. S., Frith, C. D., Perrett, P. L., Rowland, D., Young, A. W., Calder, A. J., & Dolan, R. J. (1996). A differential neural response in the human amygdala to fearful and happy facial expressions. *Nature, 383,* 812–815.

Mowrer, O. H. (1947). On the dual nature of learning-reinterpretation on conditioning and problem solving. *Harvard Education Review, 17,* 102–148.

Munck, A., Guyre, P. M., & Holbrook, N. J. (1984). Physiological regulation of glucocorticoids in stress and their regulation to pharmacological actions. *Endocrine Review, 5,* 25–44.

Nachmias, M., Gunnar, M., Mangelsdorf, S., Parritz, R. H., & Buss, K. (1996). Behavioral inhibition and stress reactivity: The moderating role of attachment security. *Child Development, 67,* 508–522.

Nauta, W. J. H. (1961). Fibre degeneration following lesions of the amygdaloid complex in the monkey. *Journal of Anatomy, 95,* 515–531.

Nauta, W. J. H., & Domesick, V. B. (1982). Neural associations of the limbic system. *Neural Basis of Behavior, 10,* 175–206.

Nemeroff, C. B. (1992). New vistas in neuropeptide research in neuropsychiatry: Focus on CRF. *Neuropsychopharmacology, 6,* 69–75.

Nemeroff, C. B., Krishnan, K. R., Reed, D., Leder, R., Beam, C., & Dunnick, N. R. (1992). Adrenal gland enlargement in major depression: A computed tomographic study. *Archives of General Psychiatry, 49,* 384–387.

Norgren, R. (1978). Projections from the nucleus of the solitary tract in the rat. *Neuroscience, 3,* 207–218.

Ohman, A. (1993). Fear and anxiety as emotional phenomena: Clinical phenomenology, evolutionary perspectives, and information-processing mechanisms. In M. Lewis & J. M. Haviland (Eds.), *Handbook of emotions* (pp. 511–536). New York: Guilford Press.

Owens, M. J., & Nemeroff, C. B. (1991). Physiology and pharmacology of corticotropin releasing hormone. *Pharmacology Review, 43,* 425–473.

Papez, J. W. (1937). A proposed mechanism of emotion. *Archives of Neurology and Psychiatry, 79,* 217–224.

Parrott, W. G., & Schulkin, J. (1993). Neuropsychology and the cognitive nature of the emotions. *Cognition and Emotion, 7,* 43–59.

Pashler, H. (1998). *The psychology of attention.* Cambridge, MA: MIT Press.

Petrovich, G. D., & Swanson, L. W. (1997). Projections from the lateral part of the central amygdalar nucleus to the postulated fear conditioning circuit. *Brain Research, 763,* 247–254.

Pfaff, D. W. (1980). *Estrogens and brain function: Neural analysis of a hormone-controlled mammalian reproductive behavior.* New York: Springer.

Phillips, R. G., & LeDoux, J. E. (1992). Differential contribution of amygdala and hippocampus to cued and contextual fear conditioning. *Behavioral Neuroscience, 106,* 274–285.

Pich, E. M., Koob, G. F., Helig, M., Menzaghi, F., Vale, W., & Weiss, F. (1993). Corticotropin-releasing factor (CRF) release from the mediobasal hypothalamus of the rat as measured by microdialysis. *Neuroscience, 55,* 695–707.

Pich, E. M., Lorang, M., Yeganeh, M., Rodriguez de Fonseca, F., Rober, J., Koob, G. F., & Weiss, F. (1995). Increase of extracellular CRF-like immunoreactivity levels in the amygdala of awake rats during restraint stress and ethanol withdrawal as measured by microdialysis. *Journal of Neuroscience, 15,* 5439–5447.

Pitkanen, A., Stefanacci, L., Farb, C. R., Go, G. G., LeDoux, J. E., & Amaral, D. G. (1995). Intrinsic connections of the rat amygdaloid complex: Projections originating in the lateral nucleus. *Journal of Comparative Neurology, 356,* 288–310.

Pitman, R. K. (1997). Overview of biological themes in PTSD. *Annals of the New York Academy of Sciences, 821,* 1–9.

Potter, E., Sutton, S., Donaldson, C., Chen, R., Perrin, M., Lewis, K., Sawchenko, P. E., & Vale, W. (1994). Distribution of corticotropin releasing hormone receptor mRNA expression in the rat brain and pituitary. *Neurobiology, 91,* 8777–8781.

Pugh, C. R., Tremblay, D., Fleshner, M., Fleshner, D., & Rudy J. W. (1997). A selective role for corticosterone in contextual fear conditioning. *Behavioral Neuroscience, 111,* 503–511.

Raadsheer, F. C., Hoogendijk, W. J. G., Stam, F. C., Tilders, F. J. H., & Swaab, D. F. (1994). Increased numbers of corticotropin-releasing hormone expressing neurons in the hypothalamic paraventricular nucleus of depressed patients. *Neuroendocrinology, 60,* 436.

Rauch, S. L., Van der Kolk, B. A., Fisler, R. E., Alpert, N. M., Orr, S. P., Savage, C. R., Fischman, S. J., Jenike, M. A., & Pitman, R. I. C. (1996). A symptom provocation study of posttraumatic stress disorder using positron emission tomography and script-driven imagery. *Archives of General Psychiatry, 53,* 380–387.

Rescorla, R. A., & Wagner, A. R. (1972). A theory of Pavlovian conditioning: Variations in the effectiveness of reinforcement and non-reinforcement. In A. Block & W. Prokasy (Eds.), *Classical conditioning: II. Current research and theory.* New York: Appleton-Century Crofts.

Ricardo, J. A., & Koh, E. T. (1978). Anatomical evidence of direct projections from the nucleus of the solitary tract to the hypothalamus, amygdala, and other forebrain structures in the rat. *Brain Research, 153,* 1–26.

Rickman, M. D., & Davidson, R. J. (1994). Personality and behavior in parents of temperamentally inhibited and uninhibited children. *Developmental Psychology, 30,* 346–354.

Richter, C. P. (1949). Domestication of the Norway rat and its implications for the problem of stress. *Proceedings of the Association for Research in Nervous and Mental Disease, 29,* 19–30.

Rogan, M. T., & LeDoux, J. E. (1996). Emotion: Systems, cells, synaptic plasticity. *Cell, 85,* 469–475.

Roozendaal, B., & McGaugh, J. L. (1997). Glucocorticoid receptor agonist and antagonist administration to the basolateral but not central amygdala modulated memory storage. *Neurobiology of Learning and Memory, 67,* 176–179.

Roozendaal, B., Quirarte, G. L., & McGaugh, J. L. (1997). Stress-activated hormonal systems and the regulation of memory and storage. *Annals of the New York Academy of Sciences, 821,* 247–258.

Rosen, J. B., & Davis, M. (1988). Enhancement of acoustic startle by electrical stimulation of the amygdala. *Behavioral Neuroscience, 102,* 195–202

Rosen, J. B., Hamerman, E., Sitcoske, M., Glowa, J. R., & Schulkin, J. (1996). Hyperexcitability: exaggerated fear-potentiated startle produced by partial amygdala kindling. *Behavioral Neuroscience, 110,* 43–50.

Rosen, J. B., Hitchcock, J. M., Miserendino, M. J., Falls, W. A., Campean, S., & Davis, M. (1992). Lesions of the perirhinal cortex but not of the frontal, medial prefrontal, visual, or insular cortex block fear-potentiated startle using a visual conditioned stimulus. *Journal of Neuroscience, 12,* 4624–4633.

Rosen, J. B., Hitchcock, J. M., Sananes, C. B., Miserendino, M. J., & Davis, M. (1991). A direct projection from the central nucleus of the amygdala to the acoustic startle pathway: anterograde and retrograde tracing studies. *Behavioral Neuroscience, 105,* 817–825.

Rosen, J. B., Pishevar, S. K., Weiss, S. R. B., Smith, M. A., Gold, P. W., & Schulkin, J. (1994). Glucocorticoid potentiation of CRH-induced seizures. *Neuroscience Letters, 174,* 113–116.

Rosen, J. B., & Schulkin, J. (1998). From normal fear to pathological anxiety. *Psychological Review, 105,* 325–350.

Sabini, J., & Silver, M. (1996). On the possible non-existence of emotions: The passions. *Journal of Theory and Social Behavior, 26,* 375–398.

Sachar, E. J., Hellman, I., Fukushima, D. K., & Gallagher, T. F. (1970). Cortisol production in depressive illness: A clinical and biochemical clarification. *Archives of General Psychiatry, 23,* 289–298.

Sapolsky, R. M. (1992). *Stress: The aging brain and the mechanisms of neuron death.* Cambridge, MA: MIT Press.

Sapolsky, R. M., Zola-Morgan, S., & Squire, L. R. (1991). Inhibition of glucocorticoid secretion by the hippocampal formation in the primate. *Journal of Neuroscience, 11,* 3695–3704.

Sartre, J. P. (1948). *The emotions.* New York: Philosophical Library.

Sawchenko, P. E. (1987). Evidence for local site of action for glucocorticoids in inhibiting corticotropin releasing hormone and vasopressin expression in the paraventricular nucleus. *Brain Research, 17,* 213–223.

Schmidt, L. A., Fox, N. A., Rubin, K. H., Sternberg, E. M., Gold, P., Smith, C. C., & Schulkin, J. (1997). Behavioral and neuroendocrine responses in shy children. *Developmental Psychobiology, 30,* 127–140.

Schmidt, L.A., Fox, N., Sternberg, E.M., Gold, P. W., Smith, C.C., & Schulkin, J. (1999). Adrenocortical reactivity and social competence in seven year olds. *Personality and Individual Differences, 26,* 977–985.

Schulkin, J. (1994). Melancholic depression and the hormones of adversity. *Current Directions in Psychology, 3,* 41–44.

Schulkin, J., Gold, P. W., & McEwen, B. S. (1998). Induction of corticotropin-releasing hormone gene expression by glucocorticoids: Implication for understanding the states of fear and anxiety, and allostatic load. *Psychoneuroendocrinology, 23,* 219–243.

Schulkin, J., McEwen, B. S., & Gold, P. W. (1994). Allostasis, amygdala, and anticipatory angst. *Neuroscience and Biobehavioral Review, 18,* 385–396.

Schwaber, J. S., Kapp, B. S., Higgins, G. A., & Rapp, P. R. (1982). Amygdaloid and basal forebrain direct connections with the nucleus of the solitary tract and the dorsal motor nucleus. *Journal of Neuroscience, 2,* 1424–1438.

Scott, S. K., Young, A. W., Calder, A. J., Hellawell, D. J., Aggleton, J. P., & Johnson, M. (1997). Impaired auditory recognition of fear and anger following bilateral amygdala lesions. *Nature, 385,* 254–257.

Selye, H. (1976). *The stress of life.* New York: McGraw-Hill. (original work published 1956)

Smith, J. E. (1977). *The behavior of communicating.* Cambridge, MA: Harvard University Press.

Spinoza, B. (1955). *On the improvement of the understanding. The ethics* (R. H. M. Elwes, Trans.). New York: Dover. (original work published 1677)

Stellar, E. (1954). The physiology of motivation. *Psychological Review, 61,* 5–22.

Stenzel-Poore, M. P., Heinrichs, S. C., Rivest, S., Koob, G. F., & Vale, W. W. (1994). Overproduction of corticotropin-releasing factor in transgenic mice: A genetic model of anxiogenic behavior. *Journal of Neuroscience, 14,* 2579–2584.

Swanson, L. W., Sawchenko, P. E., Rivier, J., & Vale, W. W. (1983). Organization of ovine corticotropin releasing hormone immunoreactive cells and fibers in the rat brain: An immunohistochemical study. *Neuroendocrinology, 36,* 165–186.

Swanson, L. W., & Simmons, D. M. (1989). Differential steroid hormone and neural influences on peptide mRNA levels in CRH cells of the paraventricular nucleus: A hybridization histochemical study in the rat. *Journal of Comparative Neurology, 285,* 413–435.

Swerdlow, N. R., Britton, K. T., & Koob, G. F. (1989). Potentiation of acoustic startle by corticotrophin-releasing factor and by fear are both reversed by alpha-helical CRF (9-41). *Neuropsychopharmacology, 2,* 285–292.

Takahashi, L. K. (1995). Glucocorticoids, the hippocampus, and behavioral inhibition in the preweaning rat. *Journal of Neuroscience, 15,* 6023–6034.

Takahashi, L. K., & Kim, H. (1994). Intracranial action of corticosterone facilitates the development of behavioral inhibition in the adrenalectomized preweaning rat. *Neuroscience Letters, 176,* 272–276.

Takahashi, L. K., & Rubin, W. W. (1993). Corticosteroid induction of threat-induced behavioral inhibition in the preweaning rat. *Behavioral Neuroscience, 107,* 860–866.

Tinbergen, N. (1951). *The study of instinct.* Oxford: Oxford University Press.

Treit, D., Pesold, C., & Rotzinger, S. (1993). Dissociating the anti-fear effects of septal and amygdaloid lesions using two pharmacologically validated models of rat anxiety. *Behavioral Neuroscience, 107,* 770–785.

Turner, B. H., & Herkenham, M. (1992). Thalamoamygdaloid projections in the rat: A test of the amygdala's role in sensory processing. *Journal of Comparative Neurology, 313,* 295–325.

Vale, W., Spiess, J., Rivier, C., & Rivier, J. (1981). Characterization of a 41-residue ovine hypothalamic peptide that stimulates the secretion of corticotropin and Beta-endorphin. *Science, 213,* 1394–1397.

Watts, A. G. (1996). The impact of physiological stimuli on the expression of CRH and other neuropeptide genes. *Frontiers in Neuroendocrinology, 17,* 281–326.

Watts, A. G., & Sanchez-Watts, G. (1995). Region-specific regulation of neuropeptide mRNAs in rat limbic forebrain neurones by aldosterone and corticosterone. *Journal of Physiology, 484,* 721–736.

Weiss, S. R., Post, R. M., Gold, P. W., Chrousos, G., Sullivan, T. L., Walker, D., & Pert, A. (1986). CRF-induced seizures and behavior: Interaction with amygdala kindling. *Brain Research, 372,* 345–351.

Wiersma, A., Baauw, A. D., Bohus, B., & Koolhaas, J. M. (1995). Behavioural activation produced by CRH but not a-helical CRH (CRH receptor agonist) when microinfused into the central nucleus of the amygdala under stress-free conditions. *Psychoneuroendocrinology, 20,* 423–432.

Windle, M. (1994). Temperamental inhibition and activation: Hormonal and psychosocial correlates and associated psychiatric disorders. *Personality and Individual Differences, 17,* 61–70.

Yehuda, R., Kahana, B., Binder-Brynes, K., Southwick, S. M., Mason, J. W., & Giller, E. L. (1995). Low urinary cortisol excretion in Holocaust survivors with posttraumatic stress disorder. *American Journal of Psychiatry, 152,* 982–986.

Yehuda, R. (1997). Sensitization of the hypothalamic-pituitary-adrenal axis in post-traumatic stress disorder. *Annals of the New York Academy of Sciences, 821,* 57–75.

# 9

## Lifelong Effects of Hormones on Brain Development

### Relationship to Health and Disease

Bruce S. McEwen

Events early in life can have profound and long-lasting influences on brain development. This has been demonstrated in animal studies of the effects of "handling" and prenatal stress on lifelong patterns of stress hormone reactivity, emotionality and brain aging (Barbazanges, Vallee, et al., 1996; Maccari et al., 1995; Meaney et al., 1996; Meaney, Aitken, Bhatnagar, & Sapolsky, 1991). One of the most powerful demonstrations of this effect is the study showing that stressing a pregnant mother rat produces effects in emotionality in the offspring that are transmitted over several generations in the absence of further experimenter-applied stress (Denenberg & Rosenberg, 1967). There are also observational studies in primates that show that female offspring of nervous mothers become nervous mothers themselves, possibly due to the behavioral transmission of the nervousness (Altmann, 1980). Indeed, the behavioral transmission of traits that appear otherwise to follow laws of genetic transmission provides a novel way to look at traditional genetic transmission. These findings reactivate interest at the level of experience and behavior in the relationship between nature, or genetic constitution, and nurture, or the influences of experience and other environmental factors.

In contrast to the early "nature-nurture" debates, when genes and environment were regarded as isolated and independent entities, modern cell and molecular biology has taught us that genes are regulated by environmental signals over the entire lifespan. In development, a common pattern is for genes to be made available for expression or to be made inaccessible for regulation at a later time by hormonal or other inter- and intracellular messengers.

In the brain, there is an additional constraint because nerve cells for the most part are born early in life and then are not replaced during the rest of the lifespan. Moreover, it has been assumed until recently that neural circuits and nerve cell structures are largely static and unchanging in adult life and that only during development is the brain plastic and subject to rewiring. However, this idea is changing, because recent studies have shown that certain regions of the adult brain display cyclic synaptogenesis in the female reproductive cycle, atrophy and elongation of dendrites after repeated stress and during hibernation, and neurogenesis that is regulated by experiences, including stress. Moreover, recent studies are also showing that the responses of the adult brain to its environment are shaped by events that occur early in brain development. For both the developmental and adult forms of neural plasticity, hormones of the gonads, adrenals, and thyroid gland play an important role. This chapter reviews studies of hormone action that illuminate these principles and illustrate our rapidly increasing understanding of the lifelong interactions between genes and environment as they affect the progression toward disease. This information will undoubtedly be applicable to the condition of extreme fear and shyness, both in terms of how it comes about and of what it means for lifelong patterns of health and disease.

## Developmental Events

Early experiences help to determine individual differences in brain function and behavior, and they do so, in part, by the actions of hormones (see figure 9.1). Gonadal, adrenal, and thyroid hormones are involved, and many of the developmental events interact with each other during the course of a lifetime.

### Sexual Differentiation

The sexual differentiation of the brain is an example of a hormonally directed event in which the presence or absence of testosterone during fetal and neonatal life causes brain development to diverge in two directions: male or female. As a result, male and female brains differ in subtle ways, in structure and connectivity, as well as in their different responses to hormonal signals (Kimura, 1992; McEwen, 1991b; Witelson, 1989; Witelson, Glezer, & Kigar, 1995). There are sex differences in numbers and distributions of synaptic connections and in the numbers of neurons in particular brain regions; in addition, male and female brains differ in that they use the same hormonal signals, androgens, estrogens, and progestins, to achieve somewhat different effects in various brain regions. For example, estrogens induce the formation of progestin receptors in female brain cells to a greater extent than in the same cells in males, and estrogens induce new synapses to form in the female hypothalamus and hippocampus, but not in these regions of the male brain (McEwen, 1991b). Androgens regulate synaptic and dendritic plasticity of specific regions of the male nervous system that are not present in the female, such as the spinal nucleus that innervates muscles of the penis (Forger & Breedlove, 1991).

Sexual differentiation has consequences for brain structures that support higher cognitive functions. Structural sex differences have been found in the human temporal cortex in both gross morphology and cortical anatomy (Witelson, 1989; Witelson et al. 1995), and sex differences have been reported in the size and shape of the anterior commissure and the corpus callosum (Allen & Gorski, 1991; Allen & Gorski, 1993; Allen, Richey, Chai, & Gorski, 1991). Sex differences in spatial learning strategies have been reported in humans and in experimental animals

## A.     Sexual   differentiation

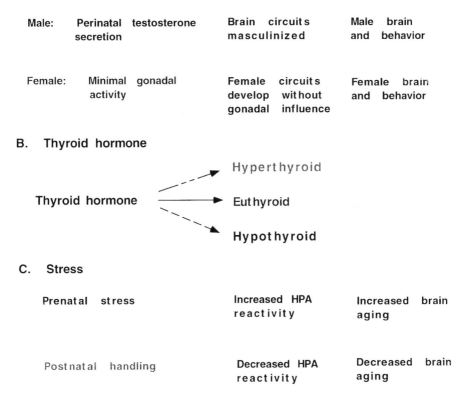

| Male: | Perinatal testosterone secretion | Brain circuits masculinized | Male brain and behavior |

| Female: | Minimal gonadal activity | Female circuits develop without gonadal influence | Female brain and behavior |

## B.   Thyroid hormone

Thyroid hormone → Hyperthyroid / Euthyroid / Hypothyroid

## C.   Stress

| Prenatal stress | Increased HPA reactivity | Increased brain aging |

| Postnatal handling | Decreased HPA reactivity | Decreased brain aging |

Figure 9.1. Developmental influences of hormones on brain development. (A) Sexual differentiation in mammals, under the influence of testosterone in males, affects brain circuitry and behavior. (B) Thyroid hormone actions operate within a range of hormone concentrations; elevations to either extreme lead to abnormalities of brain development. (C) Prenatal stress increases the rate of brain (esp. hippocampal) aging, whereas postnatal handling, in rats, reduces the rate of brain (esp. hippocampal) aging; HPA activity appears to mediate the differences in hippocampal aging in rats.

(Kimura, 1992). Indeed, the hippocampus of rats and mice shows morphological sex differences of a number of types (Tallal & McEwen, 1991) and hippocampal-dependent spatial learning shows differences between male and females that reflect the developmental actions of sex hormones on the sexual differentiation of this brain structure (Williams & Meck, 1991).

### Developmental Effects of Thyroid Hormone

Hyperthyroidism early in neonatal life alters hippocampal morphology and the neurochemistry and structure of the basal forebrain cholinergic system of rats (Gould, Woolley, & McEwen, 1991; Westlind-Danielsson, Gould, & McEwen, 1991).

In spite of these effects, sex differences in these systems persist in both basal fore-brain and hippocampus (Gould, Westlind-Danielsson, Frankfurt, & McEwen, 1990; Westlind-Danielsson et al., 1991). But these effects are not necessarily to the benefit of the treated animal. In the rat experiments cited previously, both male and female hyperthyroid animals are slower to acquire a hippocampal-dependent spatial learning task and are somewhat impaired in showing long-term potentiation in the hippocampus (Pavlides, Westlind-Danielsson, Nyborg, & McEwen, 1991). On the other hand, a strain of mice that normally shows poor spatial learning and may have a congenital deficiency of thyroid hormone secretion during eary development displays a beneficial effect of the same kind of neonatal thyroid hormone treatment (Schwegler, Crusio, Lipp, Brust, & Mueller, 1991). Thus there is an optimal level of thyroid hormone that is associated with optimal cognitive performance, and deviations in the direction of both hyper- and hypothyroidism result in deficiencies in neural development and cognitive function.

## Pre- and Postnatal Experiences and Stress Responsiveness Later in Life

Unpredictable or uncontrollable stressful experiences of a pregnant rat increase emotionality and stress hormone reactivity in offspring that last for the lifetime of the individual, whereas the gentle and repeated stimulation of newborn rat pups known as postnatal handling produces reductions in emotionality and stress hormone reactivity that also last a lifetime (Ader, 1968; Denenberg & Haltmeyer, 1967; Fride, Dan, Feldon, Halevy, & Weinstock, 1986; Levine, Haltmeyer, Karas, & Denenberg, 1967; Meaney, Aitken, Berkel, Bhatnager, & Sapolsky, 1988; Vallee et al., 1997). These effects appear to involve mediation by both the mother's behavior and by adrenal and thyroid hormone actions. More is known about the mechanism of neonatal handling. Handling involves separating the pups from the mother for 10 minutes per day for the first 2 weeks of neonatal life, and the licking of the pup by the mother appears to be an important determinant of the postnatal handling effect (Liu et al., 1997). At the same time, increasing corticosterone levels in the mother's milk mimic some of the effects of neonatal handling (Catalani et al., 1993), and thyroid hormone elevations have been suggested as a possible mediator of the neonatal handling effect, particularly regarding the elevated expression of glucocorticoid receptors in the hippocampus (Meaney, Aitken, & Sapolsky, 1987).

Studies in which both prenatal stress and postnatal handling were compared indicate that these two procedures have opposite effects on food intake, body weight, and anxiety, as well as HPA activity (Vallee et al., 1997; Vallee, Mayo, Maccari, Le Moal, & Simon, 1996). However, the two processes interact in that prenatal stress effects on HPA activity and emotionality are reversed by early postnatal "adoption" or cross-fostering of pups to new mothers (Barbazanges, Vallee, et al., 1996; Maccari et al., 1995), which is most likely a form of postnatal handling involving intense licking of the pup by the mother (Liu et al., 1997). Prenatal stress during the last week of gestation in rats increases reactivity of the HPA axis and reduces expression of the Type I adrenal steroid receptor in the hippocampus, which helps to contain basal levels of HPA activity (Henry, Kabbaj, Simon, LeMoal, & Maccari, 1994; Vallee et al., 1996). Prenatal stress also increases anxiety in an open field test and decreases basal food intake and body weight (Vallee et al., 1997; Vallee et al., 1996). It is important to note that some of these prenatal stress effects may involve a mediation by adrenal steroids (Barbazanges, Piazza, & LeMoal, & Maccari, 1996). Taken together with the fact that postnatal handling effects may also be mimicked by adrenal steroids (Catalani et al., 1993), the specific effects of adrenal steroids on the neural development of emotionality and HPA reactivity may change qualitatively as the nervous system matures.

For prenatal stress and postnatal handling, once the emotionality and the reactivity of the adrenocortical system are established by events early in life, it is the subsequent actions of the hypothalamo-pituitary-adrenal (HPA) axis in adult life that play a major role in determining the rate of brain and body aging. Increased HPA activity is associated with increased brain aging, whereas the opposite is true of animals with reduced HPA reactivity to novel situations. Rats with increased HPA reactivity show early decline of cognitive functions associated with the hippocampus (Dellu, Mayo, Vallee, LeMoal, & Simon, 1994) as well as increased propensity to self-administer drugs such as amphetamine and cocaine (Deroche, Piazza, LeMoal, & Simon, 1993; Piazza et al., 1994). In contrast, rats with a lower HPA reactivity as a result of neonatal handling have a slower rate of cognitive aging and a reduced loss of hippocampal neurons and function (Catalani et al., 1993; Meaney et al., 1994).

## Plasticity of the Adult Brain

The hippocampus is an important brain structure for spatial and declarative memory in animals and humans, as well as for memory for "context" in which positive and negative experiences have taken place (Eichenbaum & Otto, 1992; LeDoux, 1995). The hippocampus is also a vulnerable, as well as plastic, brain structure as far as sensitivity to epilepsy, ischemia, head trauma, stress, and aging (Sapolsky, 1992). Moreover, the hippocampus displays a variety of reversible changes in function and morphology as a result of the actions of circulating hormones and endogenous neurotransmitters (see figure 9.2).

### Functional and Structural Plasticity of Hippocampal Neurons

Rapid and reversible changes in hippocampal excitability of hippocampal neurons are brought about by repetitive stimulation, leading to long-term potentiation (LTP) and long-term depression (LTD) of synaptic reactivity to subsequent stimulation (Bliss & Lomo, 1973; Mulkey, Endo, Shenolikar, & Malenka, 1994). Adrenal steroid hormones modulate LTP and LTD (Coussens, Kerr, & Abraham, 1997; Diamond, Bennett, Fleshner, & Rose, 1992; Fehm, & Born, 1991; Kerr, Huggett, & Abraham, 1994; Pavlides, Kimura, Magarinos, & McEwen, 1994; Pavlides, Kimura, Magarinos, & McEwen, 1995; Pavlides, Ogawa, Kimura, & McEwen, 1996; Pavlides, Watanabe, Magarinos, & McEwen, 1995), as well as other aspects of hippocampal excitablity (Joels, 1997). Adrenal steroids produce biphasic effects on excitability that may help explain diurnal variations in hippocampal function (Barnes, McNaughton, Goddard, Douglas, & Adams, 1977; Dana & Martinez, 1984; Diamond et al., 1992), as well as both stimulatory and inhibitory effects of stress hormones on learning and memory (Lupien & McEwen, 1997). Stress exerts inhibitory effects

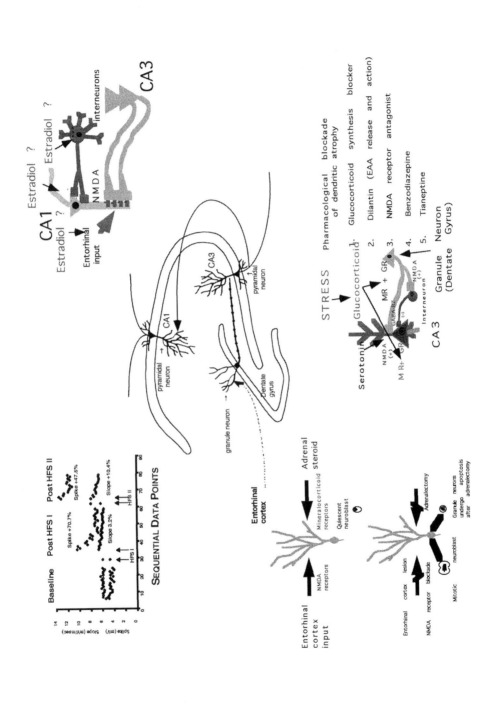

Estradiol ?
Estradiol ?
CA1
Estradiol ?
interneurons
CA3
Entorhinal
input
NMDA

CA1
pyramidal
neuron
CA3
pyramidal
neuron
granule
neuron
Dentate
gyrus

STRESS
Serotonin
Glucocorticoid
MiR + GR
M R+
GR
NMDA
(+)
GABA-IN
NMDA
(+)
Interneuron
(+)
CA3
Granule
Neuron
(Dentate
Gyrus)

Pharmacological blockade
of dendritic atrophy
Glucocorticoid synthesis blocker
2. Dilantin (EAA release and action)
3. NMDA receptor antagonist
4. Benzodiazepine
5. Tianeptine

Baseline    Post HFS I    Post HFS II
Spike +70.7%    Spike +47.6%
Slope 3.2%    Slope +10.4%
HFS II
HFS I
SEQUENTIAL DATA POINTS
Spike (mV)
Slope (mV/msec)

Entorhinal
cortex

Entorhinal
cortex
input
Adrenal
steroid
NMDA
receptors
Mineralocorticoid
receptors
Quiescent
neuroblast

Entorhinal
cortex lesion
Adrenalectomy
NMDA
receptor blockade
Mitotic
neuroblast
Granule neurons
undergo apoptosis
after adrenalectomy

on hippocampal excitability, acting in part through adrenal steroids (Diamond, Bennett, Engstrom, Fleshner, & Rose, 1989; Diamond, Fleshner, Ingersoll, & Rose, 1996; Diamond, Fleshner, & Rose, 1994), as well as through endogenous opioid peptides in the case of painful stress (Shors, Levine, & Thompson, 1990; Shors, Seib, Levine, & Thompson, 1989).

Repeated stress leads to atrophy of dendrites of neurons in the CA3 region of the hippocampus. These neurons receive a powerful excitatory input from the dentate gyrus, and the repetitive stimulation of this input in epilepsy causes some CA3 pyramidal neurons to die. The stress effect to cause atrophy of apical dendrites of these neurons appears to be a milder reaction to repeated stimulation, and over the course of 3–5 weeks of repeated stress the dendritic atrophy or remodeling is largely reversible (Conrad, Magarinos, Ledoux, McEwen, 1998; McEwen, Albeck, et al., 1995). On the other hand, prolonged psychosocial stress has been shown to result in permanent loss of CA3 pyramidal neurons in subordinate animals (Uno, Ross, Else, Suleman, & Sapolsky, 1989).

The atrophy of dendrites and the ultimate neuronal loss are mediated by adrenal steroids acting together with excitatory amino acids and a number of other neurotransmitters, including serotonin (McEwen, 1997). Dendritic remodeling, which consists of an atrophy and reduction of dendritic branching and length of the apical, but not of the basal, dendrites, is produced by repeated restraint stress in rats and repeated psychosocial stress in tree shrews (Magarinos, McEwen, Flugge, & Fuchs, 1996). The atrophy is mimicked by systemic glucocorticoid administration and can be blocked by inhibiting adrenal steroid synthesis, by blocking NMDA receptors, by blocking sodium channels with phenytoin, and by the atypical tricyclic antidepressant tianeptine, which suggests an involvement of serotonin (McEwen, Albeck, et al., 1995). The atrophy, which is reversible over 7–10d after the end of stress (Conrad et al., 1998), is associated with impairments of hippocampus-dependent spatial learning tasks (Conrad, Galea, Kuroda, & McEwen, 1996; Luine, Villegas, Martinez, & McEwen, 1994). The atrophy of dendrites in animal models may be related to atrophy of the human hippocampus determined by MRI in recurrent depressive illness (Sheline, Wang, Gado, Csernansky, & Vannier, 1996), posttraumatic stress disorder (Bremner et al., 1995; Bremner et al., 1997), Cushing's syndrome (Starkman, Gebarski, Berent, & Schteingart, 1992), and mild cognitive impairment in aging (Convit et al., 1997; Golomb et al., 1994).

Another type of plasticity within the hippocampus involves the production of new nerve cells within the dentate gyrus. Neurogenesis in this brain region continues throughout adult life and is regulated by adrenal steroids and excitatory

---

Figure 9.2. Summary of forms of plasticity in the hippocampus. Upper left: Adrenal steroids acutely modulate excitability of hippocampal neurons and biphasically modulate long-term potentiation. Lower left: Adrenal steroids contain neurogenesis and neuronal apoptosis of dentate gyrus granule neurons. Lower right: Adrenal steroids mediate stress-induced remodelling of dendrites of CA3 pyramidal neurons. Upper right: Estradiol and progesterone regulate the formation of excitatory synapses on spines of CA1 pyramidal neurons. All of these actions of steroid hormones involve interactions with excitatory amino acids acting through NMDA receptors (see text).

amino acids (Cameron, McEwen, & Gould, 1995). The size and neuron number within the dentate gyrus can be made to increase and decrease. An enriched environment increases dentate gyrus neuron number by a process that prolongs neuron survival (Kempermann, Kuhn, & Gage, 1997), whereas stress suppresses neurogenesis and can reduce dentate gyrus volume either by reducing neuron number or by reducing the branching of dendrites (Fuchs, Flugge, McEwen, Tanapat, & Gould, 1997). Whereas neurogenesis in the adult dentate gyrus was originally discovered in rodents, it has recently been found in the tree shrew and in the marmoset (Gould, McEwen, Tanapat, Galea, & Fuchs, 1997; Gould, Tanapat, McEwen, Flugge, & Fuchs, 1997), making it more likely that such a form of plasticity may also operate in the adult human brain. In small mammals that show seasonal changes in their behavior, seasonal changes in the size and functional capacity of the hippocampus may be involved (Cameron et al., 1995; Gould & McEwen, 1993).

A third type of structural plasticity in the hippocampus involves the formation of new synaptic connections between nerve cells in the CA1 region of the hippocampus of female rats under the control of ovarian hormones (McEwen, Gould, et al., 1995; Woolley & McEwen, 1994). Synapse formation and breakdown occurs during the 5d estrous cycle of the female rat, with the rising levels of estradiol causing formation of new synaptic connections and the surge of progesterone at the time of ovulation precipitating a rapid (12h) down-regulation of the newly formed synapses. Although we do not know whether the same process occurs in humans, there is evidence from neuropsychological testing that verbal memory tasks, known to depend on the hippocampus and temporal lobe, are very sensitive to estrogen absence or presence (Sherwin, 1994; Sherwin & Tulandi, 1996).

## Mechanisms for Plasticity of the Hippocampus

The hippocampus is a target brain area for the actions of hormones of the steroid/ thyroid hormone family (McEwen, Albeck, et al., 1995; McEwen, Gould, et al., 1995), which traditionally have been thought to work by regulating gene expression (Miner & Yamamoto, 1991). "Genomic" actions of steroid hormones involve intracellular receptors, whereas "nongenomic" effects of steroids involve putative cell surface receptors (McEwen, 1991a). Although this distinction is valid, it does not go far enough in addressing the variety of mechanisms that steroid hormones use to produce their effects on cells. This is because cell surface receptors may signal changes in gene expression, while genomic actions sometimes affect neuronal excitability, often doing so quite rapidly (Orchinik & McEwen, 1995).

Moreover, steroid hormones and neurotransmitters may operate together to produce effects, and sometimes these effects involve collaborations between groups of neurons (see figure 9.2). For example, a number of steroid actions in the hippocampus, described previously, involve the coparticipation of excitatory amino acids acting through NMDA receptors (McEwen, Albeck, et al., 1995; McEwen, Gould, et al., 1995). These interactions are evident for the regulation of synaptogenesis by estradiol in the CA1 pyramidal neurons of hippocampus (Gazzaley, Weiland, McEwen, & Morrison, 1996; Woolley, Gould, Frankfurt, & McEwen, 1990; Woolley, Weiland, McEwen, & Schwartzkroin, 1997) and for the induction of dendritic atrophy of CA3 neurons by repeated stress as well as by glucocorticoid injections (McEwen, Albeck, et al., 1995). Estrogen-regulated synaptogenesis is a cyclic event in the 4–5d estrous cycle of the female rat, whereas stress-induced atrophy of dendrites is slower, taking almost 3 weeks to occur and 7–10d to reverse itself. However, atrophy of dendrites of CA3 pyramidal neurons has been reported as a result of hibernation in squirrels and hamsters, and the reversal of this atrophy has been found in 1–2h after waking the animals (Magarinos, McEwen, & Pevet, in press; Popov, Bocharova, & Bragin, 1992). In addition to synaptic and dendritic plasticity, neurogenesis in the adult and developing dentate gyrus is also regulated by NMDA receptors working together with adrenal steroids (Cameron et al., 1995; Gould, Tanapat, & Cameron, 1997).

In each of these three examples of plasticity in the rat hippocampus, NMDA receptors are involved (Cameron & Gould, 1995; McEwen, Albeck, et al., 1995; McEwen, Gould, et al., 1995). Thus neurotransmission interacts with the endocrine system to regulate the structure and function of both developing and adult brain cells. One of the implications of this interaction is that experiences which cause hormone secretion and alter neural activity can govern brain structural and functional changes and they do so synergistically.

## Implications of the Plasticity and Vulnerability of the Brain for Health and Disease

### Importance of the Brain for Coping with the Environment

The brain, and in particular the limbic system, including the hippocampus, amygdala, and medial prefrontal cortex, plays a pivotal role in processing of psychosocial experiences and in determining behavioral responses. Important functions of the hippocampus and amygdala involve episodic memory and memory of emotionally-laden events, respectively, and of the context in which they have occurred (LeDoux, 1996; Phillips & LeDoux, 1992). As a result, the health and functional capacity of the brain is an essential factor in human behavior and health, because if the brain fails to perform its memory functions adequately or is programmed to overreact to certain stimuli, as in posttraumatic stress disorder, then aberrant or inappropriate behavior is likely to result. One outcome of such failure is captured in the popular adage: "Stress makes you stupid." Moreover, the forms of adult structural plasticity that have been found thus far in the hippocampus may be indicative of similar processes that occurr in other brain regions that are important for affect and cognition, such as the medial prefrontal cortex, where atrophy has been found in humans who suffer from depressive illness (Drevets et al., 1997). Another brain structure that plays an important role in cognitive function and, in particular, in the memory of events that have a strong emotional context is the amygdala (LeDoux, 1996). Fear and anxiety are an important component of chronic stress in humans (Schulkin, McEwen, & Gold, 1994).

### Homeostasis, Allostasis, and Allostatic Load

Memories of and responses to emotionally charged events are an important determinant of neuroendocrine and neural stress responses, and it is the stress hormones that produce changes in the body and brain that constitute adaptation under some conditions and also exacerbate pathophysiology that leads to disease (McEwen, 1997). What is stressful to one individual is not necessarily stressful to another, and prior experience plays an important role (Lazarus & Folkman, 1984; McEwen & Stellar, 1993). But how are stressful experiences related to health and disease? Physiological systems maintain a dynamic balance in the face of environmental challenges. Homeostasis, a term coined in the era of classical thermodynamics, has been replaced by allostasis, referring to "stability through change" (Sterling & Eyer, 1988), and it reflects modern open-system thermodynamics in which the "steady state" replaces "equilibrium." Physiological systems operate within a dynamic range of steady states, being higher at some times of day or as pushed by ongoing events, and yet they maintain internal balance.

During allostasis, physiological systems sometimes work for periods of time at higher or lower levels than average, and the increased activity of these systems can accelerate pathological processes if the elevation occurs chronically over long times. This is because the products of the elevated activity produce various effects on tissue of the body. This has been termed "allostatic load" (McEwen, 1998; McEwen & Stellar, 1993), and allostatic load is a better description for the sometimes subtle long-term influences that can compromise health than is the term *chronic stress,* which evokes images of more dramatic physiological changes than are actually needed to accelerate disease processes. In fact, very subtle increases in the operation of stress hormone secretion can lead, over long periods of time, to pathophysiological changes (McEwen, 1997). Chronic stress comprises only one of four situations that exemplify allostatic load (see figure 9.3). As shown in this figure, the other situations include the failure to habituate to the same repeated stressor, the delayed shutdown of stress responses after the stressor is eliminated, and the failure to mount an adequate allostatic response to a challenge.

Examples of allostatic load include fat deposition and progression toward diabetes and atherosclerosis, each of which is accelerated by dietary factors and by stressful events (McEwen, 1998; McEwen & Stellar, 1993). Chronic psychosocial stress elevates blood pressure and promotes atherosclerosis in cynomologous monkeys (Manuck, Kaplan, Muldoon, Adams, & Clarkson, 1991; Manuck, Kaplan, Adams, & Clarkson, 1988), and there is some evidence that lack of control on the job may have a similar effect in humans (Bosma et al., 1997; Everson et al., 1997; Marmot, Basma, Hemingway, Brunner, & Stansfeld, 1997). Chronically elevated levels of stress hormones of 10 percent or so in depressive illness are associated with calcium loss from bone (Michelson et al., 1996). Likewise, as noted previously, long-term actions of psychosocial stress, mediated by stress hormones and excitatory amino acids, cause hippocampal damage and cognitive impairment, and there is evidence for more rapid brain aging in rats that are intrinsically more reactive to novelty and that show greater stress hormones response (see above). In contrast, rats that are less reactive to novelty show evidence of slower brain aging (Meaney et al., 1994). There is now new evidence in humans for allostatic load on human cognitive function with increasing age (Lupien et al., 1994; see also McEwen & Sapolsky, 1995). In each of these examples, early experience, as well as the process of sexual differentiation, all play a role in determining an individual's susceptibility.

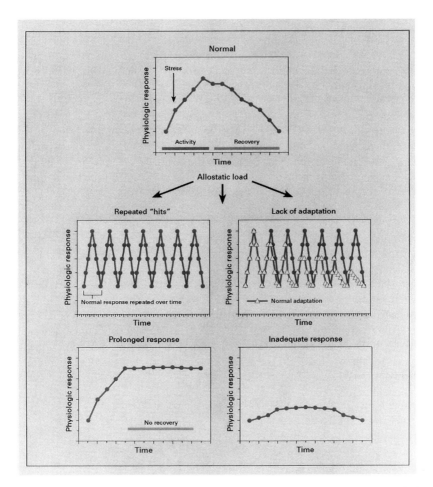

Figure 9.3. Four types of allostatic load. The top panel illustrates the normal allostatic response, in which a response is initiated by a stressor, sustained for an appropriate interval, and then turned off. The remaining panels illustrate four conditions that lead to allostatic load: *repeated "hits"* (multiple novel stressors); *lack of adaptation* to repetitions of the same stressor; *prolonged response* (delayed shutdown); and *inadequate response* that leads to compensatory hyperactivity of other mediators (e.g., inadequate secretion of glucocorticoid, resulting in increased levels of cytokines that are normally counterregulated by glucocorticoids). Figure drawn by Firdaus Dhabhar, Rockefeller University. From McEwen (1998). Copyright 1998 by *New England Journal of Medicine*. Reprinted by permission.

Importance of Sex Differences

Sex differences in brain structures and mechanisms occur in other brain regions besides the hypothalamus, such as the hippocampus, and they appear to be involved in aspects of cognitive function and other processes that go beyond the reproductive process itself, such as the higher incidence of depression in women and of substance abuse in males (Regier et al., 1988). There are also sex differences in the severity of brain damage that results from transient ischemia (Hall, Pazara, & Linseman, 1991) and sex differences in the response of the brain to lesions (Morse, Dekosky, & Scheff, 1992) and to severe chronic stress (Mizoguchi, Kunishita, Chui, & Tabira, 1992; Uno et al., 1989).

Genetic Traits as Risk Factors for Allostatic Load

So far we have neglected discussing genotype as a factor involved in determining individual differences. There is no question that the genetic traits are important in this regard, and genes that underlie diabetes, atherosclerosis, obesity, and susceptibility to depressive illness, schizophrenia, and Alzheimer's disease increase the risk that experiences and other aspects of the lifelong environment will ultimately produce disease. In other words, genetic traits contribute to allostatic load by making it more potent in certain individuals. However, it is not sufficient simply to find and describe the genes responsible for diseases; rather it is necessary to understand how these genes are involved in the pathophysiology of disease and, in particular, how they are regulated.

## Psychosocial Determinants of Health

Psychosocial interactions and social hierarchies appear to be powerful determinants of allostatic load, not only in animal societies but also in human societies, where there are reported gradients of health and disease across the entire spectrum of socioeconomic status (Adler, Boyce, Chesney, Folkman, & Syme, 1993). These gradients involve cardiovascular disease, abdominal obesity, osteoarthritis, chronic diseases, and cervical cancer (Adler et al., 1994). Moreover, the collapse of social systems, as occurred in Russia with the collapse of Communism, has increased mortality from suicide, homicide, alcoholism, and cardiovascular disease among Russian men (Bobak & Marmot, 1996).

Social interactions regulate neuroendocrine function, and social support is related to lower levels of adrenocortical activity (see Seeman & McEwen, 1996). The repeated psychosocial stress of being subordinate has been reported, in tree shrews, to cause dendritic atrophy in the hippocampus and, in vervet monkeys, to cause actual loss of hippocampal neurons (Fuchs, Uno, & Flugge, 1995; Uno et al., 1989). Psychosocial stress produces an allostatic load in cynomologous monkeys that increases atherosclerosis in dominant males in unstable social hierarchies (Manuck, Kaplan, Adams, & Clarkson, 1995) and in subordinate females (Shively & Clarkson, 1994). These are some examples of what further investigation may show is a wide range of psychosocial and environmental influences that create allostatic load and alter the progression toward disease.

## Allostatic Load in Children

If allostatic load were to begin in early development, it could have ramifications for many aspects of later life. A prime example is the phenomenon of low birth weight and its association with later cardiovascular disease, as well as Type II diabetes (Barker, 1997). Undernutrition and prenatal stress are possible causes of this condition (Barker, 1997), with the glucocorticoid enhancement of placental CRF production possibly contributing to the termination of pregnancy under some conditions (Robinson, Emanuel, Frim, & Majzoub, 1988). Prenatal stress is known to impair motor development and possibly other functions in infant primates (Schneider & Coe, 1993). It is, however, not clearly established that there are long-lasting effects of prenatal stress in primates, including humans, as there appear to be in rats (see pp. 6–7).

The condition of extreme shyness is associated with emotional problems, including loneliness, depression, social anxiety, and low self-esteem (Schmidt & Fox, 1995). Psychosomatic problems such as allergies and gastrointestinal disturbances, are also associated with extreme shyness (Bell, Jasnoski, Kagan, & King, 1990; Kagan, Snidman, Julia-Sellers, & Johnson, 1991; Schmidt & Fox, 1995). There is also a report of altered heart rate variability in shy children (Snidman, Kagan, Riordan, & Shannon, 1995). As life progresses, shyness has been associated with hypertension and increased cardiovascular disease and elevated thyroid disease in adult men, as well as lower HDL cholesterol and higher triglycerides in both sexes (Bell et al., 1993). Thus allostatic load appears to be increased by shyness, at least in markers related to cardiovascular disease. Further studies are in order to elaborate on this issue.

## Conclusion

The lifelong interplay between genes and the environment is instrumental in shaping the structure and function of the body, and this chapter reveals some of the new information indicating that the brain is a plastic and ever-changing organ of the body and is very much influenced by life experiences. Many of the processes that determine lifelong patterns of response begin early in development and are programmed by experience, acting in part through the secretion of hormones. These processes affect many structures in the brain, and we are beginning to uncover some of the events in the amygdala, hippocampus, and medial prefrontal cortex that may be responsible for lifelong patterns of emotionality and which may, in turn, increase the risk for depressive illness, as well as the rate of brain aging. In addition, traumatic events early in life, or even later in life, have been shown to affect the volume of the hippocampal formation, further emphasizing the direct impact of experiences on brain structure and function.

Key brain areas such as the hippocampus and amygdala are vital to the processing of information that affects how each individual adapts to and responds to life events, and the response of the brain through its control of endocrine and autonomic function in turn determines the degree of allostatic load that an individual will experience. The allostatic load, in turn, interacts with intrinsic genetic susceptibility to determine the progression toward declining health. It seems very likely that the condition of extreme fear and shyness contributes to a lifelong pattern of allostatic load and that structural and functional correlates will be found to exist in the brains of those individuals who are extremely shy and fearful. Other chapters in this volume deal more specifically with the role of extreme fear and shyness in successful and unsuccessful adaptation and risk for disease over the life course.

*References*

Ader, R. (1968). Effects of early experiences on emotional and physiological reactivity in the rat. *Journal of Comparative and Physiological Psychology, 66,* 264–268.
Adler, N., Boyce, W. T., Chesney, M., Folkman, S., & Syme, L. (1993). Socioeconomic inequalities in health: No easy solution. *Jounal of the American Medical Association, 269,* 3140–3145.
Adler, N. E., Boyce, W. T., Chesney, M. A., Cohen, S., Folkman, S., Kahn, R. L., & Syme, L. S. (1994). Socioeconomic status and health: The challenge of the gradient. *American Psychologist, 49,* 15–24.
Allen, L., & Gorski, R. (1991). Sexual dimorphism of the anterior commissure and massa intermedia of the human brain. *Journal of Comparative Neurology, 312,* 97–104.
Allen, L., & Gorski, R. (1993). Sexual orientation and the size of the anterior commissure in the human brain. *Proceedings of the National Academy of Science, USA, 89,* 7199–7202.
Allen, L. S., Richey, M. F., Chai, Y. M., & Gorski, R. A. (1991). Sex differences in the corpus callosum of the living human being. *Journal of Neuroscience, 11,* 933–942.
Altmann, J. (1980). *Baboon mothers and infants.* Cambridge, MA: Harvard University Press.
Barbazanges, A., Piazza, V. P., Le Moal, M., & Maccari, S. (1996). Maternal glucocorticoid secretion mediates long-term effects of prenatal stress. *Journal of Neuroscience, 15,* 3943.
Barbazanges, A., Vallee, M., Mayo, W., Day, J., Simon, H., Le Moal, M., & Maccari, S. (1996). Early and later adoptions have different long-term effects on male rat offspring. *Journal of Neuroscience, 16,* 7783–7790.
Barker, D. J. P. (1997). The fetal origins of coronary heart disease. *Acta Paediatric Supplement, 422,* 78–82.
Barnes, C. A., McNaughton, B. L., Goddard, G. V., Douglas, R. M., & Adams, R. (1977). Circadian rhythm of synaptic excitability in rat and monkey central nervous system. *Science, 19,* 91–92.
Bell, I. R., Jasnoski, M. L., Kagan, J., & King, D. S. (1990). Is allergic rhinitis more frequent in young adults with extreme shyness? A preliminary survey. *Psychosomatic Medicine, 52,* 517–525.
Bell, I. R., Martino, G. M., Meredith, K. E., Schwartz, G. E., Siani, M. M., & Morrow, F. D. (1993). Vascular disease risk factors, urinary free cortisol, and health histories in older adults: Shyness and gender interactions. *Biological Psychiatry, 35,* 37–49.
Bliss, T. V. P., & Lomo, T. (1973). Long-lasting potentiation of synaptic transmission in the dentate area of the anaesthetized rabbit following stimulation of the perforant path. *Journal of Physiology, 232,* 331–356.
Bobak, M., & Marmot, M. (1996). East-West mortality divide and its potential explanations: Proposed research agenda. *British Medical Journal, 312,* 421–425.
Bosma, H., Marmot, M. G., Hemingway, H., Nicholson, A. C., Brunner, E., & Stansfeld, S. A. (1997). Low job control and risk of coronary heart disease in Whitehall II (prospective cohort) study. *British Medical Journal, 314,* 558–565.

Bremner, J. D., Randall, P., Scott, T. M., Bronen, R. A., Seibyl, J. P., Southwick, S. M., Delaney, R. C., McCarthy, G., Charney, D. S., & Innis, R. B. (1995). MRI-based measurement of hippocampal volume in patients with combat-related posttraumatic stress disorder. *American Journal of Psychiatry, 152,* 973–981.

Bremner, J. D., Randall, P., Vermetten, E., Staib, L., Bronen, R. A., Mazure, C., Capelli, S., McCarthy, G., Innis, R. B., & Charney, D. S. (1997). Magnetic resonance imaging-based measurement of hippocampal volume in posttraumatic stress disorder related to childhood physical and sexual abuse—A preliminary report. *Biological Psychiatry, 41,* 23–32.

Cameron, H. A., & Gould, E. (1995). The control of neuronal birth and death. In C. Shaw (Ed.), *Receptor dynamics in neural development.* Boca Raton, FL: CRC Press.

Cameron, H. A., McEwen, B. S., & Gould, E. (1995). Regulation of adult neurogenesis by excitatory input and NMDA receptor activation in the dentate gyrus. *Journal of Neuroscience, 15,* 4687–4692.

Catalani, A., Marinelli, M., Scaccianoce, S., Nicolai, R., Muscolo, L. A. A., Porcu, A., Koranyi, L., Piazza, P. V., & Angelucci, L. (1993). Progeny of mothers drinking corticosterone during lactation has lower stress-induced corticosterone secretion and better cognitive performance. *Brain Research, 624,* 209–215.

Conrad, C. D., Galea, L. A. M., Kuroda, Y., & McEwen, B. S. (1996). Chronic stress impairs rat spatial memory on the Y-maze and this effect is blocked by tianeptine pretreatment. *Behavioral Neuroscience, 110,* 1321–1334.

Conrad, C., Magarinos, A.-M., Ledoux, J., & McEwen, B. S. (1998). Unpublished data.

Convit, A., de Leon, M. J., Tarshish, C., De Santi, S., Tsui, W., Rusinek, H., & George, A. (1997). Specific hippocampal volume reductions in individuals at risk for Alzheimer's disease. *Neurobiology of Aging, 18,* 131–138.

Coussens, C. M., Kerr, D. S., & Abraham, W. C. (1997). Glucocorticoid receptor activation lowers the threshold for NMDA-receptor-dependent homosynaptic long-term depression in the hippocampus through activation of voltage-dependent calcium channels. *Journal of Neurophysiology. 78,* 1–9.

Dana, R. C., & Martinez, J. L. (1984). Effect of adrenalectomy on the circadian rhythm of LTP. *Brain Research, 308,* 392–395.

Dellu, F., Mayo, W., Vallee, M., LeMoal, M., & Simon, H. (1994). Reactivity to novelty during youth as a predictive factor of cognitive impairment in the elderly: A longitudinal study in rats. *Brain Research, 653,* 51–56.

Denenberg, V. H., & Haltmeyer, G. C. (1967). Test of the monotonicity hypothesis concerning infantile stimulation and emotional reactivity. *Journal of Comparative and Physiological Psychology, 63,* 394–396.

Denenberg, V. H., & Rosenberg, K. M. (1967). Nongenetic transmission of information. *Nature, 216,* 549–550.

Deroche, V., Piazza, P. V., LeMoal, M., & Simon, H. (1993). Individual differences in the psychomotor effects of morphine are predicted by reactivity to novelty and influenced by corticosterone secretion. *Brain Research, 623* 341–344.

Diamond, D., Bennett, M., Engstrom, D., Fleshner, M., & Rose, G. (1989). Adrenalectomy reduces the threshold for hippocampal primed burst potentiation in the anesthetized rat. *Brain Research, 492,* 356–360.

Diamond, D. M., Bennett, M. C., Fleshner, M., & Rose, G. M. (1992). Inverted-U relationship between the level of peripheral corticosterone and the magnitude of hippocampal primed burst potentiation. *Hippocampus, 2,* 421–430.

Diamond, D. M., Fleshner, M., Ingersoll, N., & Rose, G. M. (1996). Psychological stress impairs spatial working memory: Relevance to electrophysiological studies of hippocampal function. *Behavioral Neuroscience, 110,* 661–672.

Diamond, D. M., Fleshner, M., & Rose, G. M. (1994). Psychological stress repeatedly blocks hippocampal primed burst potentiation in behaving rats. *Behavioural Brain Research, 62,* 1–9.

Drevets, W. C., Price, J. L., Simpson, J. R., Jr., Todd, R. D., Reich, T., Vannier, M., & Ralchle, M. E. (1997). Subgenual prefrontal cortex abnormalities in mood disorders. *Nature, 386,* 824–827.

Eichenbaum, H., & Otto, T. (1992). The hippocampus—what does it do? *Behavioural Neural Biology, 57,* 2–36.

Everson, S. A., Lynch, J. W., Chesney, M. A., Kaplan, G. A., Goldberg, D. E., Shade, S. B., Cohen, R. D., Salonen, R., & Salonen, J. T. (1997). Interaction of workplace demands and cardiovascular reactivity in progression of carotid atherosclerosis: Population based study. *British Medical Journal, 314,* 553–558.

Fehm, H., & Born, J. (1991). Evidence for entrainment of nocturnal cortisol secretion to sleep processes in human beings. *Neuroendocrinology, 53,* 171–176.

Forger, N. G., & Breedlove, S. M. (1991). Steroid influences on a mammalian neuromuscular system. *Seminars in the Neurosciences, 3,* 459–468.

Fride, E., Dan, Y., Feldon, J., Halevy, G., & Weinstock, M. (1986). Effects of prenatal stress on vulnerability to stress in prepubertal and adult rats. *Physiological Behavior, 37,* 681–687.

Fuchs, E., Flugge, G., McEwen, B. S., Tanapat, P., & Gould, E. (1997). Chronic subordination stress inhibits neurogenesis and decreases the volume of the granule cell layer. *Society for Neuroscience Abstracts, 23,* 317.

Fuchs, E., Uno, H., & Flugge, G. (1995). Chronic psychosocial stress induces morphological alterations in hippocampal pyramidal neurons of the tree shrew. *Brain Research, 673,* 275–282.

Gazzaley, A. H., Weiland, N. G., McEwen, B. S., & Morrison, J. H. (1996). Differential regulation of NMDAR1 mRNA and protein by estradiol in the rat hippocampus. *Journal of Neuroscience, 16,* 6830–6838.

Golomb, J., Kluger, A., de Leon, M. J., Ferris, S. H., Convit, A., Mittelman, M. S., Cohen, J., Rusinek, H., De Santi, S., & George, A. E. (1994). Hippocampal formation size in normal human aging: A correlate of delayed secondary memory performance. *Learning and Memory, 1,* 45–54.

Gould, E., & McEwen, B. S. (1993). Neuronal birth and death. *Current Opinion in Neurobiology, 3,* 676–682.

Gould, E., McEwen, B. S., Tanapat, P., Galea, L. A. M., & Fuchs, E. (1997). Neurogenesis in the dentate gyrus of the adult tree shrew is regulated by psychosocial stress and NMDA receptor activation. *Journal of Neuroscience, 17,* 2492–2498.

Gould, E., Tanapat, P., & Cameron, H. A. (1997). Adrenal steroids suppress granule cell death in the developing dentate gyrus through an NMDA receptor-dependent mechanism. *Developmental Brain Research, 103,* 91–93.

Gould, E., Tanapat, P., McEwen, B. S., Flugge, G., & Fuchs, E. (1997). Neurogenesis in the dentate gyrus of adult primates can be suppressed by stress. *Society for Neuroscience Abstracts, 23,* 316.

Gould, E., Westlind-Danielsson, A., Frankfurt, M., & McEwen, B. S. (1990). Sex differences and thyroid hormone sensitivity of hippocampal pyramidal neurons. *Journal Neuroscience, 10,* 996–1003.

Gould, E., Woolley, C., & McEwen, B. S. (1991). The hippocampal formation: Morphological changes induced by thyroid, gonadal and adrenal hormones. *Psychoneuroendocrinology, 16,* 67–84.

Hall, E. D., Pazara, K. E., & Linseman, K. L. (1991). Sex differences in postischemic neuronal necrosis in gerbils. *Journal of Cerebral Blood Flow and Metabolism, 11,* 292–298.

Henry, C., Kabbaj, M., Simon, H., LeMoal, M., & Maccari, S. (1994). Prenatal stress increases the hypothalamo-pituitary-adrenal axis response in young and adult rats. *Journal of Neuroendocrinology, 6,* 341–345.

Joels, M. (1997). Steroid hormones and excitability in the mammalian brain. *Frontiers in Neuroendocrinology, 18,* 2–48.

Kagan, J., Snidman, N., Julia-Sellers, M., & Johnson, M. O. (1991). Temperament and allergic symptoms. *Psychosomatic Medicine, 53,* 332–340.

Kempermann, G., Kuhn, H. G., & Gage, F. H. (1997). More hippocampal neurons in adult mice living in an enriched environment. *Nature, 586,* 493–495.

Kerr, D. S., Huggett, A. M., & Abraham, W. C. (1994). Modulation of hippocampal long-term potentiation and long-term depression by corticosteroid receptor activation. *Psychobiology, 22,* 123–133.

Kimura, D. (1992). Sex differences in the brain. *Scientific American, 267,* 119–125.

Lazarus, R. S., & Folkman, S. (1984). *Stress, appraisal and coping.* New York: Springer Verlag.

LeDoux, J. E. (1995). In search of an emotional system in the brain: Leaping from fear to emotion and consciousness. In M. Gazzaniga (Ed.), *The Cognitive Neurosciences* (pp. 1049–1061). Cambridge, MA: MIT Press.

LeDoux, J. E. (1996). *The emotional brain.* New York: Simon & Schuster.

Levine, S., Haltmeyer, G. C., Karas, G. G., & Denenberg, V. H. (1967). Physiological and behavioral effects of infantile stimulation. *Physiology and Behavior, 2,* 55–59.

Liu, D., Diorio, J., Tannenbaum, B., Caldji, C., Francis, D., Freedman, A., Sharma, S., Pearson, D., Plotsky, P. M., & Meaney, M. J. (1997). Maternal care, hippocampal glucocorticoid receptors, and hypothalamic-pituitary-adrenal responses to stress. *Science, 277,* 1659–1662.

Luine, V., Villegas, M., Martinez, C., & McEwen, B. S. (1994). Repeated stress causes reversible impairments of spatial memory performance. *Brain Research, 639,* 167–170.

Lupien, S., Lecours, A. R., Lussier, I., Schwartz, G., Nair, N. P. V., & Meaney, M. J. (1994). Basal cortisol levels and cognitive deficits in human aging. *Journal of Neuroscience, 14,* 2893–2903.

Lupien, S. J., & McEwen, B. S. (1997). The acute effects of corticosteroids on cognition: Integration of animal and human model studies. *Brain Research Review, 24,* 1–27.

Maccari, S., Piazza, P. V., Kabbaj, M., Barbazanges, A., Simon, H., & LeMoal, M. (1995). Adoption reverses the long-term impairment in glucocorticoid feedback induced by prenatal stress. *Journal of Neuroscience, 15,* 110–116.

Magarinos, A. M., McEwen, B. S., Flugge, G., & Fuchs, E. (1996). Chronic psychosocial stress causes apical dendritic atrophy of hippocampal CA3 pyramidal neurons in subordinate tree shrews. *Journal of Neuroscience, 16,* 3534–3540.

Magarinos, A.-M., McEwen, B. S., & Pevet, P. (In press). Rapid and reversible morphological changes in the apical dendrites of hippocampal CA3 pyramidal neurons during the course of hibernation in European hamsters. *Society for Neuroscience Abstracts.*

Manuck, S. B., Kaplan, J. R., Adams, M. R., & Clarkson, T. B. (1988). Studies of psychosocial influences on coronary artery atherosclerosis in cynomologous monkeys. *Health Psychology, 7,* 113–124.

Manuck, S. B., Kaplan, J. R., Muldoon, M. F., Adams, M. R., & Clarkson, T. B. (1991). The behavioral exacerbation of atherosclerosis and its inhibition by propranolol. In P. M. McCabe, N. Schneiderman, T. M. Field, & J. S. Skyler (Eds.), *Stress, coping, and disease* (pp. 51–72). Hove and London: Erlbaum.

Marmot, M. G., Bosma, H., Hemingway, H., Brunner, E., & Stansfeld, S. A. (1997). Contribution of job control and other risk factors to social variations in coronary heart disease incidence. *Lancet, 350,* 235–239.

McEwen, B. S. (1991a). Steroids affect neural activity by acting on the membrane and the genome. *Trends in Pharmacological Science, 12,* 141–147.

McEwen, B. S. (1991b). Our changing ideas about steroid effects on an ever-changing brain. *Seminars in Neurosciences, 3,* 497–507.

McEwen, B. S. (1997). Possible mechanisms for atrophy of the human hippocampus. *Molecular Psychiatry, 2,* 255–262.

McEwen, B. S. (1998). Protective and damaging effects of stress mediators. *New England Journal of Medicine, 338,* 171–179.

McEwen, B. S., Albeck, D., Cameron, H., Chao, H. M., Gould, E., Hastings, N., Kuroda, Y., Luine, V., Magarinos, A. M., McKittrick, C. R., Orchinik, M., Pavlides, C., Vaher, P., Watanabe, Y., & Weiland, N. (1995). Stress and the brain: A paradoxical role for adrenal steroids. In G. D. Litwack (Ed.), *Vitamins and hormones* (pp. 371–402). Academic Press.

McEwen, B. S., Gould, E., Orchinik, M., Weiland, N. G., & Woolley, C. S. (1995). Oestrogens and the structural and functional plasticity of neurons: Implications for memory, aging and neurodegenerative processes. In J. Goode (Ed.), *CIBA Foundation Symposium: Vol. 191. The Nonreproductive actions of sex steroids* (pp. 52–73). London: CIBA Foundation.

McEwen, B. S., & Sapolsky, R. M. (1995). Stress and cognitive function. *Current Opinion in Neurobiology, 5,* 205–216.

McEwen, B. S., & Stellar, E. (1993). Stress and the individual: Mechanisms leading to disease. *Archives of Internal Medicine, 153,* 2093–2101.

Meaney, M., Aitken, D., Berkel, H., Bhatnager, S., & Sapolsky, R. (1988). Effect of neonatal handlng of age-related impairments associated with the hippocampus. *Science, 239,* 766–768.

Meaney, M., Aitken, D., Bhatnagar, S., & Sapolsky, R. (1991). Postnatal handling attenuates certain neuroendocrine, anatomical and cognitive dysfunctions associated with aging in female rats. *Neurobiological Aging, 12,* 31–38.

Meaney, M., Aitken, D., & Sapolsky, R. (1987). Thyroid hormones influence the development of hippocampal glucocorticoid receptors in the rat: A mechanism for the effects of postnatal handling on the development of the adrenocortical stress response. *Neuroendocrinology, 45,* 278–285.

Meaney, M. J., Diorio, J., Francis, D., Widdowson, J., LaPlante, P., Caldji, C., Sharma, S., Seckl, J. R., & Plotsky, P. M. (1996). Early environmental regulation of forebrain glucocorticoid receptor gene expression: Implications for adrenocortical responses to stress. *Developmental Neuroscience, 18,* 49–72.

Meaney, M. J., Tannenbaum, B., Francis, D., Bhatnagar, S., Shanks, N., Viau, V., O'Donnell, D., & Plotsky, P. M. (1994). Early environmental programming hypothalamic-pituitary-adrenal responses to stress. *Seminars in the Neurosciences, 6,* 247–259.

Michelson, D., Stratakis, C., Hill, L., Reynolds, J., Galliven, E., Chrousos, G., & Gold, P. (1996). Bone mineral density in women with depression. *New England Journal of Medicine, 335,* 1176–1181.

Miner, J. N., & Yamamoto, K. R. (1991). Regulatory crosstalk at composite response elements. *Trends in Biochemical Science, 16,* 423–426.

Mizoguchi, K., Kunishita, T., Chui, D. H., & Tabira, T. (1992). Stress induces neuronal death in the hippocampus of castrated rats. *Neuroscience Letters, 138,* 157–160.

Morse, J. K., Dekosky, S. T., & Scheff, S. W. (1992). Neurotrophic effects of steroids on lesion-induced growth in the hippocampus. *Experimental Neurology, 118,* 47–52.

Mulkey, R. M., Endo, S., Shenolikar, S., & Malenka, R. C. (1994). Involvement of a calcineurin/inhibitor-1 phosphatase cascade in hippocampal long-term depression. *Nature, 369,* 486–488.

Orchinik, M., & McEwen, B. S. (1995). Rapid actions in the brain: a critique of genomic and non-genomic mechanisms. In M. Wehling (Ed.), *Genomic and non-genomic effects of aldosterone* (pp. 77–108). Boca Raton, FL: CRC Press.

Pavlides, C., Kimura, A., Magarinos, A. M., & McEwen, B. S. (1994). Type I adrenal steroid receptors prolong hippocampal long-term potentiation. *NeuroReport, 5,* 2673–2677.

Pavlides, C., Kimura, A., Magarinos, A. M., & McEwen, B. S. (1995). Hippocampal homosynaptic long-term depression/depotentiation induced by adrenal steroids. *Neuroscience, 68,* 379–385.

Pavlides, C., Ogawa, S., Kimura, A., & McEwen, B. S. (1996). Role of adrenal steroid mineralocorticoid and glucocorticoid receptors in long-term potentiation in the CA1 field of hippocampal slices. *Brain Research, 738*, 229–235.

Pavlides, C., Watanabe, Y., Magarinos, A. M., & McEwen, B. S. (1995). Opposing role of adrenal steroid Type I and Type II receptors in hippocampal long-term potentiation. *Neuroscience, 68*, 387–394.

Pavlides, C., Westlind-Danielsson, A., Nyborg, H., & McEwen, B. S. (1991). Neonatal hyperthyroidism disrupts hippocampal LTP and spatial learning. *Experimental Brain Research, 85*, 559–564.

Phillips, R. G., & LeDoux, J. E. (1992). Differential contribution of amygdala and hippocampus to cued and contextual fear conditioning. *Behavioural Neuroscience, 106*, 274–285.

Piazza, P. V., Marinelli, M., Jodogne, C., Deroche, V., Rouge-Pont, F., Maccari, S., LeMoal, M., & Simon, H. (1994). Inhibition of corticosterone synthesis by metyrapone decreases cocaine-induced locomotion and relapse of cocaine self-administration. *Brain Research, 658*, 259–264.

Popov, V. I., Bocharova, L. S., & Bragin, A. G. (1992). Repeated changes of dendritic morphology in the hippocampus of ground squirrels in the course of hibernation. *Neuroscience, 48*, 45–51.

Regier, D. A., Boyd, J. H., Burke, J. D., Rae, D. S., Myers, J. K., Kramer, M., Robbins, L. N., George, L. K., Karno, M,. & Locke, B. Z. (1988). One-month prevalence of mental disorders in the U.S. *Archives of General Psychiatry, 45*, 977–986.

Robinson, B. G., Emanuel, R. L., Frim, D. M., & Majzoub, J. A. (1988). Glucocorticoid stimulates expression of corticotropin-releasing hormone gene in human placenta. *Proceedings of the National Academy of Science USA, 85*, 5244–5248.

Sapolsky, R. (1992). *Stress, the aging brain and the mechanisms of neuron death.* Cambridge, MA: MIT Press.

Schmidt, L. A., & Fox, N. A. (1995). Individual differences in young adults' shyness and sociability: Personality and health correlates. *Personality and Individual Differences, 19*, 455–462.

Schneider, M. L., & Coe, C. L. (1993). Repeated social stress during pregnancy impairs neuromotor development of the primate infant. *Journal of Developmental Behavioral Pediatrics, 14*, 81–67.

Schulkin, J., McEwen, B. S., & Gold, P. W. (1994). Allostasis, amygdala, and anticipatory angst. *Neuroscience and Biobehavioral Review, 18*, 385–396.

Schwegler, H., Crusio, W. E., Lipp, H. P., Brust, I., & Mueller, G. G. (1991). Early postnatal hyperthyroidism alters hippocampal circuitry and improves radial-maze learning in adult mice. *Journal of Neuroscience, 11*, 2102–2106.

Seeman, T. E., & McEwen, B. S. (1996). The impact of social environment characteristics on neuroendocrine regulation. *Psychosomatic Medicine, 58*, 459–471.

Sheline, Y. I., Wang, P. W., Gado, M. H., Csernansky, J. C., & Vannier, M. W. (1996). Hippocampal atrophy in recurrent major depression. *Proceedings of the National Academy of Sciences, 93*, 3908–3913.

Sherwin, B. B. (1994). Estrogenic effects on memory in women. *Annals of the New York Academy of Sciences, 743*, 213–231.

Sherwin, B. B., & Tulandi, T. (1996). "Add-back" estrogen reverses cognitive deficits induced by a gonadotropin-releasing hormone agonist in women with leiomyomata uteri. *Journal of Clinical Endocrinology and Metabolism, 81*, 2545–2549.

Shively, C. A., & Clarkson, T. B. (1994). Social status incongruity and coronary artery atherosclerosis in female monkeys. *Arteriosclerosis and Thrombosis, 14*, 721–726.

Shors, T., Levine, S., & Thompson, R. (1990). Effect of adrenalectomy and demedullation on the stress-induced impairment of long-term potentiation. *Neuroendocrinology, 51*, 70–75.

Shors, T., Seib, T., Levine, S., & Thompson, R. (1989). Inescapable versus escapable shock modulates long-term potentiation in the rat hippocampus. *Science, 244,* 224–226.

Snidman, N., Kagan, J., Riordan, L., & Shannon, D. C. (1995). Cardiac function and behavioral reactivity during infancy. *Psychophysiology, 32,* 199–207.

Starkman, M. N., Gebarski, S. S., Berent, S., & Schteingart, D. E. (1992). Hippocampal formation volume, memory dysfunction, and cortisol levels in patients with Cushing's Syndrome. *Biological Psychiatry, 32,* 756–765.

Sterling, P., & Eyer, J. (1988). Allostasis: A new paradigm to explain arousal pathology. In S. Fisher & J. Reason (Eds.), *Handbook of life stress, cognition and health* (pp. 629–649). New York: Wiley.

Tallal, P., & McEwen, B. (1991). Special Issue: Neuroendocrine effects on brain development and cognition. *Psychoneuroendocrinology, 16,* 1–3.

Uno, H., Ross, T., Else, J., Suleman, M., & Sapolsky, R. (1989). Hippocampal damage associated with prolonged and fatal stress in primates. *Journal of Neuroscience, 9,* 1709–1711.

Vallee, M., Mayo, W., Dellu, F., Le Moal, M., Simon, H., & Maccari, S. (1997). Prenatal stress induces high anxiety and postnatal handling induces low anxiety in adult offspring: Correlation with stress-induced corticosterone secretion. *Journal of Neuroscience, 17,* 2626–2636.

Vallee, M., Mayo, W., Maccari, S., Le Moal, M., & Simon, H. (1996). Long-term effects of prenatal stress and handling on metabolic parameters: Relationship to corticosterone secretion response. *Brain Research, 712,* 287–292.

Westlind-Danielsson, A., Gould, E., & McEwen, B. S. (1991). Thyroid hormone causes sexually distinct neurochemical and morphological alterations in rat septal-diagonal band neurons. *Journal of Neurochemistry, 56,* 119–128.

Williams, C. L., & Meck, W. H. (1991). The organizational effects of gonadal steroids on sexually dimorphic spatial ability. *Psychoneuroendocrinology, 16,* 155–176.

Witelson, S. (1989). Hand and sex differences in the isthmus and genu of the human corpus callosum. *Brain, 112,* 799–835.

Witelson, S. F., Glezer, I. I., & Kigar, D. L. (1995). Women have greater density of neurons in posterior temporal cortex. *Journal of Neuroscience, 15,* 3418–3428.

Woolley, C., Gould, E., Frankfurt, M., & McEwen, B. S. (1990). Naturally occurring fluctuation in dendritic spine density on adult hippocampal pyramidal neurons. *Journal of Neuroscience, 10,* 4035–4039.

Woolley, C., & McEwen, B. S. (1994). Estradiol regulates hippocampal dendritic spine density via an N-methyl-D-aspartate receptor dependent mechanism. *Journal of Neuroscience, 14,* 7680–7687.

Woolley, C. S., Weiland, N. G., McEwen, B. S., & Schwartzkroin, P. A. (1997). Estradiol increases the sensitivity of hippocampal CA1 pyramidal cells to NMDA receptor-mediated synaptic input: Correlation with dendritic spine density. *Journal of Neuroscience, 17,* 1848–1859.

# The Inhibited Child "Syndrome"

### Thoughts on Its Potential Pathogenesis and Sequelae

George P. Chrousos & Philip W. Gold

The preceding chapters eloquently describe the prevailing psychoneuroendocrine state of the inhibited child as one of excessive and prolonged fear. Then they go on to report on the areas and substances of the brain likely to be involved in the generation of fear and, hence, in the pathogenesis of this syndromal state of childhood. The amygdala, hippocampus, and stress system are convincingly implicated, along with corticotropin-releasing hormone (CRH), the proopiomelanocortin (POMC)-derived peptides β-endorphin and α-melanocyte-stimulating hormone (αMSH), the catecholamines norepinephrine, epinephrine, and dopamine, and the end-hormones of the hypothalamic-pituitary-adrenal (HPA) axis, glucocorticoids. The purpose of this commentary is to integrate these data on the inhibited child and the fear response with the clinical views and thoughts of a pediatrician and a psychiatrist with a long-standing interest in stress and diseases associated with dysregulation of the stress system.

In his dialogue "The Republic," Plato described his conception of the human brain or mind (*nous*) as a three-sided construct: The *logisticon,* or cognitive part, the *thymoides,* or feeling part, and the *epithymeticon,* or instinctual part, the latter subserving basic functions, such as eating and reproduction (Simon, 1978). He suggested that both high intellectual and basal animal functions employed the same feeling component of the brain to produce emotions and, hence, influence the actions of an individual. He also proposed that disharmony between these parts of the brain could produce pathologic changes in the personality of a human being and that early life experiences determined a person's personal and intellectual development and fulfillment in adulthood.

Modern concepts have expanded on this highly intuitive edifice, and knowledge accumulated mostly in the twentieth century allows us to construct a theoretical integrated model on the basis of solid factual and inferential evidence

(Chrousos, 1996). The brain is heuristically divided into anatomic and functional parts: The cognitive brain occupies part of the cortex; the emotional brain consists of the mesocorticolimbic dopaminergic system; and the instinctual brain, which subserves many diverse functions, includes areas that generate fear, such as the amygdala, and others that maintain cardiovascular function, growth, and energy metabolism and regulate temperature, reproductive activity, pain perception, and immune function. These areas include the hypothalamus, brainstem, and peripheral nervous system. All the above systems function in concert with each other to assist the individual to preserve her- or himself and the species. The success of these basic, primal goals depends to a great extent on the ability of the brain and the rest of the organism to successfully respond to challenges with proper adaptive behavioral and physical changes.

The behavioral and physical responses of the organism to a stressful stimulus or "stressor" result in a clinical "stress syndrome" that is summarized in table II.1 (Chrousos & Gold, 1992). This syndrome can be experimentally produced in its entirety by activation of the hypothalamic and brainstem centers of the HPA axis and the autonomic nervous system. The neuroanatomical and functional interactions between these central components of the "stress system" and their regulation by the major neurotransmitter systems of the brain are summarized in figure II.1. CRH and norepinephrine are the principal central molecular regulators of the HPA axis and locus ceruleus/norepinephrine-sympathetic system and are responsible for mutual stimulation of the two centers. The stress system interacts with the amygdala, hippocampus, and mesocorticolimbic dopaminergic system and receives inputs from the periphery that concern the metabolic (leptin/NPY), circulatory, pain, and immune/inflammatory status of the individual (Chrousos, 1995, 1996). From this scheme, one sees that the basal activity of the amygdala—hence fear—could influence the activity of the stress system, while the basal activity of the stress system could influence the activity of the amygdala as well. The same is true for the hippocampus, a generator of inhibitory inputs toward the stress system primarily via activation of GABA-ergic neurotransmission. A deficient hippocampus could result in increased activity of the stress system and, hence, of the amygdala, activating the fear response. Finally, acute activation of the stress system alters the activity of the mesocorticolimbic dopaminegic system to produce emotions, while components of the latter exert inhibitory input on the stress system (Chrousos, 1998; Diorio, Viau, & Meaney, 1993; Morgan, Romanski, & LeDoux, 1993). The interrelations between the mesocorticolimbic dopaminergic system, the amygdala, and the stress system are extremely complex. Issues such as lateralization of activity, desensitization by chronic activation, and lability are extremely important. New analytical and imaging techniques will hopefully elucidate this area in the next few years.

The reciprocal crucial interaction between the major brain systems possibly involved in the genesis of the inhibited child syndrome are summarized in figure II.2a. The syndrome may involve a hyperactive or hyperreactive amygdala generating excessive and prolonged fear; an activated stress system generating peripheral physiologic and hormonal responses, such as tachycardia and hypercortisolism; a tachyphylactic or labile mesocorticolimbic dopaminergic system generating dysphoria; and/or a hypoactive hippocampus unable to inhibit and limit the activity of the stress system and amygdala (figure II.2b). This complex in-

Table II.1  The Stress System: Behavioral and Physical Adaptation
During Acute Stress

| Behavioral Adaptation | Physical Adaptation |
| --- | --- |
| *Adaptive Redirection of Behavior* | *Adaptive Redirection of Energy* |
| Increased arousal and alertness | Oxygen and nutrients directed to the CNS and stressed body site(s) |
| Increased cognition, vigilance, and focused attention | Altered cardiovascular tone, increased blood pressure and heart rate |
| Euphoria or dysphoria, depending on context | Increased respiratory rate |
| Suppression of potentially harmful activity (fear[†], flight, withdrawal); or stimulation of potentially beneficial activity (rage, fight), depending on context. | |
| Suppression of appetite and feeding behavior | Increased gluconeogenesis and lipolysis |
| Suppression of reproductive behavior | Detoxification from endogenous or exogenous toxic products |
| Suppression of immunity, $TH_1$ to $TH_2$ shift[*] | Inhibition of growth and reproductive systems |
| Containment of the stress response | Inhibition of digestion-stimulation of colonic motility |
| | Containment of the inflammatory/immune response |
| | Containment of the stress response |

[†]The inhibited child is characterized by an excessive fear response to stressors. [*]Thelper 1-supported cellular immunity; Thelper 2-supported humoral immunity. From Chrousos and Gold (1992), *Journal of the American Medical Association*.

terrelation of the above systems defines the behavioral and physical equanimity of an individual toward challenges (Chrousos, 1997, 1998). A genetically or environmentally altered interrelation, as seen in the inhibited child syndrome (figure II.2b), would be expected to make such a child vulnerable to conditions characterized by a chronically hyperactive or hyperreactive stress system, such as chronic anxiety, melancholic depression, eating disorders, substance and alcohol abuse, juvenile delinquency, personality and conduct disorders, and several psychosomatic diseases, such as generalized organ-specific chronic pain and/or fatigue syndromes (Chrousos, 1997, 1998; Clauw & Chrousos, 1997). A chronically hyperactive stress system, even intermittently, may produce in such patients its predicted somatic sequellae: abnormal growth, components of the metabolic syndrome X, such as visceral obesity, insulin resistance, hypertension, dislipidemia and discoagulation, collectively resulting in cardiovascular disease and osteoporosis (Chrousos, 1998; Johnson et al., 1996; Michelson et al., 1996; Phillips et al., 1998).

Recently, it has become apparent that the above stress-related pathological conditions occur in parallel and in conjunction with each other and in varying combinations and degrees. These states are grounded in a genetic vulnerability which is not simple Mendelian but polygenic and which allows expression of the clinical phenotype in the presence of triggers from the environment. There is no question that there is a very complex genetic background continuum in the population

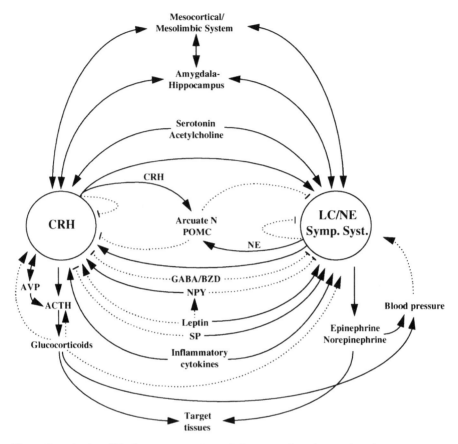

Figure II.1. A simplified representation of the central and peripheral components of the stress system, their functional interrelations, and their relations to other central systems involved in the stress response. CRH-corticotropin-releasing hormone; LC/NE-Symp. Syst., locus ceruleus/norepinephrine-sympathetic system; POMC-proopiomelanocortin; AVP-arginine-vasopressin; GABA-γ-aminobutyric acid; BZD-benzodiazepine; ACTH-corticotropin; NPY-neuropeptide Y; SP-substance P. Activation is represented by solid lines, and inhibition by dashed lines. From Chrousos & Gold (1992), *Journal of the American Medical Association*.

of human beings, from extreme resilience to extreme vulnerability to these stress-related "comorbid" states and that environmental triggers (stressors) of diminishing size would be required to cause expression of these conditions in an individual, progressively on the right side of the continuum (figure II.3, top).

What appears to be of crucial importance is that these environmental triggers or stressors may have not a transient but a permanent effect on the organism, quite reminiscent of the "organizational" effects of several hormones exerted on certain target tissues and lasting well after the exposure to the hormone has ceased. The prenatal and early life periods are particularly sensitive to these permanent effects of stressors and are, hence, "critical" periods, although sufficiently strong stressors

Acute Stress

Stress hyperresponsive
"inhibited" child

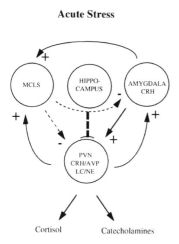

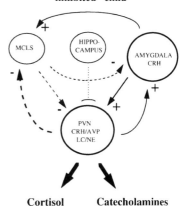

Potential somatic consequences
Growth retardation
Metabolic syndrome X
Cardiovascular disease
Osteoporosis

Figure II.2. Central neurocircuitry in the stress-hyperresponsive/inhibited child leading to a hyperactive stress system as it relates to the central neurocircuitry of the stress response (left). A hyperfunctioning amygdala, hypofunctioning hippocampus, and/or a hypofunctioning mesocorticolimbic dopaminergic system could predispose an individual to anxiety disorders and melancholic depression, along with their somatic consequences (right). Activation is represented by solid lines and inhibition by dashed lines. MCLS = mesocorticolimbic system. From Chrousos (1998), *Annals of the New York Academy of Sciences.*

may have permanent effects on the organism throughout the lifespan, as the existence of adult posttraumatic stress disorder suggests. Nevertheless, it seems that the vulnerability of the subpopulation of human beings to developing one or more of these stress-related states can be altered by exogenous triggers, with adverse stimuli shifting the entire bell-shaped curve of that subpopulation to the right and with a propitious, supportive environment shifting the same curve to the left (figure II.3, right).

The organizational effects of stress appear to be mediated to some extent by two key hormones of the stress system, corticotropin-releasing hormone (CRH) and the glucocorticoids (Coplan et al., 1996; Piazza et al., 1993). Thus, presence of stressors in the prenatal or early postnatal life is associated with concurrent elevations of these and other hormones and alterations in the responsiveness of the stress system, which are permanent and, hence, present for the remaining life of the individual. Proper responsiveness of the stress system to stressors is a crucial prerequisite for sense of well-being, adequate performance of tasks, and positive social interactions. Improper responsiveness has been associated with inadequacies in these functions and increased vulnerability to one or more of the stress-related states. Thus, depending on the genetic background of the individual and the ex-

# GENETIC CONTINUUM

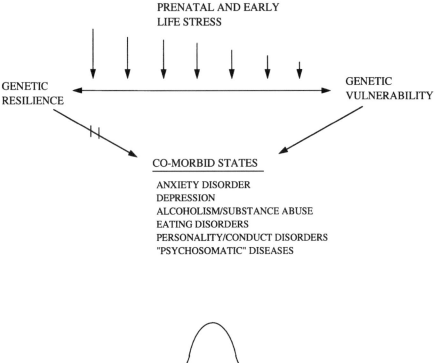

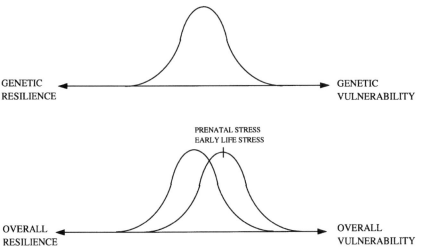

Figure II.3. (Top) The genetic continuum that defines background resiliency-vulnerability to develop one or more common developmental/behavioral states of major epidemiologic and societal impact. The vertical arrows indicate the size of environmental stressors necessary to produce a morbid state. (Bottom) Shift in vulnerability of a subpopulation affected by an early environmental stressor. From Chrousos (1997), *Annals of the New York Academy of Sciences.*

posure of this individual to adverse stimuli in prenatal and early postnatal life, one might develop any of these states in any combination and degree of severity.

These concepts of genetic vulnerability and permanent alterations of this vulnerability by exogenous stimuli at critical periods of life mediated by hormones of the stress system have been amply demonstrated in convincing rodent and non-human primate studies (Coplan et al., 1996; Piazza et al., 1993). Human data appear to agree with the experimental animal studies. An excellent example comes from the study of sexually abused preadolescent girls, who, when studied at least 2 years after the last episode of abuse took place, had changes in their hypothalamic-pituitary-adrenal axis similar to previously characterized changes observed in adult patients with melancholic depression (DeBellis et al., 1994). Interestingly, all young patients studied had mood disorders that ranged from dysthymia to depression at the time of the study. In concordance with these data, there has recently been an epidemiologic association of history of sexual abuse in patients with a psychosomatic disorder and of history of "stressful life events" in patients with melancholic depression (Clauw & Chrousos, 1997; Kendler, Kessler, et al., 1995; Kendler, Walters, et al., 1995; Scarinci, MacDonald-Haile, Bradley, & Richter, 1994). The adverse environmental stimuli in both conditions took place most frequently during the periods of childhood and puberty/adolescence.

In our opinion, the inhibited child "syndrome" is observed in individuals found in the right extreme of a Gaussian population curve (figure II.3b). It is an early-life clinical syndrome of stress system hyperactivity with increased fear sensation as a key manifestation. This syndrome could be due to genetic or early-life-induced abnormalities in the interrelations of the stress system with the amygdala, hippocampus, and mesocorticolimbic system. This syndrome thus appears heterogeneous in its pathogenesis. We believe that, depending on the genetic and constitutional vulnerabilities of the child with this syndrome and on her or his environment in the broad sense, this child may adapt to develop into a healthy, happy, successful adult.

*References*

Chrousos, G. P. (1995). The hypothalamic-pituitary-adrenal axis and immune-mediated inflammation. *New England Journal of Medicine, 332,* 1351–1362.
Chrousos, G. P. (1996). Organization and integration of the endocrine system. In M. Sperling (Ed.), *Pediatric endocrinology* (pp. 1–14). Philadelphia, PA: Saunders.
Chrousos, G. P. (1997). The future of pediatric and adolescent endocrinology. *Annals of the New York Academy of Sciences, 816,* 4–8.
Chrousos, G. P. (1998). Stressors, stress and neuroendocrine integration of the adaptive response. *Annals of the New York Academy of Sciences, 851,* 124–148.
Chrousos, G. P., & Gold, P. W. (1992). The concepts of stress and stress system disorders: Overview of physical and behavioral homeostasis. *Journal of the American Medical Association, 267,* 1244–1252.
Clauw, D. J., & Chrousos, G. P. (1997). Chronic pain and fatigue syndromes: Overlapping clinical and neuroendocrine features and potential pathogenic mechanisms. *NeuroImmunoModulation, 4,* 134–153.
Coplan, J. D., Andrews, M. W., Rosenblum, L. A., Owens, M. J., Friedman, S., Gorman, J. M., & Nemeroff, C. B. (1996). Persistent elevations of cerebrospinal fluid, con-

centrations of corticotropin-releasing factor in adult nonhuman primates exposed to early-life stressors: Implications for the pathophysiology of mood and anxiety disorders. *Proceedings of the National Academy of Sciences, USA, 93,* 1619–1623.

DeBellis, M., Chrousos, G. P., Dorn, L., Burke, L., Helmers, K., Kling, M. A., Trickett, P. K., & Putnam, F. W. (1994). Hypothalamic-pituitary-adrenal axis dysregulation in sexually abused girls. *Journal of Clinical Endocrinology and Metabolism, 78,* 249–255.

Diorio, D., Viau, V., & Meaney, M. J. (1993). The role of the medial prefrontal cortex (cingulate gyrus) in the regulation of hypothalamic-pituitary-adrenal responses to stress. *Journal of Neuroscience, 13,* 3839–3847.

Johnson, E. O., Kamilaris, T. C., Carter, C. S., Calogero, A. E., Gold, P. W., & Chrousos, G. P. (1996). Effects of early parenting on growth and development in a small primate. *Pediatric Research, 39,* 999–1005.

Kendler, K. S., Kessler, R. C., Walters, E. E., MacLean, C. J., Sham, P. C., Neale, M. C., Heath, A. C., & Eaves, L. J. (1995). Stressful events, genetic liability and onset of an episode of depression in women. *American Journal of Psyciatry, 152,* 833–842.

Kendler, K. S., Walters, E. E., Neals, M. C., Kessler, R. C., Heath, A. C., & Eaves, L. J. (1995). The structure of the genetic and environmental risk factors for six major psychiatric disorders in women. *Archives of General Psychiagry, 52,* 374–383.

Michelson, D., Stratakis C., Hill, L. Y., Reynolds, J., Galliven, E., Chrousos, G. P., & Gold, P. W. (1996). Bone mineral density is decreased in women with depression. *New England Journal of Medicine, 335,* 1176–1181.

Morgan, M. A., Romanski, L. M., & Le Doux, J. E. (1993). Extinction and emotional learning: Contribution of medical prefrontal cortex. *Neurosciences Letters, 163,* 109–113.

Phillips, D. I. W., Barker, J. P., Fall, C. H. D, Seckl, J. R., Whorwood, C. B., Wood, P. J., & Walker, B. R. (1998). Elevated plasma cortisol concentrations: A link between low birth weight and the insulin resistance syndrome? *Journal of Clinical Endocrinology and Metabolism, 83,* 757–760.

Piazza, P. V., Deroche, V., Deminere, J., Maccadi, S., Le Moal, M., & Simon, H. (1993). Corticosterone in the range of stress-induced levels possesses reinforcing properties: Implications for sensation-seeking behaviors. *Proceedings of the National Academy of Sciences, USA, 90,* 11738–11742.

Scarinci, I. C., MacDonald-Haile, J., Bradley, L. A., & Richter, J. E. (1994). Altered pain perception and psychosocial features among women with gastrointestinal disorders and history of abuse: A preliminary model. *American Journal of Medicine, 97,* 108–118.

Simon, B., (1978). *Mind and madness in ancient Greece: The classical roots of modern psychiatry.* Ithaca, NY: Cornell University Press.

# PART III

## DEVELOPMENTAL OUTCOMES
## AND CLINICAL PERSPECTIVES

# 10

## The Natural Course of Shyness and Related Syndromes

Deborah C. Beidel & Samuel M. Turner

Longitudinal studies of children's temperament reveal that certain early-appearing characteristics exert significant influence on later behavior, functioning, and perhaps psychopathology (Thomas & Chess, 1986). Some behaviors (e.g., aggression) are stable from middle childhood through adolescence and young adulthood (Kagan & Moss, 1962). However, prior to middle childhood, there are few behaviors that show such long-term persistence (Caspi & Silva, 1995). Notable exceptions are early passivity and fearfulness, where existence of these characteristics prior to age 3 predicted related behaviors much later in life (Kagan & Moss, 1962). Relatedly, more recent research also indicates that childhood *social* fears are nontransient (Achenbach, 1985) and that onset of social anxiety prior to age 11 predicted nonrecovery in adulthood (Davidson, 1993).

Children's fears and difficulties in social interactions usually are apparent to parents, teachers, and professionals. Various terms are used to describe these problematic behaviors (i.e., socially isolated, shy, behaviorally inhibited, socially phobic) and various fields of psychology (social, developmental, and clinical) have studied children's difficulties in social engagement and social interactions. In addition to being persistent, these behavioral styles have been related to serious detrimental outcomes. In this chapter, we draw together these various psychological literatures to examine the short and long-term effects of three constructs commonly used to describe social reticence (behavioral inhibition, social isolation, and shyness) and their relationship to social phobia.

### Conceptualization of Shyness

Among the constructs listed above, shyness probably is most commonly used by lay persons and professionals to describe individuals who are reticent to engage in social interactions or who are socially withdrawn. The number of individuals who report feeling shy at some time in their lives is large. For example, over 40 percent of college students considered themselves to be generally shy and over 90 percent considered themselves to have been shy at some time in their lives (Zimbardo, Pilkonis, & Norwood, 1975). These figures suggest that shyness may be experienced at some time by virtually everyone. For some, shyness may be a temporary state resulting from specific situational circumstances (Vernberg, Abwender, Ewell, & Beery, 1992). For others, shy feelings and associated behavior are highly consistent across time and social settings (Turner, Beidel, & Townsley, 1990). Buss and Plomin (1984) termed this consistency "temperamental shyness" and hypothesized that it resulted from a high level of negative emotionality coupled with a high desire for sociability. In other words, temperamental shyness consists of both a desire to interact with others and anxious worry about doing so.

In a review of shyness, Turner et al. (1990) examined various aspects of its clinical presentation, including somatic symptoms, cognitive features, behavioral responses, daily functioning, and longitudinal course. Table 10.1 lists the similarities and differences between social phobia and shyness discussed in Turner et al. (1990). This review revealed that those who are shy often have increased cardiac responses during social performance situations and commonly report fears of negative evaluation. Also, avoidance of social encounters is a defining characteristic, and social skill deficits have been reported. Finally, shyness impairs daily functioning, at least for a subset of those who suffer from it. For example, 46 percent of shy fifth-graders felt that their shyness was problematic and were interested in treatment (Lazarus, 1982). Similarly, 63 percent of shy college students felt that their shyness was a "real problem," resulting in difficulty making friends, feelings of loneliness and depression, lack of assertiveness, and self-preoccupation when in social encounters (Zimbardo et al., 1975). Shy children were rated by their teachers as less friendly and sociable, less likely to be leaders, and more somber and withdrawn (Caspi, Elder, & Bem, 1988). In addition to these concurrent clinical correlates, shyness can result in long-term impairment in a number of areas, and it is to this area that we now turn our attention.

## Short- and Long-Term Outcome of Shyness

The popular conception of shyness is that it is a relatively mild, common and transitory condition. Indeed, some shy individuals appear to outgrow their social reticence over time (Zimbardo et al., 1975). In a retrospective study using college students selected for their extreme scores on a shyness battery, Bruch, Giordano, and Pearl (1986) examined various characteristics of shyness, including stability (see Bruch et al., 1986 for details of the battery and cutoff scores). Interestingly, almost half of the currently not-shy group reported feeling shy during their early childhood years. When this group was divided into those who were never shy or those who were previously shy, the latter group had significantly more severe feelings of shyness during junior high school. Thus for these students the process of becoming less shy appears to have occurred during high school and college. However, exactly how or why this happened remains unclear. Similarly, there are no known

Table 10.1  Similarities and Differences Between
Social Phobia and Shyness.

*Characteristics of both groups*

   Increased physiological (cardiovascular) responses
   Negative cognitions when in social encounters
   Behavioral avoidance of social situations
   Social skills deficits

*Characteristics of social phobia*

   Lower prevalence rate in the general population
   More chronic course of disorder
   More pervasive functional impairment
   Later average age of onset

(Adapted from Turner et al., 1990)

features that have been demonstrated to clearly differentiate those with temporary
shyness from those who suffer the more chronic pattern.

A prospective study of 39 children living in Munich, Germany (Engfer, 1993), examined conditions that increased or decreased shyness between birth and 6.3 years
of age. Between these ages, 12 children showed substantial changes in shy behavior. Six changed from the high- to low-shy classification, and six changed in the opposite direction (low to high shyness). Although the small sample size means that
the data must be interpreted cautiously, there are so few prospective studies that the
results have heuristic value. Interestingly, more girls (33 percent) than boys (<10
percent) "outgrew" their shyness, indicating that shyness in boys was more stable.
Consistently, boys' shyness at 6.3 years could be predicted from their 33-month ratings. However, this was not the case for girls. Several features of these findings war-
rant comment. First, clearly not all of those who manifest early-onset shyness remain shy. Second, those who are not shy early on can develop shyness during later
years. Finally, early-appearing shyness appears to be more predictive of later shyness in males than it does in females. One might speculate that socialization pattern differences between males and females could account for this difference.

Despite gender differences in stability, children who became more shy at 6.3
years were rated by their mothers as having been less soothable, as well as having
had more problems with sleeping and eating during infancy. At 8 months, mothers rated them as moody and unhappy, and at 43 months as less socially competent. This latter finding is important because it suggests that shy children who are
rated as more socially competent at an early age become less shy, perhaps as a result of their ability to interact appropriately with others.

In addition to these short-term outcomes, there are two long-term prospective
studies that identify adult outcomes of preadolescent shyness (Caspi et al., 1988;
Kerr, Lambert, & Bem, 1996). Caspi et al. (1988) studied American children ($n =$
182) and reported 30-year follow-up data. Kerr et al. (1996) examined a Swedish
sample ($n = 169$) using 25-year follow-up data. Both studies also included assessment of nonshy peers. Table 10.2 presents an overview of the outcomes of shyness

Table 10.2  Life Course of Shyness for American and Swedish Children.

| Behavior | American boys | American girls | Swedish boys | Swedish girls |
|---|---|---|---|---|
| Later age of marriage | yes | no | yes | no |
| Later age of parenthood | yes | no | yes | no |
| Later Entry into stable careers | yes | | no | |
| Lower occupational achievement | yes | | no | |
| Less occupational stability | yes | | no | |
| Limited or no work history | | no | | ? |
| Lower likelihood of attending college | | yes | | yes |

(Adapted from Caspi et al., 1988 and Kerr et al., 1996)

in both of these samples. In both instances, shyness was determined by maternal ratings of social withdrawal and emotional inhibition when the children were 8–10 years of age. Both studies used virtually identical variables to determine social adjustment. The outcome illustrates some interesting consistencies, as well as perhaps some cultural variations. The results indicated that American and Swedish males who were shy as children married later and became fathers at a later age than their nonshy peers. Swedish men did not manifest occupational impairment in adulthood. However, American men who were shy as children entered stable career paths significantly later (i.e., 3 years later) than their nonshy American peers. In other words, shy boys took longer to find an occupation that developed into a stable career. In turn, that delay predicted both lower occupational achievement and less occupational stability.

Among girls, age at marriage and motherhood did not differentiate either the American or Swedish shy samples from their nonshy counterparts. For American women, 56 percent of those who were shy as girls either had no work history or permanently ended employment with the onset of marriage or childbirth. Only 36 percent of the nonshy American women were characterized by this pattern, a difference that was statistically significant. Furthermore, both Swedish and American women who were shy as children had lower levels of academic achievement than nonshy girls. This particularly was striking in the Swedish sample, in which the rate of college attendance for nonshy girls was 44 percent in comparison with 0 percent for the shy girls. Thus, shyness appears to result in some long-term impairments, although the specific outcome appears to be influenced by gender. Shyness in boys delays the achievement of some social milestones such as marriage and parenthood. Furthermore, for American males there was a delay in occupational adjustment (i.e., a later age at which they achieved a stable career path). The long-term effects for shyness in girls were different but nonetheless evident. Shy girls followed a traditional life path, with marriage and motherhood at the same age as their nonshy peers. They were, however, less likely to work outside the home or to attend college, again indicative of a more traditional female role. One might speculate whether the presence of shyness influenced the choice of these women because Turner, Beidel, Dancu, and Keyes (1986) found that social anxiety influenced occupational choice.

In summary, the term *shyness* is used to describe individuals who have considerable reticence about engaging in social discourse. Extant studies of shyness reveal it to be a fairly common experience for a sizable segment of the population at least at some time during their lives. Although the experience of being shy appears to be a temporary condition for many, for others it is chronic. Currently, there is no way to differentiate temporary shyness states from the more chronic pattern. What is known, however, is that early-onset shyness can delay the achievement of adult developmental milestones.

## The Construct of Behavioral Inhibition

This term describes a group of behaviors, initially appearing in toddlers, that are characterized by uneasiness, wariness, or avoidance of unfamiliar situations, people, objects, or events (Garcia-Coll, Kagan, & Reznick, 1984)—behaviors which sometimes also are associated with shyness. For example, children with behavioral inhibition (BI) show increased heart rates when in the presence of unfamiliar people or events (Garcia-Coll et al., 1984), and those who are shy have increased heart rate in social-performance situations (Turner et al., 1990). Children with BI are slow to verbally engage unfamiliar individuals (Reznick et al., 1986), as are shy children (Beidel, Turner, & Morris, in press). Thus, there has been speculation that the earliest manifestation of shyness might be reflected in the construct known as behavioral inhibition (e.g., Turner et al., 1990).

Identified in approximately 10–20 percent of Caucasian children, behavioral inhibition has both behavioral and physiological correlates. Among the latter, higher and more stable heart rates (less heart rate variability) characterize those who are behaviorally inhibited (Garcia-Coll et al., 1984). Other physiological variables include pupillary dilation (those with behavioral inhibition have larger pupillary dilations during resting and task phases; Reznick et al., 1986), salivary cortisol (those who are behaviorally inhibited have higher overall salivary cortisol levels; Reznick et al., 1986), and norepinephrine (there is a modest correlation between norepinephrine and behavioral inhibition; Kagan, Reznick, & Snidman, 1987). All of these features are detected only under specific challenge conditions.

Although physiological correlates of behavioral inhibition have been assessed, it is the overt behaviors that have been studied most frequently. In an initial report, 21-month-old toddlers were assessed in several unfamiliar or novel encounters (challenge conditions). Those who responded with crying, fretting, distressful vocalizations or facial expressions, physical withdrawal, and the absence of initiations or interactions with the experimenter were considered behaviorally inhibited (Garcia-Coll et al., 1984). Again, the similarities of these behaviors to those often considered descriptive of shyness (in older children and adults) is striking. Although the specific behaviors exhibited by toddlers varied with the particular task, overall, 28 percent of children were judged to be consistently behaviorally inhibited. Another 32 percent were judged as consistently uninhibited, and the remainder could not be classified. A quantitative index of behavioral inhibition was constructed for this study that included the behaviors listed here, as well as length of time to initiate interactions, inhibition of play, and distressful responses to experimenters or objects. It is this index that is the object of the stability and outcome studies described in the next section.

Before examining these stability data, it is important to note variations in the method of determining behavioral inhibition. Kagan and colleagues have relied on direct observation of children in order to determine inhibited status. Other investigators used ratings by parents or independent observers (e.g., Broberg, 1993). Despite the different assessment methods, behavioral inhibition, its correlates, and its stability estimates are markedly similar across research laboratories. Issues of stability are a particularly important focus for this chapter, and, along with the short-term and long-term outcomes of behavioral inhibition, they are discussed in the following section.

## Short- and Long-Term Outcome of Behavioral Inhibition

Prior to describing the results of these investigations, it is important to note that the developmental appropriateness of the tasks used to define inhibited behavior vary with the child's age. Thus, one caveat when evaluating stability estimates for behavioral inhibition (or social isolation or shyness) is whether the tasks used at different ages were equated for their ability to produce the desired response. Often no assurance is provided (Turner, Beidel, & Wolff, 1996). Stevenson-Hinde and Shouldice (1993) highlighted other developmental issues that also merit consideration. These include developmental changes in overt behavioral expression of a construct and, with maturation, a narrowing of the range of objects that evoke fear or wariness. Without consideration of developmental maturation, researchers may erroneously assume construct instability when the correct interpretation is merely a change in overt behavior (e.g., separation fears, for example, expressed as clinging to mother at a young age vs. repeated questioning regarding her whereabouts at an older age).

Behavioral inhibition is most commonly linked to studies by Kagan and his colleagues. The Harvard group that was originally assessed at age 21 months (Garcia-Coll et al., 1984) has been followed for a number of years. The behavioral index has been the most common subject of stability analysis, and follow-up investigations have been conducted over at least a 12-year time period. Initial stability coefficients were reported 1 month ($n = 58$) and 10 months ($n = 40$) after the initial assessment (Garcia-Coll et al., 1984). The 1-month correlation coefficient, which used the same tasks as the initial assessment, was $r = .63$, which was statistically significant. Ten months later (i.e., at 31 months of age), children participated in assessments of behavioral inhibition that were conducted both in the laboratory and at the children's homes. Both outcomes were correlated with the original (21-month) index, which was conducted in a laboratory setting. The correlation of the 21-month index with the home index at 31 months was $r = .39$ and with the laboratory index at 31 months, $r = .66$. Both correlations were statistically significant. The higher correlation of the original index with the 31-month laboratory index was probably due to the similarity of the two laboratory-based assessments.

Another follow-up assessment occurred at age 4 (Kagan, Reznick, Clarke, Snidman, & Garcia-Coll, 1984). Among children classified as behaviorally inhibited at 21 months, 59 percent (13/22) retained this classification at age 4. The other nine children were less inhibited but had not changed enough to be classified as uninhibited. One factor predictive of lessening inhibition was heart rate variability at 21 months of age. Fifty-five percent (5/9) of the children who could no longer be classified as behaviorally inhibited at age 4 had variable (unstable) heart rates at 21 months, whereas 11 of 13 who retained their classification at age 4 had stable heart rates at 21 months of age. Recall that stable heart rates were more characteristic of behaviorally inhibited children overall at the initial assessment. Therefore, children who had less consistency between their behavioral and physiological symptoms were more likely to change classification (i.e., become somewhat less inhibited) at a later date.

Children were reassessed at 5.5 years of age (Reznick et al., 1986). When compared with their uninhibited peers ($n = 22$), those who were originally classified as behaviorally inhibited ($n = 24$) continued to exhibit inhibited behavior, such as being cautious and restrained during tasks that were considered challenging or risky. In addition, there were significant correlations between mothers' ratings of children's shyness at age 5½ and their behavioral inhibition index at 21 months ($r = .33$ and $r = .36$). Interestingly, however, the correlation between mother's ratings of shyness at 5½ years and the behavioral inhibition index of 5½ years was $r = .33$. A higher correlation might have been expected because the assessments were conducted at the same time. It suggests, however, that although behavioral inhibition and shyness are significantly correlated, they may not be identical constructs.

Two years later (7.5 years chronological age; Kagan, Reznick, & Snidman, 1988) there was still moderate stability of behavioral inhibition, as indicated by correlation coefficients between the behavioral inhibition index at 7½ years and those from the 21-month, 4-year, and 5½-year indexes ($r = .67, .54,$ and $.57$, respectively). Furthermore, mothers' ratings of shyness at 7.5 years were substantially correlated with behavioral inhibition indexes at 21-months, 4 years, and 5½ years ($r = .66, .66,$ and $.63$, respectively). Although the reason for this increase in the strength of the correlation from the earlier Resnick et al. (1986) study is unclear, maturation factors such as a narrowing range of fears (Stevenson-Hinde & Shouldice, 1993) may have played a role. Thus, expression of shyness may change in form from 5½ to 7½ years such that it is more easily identified at the later age.

With respect to long-term stability, one recent investigation examined correlates of behavioral inhibition, specifically, inhibited and noninhibited youths' responses on the Stroop Color Naming Task (Schwartz, Snidman, & Kagan, 1996). Latency to respond to positive, threat, or neutral words was assessed in children now aged 13.3 years, 41 of whom were formerly classified as behaviorally inhibited and 33 as uninhibited. Longer latencies to respond to threat words usually is considered a sign of anxious pathology. There were no significant differences in average latency across all words and no differences in average latency for any particular group of words. However, when the words with the longest latencies for each subject were examined, there was a significant group difference in the percentage of words that were from the threat category. Children formerly classified as behaviorally inhibited had a significantly larger proportion of threat words in their longest latency group than children in the other classifications. One interpretation of this finding is that threat words generated a more intense emotional arousal or a greater number of associations in the inhibited children, thus inhibiting their ability to respond to the word quickly. However, because the overall latency to respond to threat words did not discriminate the groups, these findings cannot be interpreted unambiguously. Yet, the results do suggest that even 12 years later, children classified as behaviorally inhibited still can be differentiated from their uninhibited peers on some dimensions.

Other investigators, using different but similar operational definitions of behavioral inhibition, also have reported moderate stability coefficients across the same developmental period. Broberg (1993) assessed 144 Swedish firstborn children at 16 months, 28 months, and 40 months of age. Those who were rated by their mothers and an independent observer as inhibited at 16 months also were significantly more likely to be inhibited at 28 and 40 months of age. Similarly, Schmidt et al. (1997) reported that 4-month-old infants who displayed a behavioral profile characterized by high motor activity and negative affect were more likely to be rated by their mothers as shy when they were 4 years old. Infants who were rated as fearful and wary of novel stimuli at 14 months of age were more likely, at 4 years of age, to display social wariness during peer play activities and more likely to be rated by their mothers as shy. Also, Asendorpf (1990, 1993) conducted a 4-year study (ages 3 years 9 months to 8 years) using a sample of children previously unselected for behavioral inhibition. Inhibition scores were calculated for interactions with unfamiliar people (adults or children) in an unfamiliar setting, an unfamiliar peer in a familiar environment, and a familiar peer in a familiar environment. Correlations between inhibition ratings at 4 and 8 years were as follows: unfamiliar peers in unfamiliar environments, $r = .49$ to $.75$; unfamiliar peers in familiar environments, $r = .25$ to $.55$; familiar peers in familiar environments, $r = .00$ to $.20$. These results suggest that stability of the behavioral construct is influenced by the parameters of the setting (i.e., in this case, unfamiliarity) in addition to the development factors addressed earlier.

Rubin, Hastings, Stewart, Henderson, and Chen (1997) also addressed the need to examine the type of situation used to assess the presence of behavioral inhibition. This study examined the stability of expressions of behavioral inhibition using three common behavioral inhibition paradigms: nonsocial (child is approached by a toy robot), adult-social (child is approached by an unfamiliar adult) and peer-social (child is approached by an unfamiliar, same-aged peer) in infants who were 24 months old. Only 31 percent of children who showed strong behavioral inhibition in one setting showed strong inhibition in a second setting. The authors concluded that behavioral inhibition (at least at 24 months) was multifaceted and context-dependent. In summary, despite the particular strength of the correlation and even across a period characterized by rapid physical and mental development, some children who initially are determined to be behaviorally inhibited remain that way, particularly those who manifest both overt behavioral and physiological indexes at the earliest stages of identification. However, the stability of the coefficients is dependent on the environmental context and specific aspects of the assessment paradigm.

Using a longer follow-up period, the Harvard cohorts of inhibited and uninhibited children (initially assessed at either 21 or 31 months of age) were re-assessed at 13 years with the Youth Self Report (YSR) and the Child Behavior Checklist (CBCL) (Schwartz et al., 1996). Those who were judged as inhibited at 21 months of age had significantly lower scores than uninhibited children on the YSR Total Externalizing, Delinquent Behavior, and Aggressive Behavior scales and on the

CBCL Total Externalizing and Aggressive Behavior scales. Similar results were found for the cohort originally assessed at age 31 months, but they were statistically significant only for the uninhibited males. These results suggest that those rated as uninhibited had higher ratings of "acting out" behaviors such as hyperactivity and oppositional behaviors. However, none of the YSR or CBCL scores were in the clinically significant range suggesting that perhaps these uninhibited children were just more "outgoing" than their peers.

Recent studies have suggested that parental behavior can exert substantial influence on the stability of behavioral inhibition. For example, infant boys rated as high on negativity and low on positivity had high inhibition when they were toddlers. However, there also was a relationship between parental "sensitivity" and maintenance of inhibition (Park, Belsky, Putnam, & Crnic, 1997). Highly sensitive parents were those who adjusted their behavior to meet the child's goals and needs, whereas insensitivity was defined as the degree to which parents inserted their own goals and agenda on the child without regard to the child. Interestingly, parents who were rated as sensitive were more likely to support the development of inhibition in their sons, whereas negative and intrusive controlling behavior (insensitive pattern) were more likely to result in a lessening of behavioral inhibition. The results were interpreted as suggesting that parents who demanded different behavior rather than supporting inhibited behavior from their children were more likely to facilitate a decrease in their child's inhibited behaviors. Similarly, Arcus et al. (1992; cited in Park et al. 1997) reported that mothers of high reactive infants (a precursor to behavioral inhibition) who used direct limit-setting strategies and less frequently responded to frets and cries dampened the development of fearful, inhibited behaviors in their infants. Thus, parental behaviors may play a role in the stability of behavioral inhibition in children.

In a study that did not use the Harvard cohort but examined correlates and longer-term outcome of behavioral inhibition, Gest (1997) reported a correlation coefficient of $r = .57$ between ratings of behavioral inhibition at preadolescence (ages 8–12) and in early adulthood (ages 17–24). Ratings at age 12 were based on an interview and observation of the child during a series of laboratory-based tasks (similar to those used by Kagan and colleagues). At ages 17 to 24, ratings were based on 22 5-point observer rating scales that assessed interpersonal, cognitive, and affective behavior. Those with high scores were ill at ease, communicated hesitantly and without expression, and seldom initiated contact by talking, smiling, or joking. Structural equation modeling was used to determine the relationship between childhood behavioral inhibition and adult outcomes (peer social success, emotional distress, and life-course timing). The results indicated that childhood behavioral inhibition was negatively associated with peer social success (defined as a less positive and less active social life) in early adulthood. It also was negatively related to moving away from the family of origin at a later age and, for males, to higher negative emotionality (as assessed by the Multidimensional Personality Questionnaire; Tellegen, 1982).

Examining adult outcomes based on toddler behavior, Caspi and Silva (1995) reported that, as adults, inhibited children who were shy and fearful at age 3 had an overcontrolled restrained behavioral style and a nonassertive interpersonal attitude. As adults, they preferred safety over dangerous activities, were cautious rather than impulsive, and were unlikely to favor aggressive behaviors. Similarly, they were socially passive, describing themselves as submissive, not fond of leadership roles, and having minimal desire to influence others. Interestingly, this description is very similar to the diagnostic criteria for a personality style known in the clinical literature as *avoidant personality disorder.* The boundary between social phobia and avoidant personality disorder is not clearly delineated, and the two syndromes overlap considerably.

The relationship of early-appearing temperament (age 3) and adult psychiatric disorder (including anxiety disorders) was reported by Caspi, Moffit, Newman, and Silva (1996). The sample in this study consisted of participants in a longitudinal sample in New Zealand. Diagnosis at age 21 was made with the Diagnostic Interview Schedule (DIS), and determined through the use of a computer algorithm. At age 3, the children were divided into five groups: undercontrolled (those who were restless, impulsive, and distractable); inhibited (those who were shy, fearful, and easily upset); well adjusted (capable of self-control, self-confident, not easy to upset); confident (zealous, friendly); and reserved (slightly cautious). At age 21, there was a weak link overall between early-appearing behavior style and psychopathology, but it did not quite reach the traditional .05 criterion level ($p < .07$). Although there did not appear to be a specific relationship to anxiety disorders, in general those who were undercontrolled or inhibited were significantly more likely to manifest multiple disorders. Thus, these findings support the contention that those who are undercontrolled or inhibited (as defined by study criteria) at an early age are at greater risk for mental health difficulties during adulthood. Those considered to be undercontrolled were more likely to meet diagnostic criteria for antisocial personality disorder and to be involved in crime than those in the other group. On the other hand, those who were considered to be inhibited at age 3 were more likely to meet criteria for depression. Both groups were more likely to attempt suicide, and boys in both groups were more likely to have alcohol-related problems. These findings were found to be unrelated to social class. Although the effect sizes were small, the findings are impressive, given the 18-year time span, and provide some of the strongest evidence to date that early-appearing behavioral styles are related to adult psychiatric diagnosis.

## Relationship of Behavioral Inhibition to Anxiety Disorders

There is some evidence that stable behavioral inhibition is associated with increased risk for the development of anxiety disorders. For example, children who were behaviorally inhibited at 21 months were described by their parents as "shy" at 5.5 years (Reznick et al., 1986). Again, children who manifested both the behavioral and physiological aspects of behavioral inhibition were the ones most likely to exhibit anxious behaviors. Mothers reported that fears of the dark, elevators, heights, and bugs were common among these children. Consistently, Gersten (1989) found that children who were inhibited at 21 months of age were significantly more likely to be socially isolated in kindergarten, whereas Broberg (1993) reported that behavioral inhibition was strongly correlated with mothers' ratings of restricted sociability and risk avoidance. Asendorpf (1991) found a significant positive correlation between failed social interactions and inhibition. Increases in the frequency of failed interactions resulted in enhanced inhibited behavior, thus establishing a spiralling inhibition effect. This finding is important because it suggests a mechanism for how arrested social development can occur and why those with social anxiety sometimes show social skill deficits (Beidel, Turner, & Morris, in press).

Hirschfeld et al. (1992) reported that children who maintained their classification as behaviorally inhibited across a 6-year period were significantly more likely to have any anxiety disorder, more than two anxiety disorders, and phobic disorders than were children who were originally classified as uninhibited or who were classified at various times as behaviorally inhibited or uninhibited (unstable inhibited). In a second study that included some of the original Harvard cohort, Biederman et al. (1993) found that children previously classified as behaviorally inhibited were more likely to have four or more disorders in general, and two or more anxiety disorders. In addition, behaviorally inhibited children were more likely to have avoidant disorder, separation anxiety disorder, and agoraphobia. The rates of disorders at follow-up were higher than the rates detected at the baseline assessment (3 years earlier). When the stable inhibited sample was further subdivided into those who did or did not have a disorder at baseline, even those without a disorder at the initial assessment were more likely at follow-up to have two or more anxiety disorders, avoidant disorder, or separation anxiety disorder. Similarly, Kagan (1997) reported that extensive clinical interviews with 13- to 14-year-old adolescents who were part of the original two Harvard cohorts revealed that social phobia was "more frequent" among inhibited than uninhibited adolescents, whereas specific phobias, separation anxiety, or compulsive symptoms did not differentiate the two groups. Unfortunately, this report did not provide more specific data, and it is unclear if the descriptor "more frequent" represented a statistically significant difference. However, these data lend credence to the observation of Stevenson-Hinde and Shouldice (1993), reported earlier; that is, that with maturation there is a narrowing of the range of objects that a child fears. In this case, one might hypothesize that there is a narrowing of focus from a general fear of novelty to the emergence of specific, though not always identical, fears.

In summary, there is evidence for stability of behavioral inhibition over time, albeit the correlations are only moderate. In addition, correlates of behavioral inhibition include theoretically related constructs and disorders such as shyness, specific fears, separation anxiety, and social isolation.

## Social Isolation

Behavioral inhibition is associated with socially reclusive or isolative behaviors (Rubin & Mills, 1988; see the next section). Social isolation, however, is a multidimensional construct, resulting from several different causes. For example, some children who choose to engage in quiet, constructive, or exploratory play when in social settings are considered passively isolated (Rubin & Mills, 1988). Other children are deliberately socially isolated by peers because of their cognitive immaturity and rambunctious behavior. Those who engage in this pattern, termed active-immature behavior, are disliked and rejected by peers. Rubin and Mills (1988) examined the concurrent relationships among social isolation, social behavior, and emotional distress. The results indicated that passive isolation is negatively related to the frequency of social behavior in second- and fourth-grade students, to measures of social self-perception in fourth-grade students, and to measures of inter-nalizing behaviors in fifth-grade children. Furthermore, measures of peer rejection and acceptance became increasingly correlated with passive withdrawal as chil-dren matured (from second through fifth grades), highlighting the ever-spiralling interaction of these variables. Interestingly, studies from the clinical literature have reported similar relationships between emotionality and peer social status. Strauss, Lahey, Frick, Frame, and Hynd (1988) reported that children most likely to be ignored by their peers were those with the highest level of anxiety. Therefore, it is likely that many children who are passively isolated (or who passively isolate themselves) suffer from internalizing disorders such as anxiety and depression.

## Short- and Long-Term Outcome of Social Isolation/Withdrawal

Similar to behavioral inhibition, social withdrawal also appears to be a relatively stable behavioral characteristic (Rubin, Stewart, & Coplan, 1995). Behavioral ob-servations of social withdrawal in children resulted in significant correlations at ages 5 and 7 and at ages 7 and 9. Similarly, peer assessments of socially withdrawn behaviors were found to be stable across ages 7, 9, and 10 years.

Also, similar to behavioral inhibition, both short- and long-term detrimental effects of social isolation/withdrawal in young children have been documented clearly. For example, socially isolated children were significantly more likely than others to use nonassertive, compliant problem-solving strategies in kindergarten (Rubin, Daniels-Beirness, & Bream, 1984). When these children ($n = 37$) were re-assessed 1 year later, isolated kindergarten play predicted poor quantitative and qualitative social problem-solving skills in first grade. Quantitative (the ability to produce multiple solutions to a single problem) and qualitative (flexibility when confronted with a social problem) social problem-solving skills are considered in-dicative of social competence in childhood (Rubin et al., 1984), and as noted ear-lier, social problem-solving skills deficits are more common in anxious withdrawn children. Thus, there appears to be a pattern, at least in the short term, of social isolation and inadequate social competence, although it is unclear whether isola-tion functions as an etiological or maintenance factor or whether it acts in both ways.

With respect to the short-term outcome of social withdrawal, Kerr, Tremblay, Pagani, and Vitaro (1997) reported that behavioral inhibition served as a protective factor against the later (3 years later) development of delinquency in socially with-drawn children. Children who were socially withdrawn but also disruptive (and not behaviorally inhibited) were at increased risk for delinquency and depression. However, those who were withdrawn but inhibited did not manifest this later neg-ative outcome. The authors hypothesized that behavioral inhibition was responsi-ble for the suppression of delinquent behavior because delinquency was primarily a social phenomenon. Thus, children who were inhibited and withdrawn did not enter into the type of situations in which delinquent behavior occurs and/or did not socialize with other children (delinquent acts usually occur in the company of deviant friends). Despite the negative outcomes normally associated with behav-ioral inhibition, in this case, it seemed to be associated with the lack of occurrence of antisocial behavior.

In the Rubin and Mills (1988) study cited earlier in this chapter, the authors examined the relationship of early-appearing social isolation (passive isolation or active rejection) to later indicants of social adjustment and emotional distress. Both patterns can result in social isolation by other children, but passive isolation appears to be more consistent with other descriptions of social withdrawal. Furthermore, it is this pattern of social isolation that appears stable across several years (in this case Grades 2 through 5) and is predictive of subsequent difficulties. Second-graders who engaged in passive isolation (particularly when this isolation was coupled with negative self-perception of social competence) were more likely to display depression and loneliness in the fifth grade (Rubin & Mills, 1988). It seems as though those children who are passively socially isolated manifest behaviors similar to those labeled shy or behaviorally inhibited, but studies examining such a relationship have yet to be conducted.

In a short-term (6-month) longitudinal study, Adalbjarnardottir (1995) examined the relationship between social withdrawal, social anxiety, and interpersonal problem-solving skills in third- and sixth-grade children. Overall, those children who were socially withdrawn had significantly poorer problem-solving skills. Over the 6-month period, third-grade children who became less socially withdrawn showed greater improvement in interpersonal problem-solving skills at the follow-up assessment than children who maintained their original level of social withdrawal. However, this change was not evident in sixth-grade children. Furthermore, it was not possible to determine the direction of the relationship between problem-solving skills and social withdrawal (i.e., did changes in withdrawal precede change in problem-solving skills or vice versa?)

In a study of the early to middle childhood years, Hymel, Rubin, Rowden, and LeMare (1990) examined the ability of early social difficulties (Grade 2) to predict later indices of externalizing and internalizing disorders (Grade 5). Whereas peer rejection in Grade 2 was predictive of aggression and externalizing behaviors (conduct problems and hyperactivity at later ages), the outcome was quite different for those whose Grade 2 behavior was characterized by social isolation. In those cases, socially isolated peers (who had lower perceptions of social competence and poor peer acceptance) developed internalizing problems (anxiety, depression) in middle childhood (Grade 5). However, the results were not specific for social fears but rather only predicted a more general anxious or depressive mood state (Hymel et al., 1990).

Rubin et al. (1995) reported that a constellation of behaviors at age 7, consisting of early passive withdrawal, anxiety, and negative self-perceptions of social competence, was significantly associated with measures of depression, loneliness, and anxiety at age 11. In addition, behavioral observations of social withdrawal, combined with peer and teacher ratings of passive withdrawal, predicted negative self-esteem, loneliness, and a feeling of not belonging to family or a peer group when the children were in 9th grade (approximately age 14). Although these children were not clinically assessed to determine presence of psychopathology, scores on the measures of loneliness, depression, and anxiety indicated a positive relationship between social isolation and negative emotion.

The lack of a prediction specifically for social fear is consistent with the prediction data for behavioral inhibition. It appears that factors such as social isolation and behavioral inhibition may lead, in the elementary school years, to the development of disruptions in emotion, most specifically anxiety and depression. As discussed in the next section, it may be that the emergence of these mood states and further socially isolative experiences interact synergistically to result in discrete psychological disorders, one of which may be social phobia.

## Similarities Among Shyness, Social Withdrawal, and Behavioral Inhibition

A comparison of the descriptions of passive isolation/social withdrawal and shyness and behavioral inhibition suggest that there may be some overlap but that these terms probably do not describe the same condition. Behavioral inhibition is characterized by withdrawal, avoidance, and fear of unfamiliar situations, persons, objects, and events (Garcia-Coll et al., 1984). Passive isolation, as noted previously, is characterized by quiet, constructive, or exploratory play. Although one might hypothesize that the motivation behind such passive isolation is fear of social encounters, other factors also could account for the reclusive behavior. Thus, some children might be classified as both behaviorally inhibited and passively isolated, but others may actually fit into only one of the two categories. Similarly, shyness is characterized by social withdrawal and by physical and cognitive correlates suggestive of anxious emotionality.

In addition to the overlap in their clinical presentation, the outcomes of these three early-appearing conditions appear to be quite similar. With respect to the known short-term and long-term outcomes, there are several intriguing areas of overlap. First, all three as a group show moderate levels of stability at least through the childhood years (e.g., Bruch et al., 1986; Kagan et al., 1988; Rubin & Mills, 1988), although some data on behavioral inhibition suggest that the degree of stability may in part vary as a function of setting familiarity (Asendorpf, 1991). The presence of any of these conditions appears to affect social competence. Behaviorally inhibited toddlers, for instance, show patterns of social withdrawal and isolation when they enter kindergarten and first grade (Kagan et al., 1988). Similarly, passively isolated kindergartners had poorer social problem-solving skills in later childhood (Rubin et al., 1984). Anxious-withdrawn children and average children (kindergarten, Grade 2, and Grade 4) also had significantly fewer social problem-solving situations, produced fewer socially assertive strategies, and were less successful in their socialization attempts (Stewart & Rubin, 1995). Consistently, shy first-graders had a history of impaired social competence, as determined by mothers' retrospective reports (Engfer, 1993). Thus, there appears to be an interrelationship among these three constructs that transcends their overlapping clinical descriptors. In each case, the presence of the condition, either concurrently or prospectively in the short term, was associated with poor social competence and social problem-solving abilities.

In addition to their relationship to poor social competence, both a history of stable behavioral inhibition and a history of social isolation predict the presence of negative emotionality in later childhood years. Stable behavioral inhibition was associated with the later presence of several different anxiety disorders (Hirschfeld et al., 1992). Early isolation predicted the later presence of anxiety, depression, and loneliness in middle childhood (Rubin & Mills, 1988). Additionally, children who were initially identified as behaviorally inhibited were significantly less likely to have scores indicative of externalizing problems (aggression, hyperactivity; Schwartz et al., 1996). These data suggest that the early presence of behavioral inhibition or social isolation does not necessarily lead to one particular disorder but may be a factor predisposing one to the development of different disorders, most likely those that fall along the internalizing continuum.

Studies of adult outcomes of behaviorally inhibited or shy children are few, but what data do exist show some consistency. As adults, behaviorally inhibited children lived with their family of origin for a longer period of time and reported less satisfying social interactions with peers (Gest, 1997). Shy boys reached adult developmental milestones of marriage and fatherhood later than their nonshy peers, and some were delayed in the establishment of a stable career. As adults, shy girls were more likely to exemplify traditional female roles of marriage and motherhood. Similarly, they were less likely to attend college or work outside the home.

There are some differences in the number of individuals who have been determined to have these conditions. Behavioral inhibition, for example, appears to affect about 20 percent of the Caucasian population in the United States (although this is a projection from the Harvard sample and not the result of an epidemiological study). Shyness, in contrast, appears to be a self-identifying descriptor used by up to 40 percent of college students. Furthermore, these conditions are not immutable. Follow-up studies of both behavioral inhibition and shyness indicate that a subset of children do appear to outgrow these conditions. With respect to behavioral inhibition, discordance between the physiological and behavioral indexes was a factor that indicated those who had a less stable condition. Interestingly, differences in cardiac reactivity between inhibited and uninhibited boys was much stronger than between the groups of girls, with inhibited boys having the least cardiac variability in the initial study on behavioral inhibition (Garcia-Coll et al., 1984). Thus, one important avenue for future research is to more clearly determine which children are likely to outgrow these early-appearing conditions. Isolation of the important factors that determine these various patterns could lead to intervention strategies that could be applied to those not likely to change spontaneously.

How do these findings relate to the clinical disorder known as social phobia? Social phobia is a fear that the individual will do or say something in front of others that will be perceived as humiliating or embarrassing (*Diagnostic and Statistical Manual of Mental Disorders,* American Psychiatric Association, 1994). Common social fears include fear of speaking or otherwise performing in front of others, eating or drinking in front of others, using public bathrooms, or engaging in general social interactions, such as at meetings or parties. To date, most studies of social phobia have focused on the psychopathology or treatment of this condition, and there appear to be some areas of overlap. The long-term outcomes of those who were identified during early childhood as behaviorally inhibited indicated the presence of social skill impairments, deficits which also have been noted to occur in socially phobic children (Beidel et al., in press) and adults (Turner, Beidel, Cooley, Woody, & Messer, 1994). Similarly, Caspi and Silva's (1995) description of the long-term outcome of behavioral inhibition (i.e., overcontrolled restrained behavior, nonassertion, and preference for familiar rather than unfamiliar situations) is also similar to the features characteristic of avoidant personality disorder. Thus,

Table 10.3 Percentage of individuals with social phobia (SP) or no psychiatric disorder who had a history of childhood shyness and trauma.

|  | No disorder | Specific SP | Generalized SP | $p$ |
|---|---|---|---|---|
| Childhood shyness | 52%[a] | 56%[ab] | 76%[b] | .06 |
| Traumatic event | 20%[a] | 56%[b] | 40%[ab] | .05 |

Data not sharing superscripts are significantly different at $p < .05$. (Adapted from Stemberger et al., 1995)

these overlapping behavioral features further strengthen the notion that there are relationships among these conditions.

In one of the few attempts to address the etiology of social phobia, Stemberger, Turner, Beidel, and Calhoun (1995) retrospectively examined whether histories of childhood shyness or traumatic conditioning experiences were more common in the backgrounds of those with social phobia than of those without psychiatric disorders. Table 10.3 provides a breakdown of the percentage of these adult individuals who had a history of childhood shyness and traumatic events. The results indicated that both a history of traumatic conditioning episodes and a history of childhood shyness predicted the presence of social phobia, although other factors, currently unidentified, also appeared to play a role. Some of these factors may include a history of behavioral inhibition or social isolation, or perhaps all of these constructs are used to describe the same (or similar) syndrome, having been studied separately by social, developmental, and clinical psychologists.

### A Model for the Interrelationships Among Shyness, Behavioral Inhibition. Social Isolation, and Shyness

Figure 10.1 presents a hypothetical model that depicts the relationships among shyness, social isolation, behavioral inhibition, and social phobia. As illustrated, shyness and social isolation are represented by the two larger circles, because the literature suggests that these constructs encompass the largest number of individuals. The area marked *behavioral inhibition* represents a smaller group of children (based on the currently available literature), and the cross-hatched area illustrates what we believe are the boundaries among these conditions and the clinical syndrome known as social phobia. The model describes the following relationships.

First, Bruch et al. (1986) described two subcategories of shyness, one of which was called *cognitively shy.* These children were socially reticent but without an anxious physiological temperament. In the proposed model, these children would be in the domain of shyness but without behavioral inhibition and without anxious temperament. Indeed, one might call this group "temporarily shy," as Bruch et al. (1986) suggested that they were the ones most likely to outgrow their shyness.

In contrast, Bruch et al.'s (1986) second group of children consisted of those who were cognitively shy but also had anxious physiology. This group had an earlier onset of their disorder, suggesting that this type of shyness might be temperamental, as has been suggested for behavioral inhibition (i.e., fear of unfamiliar people,

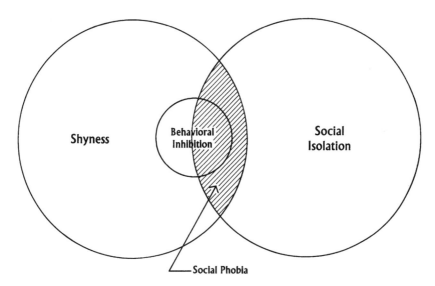

Figure 10.1. Proposed relationships among shyness, social isolation, behavioral inhibition, and social phobia.

objects, and situations). Based on the behavioral and physiological similarities between shyness and behavioral inhibition, the available literature at this time suggests that behaviorally inhibited children are shy children and that the construct of behavioral inhibition may represent a subcategory of shyness (see figure 10.1). Because of their anxious temperament (for which there appears to be a biological basis), these behaviorally inhibited and shy children might be referred to as the *permanently shy.*

As noted earlier in this chapter, there are many reasons why a child might be socially isolated. For example, children with conduct disorders or attention deficit disorder often are socially isolated from others. However, in that case, the social isolation is a result of active rejection by others because of the child's negative behavior. Other individuals may choose to socially isolate themselves. These individuals often are referred to in the clinical literature as schizoid because they prefer the company of objects and ideas to the company of other people. Also, there are those individuals who are passively isolated. It is this group which shows behaviors also described by those who are shy. In our model, this subgroup is represented by the overlap between the circles that represent shyness and social isolation.

Finally, the diagnostic criteria for social phobia not only includes feelings of shyness, physiological arousal, and social avoidance/isolation, but must include either functional impairment or substantial distress about having the disorder. In our model, we have represented social phobia by the cross-hatched area. As depicted, there may be several pathways by which one develops social phobia. In this model, there are some individuals who have both shyness and social isolation but need not necessarily have an anxious temperament. In this instance, social phobia may be a conditioned fear response acquired as a result of a traumatic event and which tends to be more characteristic of those who develop the more circum-scribed pattern of social phobia referred to as the specific subtype (Stemberger et al., 1995). Others with social phobia may have had all three of the conditions ex-amined in this chapter: behavioral inhibition, social isolation, and shyness.

In summary, those with social phobia may develop this condition through var-ious etiological pathways. Not everyone who manifests what appear to be predis-positional factors (behavioral inhibition, shyness, or social isolation) necessarily develop social phobia. To date, the mechanism by which these factors evolve into the disorder remain unclear.

## Conclusions

We noted in the introduction to this chapter that social reticence has been studied by psychologists from several subspecialties. Early studies of shyness largely have been carried out by social psychologists; studies of behavioral inhibition and so-cially isolative or neglected children largely have been studied by developmental psychologists. Finally, in recent years clinical psychologists have studied social phobia in adults and in children and adolescents. As we noted, there is much over-lap in these syndromes, as well as some differences. However, it is likely that at least some of the children in these various categories suffer from the same condi-tion, and our model proposes one heuristic conceptualization of the relationships among these constructs. For example, it is likely that children described as behav-iorally inhibited also are shy, are neglected by their peers, and could meet criteria for the clinical diagnosis of social phobia. Virtually no studies are available that address the relationship of these syndromes, and the exact nature of these rela-tionships remain to be unraveled by future research. However, it is tempting to speculate that the fear of novelty and social reticence identified in studies of be-havioral inhibition is a precursor of shyness. At the very least, this is the case for some shyness, perhaps the early-onset and persistent variety. Similarly, those who are shy appear to be at greatest risk for being neglected by their peers. Finally, those who do not "outgrow" their shyness at a reasonably early age may be at particular risk for developing social phobia.

*References*

Achenbach, T. M. (1985). Assessment of anxiety in children. In A. H. Tuma & J. D. Maser (Eds.), *Anxiety and the anxiety disorders* (pp. 707–734). Hillsdale, NJ: Erlbaum.

Adalbjarnardottir, S. (1995). How schoolchildren propose to negotiate: The role of so-cial withdrawal, social anxiety and locus of control. *Child Development, 66,* 1739–1751.

American Psychiatric Association (1994). *Diagnostic and statistical manual of mental disorders (4th ed.).* Washington, DC: Author.

Asendorpf, J. B. (1990). Development of inhibition during childhood: Evidence for sit-uational specificity and a two-factor model. *Developmental Psychology, 26,* 721–730.

Asendorpf, J. B. (1991). Development of inhibited children's coping with unfamiliarity. *Child Development, 62,* 1460–1474.

Asendorpf, J. B. (1993). Beyond temperament: A two-factor coping model of the development of inhibition during childhood. In K. H. Rubin & J. B. Asendorpf (Eds.), *Social withdrawal, inhibition and shyness in childhood* (pp. 265–290). Hillsdale, NJ: Erlbaum.

Beidel, D. C., Turner, S. M., & Morris, T. L. (in press). Psychopathology of childhood social phobia. *Journal of the American Academy of Child and Adolescent Psychiatry.*

Biederman, J., Rosenbaum, J. F., Bolduc-Murphy, E. A., Faraone, S. V., Chaloff, J., Hirshfeld, D. R., & Kagan, J. (1993). A three-year follow-up of children with and without behavioral inhibition. *Journal of the American Academy of Child and Adolescent Psychiatry, 32,* 814–821.

Broberg, A. G. (1993). Inhibition and children's experiences of out-of-home care. In K. H. Rubin & J. B. Asendorpf (Eds.), *Social withdrawal, inhibition and shyness in childhood* (pp. 151–176). Hillsdale, NJ: Erlbaum.

Bruch, M. A., Giordano, S., & Pearl, L. (1986). Differences between fearful and self-consciousness shy subtypes in background and current adjustment. *Journal of Research in Personality, 20,* 172–186.

Buss, A. H., & Plomin, R. (1984). *Temperament: Early developing personality traits.* Hillsdale, NY: Erlbaum.

Caspi, A., Elder, G. H., & Bem, D. J. (1988). Moving away from the world: Life-course patterns of shy children. *Developmental Psychology, 24,* 824–831.

Caspi, A., Moffit, T. E., Newman, D. L., & Silva, P. A. (1996). Behavioral observations at age 3 years predict adult psychiatric disorders. *Archives of General Psychiatry, 53,* 1033–1039.

Caspi, A., & Silva, P. A. (1995). Temperamental qualities at age three predict personality traits in young adulthood: Longitudinal evidence from a birth cohort. *Child Development, 66,* 486–498.

Davidson, J. (1993, March). *Childhood histories of adult social phobics.* Paper presented at the annual convention of the Anxiety Disorders Association, Charleston, SC.

Engfer, A. (1993). Antecedents and consequences of shyness in boys and girls: A 6-year longitudinal study. In K. H. Rubin & J. B. Asendorpf (Eds.), *Social withdrawal, inhibition and shyness in childhood* (pp. 49–79). Hillsdale, NJ: Erlbaum.

Garcia-Coll, C., Kagan, J., & Reznick, J. S. (1984). Behavioral inhibition in young children. *Child Development, 55,* 1005–1019.

Gersten, M. (1989). Behavioral inhibition in the classroom. In S. Reznick (Ed.), *Perspectives on behavioral inhibition* (pp. 100–124). Chicago: University of Chicago Press.

Gest, S. D. (1997). Behavioral inhibition: Stability and associations with adaptation from childhood to early adulthood. *Journal of Personality and Social Psychology, 72,* 467–475.

Hirschfeld, D. R., Rosenbaum, J. F., Biederman, J., Bolduc, E. A., Faraone, S. V., Snidman, N., Reznick, J. S., & Kagan, J. (1992). Stable behavioral inhibition and its association with anxiety disorder. *Journal of the American Academy of Child and Adolescent Psychiatry, 31,* 103–111.

Hymel, S., Rubin, K. H., Rowden, L., & LeMare, L. (1990). Children's peer relationships: Longitudinal prediction of internalizing and externalizing problems from middle to late childhood. *Child Development, 61,* 2004–2021.

Kagan, J. (1997). Temperament and the reactions to unfamiliarity. *Child Development, 68,* 139–143.

Kagan, J., & Moss, H. A. (1962). *Birth to maturity.* New York: Wiley.

Kagan, J., Reznick, J. S., Clarke, C., Snidman, N., & Garcia-Coll, C. (1984). Behavioral inhibition to the unfamiliar. *Child Development, 55,* 2212–2225.

Kagan, J., Reznick, J. S., & Snidman, N. (1987). The physiology and psychology of behavioral inhibition in children. *Child Development, 58,* 1459–1473.

Kagan, J., Reznick, J. S., & Snidman, N. (1988). Biological bases of childhood shyness, *Science, 240,* 167–171.

Kerr, M., Lambert, W. W., & Bem, D. J. (1996). Life course sequelae of childhood shyness in Sweden: Comparison with the United States. *Developmental Psychology, 32,* 1100–1105.

Kerr, M., Tremblay, R. E., Pagani, L., & Vitaro, F. (1997). Boys' behavioral inhibition and the risk of later delinquency. *Archives of General Psychiatry, 54,* 809–816.

Lazarus, P. J. (1982). Incidence of shyness in elementary-school age children. *Psychological Reports, 51,* 904–906.

Park, S. Y., Belsky, J., Putnam, S., & Crnic, K. (1997). Infant emotionality, parenting and 3-year inhibition: Exploring stability and lawful discontinuity in a male sample. *Developmental Psychology, 33,* 218–227.

Reznick, J. S., Kagan, J., Snidman, N., Gersten, M., Baak, K., & Rosenberg, A. (1986). Inhibited and uninhibited children: A follow-up study. *Child Development, 57,* 660–680.

Rubin, K. H., Daniels-Beirness, T., & Bream, L. (1984). Concurrent and predictive correlates of sociometric status in kindergarten and Grade 1 children. *Merrill-Palmer Quarterly, 29,* 337–351.

Rubin, K. H., Hastings, P. D., Stewart, S. L., Henderson, H. A., & Chen, X. (1997). The consistency and concomitants of inhibition: Some of the children, all of the time. *Child Development, 68,* 467–483.

Rubin, K. H., & Mills, R. S. L. (1988). The many faces of social isolation in childhood. *Journal of Consulting and Clinical Psychology, 56,* 916–924.

Rubin, K. H., Stewart, S. L., & Coplan, R. J. (1995). Social withdrawal in childhood: Conceptual and empirical perspectives. In T. H. Ollendick and R. J. Prinz (Eds.), *Advances in clinical child psychology* (pp. 157–196). New York: Plenum Press.

Schmidt, L. A., Fox, N. A., Rubin, K. H., Sternberg, E. M., Gold, P. W., Smith, C. C., & Schulkin, J. (1997). Behavioral and neuroendocrine responses in shy children. *Developmental Psychobiology, 30,* 127–140.

Schwartz, C. E., Snidman, N., & Kagan, J. (1996). Early temperamental predictors of Stroop interface to threatening information at adolescence. *Journal of Anxiety Disorders, 10,* 89–96.

Stemberger, R. M., Turner, S. M., Beidel, D. C., & Calhoun, K. C. (1995). Social phobia: An analysis of possible developmental factors. *Journal of Abnormal Psychology, 104,* 526–531.

Stevenson-Hinde, J., & Shouldice, A. (1993). Wariness to strangers: A behavioral systems perspective revisited. In K.H. Rubin and J.B. Asendorpf (Eds.), *Social withdrawal, inhibition and shyness in childhood* (pp. 117–150). Hillsdale, NJ: Erlbaum.

Stewart, S. L., & Rubin, K. H. (1995). The social problem-solving skills of anxious-withdrawn children. *Development and Psychopathology, 7,* 323–336.

Strauss, C. C., Lahey, B. B., Frick, P., Frame, C. L., & Hynd, G. W. (1988). Peer social status of children with anxiety disorders. *Journal of Consulting and Clinical Psychology, 56,* 137–141.

Tellegen, A. (1982). *A brief manual for the Multidimensional Personality Questionnaire.* Unpublished manuscript, University of Minnesota Minneapolis.

Thomas, A., & Chess, S. (1986). The New York Longitudinal Study: From infancy to early adult life. In R. Plomin & J. Dunn (Eds.), *The study of temperament: Changes, continuities, and challenges* (pp. 39–52). Hillsdale, NJ: Erlbaum.

Turner, S. M., Beidel, D. C., Cooley, M. R., Woody, S., & Messer, S. (1994). A multi-component behavioral treatment for social phobia: Social Effectiveness Therapy. *Behaviour Research and Therapy, 32,* 381–390.

Turner, S. M., Beidel, D. C., Dancu, C. V., & Keyes, D. J. (1986). Psychopathology of social phobia and comparison to avoidant personality disorder. *Journal of Abnormal Psychology, 95,* 389–394.

Turner, S. M., Beidel, D. C., & Townsley, R. M. (1990). Social phobia: Relationship to shyness. *Behaviour Research and Therapy, 28,* 497–505.

Turner, S. M., Beidel, D. C., & Wolff, P. L. (1996). Is behavioral inhibition related to the anxiety disorders? *Clinical Psychology Review, 16,* 157–172.

Vernberg, E. M., Abwender, D. A., Ewell, K. K., & Beery, S. H. (1992). Social anxiety and peer relationships in early adolescence: A prospective analysis. *Journal of Clinical Child Psychology, 21,* 189–196.
Zimbardo, P. G., Pilkonis, P. A., & Norwood, R. M. (1975). The social disease called shyness. *Psychology Today, 8,* 68–72.

# 11

## Varieties of Shyness in Adolescence and Adulthood

Jonathan M. Cheek & Elena N. Krasnoperova

The idea that shyness is rooted in a biological predisposition is as old as the field of psychology. William James (1890) quoted Darwin's discussion of shyness and included it in his list of basic human instincts. Baldwin (1894) also interpreted the emergence of bashfulness during the first year of life as an organic stage in the expression of instinctive emotion. Drawing on observations from his medical practice, Campbell (1896) claimed that "no fact is more certain than that shyness runs in families" (p. 805). Recent work in behavior genetics tends to support these early speculations about the contribution of an inherited biological predisposition to the origins of shyness (Plomin & Daniels, 1986).

From an evolutionary perspective on emotional development, a moderate amount of wariness regarding strangers and unfamiliar or unpredictable situations has considerable adaptive value (Izard & Hyson, 1986; Wilson, Clark, Coleman, & Dearstyne, 1994). Social anxiety is functional when it motivates preparation and rehearsal for important interpersonal events. As a social emotion, shyness also helps to facilitate cooperative group living by inhibiting individual behavior that is socially unacceptable (Ford, 1987; Keltner, Young, & Buswell, 1997). The complete absence of susceptibility to feeling shy has been recognized as an antisocial characteristic since at least the time of the ancient Greeks (Plutarch, 1906). On the other hand, excessive susceptibility to social anxiety may become so intense that shyness loses its adaptive value (Lopreato, 1984; Trower, Gilbert, & Sherling, 1990).

Shyness is a remarkably common experience. Less than 10 percent of respondents to a cross-cultural survey reported that they had never felt shy (Zimbardo, 1977). Ratings of shyness-eliciting events reveal that interactions with strangers, especially those of the opposite sex or in positions of authority; encounters requiring assertive behavior; and explicitly evaluative settings, such as interviews, provoke the strongest feelings of social anxiety (Russell, Cutrona, & Jones, 1986;

Watson & Cheek, 1986). Even though situational shyness as a transitory emotional state appears to be a normal aspect of human development and everyday adult life, for some people it becomes much more than a temporary response. About 30 to 40 percent of Americans label themselves as dispositionally shy persons (Gough & Heilbrun, 1983; Lazarus, 1982; Pilkonis, Heape, & Klein, 1980; Zimbardo, Pilkonis, & Norwood, 1975). Three-quarters of the shy respondents said that they did not like being so shy, and two-thirds of them considered their shyness to be a personal problem.

Although some psychologists have argued that the positive connotations of shyness, such as modesty or sensitivity, should be emphasized (Aron, 1996; Gough & Thorne, 1986; Keen, 1978), it is generally viewed as an undesirable personality characteristic, especially for men (Bem, 1981; Hampson, Goldberg, & John, 1987). Shy adolescents tend to regard their shyness as an unacceptable and even shameful characteristic, and shy adults often complain that their problem is not taken seriously enough by other people (Harris, 1984a; Ishiyama, 1984). A growing body of contemporary research supports this negative image of shyness as a personality trait. Rather than simply promoting cooperative social life, an enduring tendency to experience shyness frequently, intensely, and in a wide range of situations creates self-defeating behavior patterns (Cheek & Briggs, 1990; Cheek & Melchior, 1990). As a result, dispositional shyness can become a barrier to personal well-being, social adjustment, and occupational fulfillment (Jones, Cheek, & Briggs, 1986).

In this chapter we review research and theory on shyness with a focus on the varieties of shyness that are experienced during adolescence and adulthood. After considering the distinction between early- and later-developing shyness, we describe the three-component model of adult shyness. Then we introduce a new approach to withdrawn and dependent subtypes of shyness. Finally, we conclude with some implications of our approach for future directions in theory, research, and treatment.

## Early- versus Later-Developing Shyness

Shyness fulfills the two key criteria in the definition of a *temperament:* "inherited personality traits present in early childhood" (Buss & Plomin, 1984, p. 84). Therefore it may seem puzzling that Kagan (1994) has concluded that "most adults who say they are shy do not belong to the temperamental category favoring this quality" (p. 42). The solution to this puzzle may depend on the time at which shyness first becomes a salient characteristic for a particular individual. Baldwin (1894) described a developmental distinction between "primary" or "organic" bashfulness, the shyness seen in infants, young children, and animals, and "true" bashfulness, the kind of shyness seen in humans only after age 3, "which shows reflection in its simpler form, upon self and the actions of self [and] represents the child's direct application of what he knows of persons to his own inner life" (p. 439). McDougall (1963) extended Baldwin's analysis to explain the development of individual differences in the trait shyness, and he suggested a third stage of development in which the intensification of self-consciousness at the onset of puberty interacts with the development of the self-regarding sentiment to shape shyness and modesty as qualities of adult character and conduct (see table 11.1).

Table 11.1  Ages and Stages in the Development of Shyness.

| Age | Stage |
| --- | --- |
| 0 | temperamental "organic" bashfulness (Baldwin, 1894) |
|   | early developing shyness (Buss, 1980; Kagan & Reznick, 1986) |
| 4 | "true" bashfulness with simpler form of self-reflection (Baldwin, 1894) |
|   | first appearance of self-conscious shyness (Buss, 1986) |
| 8 | prepuberty intensification of self-consciousness (McDougall, 1963) |
|   | increased use of social comparison in self-evaluation (Harter, 1986) |
| 14 | peak of adolescent self-consciousness, higher for females than males |
|   | (Elkind & Bowen, 1979; Simmons & Rosenberg, 1975; Zimbardo, 1977) |

More recently, Buss (1980, 1986) has proposed a distinction between early-developing fearful shyness and later-developing self-conscious shyness that is framed in the language of contemporary research on temperament and personality development. The fearful type of shyness typically emerges during the 1st year of life and is influenced by temperamental qualities of wariness and emotionality that include a substantial genetic component (Kagan & Reznick, 1986; Plomin & Rowe, 1979). Because the effects of these temperamental factors precede the development of a cognitive self-concept, Buss specifically excluded low self-esteem as a potential cause of early-developing shyness. In light of attachment theory (Bowlby, 1988), however, it might be better to conceptualize a concurrent transactional development of temperament and the "working model" of emotional self-esteem during early childhood, even though such a theoretical integration is controversial (e.g., Sroufe, 1985; cf. Lamb, 1982).

Buss's self-conscious type of shyness first appears around age 4 or 5 when the cognitive self has already begun to develop, becomes more intense around age 8 as social comparison processes become more salient in self-evaluation (Harter, 1986), and peaks between 14 and 17 as adolescents cope with cognitive egocentrism (the "imaginary audience" phenomenon) and identity issues (Adams, Abraham, & Markstrom, 1987; Cheek, Carpentieri, Smith, Rierdan, & Koff, 1986; Hauck, Martens, & Wetzel, 1986). The peak of adolescent self-consciousness is significantly higher for females than for males, at least in American society (Elkind & Bowen, 1979; Simmons & Rosenberg, 1975; Zimbardo, 1977). In contrast to the fearfulness and somatic anxiety that characterizes early-developing shyness, later-developing shyness involves cognitive symptoms of psychic anxiety such as painful self-consciousness and anxious self-preoccupation (e.g., Crozier, 1979; Ishiyama, 1984).

Because adolescent self-consciousness declines significantly after age 14 or 15, whereas the influence of inherited temperament should be more stable, it seems reasonable that shyness would be a more enduring characteristic for people who were first shy in early childhood than for those who were first shy in later childhood or early adolescence. As part of our research on subtypes of shyness that is reported later in this chapter, we asked 590 college students whether they considered themselves currently shy and, if not, whether there had been some previous period in their lives during which they had considered themselves to be shy persons. The 48 percent of respondents who were currently shy and the 38 percent who were previously shy identified the age range in which they first remember be-

Table 11.2  Frequency Distribution for Self-Reports of the Time of First Shyness.

|  | Currently shy respondents | Previously shy respondents |
|---|---|---|
| *Years of late-developing self-conscious shyness* | | |
| On entering college | 16 | 5 |
| On entering high school | 30 | 35 |
| On entering junior high school | 52 | 51 |
| During later elementary school years | 31 | 37 |
| On entering elementary school | 29 | 45 |
| Subtotal | **158** | **173** |
| *Years of early-developing fearful shyness* | | |
| Before starting elementary school | 16 | 27 |
| As long as I can remember | 112 | 21 |
| Subtotal | **128** | **48** |
| Totals | 286 | 221 |

$\chi^2 = 29.19, p < .01.$

ing shy. Their answers are presented in table 11.2 (which replicates in a larger sample the results in table 1 of Cheek et al., 1986).

Our new data are quite consistent with previous surveys that employed retrospective reports of college students and that have revealed four findings relevant to Buss's conceptualization: (1) about 40 percent of currently shy respondents indicated that they had been shy since early childhood; (2) early-developing shyness is more enduring, with about 75 percent of those who said they were shy in early childhood reporting still being shy currently but only about 50 percent of those who were first shy during late childhood or early adolescence saying that they are currently shy; (3) the respondents with early-developing shyness also had developed cognitive symptoms of shyness on entering adolescence, so that they differed from those with later-developing shyness by having more somatic anxiety symptoms but did not have fewer cognitive symptoms; and (4) early-developing shyness appears to be more of an adjustment problem, with males in that group reporting the most behavioral symptoms of shyness (Alden & Cappe,1988; Bruch, Giordano, & Pearl, 1986; Cheek, et al., 1986; Shedlack, 1987).

The ongoing longitudinal study of childhood behavioral inhibition to the unfamiliar being conducted by Kagan and his colleagues is relevant to both types of shyness described by Buss. Kagan's construct is essentially equivalent to Buss's early-developing shyness (e.g., Kagan & Reznick, 1986), and the results from 21 months to age 5 support Buss's ideas about the physiological correlates and enduring quality of early-developing shyness (see also Rothbart & Mauro, 1990; Schmidt et al., 1997). A more recent assessment occurred at age 7, which is after the time when later-developing shyness theoretically begins to emerge. At this point, about three-fourths of the children who were extremely shy when they were 21 months old were still shy, and about three-fourths of those not previously shy continued to be uninhibited (Kagan, Reznick, Snidman, Gibbons, & Johnson, 1988). The first finding suggests that beneficial socialization experiences can ameliorate the impact of a problematic temperament, for, as James (1890) argued, in humans an instinct is only expressed in its pure form once and is thereafter subject to modification through interaction with the environment (see also Buss & Plomin, 1984).

Although Kagan et al. (1988) do not invoke it, Buss's theory may also help to explain the finding that one-fourth of the previously uninhibited children had become shy. This outcome is, in fact, absolutely necessary if his construct of later-developing shyness is valid. If no one becomes shy for the first time after age 5, then Buss's theory of a distinct type of shyness that primarily involves self-concept disturbances, rather than infant temperament, would be superfluous. Buss and Plomin (1984) have suggested that the later-developing self-conscious kind of shyness has no genetic component, but Cheek and Melchior (1990) speculated that research that points to separate genetic factors that contribute to somatic and psychic anxiety symptoms might be applied eventually to a developmental model of shyness (cf. Kendler, Heath, Martin, & Eaves, 1987; Scarr, 1987).

The early-late distinction implies that the ordering consistency assessed by test-retest stability for shyness should be high from infancy to age 5; more variable for assessments during middle childhood, depending on the exact age of each measurement; and then increasingly stable once again within adolescence and adulthood. The results from Kagan's project so far and from several other longitudinal studies generally support these expectations, although no one has yet analyzed longitudinal data specifically to test Buss's theory (for reviews see Cheek et al., 1986, and Moskowitz, Ledingham, & Schwartzman, 1985).

In Kagan's laboratory a recent study of maternal behavior and infant temperament during the first year by Arcus (1991) found that mothers of temperamentally highly reactive infants who were direct in their limit setting and not overly responsive to fretting and crying appeared to be reducing the amount of behavioral inhibition subsequently displayed by their infants. As Plomin and Daniels (1986) have pointed out, however, findings of family environmental influences on shyness do not necessarily undermine interpretations of the substantial genetic component found in early-developing shyness (within a studied population or group). In their study, the emotional expressiveness factor of a family environment measure had a much stronger negative correlation with infant shyness in nonadoptive families (i.e., biological parents were present) than in adoptive families. This is an important example of how genotype-environment correlations may influence the course of personality development (Scarr, 1987).

Three prospective studies that traced the consequences of shyness from middle or late childhood into adulthood (average age about 35) found meaningful continuities in the trait and a coherent influence on the shy person's style of life but uncovered little psychopathology (Caspi, Elder, & Bem, 1988; Kerr, Lambert, & Bem, 1996; Morris, Soroker, & Burruss, 1954). Gilmartin's (1987) retrospective study of extremely shy adult men, however, indicates that early-developing shyness sometimes can have devastating consequences in terms of loneliness, underemployment, and unhappiness. To the extent that it can be inferred from retrospective reports, it appears that these men would fit Kagan's definition of behavioral inhibition as a qualitative category, because they report somatic anxiety symptoms and other physical complaints such as allergies that date back to early childhood. It seems possible, then, that children who meet all the criteria for categorization as behaviorally inhibited in temperament, a group estimated to be about 15 to 20 percent of the population, may be at much greater risk for developing social phobia later in life than children who are merely shy around strangers (Kagan, 1997; Kagan, Snidman, & Arcus, 1993).

The socially phobic men in Gilmartin's (1987) study reported that their childhood relationships with *both* their peers and their parents, especially their mothers, were simply terrible. In contrast, the typical pattern for shy children is poor relationships with peers but positive interactions at home, especially with their mothers (Stevenson-Hinde & Hinde, 1986). Thus, in spite of the strength of findings from temperament research, it appears that the home environment is also a decisive factor for developmental outcomes of shyness, even in extreme cases (Bruch & Cheek, 1995).

We also should point out that broader cultural values influence both the prevalence of shyness and the extent to which it is perceived as a problem (Klopf, 1984; Zimbardo, 1977; see Murphy, 1947, chapter 40, for a theoretical discussion of the degree of fit between a culture and the biological individuality of its members). For example, the Japanese tend to be substantially more shy than European Americans, whereas Israelis tend to be significantly less shy. Moreover, the influence of culture on shyness may vary according to the age or gender of the shy person (Chen, Rubin, & Li, 1995; Kerr, Lambert, Stattin, & Klackenberg-Larsson, 1994). As a result, there are many complex issues to be addressed in future longitudinal studies of the development of shyness.

## Three Components of Adolescent and Adult Shyness

In spite of some debates about the precise definition of shyness as a psychological construct (Cheek & Watson, 1989; Harris, 1984b; Leary, 1986), there is considerable agreement among clinical, psychometric, experimental, and observational studies concerning the typical reactions of shy adolescents and adults during social interactions: global feelings of tension, specific physiological symptoms, painful self-consciousness, worry about being evaluated negatively by others, awkwardness, inhibition, and reticence (Briggs, Cheek, & Jones, 1986).

We believe that the best way to organize this list of typical shyness symptoms is to employ the standard tripartite division of experience into three components: affect, cognition, and observable behavior. This trichotomy of feeling, thinking, and acting has a long history in psychology (Breckler, 1984). Recently, Buss (1984) has advocated the formal elaboration of a three-component model of shyness. Jones, Briggs, and Smith (1986), however, conducted a factor analysis of 88 shyness items from five personality scales and concluded that "there are persuasive reasons to suspect that a single dimension underlies the construct of shyness" (p. 638). We do not question their factor analysis; it is quite consistent with our own factor analytic work that indicates only one major factor in shyness items (Cheek & Buss, 1981, p. 332; Cheek & Melchior, 1985). Rather, it is the research described later, employing a variety of methods other than factor analysis, that has persuaded us to continue to hold our previously stated preference for the three-component rather than the unidimensional conceptualization of shyness (Cheek & Briggs, 1990; Cheek & Melchior, 1990).

The first category of shyness symptoms includes global feelings of emotional arousal and specific physiological complaints, such as upset stomach, pounding heart, sweating, or blushing. These reactions define the somatic anxiety component of shyness. Several surveys of high school and college students indicate that from 40 to 60 percent of shy students experience difficulties with multiple symptoms in this category (Cheek & Melchior, 1985; Fatis, 1983; Ishiyama, 1984). In a study that employed content codings of free descriptions by shy women, 38 percent of them volunteered at least one somatic anxiety symptom when describing why they consider themselves shy (Cheek & Watson, 1989). The somatic component is clearly an important aspect of shyness, but these results also help to clarify why it has been relatively easy for researchers to identify a subtype of socially anxious individuals who are not troubled by somatic arousal symptoms (e.g., McEwan & Devins, 1983; Turner & Beidel, 1985).

Acute public self-consciousness, self-deprecating thoughts, and worries about being evaluated negatively by others constitute the second, the cognitive, component of shyness. The argument for distinguishing the somatic and cognitive components of shyness is based on the general distinction between somatic anxiety and psychic anxiety (Buss, 1962; Schalling, 1975), which continues to receive empirical support (Deffenbacher & Hazaleus, 1985; Fox & Houston, 1983). Between 60 and 90 percent of shy students identified various cognitive symptoms as part of their shyness (Cheek & Melchior, 1985; Fatis, 1983; Ishiyama, 1984). However, only 44 percent of the shy adults in the Cheek and Watson (1989) study described specific cognitive symptoms. Although this figure is unusually low (cf. Turner & Beidel, 1985), even among men and women clinically diagnosed as socially phobic, there is a meaningful amount of variability in public self-consciousness and other cognitive symptoms of anxiety (Hope & Heimberg, 1988).

The third component concerns the social competence of shy people. The relative absence of normally expected social responsiveness defines the quietness and withdrawal typical of shy people (Buss, 1984). Nonverbal aspects of the behavioral component of shyness include awkward body language and gaze aversion. About two-thirds of the shy respondents in the studies described previously reported behavioral symptoms of shyness. Similarly, the results of several laboratory experiments indicate that most, but not all, shy people show observable deficits in social skills (e.g., Cheek & Buss, 1981; Curran, Wallander, & Fischetti, 1980; Halford & Foddy, 1982; Paulhus & Morgan, 1997; Schroeder & Ketrow, 1997).

All three components of shyness are important, but none of them is a universal aspect of the experience of shy people. In order to investigate the degree of relationship among the three components, we wrote a short paragraph describing each component of shyness (see table 11.3) and asked two groups of college students to rate on a 5-point scale how frequently they experienced each aspect of shyness (Cheek & Melchior, 1985; Melchior & Cheek, 1987). The intercorrelations among the somatic, cognitive, and behavioral components ranged from .23 to .48, with an average of .30 for men ($n = 266$) and .39 for women ($n = 313$). The results from this rating method suggest more meaningful discrimination among the components of shyness than do the factor analyses of inventory items described earlier (e.g., Jones, Briggs, & Smith, 1986; see also, Leary, Atherton, Hill, & Hur, 1986). Moreover, in the codings of self-descriptions by shy women, 43 per-

Table 11.3 Questionnaire Paragraphs for the Three Components of Shyness.

INSTRUCTIONS: Experiences of shyness can be classified into three distinct categories, concerned with *physiological reactions, observable behaviors*, and *thoughts and worries*. Please read the detailed descriptions of each below, and answer the following questions based on these descriptions.

*Physiological reactions:*

This category of shyness could also be called "physical shyness." Physical feelings such as "butterflies in the stomach," heart pounding, blushing, increased pulse rate, and dry mouth are all examples of physiological reactions. General physical tenseness and uneasiness is also a good way to classify these reactions.

1. Physiological symptoms are an aspect of my shyness:

| 1 | 2 | 3 | 4 | 5 |
|---|---|---|---|---|
| Never | Rarely | Sometimes | Usually | Always |

*Observable behaviors:*

This category of shyness is concerned with actions that might indicate to others that you are feeling shy. For example, having trouble speaking, being unable to make eye contact, or simply not interacting with others (at a party, for instance) are all observable behaviors that may suggest shyness.

2. Observable behaviors are an aspect of my shyness:

| 1 | 2 | 3 | 4 | 5 |
|---|---|---|---|---|
| Never | Rarely | Sometimes | Usually | Always |

*Thoughts and worries:*

This category includes such things as thinking about the situation that is making you feel shy (i.e., how terrible it is, that you want to leave), or being concerned with what others may be thinking about you and the impression that you are making, feeling insecure, feeling very self-conscious or distracted. This category encompasses a wide range of experiences, but they all deal with thoughts and worries, as opposed to physical feelings or behaviors.

3. Thoughts and worries are an aspect of my shyness:

| 1 | 2 | 3 | 4 | 5 |
|---|---|---|---|---|
| Never | Rarely | Sometimes | Usually | Always |

(Adapted from Cheek & Melchior, 1985)

cent of them gave responses from only one shyness component category, 37 percent reported symptoms from two categories, and only 12 percent mentioned symptoms of all three components; the remaining 8 percent defined their shyness exclusively in terms of its consequences (e.g., being alone, not getting a job, etc.; Cheek & Watson, 1989).

Evidence that supports the three-component model suggests that shyness as a global or nomothetic trait should be conceptualized as a personality syndrome that involves varying degrees of these three types of reactions (Cheek & Melchior, 1990). But do the three components converge toward defining such a global psychological construct? To find out, we correlated the self-ratings on each component with scores on a recently revised and expanded version of the Cheek and Buss (1981) scale for assessing global shyness. This 20-item scale has an alpha coefficient of

.91, 45-day test-retest reliability of .91, a .69 correlation with aggregated ratings of shyness made by family members and close friends, and a correlation of .96 with the original scale (Cheek & Melchior, 1985; Melchior & Cheek, 1990). The self-ratings of the somatic, cognitive, and behavioral components all correlated between .40 and .68 with the global shyness scale for each gender in both of our samples (average $r = .50$, $N = 579$; Melchior & Cheek, 1987).

The research reviewed in this section validates Buss's (1984) theoretical argument that it is reasonable to infer shyness when symptoms of at least one of the three components are experienced as a problem in a social context, as well as his contention that "it makes little sense to suggest that any one of the components represents shyness to the exclusion of the other two" (p. 40). From the perspective of the three-component syndrome model, dispositional shyness is defined as the tendency to feel tense, worried, or awkward during social interactions, especially with unfamiliar people (Cheek & Briggs, 1990). Although the focus of this definition is on reactions that occur during face-to-face encounters, it should be noted that feelings of shyness often are experienced when anticipating or imagining social interactions (Buss, 1980; Leary, 1986). It also should be clear that discomfort or inhibition of social behavior due to fatigue, illness, moodiness, or unusual circumstances, such as the threat of physical harm, are excluded from the definition of shyness (Buss, 1980; Jones, Briggs, & Smith, 1986).

Regardless of their relative positions in experiencing the somatic, cognitive, and behavioral components of shyness, shy people have one obvious thing in common: They think of themselves as being shy. Rather than being a trivial observation, this may be a crucial insight for understanding the psychology of shyness. Shy people seem to have broad commonalities at the metacognitive level of psychological functioning (see table 11.4). Metacognition is defined as higher-order cognitive processing that involves awareness of one's current psychological state or overt behavior (Flavell, 1979). The distinctive self-concept processes of shy people suggest that maladaptive metacognition is the unifying theme in the experience of shyness during adulthood (Cheek & Melchior, 1990).

Viewed at this higher level of metacognitive functioning, shyness may be conceptualized as the tendency to become anxiously self-preoccupied about social interactions (Crozier, 1979, 1982). As Hartman (1986) put it, shy people become "preoccupied with metacognition: thoughts about their physiological arousal, ongoing performance, and other's perceptions of them as socially incompetent, inappropriately nervous, or psychologically inadequate" (p. 269). Because this tendency represents only one specific aspect of metacognition, Cheek and Melchior (1990) referred to the shy person's metacognitive processing of self-relevant social cognitions as *meta-self-consciousness* (cf. Dissanayake, 1988).

The pervasiveness of the self-concept processes summarized in table 11.4 suggests that the cognitive component is the predominant aspect of adult shyness. That is, shy people's cognitions regarding their somatic anxiety symptoms and degree of social skill may be more consequential than their objectively assessed levels of tension or awkwardness (Cheek & Melchior, 1990). The metacognitive model of shyness implies that, in addition to help for their specific shyness symptoms, therapy for shy adults should include cognitive approaches that address self-concept disturbances and anxious self-preoccupation (Alden & Cappe, 1986).

Table 11.4  Summary of Shy People's Cognitive and Metacognitive Tendencies Before, During, and After Confronting Shyness-Eliciting Situations.

Unlike those who are not shy, dispositionally shy people tend to:
1. Perceive that a social interaction will be explicitly evaluative.
2. Expect that their behavior will be inadequate and that they will be evaluated negatively.
3. Hold "irrational beliefs" about how good their social performance should be and how much approval they should get from others.
4. Think about "who does this situation want me to be?" rather than "how can I be me in this situation?"
5. Adopt a strategy of trying to get along rather than trying to get ahead.
6. Become anxiously self-preoccupied and not pay enough attention to others.
7. Judge themselves more negatively than others judge them.
8. Blame themselves for social failures and attribute successes to external factors.
9. Accept negative feedback and resist or reject positive feedback.
10. Remember negative self-relevant information and experiences.

From Cheek and Melchior (1990). Copyright 1990 by Plenum Press. Reprinted by permission.

## Withdrawn and Dependent Subtypes of Adolescent and Adult Shyness

According to recent estimates, approximately 40 to 50 percent of American college students consider themselves shy (Carducci & Zimbardo, 1997), which is consistent with the new data we presented in table 11.2. Given the large number of shy people, it is reasonable to expect that there is substantial heterogeneity among them, not only in terms of the three components of shyness symptoms but also in terms of social motivation. Indeed, previous research has demonstrated that there is a wide range of individual differences among shy college students in sociability (Cheek & Buss, 1981), dependency (Das, 1991), and social avoidance (Pilkonis, 1977). It is possible that there might be several distinct subtypes of shyness that could be based on individual differences in preferred or habitual interpersonal styles. An identification of these subtypes would help to resolve a long-standing controversy in the shyness literature: the relative emphasis on withdrawal versus dependency in the characterization of shy people's interpersonal styles.

The withdrawal model equates shyness with inhibition, reticence, and social avoidance. For example, Caspi, Elder, and Bem (1988) characterized life-course patterns of shy children in terms of Horney's (1945) interpersonal style "moving away from the world" and used the terms *shy* and *withdrawn* interchangeably (p. 824). We see at least two problems with this emphasis. First, not all socially withdrawn children are shy; some may be simply unsociable, and others may have been actively rejected by their peers (Harrist, Zaia, Bates, Dodge, & Pettit, 1997). Second, not all shy children are socially withdrawn; in fact, Conn (1941), another child psychologist who was influenced by Horney, emphasized dependency and conformity to the standards of others in his report of play interviews with shy children.

In the literature on adolescent and adult shyness, Lewinsky (1941) emphasized a dependent interpersonal style of "going along to get along" that many shy people adopt in social situations, and some research on the social behavior of shy people has supported the interpretation that a protective self-presentational style is a predominant characteristic of shyness (Arkin, Lake, & Baumgardner, 1986; Leary & Kowalski, 1995; Meleshko & Alden, 1993). In laboratory experiments, shy people have been shown to change their views to please an authority figure and to conform with a majority opinion (e.g., Santee & Maslach, 1982; Turner, 1977). Such an overly compliant interpersonal style resembles Horney's (1945) "moving toward people" type, rather than her "moving away" type, which was invoked by Caspi et al. (1988). According to Horney, the tendency to move toward people represents a self-effacing, "compulsive compliance" solution of basic insecurity, whereas the tendency to move away from people represents a self-sufficient, "compulsive detachment" solution of insecurity.

It is plausible that both of these conceptualizations of shyness are partially true in that each of them describes a subtype of shyness. Following Horney (1945), shy people have in common feelings of insecurity and neurotic conflict, but they might choose different solutions in trying to adapt to or ameliorate their negative feelings. Some shy people withdraw from social interactions, choosing the compulsive detachment solution. Others become excessively dependent on other people, choosing the compulsive compliance solution. Yet other shy people oscillate between excessive withdrawal and excessive dependency.

These subtypes of shy people are likely to differ in their beliefs about the trustworthiness of other people, in their affiliative needs, and in their interpersonal outcomes, such as loneliness. "Dependent" shy people are hypothesized to be more trusting of others, more affiliative, and less lonely than "withdrawn" shy people. It is unclear how shy people who are both "dependent" and "withdrawn" compare to the other shy subtypes. According to some theorists (Horney, 1945; Shaver et al., 1996), such people could be better off than the "pure" groups, because valuing both independence and interpersonal relationships gives them flexibility and resourcefulness. According to others (e.g., Coyne & Whiffen, 1995), such people will be worse off than the "pure" groups, because excessive concerns with either independence or interpersonal relationships increase vulnerability to psychopathology (e.g., Adler, 1935/1979; Blatt, 1990; Robins et al., 1994), and concerns with both could double this vulnerability. From this perspective, shy people who have strong tendencies toward both dependency and withdrawal would experience frequent approach-avoidance conflicts (for a review of conflict models of shyness, see Cheek & Melchior, 1990, pp. 53–54).

One way to explore the theoretical distinction between withdrawn and dependent shy people has been to distinguish between shy-sociable and shy-unsociable individuals (Cheek & Buss, 1981). This approach has been successful for differentiating shyness from sociability, but it has not proven to be entirely satisfactory as a method for classifying subtypes of shyness (e.g, Arkin & Grove, 1990; Asendorpf & Meier, 1993; Bruch, Gorsky, Collins, & Berger, 1989; Bruch, Rivet, Heimberg, Hunt, & McIntosh, 1999; Czeschlik & Nurk, 1995; Duggan & Brennan, 1994; Eisenberg, Fabes, & Murphy, 1995; Neto, 1996; Page, 1990; Schmidt, 1999; Schmidt & Fox, 1994, 1995). We (Krasnoperova & Cheek, 1995) proposed an alternative classification technique based on attachment theory (Bartholomew & Horowitz, 1991). On the basis of a single-item self-report measure of attachment style we identified four subtypes of shy people: shy-secure, shy-dismissing, shy-preoccupied, and shy-fearful. The shy-preoccupied and the shy-fearful types were hypothesized to represent the dependent versus withdrawn distinction. We found that shy-preoccupied individuals were more sociable, more dependent, and less avoidant than shy-fearful individuals. However, contrary to expectations, the two subtypes did not differ on loneliness.

A group that did differ on loneliness from the other subtypes was the shy-secure group. In addition to being less lonely than the other shy subtypes, the shy-secure group was also less shy and less avoidant than the shy-fearful group. It did not differ from either the shy-preoccupied or the shy-fearful group on sociability or dependency. Thus it appears that some shy people have found their niche and learned to cope with their shyness and are therefore less likely to suffer from the negative interpersonal consequences of shyness, such as loneliness. As might be expected from Bartholomew and Horowitz's (1991) interpretation of attachment theory, the shy-dismissing individuals were as unsociable, avoidant, and lonely as the shy-fearful group, but they scored significantly higher on self-esteem than both the shy-preoccupied and the shy-fearful groups.

Although some of the results reported in Krasnoperova and Cheek (1995) appear promising, a potential problem with the attachment-style classification of shyness is that it is based on a single-item measure of attachment (cf. Carver, 1997). Even more importantly, it is unclear whether an attachment style, which represents people's feelings in close relationships, is the same as a general tendency to move away or move toward other people. Thus we looked for an alternative classification technique of shyness subtypes.

Because the attachment-based subtypes of shy people differed on dependency and avoidance, as measured by the Personal Style Inventory (PSI; Robins et al., 1994), we examined this scale more closely. The PSI assesses individual differences along two fairly orthogonal dimensions, sociotropy and autonomy, both of which are considered to be risk factors for depression (Arieti & Bemporad, 1980; Blatt, Quinlan, Chevron, McDonald, & Zuroff, 1982; Beck, 1983). "Sociotropic" individuals are thought to be excessively invested in positive exchanges with other people and to have heightened needs for acceptance, understanding, support, and guidance. "Autonomous" individuals are thought to be excessively concerned with the achievement of internalized standards and goals. The proposed vulnerability factors are hypothesized to derive from different developmental experiences, to confer vulnerability to depression in response to different life events, and to result in different patterns of depressive symptoms. It has also been suggested that sociotropic and autonomous depressed individuals might benefit from different types of therapy (Beck, 1983; Blatt & Maroudas, 1992; Robins & Hayes, 1993).

The PSI (Robins et al., 1994) assesses three sociotropic constructs—excessive concerns about what others think, dependency, and pleasing others—and three autonomous constructs—excessive perfectionism, need for control, and defensive separation from others. From inspection of the items, it appeared to us that two of the sociotropy subscales, Dependency, consisting of items such as "I find it difficult to be separated from people I love" and "I like to be certain that there is somebody close I can contact in case something unpleasant happens to me" and *Pleasing Others,* consisting of items such as "I often put other people's needs before my own" and "I worry a lot about hurting or offending other people," seemed to tap into Horney's (1945) conceptualization of the tendency to move toward others. One of the autonomy subscales, *Defensive Separation,* consisting of items such as "I tend to keep other people at a distance" and "I don't like relying on others for help," seemed to tap into her conceptualization of the tendency to move away from others.

Therefore, we reassigned the shy participants from our attachment study (Krasnoperova & Cheek, 1995) to four new groups, based on their scores on an index of moving toward others (a weighted sum of Dependency and Pleasing Others subscales of the PSI) and an index of moving away from others (the Defensive Separation subscale of the PSI). We also conducted a replication study with a larger sample of male and female participants. The correlations among the measures used to classify these subtypes of shyness are presented in table 11.5.

Three sets of planned comparisons were conducted in each of the two data sets. First, dependent shy people were compared with withdrawn shy people. We hypothesized that dependent shy people would be less lonely than withdrawn shy people. Second, shy people who were low on both dependency and withdrawal were compared against the other three groups. Because they are conceptually analogous to the securely-attached shy group, we hypothesized that they would be less lonely than the other shy subtypes. Finally, shy people who were high on both dependency and withdrawal were compared with the other three groups. We were less sure about specific hypotheses for this group because of the lack of theoretical consensus on whether valuing both independence and interpersonal relationships gives one flexibility or whether it makes one more vulnerable to psychopathology than valuing either of those domains alone. We also explored differences among the four shy subtypes on measures of various aspects of shyness, self-esteem, affiliative needs, self-consciousness, and emotionality.

## First Study

Two hundred and one female undergraduates at a liberal arts college for women completed an extensive set of questionnaires which included the following measures: the Shyness Syndrome Inventory (Cheek & Melchior, 1985); the Personal Style Inventory (Robins et al., 1994); the Relationship Questionnaire that measures adult attachment styles (Bartholomew & Horowitz, 1991); the Self-Consciousness Inventory (Fenigstein, Scheier, & Buss, 1975); the Self-Esteem Scale (Rosenberg, 1965), and the General Emotionality subscale of the EASI-III Temperament Survey (Buss & Plomin, 1975). The questionnaire packet also included the Interpersonal Orientation Scale (Hill, 1987), which assesses four dimensions of affiliative need: need for emotional support or comfort (e.g., "If I feel unhappy or kind of depressed, I usually try to be around other people to make me feel better"), need for positive stimulation (e.g., "I think being close to others, listening to them, and relating to them on a one-to-one level is one of my favorite and most satisfying pastimes"), need for attention, recognition, and praise (e.g., "I often have a strong need to be around people who are impressed with what I am like and what I do"), and the need for social comparison (e.g., "When I am not certain about how well I am doing at something, I usually like to be around others so that I can compare myself to them"). Finally, the packet included the Differential Loneliness Scale (Schmidt & Sermat, 1983), which assesses the quality and quantity of respondents' interactions in four kinds of relationships: romantic-sexual relationships (e.g., "I am an impor-

Table 11.5 Correlations among Measures of Shyness, Dependency, Withdrawal, and Attachment Styles.

| | Measures | | | | | | |
|---|---|---|---|---|---|---|---|
| Measures | 1 | 2 | 3 | 4 | 5 | 6 | 7 |
| 1 Shyness | **.92** | .20 | .33 | −.30 | −.10 | .17 | .33 |
| 2 Composite of Dependency and Pleasing Others | .33 | **.82** | .07 | .07 | −.20 | .28 | .16 |
| 3 Defensive Separation | .42 | −.09 | **.78** | −.43 | .23 | .05 | .40 |
| 4 Secure Style | −.39 | −.03 | −.52 | **(−)** | −.11 | −.06 | −.44 |
| 5 Dismissing Style | .00 | −.40 | .46 | −.17 | **(−)** | −.26 | −.05 |
| 6 Preoccupied Style | .20 | .40 | −.14 | −.07 | −.29 | **(−)** | .04 |
| 7 Fearful Style | .36 | .09 | .52 | −.63 | .07 | .05 | **(−)** |

*Note.* Correlation coefficients below the diagonal are from the first study ($N = 201$). Correlation coefficients shown above the diagonal are from the second study ($N = 389$). Along the diagonal, in boldface, are the alpha coefficients, averaged across the two samples. Alpha coefficients could not be computed for the four attachment style measures because each measure consisted of a single-item rating scale.

tant part of the emotional and physical well-being of my partner"), friendships (e.g., "Few of my friends understand me the way I want to be understood"), relationships with family (e.g., "I don't get along very well with my family"), and relationships with larger groups or community (e.g., "People in my community aren't really interested in what I think or feel").

In this study, the shy group consisted of 84 women (42 percent of the sample) who gave an affirmative answer to the question, "Do you consider yourself to be shy?" The shy group was divided into four subgroups based on their scores on the Defensive Separation subscale of the PSI (an index of "moving away from people") and a weighted sum of the Dependency and Pleasing Others subscales of the PSI (an index of "moving toward people"). Shy participants who were above the shy group's median on the index of moving toward people and below the median on the index of moving away from people were labeled "dependent", and those who were above the shy group's median on the index of moving away from people and below the median on the index of moving toward people were labeled "withdrawn." Based on the conventions used in the literature concerning risk factors for depression and the results of our attachment study (Krasnoperova & Cheek, 1995), shy participants who scored below the median on both indices were labeled "secure." After consideration of their "double-risk" factors for depression and their similarity to theoretical definitions of conflict models of shyness (Cheek & Melchior, 1990), those who scored above the median on both indices were labeled "conflicted."

The results of planned comparisons (*t*-tests) between the dependent and the withdrawn shy subtypes are shown in the middle columns of table 11.6. The two groups did not differ on overall shyness, on the frequency with which they experienced different symptoms of shyness, or on how problematic they considered their shyness to be. They differed on all measures of attachment, with shy-dependent participants rating themselves higher on secure and preoccupied styles and lower on dismissing-avoidant and fearful-avoidant styles than shy-withdrawn par-

Table 11.6 Differences among the Shy Subtypes in the First Study.

| Measures | | Secure ($n = 19$) | Dependent ($n = 25$) | Withdrawn ($n = 23$) | Conflicted ($n = 17$) |
|---|---|---|---|---|---|
| Shyness | $M$ | 60.21$_x$ | 62.84$_a$ | 68.26$_a$ | 69.00 |
| | $SD$ | 12.62 | 12.48 | 11.47 | 12.14 |
| Physiological symptoms | $M$ | 2.74 | 3.04$_a$ | 2.78$_a$ | 2.47 |
| | $SD$ | 0.65 | 0.93 | 0.95 | 1.01 |
| Behavioral symptoms | $M$ | 3.05 | 3.24$_a$ | 3.30$_a$ | 3.12 |
| | $SD$ | 1.03 | 0.97 | 0.70 | 0.93 |
| Cognitive symptoms | $M$ | 3.47 | 3.80$_a$ | 3.87$_a$ | 4.00 |
| | $SD$ | 0.84 | 1.04 | 1.10 | 1.00 |
| How much of a problem | $M$ | 3.63$_x$ | 4.12$_a$ | 4.26$_a$ | 4.35 |
| is shyness? | $SD$ | 1.01 | 1.24 | 1.21 | 1.11 |
| Adult attachment styles: | | | | | |
| Secure style | $M$ | 4.53$_x$ | 4.28$_a$ | 2.96$_b$ | 2.65$_y$ |
| | $SD$ | 1.54 | 2.17 | 1.72 | 1.46 |
| Dismissing-avoidant | $M$ | 3.72 | 2.52$_a$ | 4.57$_b$ | 4.18 |
| style | $SD$ | 1.90 | 1.36 | 1.59 | 1.43 |
| Preoccupied style | $M$ | 2.61 | 4.08$_a$ | 2.22$_b$ | 3.88 |
| | $SD$ | 1.46 | 2.14 | 1.73 | 2.12 |
| Fearful-avoidant style | $M$ | 3.39$_x$ | 3.52$_a$ | 5.00$_b$ | 5.06$_y$ |
| | $SD$ | 2.12 | 2.24 | 1.54 | 1.89 |
| Interpersonal Orientation Scales: | | | | | |
| Emotional support | $M$ | 20.26 | 22.64$_a$ | 13.13$_b$ | 20.53 |
| | $SD$ | 4.85 | 4.67 | 4.39 | 4.64 |
| Attention | $M$ | 13.89$_x$ | 17.12$_a$ | 15.48$_a$ | 18.47$_y$ |
| | $SD$ | 5.79 | 5.36 | 4.22 | 4.53 |
| Positive stimulation | $M$ | 29.16 | 34.16$_a$ | 27.13$_b$ | 29.65 |
| | $SD$ | 5.64 | 3.74 | 5.19 | 5.27 |
| Social comparison | $M$ | 14.16$_x$ | 17.12$_a$ | 15.00$_b$ | 17.06 |
| | $SD$ | 3.98 | 3.13 | 4.07 | 2.19 |
| Private self- | $M$ | 34.89$_x$ | 36.80$_a$ | 40.13$_a$ | 37.82 |
| consciousness | $SD$ | 6.82 | 6.03 | 6.14 | 6.72 |
| Public self- | $M$ | 23.42$_x$ | 27.84$_a$ | 26.52$_a$ | 28.06 |
| consciousness | $SD$ | 7.34 | 4.76 | 4.82 | 3.65 |
| Self-esteem | $M$ | 30.37 | 28.68$_a$ | 30.48$_a$ | 27.35 |
| | $SD$ | 5.26 | 5.15 | 5.12 | 6.09 |
| General emotionality | $M$ | 15.11 | 17.28$_a$ | 14.00$_b$ | 17.18 |
| | $SD$ | 2.81 | 3.65 | 3.85 | 3.71 |
| Differential Loneliness Scales: | | | | | |
| Loneliness in romantic | $M$ | 5.00 | 5.32$_a$ | 6.28$_a$ | 5.29 |
| relationships | $SD$ | 3.51 | 3.15 | 3.20 | 3.58 |
| Loneliness in family | $M$ | 2.21$_x$ | 3.04$_a$ | 6.02$_b$ | 4.47 |
| | $SD$ | 2.25 | 3.68 | 4.91 | 4.35 |
| Loneliness in | $M$ | 3.58$_x$ | 4.04$_a$ | 7.07$_b$ | 6.47 |
| friendships | $SD$ | 3.13 | 2.95 | 4.14 | 4.29 |
| Loneliness in | $M$ | 1.58 | 1.28$_a$ | 2.09$_a$ | 2.41 |
| community | $SD$ | 1.92 | 1.46 | 1.90 | 1.87 |
| Overall loneliness | $M$ | 12.37$_x$ | 13.68$_a$ | 21.46$_b$ | 18.65 |
| | $SD$ | 5.73 | 7.52 | 10.02 | 11.69 |

Note. Planned comparisons were conducted to compare dependent and withdrawn subtypes of shyness. When the means of the two groups are different at $p < .05$, they are designated by different subscripts, "a" and "b." Otherwise, they both share subscript "a." In addition, contrasts were carried out to compare the secure shy group that is low on both dependency and withdrawal with all other groups and to compare the conflicted shy group that is high on both dependency and withdrawal with all other groups. When the mean of the secure group is different from the mean of the other three groups at $p < .05$, it is designated by an "x" subscript. When the mean of the conflicted group is different from the mean of the other three groups at $p < .05$, it is designated by a "y" subscript.

ticipants. Shy-dependent participants also scored higher on the need for emotional support, positive stimulation, and social comparison than did shy-withdrawn participants. The two groups did not differ on private or public self-consciousness or on self-esteem. Shy-dependent participants rated themselves as more emotional than did shy-withdrawn participants. Importantly, and as predicted, shy-dependent participants were less lonely than shy-withdrawn participants in family relationships, in friendships, and overall.

Planned orthogonal contrasts were carried out to compare the shy-secure group with a group composed of the other three subtypes of shyness. As shown in table 11.6, shy-secure participants were less shy and considered their shyness to be less problematic than the other groups. They rated themselves as more secure and less fearfully avoidant than the other groups, while not differing in their ratings of the other attachment styles. They had less need for attention and for social comparison and were less privately and publicly self-conscious than the other groups. They did not differ from the other groups in self-esteem or general emotionality. Importantly, and as predicted, they were less lonely in family relationships, in friendships, and overall, than the other three groups.

Similar contrasts were carried out to compare the shy-conflicted group with the other three subtypes of shyness. As shown in table 11.6, the shy-conflicted group did not differ from the other groups on any measure of shyness. Shy-conflicted participants rated themselves as less secure and more fearfully avoidant than the other groups. They had a higher need for attention than the other groups, while not differing on the need for emotional support, positive stimulation, and social comparison. Finally, they did not differ from the other groups on self-consciousness, self-esteem, general emotionality, or any measure of loneliness.

To summarize, the first study revealed differences between the dependent and the withdrawn subtypes of shyness on measures of attachment, affiliative needs, emotionality, and loneliness. The shy-secure group differed from the other groups on shyness, attachment, self-consciousness, and loneliness. The shy-conflicted group differed from the other groups on ratings of secure and fearful-avoidant attachment and on the need for attention.

We attempted to replicate and extend these results in a larger sample. In contrast to the first study, which employed a female-only sample, the replication sample included both men and women to examine whether the differences found among the shy subtypes generalize across the two sexes.

## Second Study

Three hundred and eighty-nine undergraduates (156 male, 232 female, 1 failed to indicate sex) from a large state university in California completed a set of questionnaires that was similar to that used in the first study. Scales that measured self-consciousness and emotionality were omitted, and a measure of depression (the Center for Epidemiological Studies Depression Scale; Radloff, 1977) was added. Two hundred and three participants (52 percent of the sample) who gave an affirmative answer to the question, "Do you consider yourself to be shy?" were divided into the four subgroups (dependent, withdrawn, secure, conflicted) in the same manner as in the first study, using the medians from the shy participants in the second study as cutoff points.

Table 11.7 Differences among the Shy Subtypes in the Second Study.

| Measures | | Secure (n = 62) | Dependent (n = 49) | Withdrawn (n = 41) | Conflicted (n = 51) |
|---|---|---|---|---|---|
| Shyness | M | 59.15$_x$ | 61.20$_a$ | 62.90$_a$ | 64.80$_y$ |
| | SD | 10.39 | 8.76 | 8.60 | 11.65 |
| Physiological | M | 2.90 | 3.00$_a$ | 2.93$_a$ | 3.39$_y$ |
| symptoms | SD | 0.92 | 0.87 | 0.86 | 0.92 |
| Behavioral symptoms | M | 3.06$_x$ | 3.16$_a$ | 3.35$_a$ | 3.51$_y$ |
| | SD | 0.83 | 0.66 | 0.74 | 0.81 |
| Cognitive symptoms | M | 3.02$_x$ | 3.41$_a$ | 3.33$_a$ | 3.41 |
| | SD | 0.88 | 0.89 | 0.92 | 1.02 |
| How much of a | M | 3.82$_x$ | 4.04$_a$ | 4.54$_b$ | 4.27 |
| problem is shyness? | SD | 1.37 | 1.02 | 1.03 | 1.23 |
| Adult attachment styles: | | | | | |
| Secure style | M | 3.98 | 4.59$_a$ | 2.98$_b$ | 3.18$_y$ |
| | SD | 1.82 | 1.68 | 1.75 | 1.75 |
| Dismissing-avoidant | M | 3.52 | 3.19$_a$ | 4.32$_b$ | 3.90 |
| style | SD | 1.42 | 1.47 | 1.93 | 1.65 |
| Preoccupied style | M | 2.98$_x$ | 3.56$_a$ | 3.27$_a$ | 3.92$_y$ |
| | SD | 1.74 | 2.03 | 1.80 | 1.92 |
| Fearful-avoidant | M | 3.43$_x$ | 3.94$_a$ | 4.41$_a$ | 4.88$_y$ |
| style | SD | 1.72 | 1.78 | 1.97 | 2.01 |
| Interpersonal Orientation Scales: | | | | | |
| Emotional support | M | 18.05 | 22.16$_a$ | 15.29$_b$ | 18.43 |
| | SD | 4.48 | 4.04 | 4.84 | 5.63 |
| Attention | M | 15.60$_x$ | 17.82$_a$ | 16.80$_a$ | 18.94$_y$ |
| | SD | 4.29 | 4.24 | 5.27 | 5.81 |
| Positive stimulation | M | 27.72$_x$ | 31.69$_a$ | 26.24$_b$ | 30.61$_y$ |
| | SD | 5.75 | 5.09 | 6.55 | 6.14 |
| Social comparison | M | 14.35$_x$ | 16.78$_a$ | 14.39$_b$ | 17.10$_y$ |
| | SD | 3.53 | 3.01 | 3.89 | 3.28 |
| Self-esteem | M | 29.87 | 30.85$_a$ | 29.80$_a$ | 27.64$_y$ |
| | SD | 5.48 | 4.14 | 5.58 | 5.67 |
| Depression | M | 37.66$_x$ | 39.98$_a$ | 40.24$_a$ | 45.52$_y$ |
| | SD | 10.52 | 10.46 | 10.07 | 11.64 |
| Differential Loneliness Scales: | | | | | |
| Loneliness in romantic | M | 4.35 | 3.55$_a$ | 6.10$_b$ | 5.11 |
| relationships | SD | 3.13 | 3.42 | 3.24 | 3.61 |
| Loneliness in family | M | 4.56 | 3.98$_a$ | 5.83$_b$ | 6.69$_y$ |
| | SD | 3.06 | 3.72 | 3.96 | 3.69 |
| Loneliness in | M | 4.60$_x$ | 4.71$_a$ | 8.44$_b$ | 6.41 |
| friendships | SD | 2.66 | 3.20 | 4.10 | 3.26 |
| Loneliness in | M | 1.80$_x$ | 1.76$_a$ | 3.51$_b$ | 2.74 |
| community | SD | 1.63 | 1.55 | 1.87 | 1.69 |
| Overall loneliness | M | 15.30$_x$ | 14.00$_a$ | 23.88$_b$ | 20.94$_y$ |
| | SD | 7.56 | 6.76 | 9.31 | 9.21 |

Note. Planned comparisons were conducted to compare dependent and withdrawn subtypes of shyness. When the means of the two groups are different at $p < .05$, they are designated by different subscripts, "a" and "b." Otherwise, they both share subscript "a." In addition, contrasts were carried out to compare the secure shy group that is low on both dependency and withdrawal with all other groups and to compare the conflicted shy group that is high on both dependency and withdrawal with all other groups. When the mean of the secure group is different from the mean of the other three groups at $p < .05$, it is designated by an "x" subscript. When the mean of the conflicted group is different from the mean of the other three groups at $p < .05$, it is designated by a "y" subscript.

In the first set of analyses, we sought to establish whether participants' sex interacted with the shyness subtypes on any of the dependent variables. To this end, we carried out two-way analyses of variance, with the shy subtype and the participants' sex as two independent variables. None of the interactions or main effects involving sex of participant were significant. Therefore, the data for males and females were combined for all subsequent analyses.

The remaining analyses were analogous to those in the first study. First, we compared the dependent shy and the withdrawn shy subtypes. As shown in the middle columns of table 11.7, the two groups did not differ on overall shyness or on the frequency with which they experienced different symptoms of shyness. However, shy-withdrawn participants considered their shyness to be more problematic than did the shy-dependent participants. Shy-dependent participants rated themselves as more secure and less dismissing-avoidant than did shy-withdrawn participants. Shy-dependent participants also had higher need for emotional support, positive stimulation, and social comparison than did shy-withdrawn participants. The two subtypes did not differ from each other in self-esteem or depression. Finally, as predicted, shy-withdrawn participants were more lonely in all four types of relationships (romantic, family, friendships, community) and more lonely overall than shy-dependent participants.

Planned orthogonal contrasts between the shy-secure group and the other three groups revealed that the secure participants were less shy, experienced fewer behavioral and cognitive symptoms of shyness, and considered their shyness to be less problematic than did the other shy subtypes. They rated themselves as less preoccupied and less fearfully avoidant than the other groups. They had a lower need for attention, positive stimulation, and social comparison than the other groups. Finally, the shy-secure participants were less depressed and less lonely in friendships, in community, and overall than the other groups.

Planned orthogonal contrasts between the shy-conflicted group and the other three groups revealed that the conflicted participants were more shy and experienced more physiological and behavioral symptoms of shyness than the other shy subtypes. They were less secure, more preoccupied, and more fearfully avoidant than the other groups. Shy-conflicted participants had a higher need for attention, positive stimulation, and social comparison than the other groups. They also had lower self-esteem, were more depressed, and were more lonely in family relationships and overall than the other groups (cf. Joiner, 1997).

To summarize, the second study demonstrated that shy-dependent participants had higher affiliative needs and were less lonely than were shy-withdrawn participants. Participants who were low on both dependency and withdrawal (the secure group) were less shy, had lower affiliative needs, and were less lonely and less depressed than participants who were high on dependency, withdrawal, or both. Finally, participants who were high on both dependency and withdrawal (the conflicted group) were more shy, less securely attached, and had higher affiliative needs and lower self-esteem than the other shy participants. They were also more depressed and more lonely than the other shy participants.

There is considerable overlap in the results of the two studies. The results of comparisons between shy-dependent and shy-withdrawn participants and between shy-secure participants and all other shy participants are highly consistent across the two studies. A discrepancy in the results of the two studies occurs in comparisons between shy-conflicted participants and all other shy participants. The second study demonstrated many more differences than the first study, including differences in the important outcomes of depression and loneliness. One possible reason for the larger number of significant results in the second study is its greater statistical power due to a larger sample size. Another reason is that the sample used in the second study was more diverse. It included both men and women, it was more ethnically diverse, and it consisted of students from a large state university rather than from a small and select women's college.

The four-group subtype of shyness approach that we have introduced here appears to be superior on both empirical and theoretical grounds to Cheek and Buss's (1981) two-group classification of shy individuals into shy-sociable and shy-unsociable. First, it permits identification of a relatively better adjusted, more psychologically secure shy group (cf. Aron & Aron, 1997; Gough & Thorne, 1986). Second, using measures of both dependency and withdrawal allows a more precise classification of what used to be called the shy-sociable and the shy-unsociable groups. Third, the four-group approach separates out the conflicted shy group, whose members are high on both dependency and withdrawal. This group may present more difficult and complex treatment issues, because conflicted shy people need help in two areas simultaneously: how not to be too passively dependent on others and how not to be too disconnected from others (cf. Alden & Capreol, 1993).

Let us clarify another point about our four shy subtypes, especially about the key distinction between shy-dependent and shy-withdrawn groups. The dependent subtype of shyness represents only one of the various possible dependent interpersonal styles (Bornstein, 1996; Pincus & Gurtman, 1995). Similarly, the withdrawn subtype of shyness is only one of the various possible avoidant interpersonal styles (Birtchnell, 1996). In particular, it is not the same as Bartholomew and Horowitz's (1991) dismissing-avoidant style, because a dismissing-avoidant person has a positive self-concept, whereas a shy person generally does not have a positive self-concept (Cheek & Melchior, 1990). So, for example, we did not obtain a significant difference between shy-withdrawn and shy-dependent groups on self-esteem in either of the two studies. Even though our self-report data concerning these four subtypes of shyness must be considered somewhat preliminary, we believe that this new typology is sufficiently promising to merit both further basic research and investigation of treatment implications.

## Conclusion

Shyness is the personality trait with the strongest genetic component (Plomin & Daniels, 1986), yet it is also a trait that involves pervasive and consequential disturbances in conscious self-concept processes (see table 11.4). Future research along the lines presented in the first two sections of this volume appears likely to validate Allport's (1937) conceptualization of personality traits as "neuropsychic entities" (Briggs, 1985). Nevertheless, we think Rowe (1987) put it too strongly when he concluded that "genotypes must be the organizing force behind behavioral development" (p. 224). In our view, innate tendencies are the fundamental postulates for understanding social behavior, not because they can explain behavior directly but because they enter into the complex transactional processes of personality development and current self-interpretation (Cheek, 1985; Cheek & Hogan 1983).

Personality traits exist at different levels of biological, emotional, cognitive, interpersonal, and cultural functioning (e.g., Barkow, 1980; Hyland, 1985). Because humans are complex, self-constructing living systems, no narrow approach to the psychology of shyness, whether based on genetics, physiology, learning, emotion, self-esteem, psychodynamics, self-attention, self-efficacy, or self-presentation, can succeed by itself (Cheek & Briggs, 1990). Our understanding of shyness will advance to the extent that psychologists are able to develop a biocultural-systems theory of personality, social behavior, and psychopathology. Future research should continue to investigate individual differences among shy people (e.g., Cheek & Watson, 1989), the impact of shyness on individual lives (e.g., Wright, 1930), the interpersonal dynamics of shy people in relationships (e.g., Read & Miller, 1989), and the psychodynamic patterns that maintain shyness across the life span (e.g., Thorne, 1989).

At present, the self-concept processes typical of shy people provide an interesting challenge to psychologists who are developing new cognitive therapies for shyness, especially because the shy can be surprisingly difficult clients (e.g., Nocita & Stiles, 1986). Nevertheless, research on combining cognitive restructuring, social skills training, and systematic desensitization and investigations of potential interactions between client characteristics and treatment strategies indicate that progress is being made in the development of effective techniques for overcoming shyness (Cappe & Alden, 1986; Carducci, 1999; Cheek & Cheek, 1989; Elder, Edelstein, & Fremouw, 1981; Henderson, 1992; Turner & Beidel, 1985; Watson, 1986). Because cognitive-behavioral and pharmacological treatments for extreme shyness and social phobia have become predominant (e.g., Beidel & Turner, 1998), we suggest that more attention should be paid to psychodynamic considerations that involve the shame, hypersensitive narcissism, and covert hostility that often lurk beneath the self-effacing surface of shy people (e.g., Gabbard, 1989; Hendin & Cheek, 1997; Zerbe, 1995).

From our theoretical perspective, we view the "constructivistic" approach to cognitive therapy, which focuses on the developmental deep structures of self-organization and attachment, as being particularly promising for the treatment of shyness (Guidano, 1986; for a case illustration see Leahy, 1985). We conclude that the personal revolution necessary for reorganizing the shy person's self-concept and social behavior is a difficult but achievable goal.

*References*

Adams, G. R., Abraham, K. G., & Markstrom, C. A. (1987). The relations among identity development, self-consciousness, and self-focusing during middle and late adolescence. *Developmental Psychology, 23,* 292–297.

Adler, A. (1979). Typology of meeting life problems. In H. L. Ansbacher & R. R. Ansbacher (Eds.), *Superiority and social interest* (3rd ed., pp. 66–70). New York: Norton. (Original work published 1935)

Alden, L., & Cappe, R. (1986). Interpersonal process training for shy clients. In W. H. Jones, J. M. Cheek, & S. R. Briggs (Eds.), *Shyness: Perspectives on research and treatment* (pp. 343–355). New York: Plenum.

Alden, L., & Cappe, R. (1988). Characteristics predicting social functioning and treatment response in clients impaired by extreme shyness: Age of onset and the public/private shyness distinction. *Canadian Journal of Behavioural Science, 20,* 40–49.

Alden, L., & Capreol, M. J. (1993). Avoidant personality disorder: Interpersonal problems as predictors of treatment response. *Behavior Therapy, 24,* 357–376.

Allport, G. W. (1937). *Personality: A psychological interpretation.* New York: Holt.

Arcus, D. M. (1991). *The experiential modification of temperamental bias in inhibited and uninhibited children.* Unpublished doctoral dissertation, Harvard University.

Arieti, S., & Bemporad, J. (1980). The psychological organization of depression. *American Journal of Psychiatry, 136,* 1365–1369.

Arkin, R. M., & Grove, T. (1990). Shyness, sociability, and patterns of everyday affiliation. *Journal of Social and Personal Relationships, 7,* 273–281.

Arkin, R. M., Lake, E. A., & Baumgardner, A. B. (1986). Shyness and self-presentation. In W. H. Jones, J. M. Cheek, & S. R. Briggs (Eds.), *Shyness: Perspectives on research and treatment* (pp. 189–203). New York: Plenum.

Aron, E. N. (1996). *The highly sensitive person: How to thrive when the world overwhelms you.* Secaucus, NJ: Carol.

Aron, E. N., & Aron, A. (1997). Sensory-processing sensitivity and its relation to introversion and emotionality. *Journal of Personality and Social Psychology, 73,* 345–368.

Asendorpf, J. B., & Meier, G. H. (1993). Personality effects on children's speech in everyday life: Sociability-mediated exposure and shyness-mediated reactivity to social situations. *Journal of Personality and Social Psychology, 64,* 1072–1083.

Baldwin, J. M. (1894). Bashfulness in children. *Educational Review, 8,* 434–441.

Barkow, J. H. (1980). Sociobiology: Is this the new theory of human nature? In A. Montagu (Ed.), *Sociobiology examined* (pp. 171–197). New York: Oxford.

Bartholomew, K., & Horowitz, L. (1991). Attachment styles among adults: A test of a four-category model. *Journal of Personality and Social Psychology, 61,* 226–244.

Beck, A. T. (1983). Cognitive therapy of depression: New perspectives. In P. J. Clayton & J. E. Barrett (Eds.), *Treatment of depression: Old controversies and new approaches* (pp. 265–290). New York: Raven Press.

Beidel, D. C., & Turner, S. M. (1998). *Shy children, phobic adults: Nature and treatment of social phobia.* Washington, DC: American Psychological Association.

Bem, S. L. (1981). *Bem sex-role inventory professional manual.* Palo Alto, CA: Consulting Psychologists Press.

Birtchnell, J. (1996). Detachment. In C. G. Costello (Ed.), *Personality characteristics of the personality disordered* (pp. 173–205). New York: Wiley.

Blatt, S. J. (1990). Interpersonal relatedness and self-definition: Two personality configurations and their implications for psychopathology and psychotherapy. In J. L. Singer (Ed.), *Repression and dissociation: Implications for personality theory, psychopathology, and health* (pp. 299–336). Chicago: University of Chicago Press.

Blatt, S. J., & Maroudas, C. (1992). Convergences among psychoanalytic and cognitive-behavioral theories of depression. *Psychoanalytic Psychology, 9,* 157–190.

Blatt, S. J., Quinlan, D. M., Chevron, E. S., McDonald, C., & Zuroff, D. C. (1982). Dependency and self-criticism: Psychological dimensions of depression. *Journal of Consulting and Clinical Psychology, 50,* 113–124.

Bornstein, R. F. (1996). Dependency. In C. G. Costello (Ed.), *Personality characteristics of the personality disordered* (pp. 120–145). New York: Wiley.

Bowlby, J. (1988). *A secure base.* New York: Basic Books.

Breckler, S. J. (1984). Empirical validation of affect, behavior, and cognition as distinct components of attitude. *Journal of Personality and Social Psychology, 47,* 1191–1205.

Briggs, S. R. (1985). A trait account of social shyness. In P. Shaver (Ed.), *Review of personality and social psychology* (Vol. 6, pp. 35–64). Beverly Hills, CA: Sage.

Briggs, S. R., Cheek, J. M., & Jones, W. H. (1986). Introduction. In W. H. Jones, J. M. Cheek, & S. R. Briggs (Eds.), *Shyness: Perspectives on research and treatment* (pp. 1–14). New York: Plenum.

Bruch, M. A., & Cheek, J. M. (1995). Developmental factors in childhood and adolescent shyness. In R. Heimberg, M. R. Liebowitz, D. A. Hope, & F. R. Schneier (Eds.), *Social phobia: Diagnosis, assessment, and treatment* (pp. 163–182). New York: Guilford.

Bruch, M. A., Giordano, S., & Pearl, L. (1986). Differences between fearful and self-conscious shy subtypes in background and adjustment. *Journal of Research in Personality, 20,* 172–186.

Bruch, M. A., Gorsky, J. M., Collins, T. M., & Berger, P. A. (1989). Shyness and sociability re-examined: A multicomponent analysis. *Journal of Personality and Social Psychology, 57,* 904–915.

Bruch, M. A., Rivet, K. M., Heimberg, R. G., Hunt, A., & McIntosh, B. (1999). Shyness and sociotropy: Additive and interactive relations in predicting interpersonal concerns. *Journal of Personality, 67,* 373–406.

Buss, A. H. (1962). Two anxiety factors in psychiatric patients. *Journal of Abnormal and Social Psychology, 65,* 426–427.

Buss, A. H. (1980). *Self-consciousness and social anxiety.* San Francisco: Freeman.

Buss, A. H. (1984). A conception of shyness. In J. A. Daly & J. C. McCroskey (Eds.), *Avoiding communication* (pp. 39–49). Beverly Hills, CA: Sage.

Buss, A. H. (1986). A theory of shyness. In W. H. Jones, J. M. Cheek, & S. R. Briggs (Eds.), *Shyness: Perspectives on research and treatment* (pp. 39–46). New York: Plenum Press.

Buss, A. H., & Plomin, R. (1975). *A temperament theory of personality development.* New York: Wiley-Interscience.

Buss, A. H., & Plomin, R. (1984). *Temperament: Early developing personality traits.* Hillsdale, NJ: Erlbaum.

Campbell, H. (1896). Morbid shyness. *British Medical Journal, 2,* 805–807.

Cappe, R. F., & Alden, L. E. (1986). A comparison of treatment strategies for clients functionally impaired by extreme shyness and social avoidance. *Journal of Consulting and Clinical Psychology, 54,* 796–801.

Carducci, B. J. (1999). *Shyness: A bold new approach.* New York: Harper Collins.

Carducci, B. J., & Zimbardo, P. G. (1997). Are you shy? In M. H. Davis (Ed.), *Annual editions: Social psychology 1997/98* (pp. 35–41). Guilford, CT: Dushkin/Brown & Benchmark.

Carver, C. S. (1997). Adult attachment and personality: Converging evidence and a new measure. *Personality and Social Psychology Bulletin, 23,* 865–883.

Caspi, A., Elder, G. H., & Bem, D. J. (1988). Moving away from the world: Life-course patterns of shy children. *Developmental Psychology, 24,* 824–831.

Cheek, J. M. (1985). Toward a more inclusive integration of evolutionary biology and personality psychology [Comment]. *American Psychologist, 40,* 1269–1270.

Cheek, J. M., & Briggs, S. R. (1990). Shyness as a personality trait. In W. R. Crozier (Ed.), *Shyness and embarrassment: Perspectives from social psychology* (pp. 315–337). New York: Cambridge University Press.

Cheek, J. M., & Buss, A. H. (1981). Shyness and sociability. *Journal of Personality and Social Psychology, 41,* 330–339.

Cheek, J. M., Carpentieri, A. M., Smith, T. G., Rierdan, J., & Koff, E. (1986). Adolescent shyness. In W. H. Jones, J. M. Cheek, & S. R. Briggs (Eds.), *Shyness: Perspectives on research and treatment* (pp. 105–115). New York: Plenum Press.

Cheek, J. M., & Cheek, B. (1989). *Conquering shyness.* New York: Putnam.

Cheek, J. M., & Hogan, R. (1983). Self-concepts, self-presentations, and moral judgments. In J. Suls & A. G. Greenwald (Eds.), *Psychological perspectives on the self* (Vol. 2, pp. 249–273). Hillsdale, NJ: Erlbaum.

Cheek, J. M., & Melchior, L. A. (1985, August). Measuring the three components of shyness. In M. H. Davis & S. L. Franzoi (Co-chairs), *Emotion, personality, and personal well-being.* Symposium conducted at the annual meeting of the American Psychological Association, Los Angeles, CA.

Cheek, J. M., & Melchior, L. A. (1990). Shyness, self-esteem, and self-consciousness. In

H. Leitenberg (Ed.), *Handbook of social and evaluation anxiety* (pp. 47–82). New York: Plenum Press.

Cheek, J. M., & Watson, A. K. (1989). The definition of shyness: Psychological imperialism or construct validity? *Journal of Social Behavior and Personality, 4,* 85–95.

Chen, X., Rubin, K. H., & Li, Z. (1995). Social functioning and adjustment in Chinese children: A longitudinal study. *Developmental Psychology, 31,* 531–539.

Conn, J. H. (1941). The timid, dependent child. *Journal of Pediatrics, 19,* 91–102.

Coyne, J. C., & Whiffen, V. E. (1995). Issues in personality as diathesis for depression: The case of sociotropy-dependency and autonomy-self-criticism. *Psychological Bulletin, 118,* 358–378.

Crozier, W. R. (1979). Shyness as anxious self-preoccupation. *Psychological Reports, 44,* 959–962.

Crozier, W. R. (1982). Explanations of social shyness. *Current Psychological Reviews, 2,* 47–60.

Curran, J. P., Wallander, J. L., & Fischetti, M. (1980). The importance of behavioral and cognitive factors in heterosexual-social anxiety. *Journal of Personality, 48,* 285–292.

Czeschlik, T., & Nurk, H.-C. (1995). Shyness and sociability: Factor structure in a German sample. *European Journal of Psychological Assessment, 11,* 122–127.

Das, S. K. (1991). *Three interpersonal styles of shyness: Shy-secure, shy-avoidant, and shy-ambivalent.* Unpublished thesis, Wellesley College, Wellesley, MA.

Deffenbacher, J. L., & Hazaleus, S. L. (1985). Cognitive, emotional, and physiological components of test anxiety. *Cognitive Therapy and Research, 9,* 169–180.

Dissanayake, E. (1988). *What is art for?* Seattle: University of Washington Press.

Duggan, E. S., & Brennan, K. A. (1994). Social avoidance and its relation to Bartholomew's adult attachment typology. *Journal of Social and Personal Relationships, 11,* 147–153.

Eisenberg, N., Fabes, R. A., & Murphy, B. C. (1995). Relations of shyness and low sociability to regulation and emotionality. *Journal of Personality and Social Psychology, 68,* 505–517.

Elder, J. P., Edelstein, B. A., & Fremouw, W. J. (1981). Client by treatment interactions in response acquisition and cognitive restructuring approaches. *Cognitive Therapy and Research, 5,* 203–210.

Elkind, D., & Bowen, R. (1979). Imaginary audience behavior in children and adolescents. *Developmental Psychology, 15,* 38–44.

Fatis, M. (1983). Degree of shyness and self-reported physiological, behavioral, and cognitive reactions. *Psychological Reports, 52,* 351–354.

Fenigstein, A., Scheier, M. F., & Buss, A. H. (1975). Public and private self-consciousness: Assessment and theory. *Journal of Consulting and Clinical Psychology, 43,* 522–527.

Flavell, J. H. (1979). Metacognition and cognitive monitoring: A new area of cognitive-developmental inquiry. *American Psychologist, 34,* 906–911.

Ford, D. H. (1987). *Humans as self-constructing living systems.* Hillsdale, NJ: Erlbaum.

Fox, J. E., & Houston, B.K. (1983). Distinguishing between cognitive and somatic trait and state anxiety in children. *Journal of Personality and Social Psychology, 45,* 862–870.

Gabbard, G. O. (1989). Two subtypes of narcissistic personality disorder. *Bulletin of the Menninger Clinic, 53,* 527–532.

Gilmartin, B. G. (1987). *Shyness and love: Causes, consequences, and treatment.* Lanham, MD: University Press of America.

Gough, H. G., & Heilbrun, A. B. (1983). *The Adjective Check List Manual—1983 edition.* Palo Alto, CA: Consulting Psychologists Press.

Gough, H. G., & Thorne, A. (1986). Positive, negative, and balanced shyness: Self-definitions and the reactions of others. In W. H. Jones, J. M. Cheek, & S. R. Briggs

(Eds.), *Shyness: Perspectives on research and treatment* (pp. 205–225). New York: Plenum Press.

Guidano, V. F. (1986). The self as mediator of cognitive change in psychotherapy. In L. M. Hartman & K. R. Blankstein (Eds.), *Perception of self in emotional disorder and psychotherapy* (pp. 305–330). New York: Plenum Press.

Halford, K., & Foddy, M. (1982). Cognitive and social skills correlates of social anxiety. *British Journal of Clinical Psychology, 21,* 17–28.

Hampson, S. E., Goldberg, L. R., & John, O. P. (1987). Category-breadth and social-desirability values for 573 personality terms. *European Journal of Personality, 1,* 241–258.

Harris, P. R. (1984a). The hidden face of shyness: A message from the shy for researchers and practitioners. *Human Relations, 37,* 1079–1093.

Harris, P. R. (1984b). Shyness and psychological imperialism: On the dangers of ignoring the ordinary language roots of the terms we deal with. *European Journal of Social Psychology, 14,* 169–181.

Harrist, A. W., Zaia, A. F., Bates, J. E., Dodge, K. A., & Pettit, G. S. (1997). Subtypes of social withdrawal in early childhood: Sociometric status and social-cognitive differences across four years. *Child Development, 68,* 278–294.

Harter, S. (1986). Processes underlying the construction, maintenance, and enhancement of self-concept in children. In J. Suls & A. G. Greenwald (Eds.), *Psychological perspectives on the self* (Vol. 3, pp. 137–181). Hillsdale, NJ: Erlbaum.

Hartman, L. M. (1986). Social anxiety, problem drinking, and self-awareness. In L. M. Hartman & K. R. Blankstein (Eds.), *Perception of self in emotional disorder and psychotherapy* (pp. 265–282). New York: Plenum Press.

Hauck, W. E., Martens, M., & Wetzel, M. (1986). Shyness, group dependence, and self-concept: Attributes of the imaginary audience. *Adolescence, 21,* 529–534.

Henderson, L. (1992). Shyness groups. In M. McKay & K. Paleg (Eds.), *Focal group psychotherapy* (pp. 29–66). Oakland, CA: New Harbinger.

Hendin, H. M., & Cheek, J. M. (1997, July). *Shyness, hypersensitive narcissism, and shame.* Paper presented at the International Conference on Shyness and Self-Consciousness, University of Wales, Cardiff.

Hill, C. A. (1987). Affiliation motivation: People who need people . . . But in different ways. *Journal of Personality and Social Psychology, 52,* 1008–1018.

Hope, D. A., & Heimberg, R. G. (1988). Public and private self-consciousness and social phobia. *Journal of Personality Assessment, 52,* 629–639.

Horney, K. (1945). *Our inner conflicts.* New York: Norton.

Hyland, M. E. (1985). Do person variables exist in different ways? *American Psychologist, 40,* 1003–1010.

Ishiyama, F. I. (1984). Shyness: Anxious social sensitivity and self-isolating tendency. *Adolescence, 19,* 903–911.

Izard, C. E., & Hyson, M. C. (1986). Shyness as a discrete emotion. In W. H. Jones, J. M. Cheek, & S. R. Briggs (Eds.), *Shyness: Perspectives on research and treatment* (pp. 147–160). New York: Plenum Press.

James, W. (1890). *The principles of psychology* (Vol. 2). New York: Holt.

Joiner, T. E., Jr. (1997). Shyness and low social support as interactive diatheses, with loneliness as mediator: Testing an interpersonal-personality view of vulnerability to depressive symptoms. *Journal of Abnormal Psychology, 106,* 386–394.

Jones, W. H., Briggs, S. R., & Smith, T. G. (1986). Shyness: Conceptualization and measurement. *Journal of Personality and Social Psychology, 51,* 629–639.

Jones, W. H., Cheek, J. M., & Briggs, S. R. (Eds.). (1986). *Shyness: Perspectives on research and treatment.* New York: Plenum Press.

Kagan, J. (1994). *Galen's prophecy: Temperament in human nature.* New York: Basic Books.

Kagan, J. (1997). Temperament and the reactions to unfamiliarity. *Child Development, 68,* 139–143.

Kagan, J., & Reznick, S. J. (1986). Shyness and temperament. In W. H. Jones, J. M. Cheek, & S. R. Briggs (Eds.), *Shyness: Perspectives on research and treatment* (pp. 81–90). New York: Plenum Press.

Kagan, J., Reznick, J. S., Snidman, N., Gibbons, J., & Johnson, M. O. (1988). Childhood derivatives of inhibition and lack of inhibition to the unfamiliar. *Child Development, 59,* 1580–1589.

Kagan, J., Snidman, N., & Arcus, D. (1993). On the temperamental categories of inhibited and uninhibited children. In K. H. Rubin & J. B. Asendorpf (Eds.), *Social withdrawal, inhibition, and shyness in childhood* (pp. 19–28). Hillsdale, NJ: Erlbaum.

Keen, S. (1978). Deliver us from shyness clinics. *Psychology Today, 12* (3), 18–19.

Keltner, D., Young, R. C., & Buswell, B. N. (1997). Appeasement in human emotion, social practice, and personality. *Aggressive Behavior, 23,* 359–374.

Kendler, K. S., Heath, A. C., Martin, N. G., & Eaves, L. J. (1987). Symptoms of anxiety and symptoms of depression: Same genes, different environments? *Archives of General Psychiatry, 44,* 451–457.

Kerr, M., Lambert, W. W., & Bem, D. J. (1996). Life course sequelae of childhood shyness in Sweden: Comparison with the United States. *Developmental Psychology, 32,* 1100–1105.

Kerr, M., Lambert, W. W., Stattin, H., & Klackenberg-Larsson, I. (1994). Stability of inhibition in a Swedish longitudinal sample. *Child Development, 65,* 138–146.

Klopf, D. W. (1984). Cross-cultural apprehension research: A summary of Pacific Basin Studies. In J. A. Daly & J. C. McCroskey (Eds.), *Avoiding communication* (pp. 157–169). Beverly Hills, CA: Sage.

Krasnoperova, E. N., & Cheek, J. M. (1995, August). *Attachment styles as subtypes of shyness.* Paper presented at the meeting of the American Psychological Association, New York, NY.

Lamb, M. E. (1982). Individual differences in infant sociability: Their origins and implications for cognitive development. In H. W. Reese & L. P. Lipsitt (Eds.), *Advances in Child Development and Behavior* (Vol. 16, pp. 213–239). New York: Academic Press.

Lazarus, P. J. (1982). Incidence of shyness in elementary-school age children. *Psychological Reports, 51,* 904–906.

Leahy, R. L. (1985). The costs of development: Clinical implications. In R. L. Leahy (Ed.), *The development of the self* (pp. 267–294). New York: Academic Press.

Leary, M. R. (1986). Affective and behavioral components of shyness. In W. H. Jones, J. M. Cheek, & S. R. Briggs (Eds.), *Shyness: Perspectives on research and treatment* (pp. 27–38). New York: Plenum Press.

Leary, M. R., Atherton, S. C., Hill, S., & Hur, C. (1986). Attributional mediators of social inhibition and avoidance. *Journal of Personality, 54,* 704–716.

Leary, M. R., & Kowalski, R. M. (1995). *Social anxiety.* New York: Guilford Press.

Lewinsky, H. (1941). The nature of shyness. *British Journal of Psychology, 32,* 105–113.

Lopreato, J. (1984). *Human nature and biocultural evolution.* London: Allen & Unwin.

McDougall, W. (1963). *An introduction to social psychology* (31st ed.). London: Methuen.

McEwan, K. L., & Devins, G. M. (1983). Is increased arousal in social anxiety noticed by others? *Journal of Abnormal Psychology, 92,* 417–421.

Melchior, L. A. & Cheek, J. M. (1987). [Shyness correlations]. Unpublished raw data, University of Michigan.

Melchior, L. A., & Cheek, J. M. (1990). Shyness and anxious self-preoccupation during a social interaction. *Journal of Social Behavior and Personality, 5,* 117–130.

Meleshko, K. G. A., & Alden, L. E. (1993). Anxiety and self-disclosure: Toward a motivational model. *Journal of Personality and Social Psychology, 64,* 1000–1009.

Morris, D. P., Soroker, M. A., & Burruss, G. (1954). Follow-up studies of shy, withdrawn children: I. Evaluation of later adjustment. *American Journal of Orthopsychiatry, 24,* 743–754.

Moskowitz, D. S., Ledingham, J. E., & Schwartzman, A. E. (1985). Stability and change in aggression and withdrawal in middle childhood and adolescence. *Journal of Abnormal Psychology, 94,* 30–41.

Murphy, G. (1947). *Personality: A biosocial approach to origins and structure.* New York: Harper.

Neto, F. (1996). Correlates of Portuguese college students' shyness and sociability. *Psychological Reports, 78,* 79–82.

Nocita, A., & Stiles, W. B. (1986). Client introversion and counseling session impact. *Journal of Counseling Psychology, 33,* 235–241.

Page, R. M. (1990). Shyness and sociability: A dangerous combination for illicit substance abuse in adolescent males? *Adolescence, 25,* 803–806.

Paulhus, D. L., & Morgan, K. L. (1997). Perceptions of intelligence in leaderless groups: The dynamic effects of shyness and acquaintance. *Journal of Personality and Social Psychology, 72,* 581–591.

Pilkonis, P. A. (1977). Shyness, public and private, and its relationship to other measures of social behavior. *Journal of Personality, 45,* 585–595.

Pilkonis, P. A., Heape, C., & Klein, R. H. (1980). Treating shyness and other psychiatric difficulties in psychiatric outpatients. *Communication Education, 29,* 250–255.

Pincus, A. L., & Gurtman, M. B. (1995). The three faces of interpersonal dependency: Structural analyses of self-reported dependency measures. *Journal of Personality and Social Psychology, 69,* 744–758.

Plomin, R., & Daniels, D. (1986). Genetics and shyness. In W. H. Jones, J. M. Cheek, & S. R. Briggs (Eds.), *Shyness: Perspectives on research and treatment* (pp. 63–80). New York: Plenum Press.

Plomin, R., & Rowe, D. C. (1979). Genetic and environmental etiology of social behavior in infancy. *Developmental Psychology, 15,* 62–72.

Plutarch (1906). Of bashfulness. In R. W. Emerson (Ed.), *Plutarch's essays and miscellanies.* Boston: Little, Brown.

Radloff, L. S. (1977). The CES-D Scale: A new self-report depression scale for research in the general population. *Applied Psychological Measurement, 1,* 385–401.

Read, S. J., & Miller, L. C. (1989). Inter-personalism: Toward a goal-based theory of persons in relationships. In L. A. Pervin (Ed.), *Goal concepts in personality and social psychology* (pp. 413–472). Hillsdale, NJ: Erlbaum.

Robins, C. J., & Hayes, A. M. (1993). An appraisal of cognitive therapy. *Journal of Consulting and Clinical Psychology, 61,* 205–214.

Robins, C. J., Ladd, J., Welkowitz, J., Blaney, P. H., Diaz, R., & Kutcher, G. (1994). The Personal Style Inventory: Preliminary validation studies of new measures of sociotropy and autonomy. *Journal of Psychopathology and Behavioral Assessment, 16,* 277–301.

Rosenberg, M. (1965). *Society and the adolescent self-image.* Princeton, NJ: Princeton University Press.

Rothbart, M. K., & Mauro, J. A. (1990). Temperament, behavioral inhibition, and shyness in childhood. In H. Leitenberg (Ed.), *Handbook of social and evaluation anxiety* (pp. 139–160). New York: Plenum Press.

Rowe, D. C. (1987). Resolving the person-situation debate: Invitation to an interdisciplinary dialogue. *American Psychologist, 42,* 218–227.

Russell, D., Cutrona, C., & Jones, W. H. (1986). A trait-situational analysis of shyness. In W. H. Jones, J. M. Cheek, & S. R. Briggs, (Eds.), *Shyness: Perspectives on research and treatment* (pp. 239–249). New York: Plenum Press.

Santee, R. T., & Maslach, C. (1982). To agree or not to agree: Personal dissent and social pressure to conform. *Journal of Personality and Social Psychology, 42,* 690–700.

Scarr, S. (1987). Personality and experience: Individual encounters with the world. In J. Aronoff, A. I. Rabin, & R. A. Zucker (Eds.), *The emergence of personality* (pp. 49–78). New York: Springer.

Schalling, D. S. (1975). Types of anxiety and types of stressors as related to personality.

In C. D. Spielberger & I. G. Sarason (Eds.), *Stress and anxiety* (Vol. 1, pp. 279–283). Washington, DC: Hemisphere.

Schmidt, L. A. (1999). Frontal brain electrical activity (EEG) in shyness and sociability. *Psychological Science, 10,* 316–320.

Schmidt, L. A., & Fox, N. A. (1994). Patterns of cortical electrophysiology and autonomic activity in adults' shyness and sociability. *Biological Psychology, 38,* 183–198.

Schmidt, L. A., & Fox, N. A. (1995). Individual differences in young adults' shyness and sociability: Personality and health correlates. *Personality and Individual Differences, 19,* 455–462.

Schmidt, L. A., Fox, N. A., Rubin, K. H., Sternberg, E. M., Gold, P. W., Smith, C. C., & Schulkin, J. (1997). Behavioral and neuroendocrine responses in shy children. *Developmental Psychobiology, 30,* 127–140.

Schmidt, N., & Sermat, V. (1983). Measuring loneliness in different relationships. *Journal of Personality and Social Psychology, 44,* 1038–1047.

Schroeder, J. E., & Ketrow, S. M. (1997). Social anxiety and performance in an interpersonal perception task. *Psychological Reports, 81,* 991–996.

Shaver, P. R., Papalia, D., Clark, C. L., Koski, L. R., Tidwell, M. C., & Nalbone, D. (1996). Androgyny and attachment security: Two related models of optimal personality. *Personality and Social Psychology Bulletin, 22,* 582–597.

Shedlack, S. M. (1987). *The definition and development of shyness.* Unpublished B. A. honors thesis, Wellesley College, Wellesley, MA.

Simmons, R. G., & Rosenberg, F. (1975). Sex, sex roles, and self-image. *Journal of Youth and Adolescence, 4,* 229–258.

Sroufe, L. A. (1985). Attachment classification from the perspective of infant-caregiver relationships and infant temperament. *Child Development, 56,* 1–14.

Stevenson-Hinde, J., & Hinde, R. A. (1986). Changes in associations between characteristics and interactions. In R. Plomin & J. Dunn (Eds.), *The study of temperament: Changes, continuities, and challenges* (pp. 115–129). Hillsdale, NJ: Erlbaum.

Thorne, A. (1989). Conditional patterns, transference, and the coherence of personality across time. In D. M. Buss & N. Cantor (Eds.), *Personality psychology: Recent trends and emerging directions* (pp. 149–159). New York: Springer-Verlag.

Trower, P., Gilbert, P., & Sherling, G. (1990). Social anxiety, evolution, and self-presentation. In H. Leitenberg (Ed.), *Handbook of social and evaluation anxiety* (pp. 11–45). New York: Plenum Press.

Turner, R. G. (1977). Self-consciousness and anticipatory belief change. *Personality and Social Psychology Bulletin, 3,* 438–441.

Turner, S. M., & Beidel, D. C. (1985). Empirically derived subtypes of social anxiety. *Behavior Therapy, 16,* 384–392.

Watson, A. K. (1986). Alleviation of communication apprehension: An individualized approach. *Texas Speech Communication Journal, 11,* 3–13.

Watson, A. K., & Cheek, J. M. (1986). Shyness situations: Perspectives of a diverse sample of shy females. *Psychological Reports, 59,* 1040–1042.

Wilson, D. S., Clark, A. B., Coleman, K., & Dearstyne, T. (1994). Shyness and boldness in humans and other animals. *Trends in Ecology and Evolution, 9,* 442–446.

Wright, M. B. (1930). Shyness. *Psyche, 11,* 32–42.

Zerbe, K. J. (1995). Uncharted waters: Psychodynamic considerations in the diagnosis and treatment of social phobia. In W. W. Menninger (Ed.), *Fear of humiliation: Integrated treatment of social phobia and comorbid conditions* (pp. 1–17). Northvale, NJ: Aronson.

Zimbardo, P. G. (1977). *Shyness.* Reading, MA: Addison-Wesley.

Zimbardo, P. G., Pilkonis, P., & Norwood, R. (1975). The social disease called shyness. *Psychology Today, 8,* 69–72.

# 12

## High Sensitivity as One Source of Fearfulness and Shyness

### Preliminary Research and Clinical Implications

Elaine N. Aron

This chapter suggests that there may be a different way to understand at least some of what is inherited which predisposes certain individuals to feel extreme fear and shyness. This new understanding focuses on differences in the processing of sensory information: Many or most individuals are *not* sensitive to subtle cues, not reflective, not easily overstimulated (and indeed often seek extra stimulation), and therefore appear bold, nonfearful, or even impulsive in their behavior. However, there is a minority of individuals, about 15 percent (Kagan, 1994), who are born with a temperamental difference that, according to diverse research, makes them more reflective, sensitive to subtle stimuli, uncomfortable with novelty (with greater sensitivity to subtle stimuli, more would be seen as novel, and novelty would be more stimulating), and easily overstimulated. As a result, those with this difference would appear cautious, inhibited, or shy. The expression of this temperamental quality in adulthood I have called the trait of high sensory-processing sensitivity (Aron & Aron, 1997).

Research evidence for the existence of a trait of sensitivity to subtle cues will be reviewed. It should be noted that the emphasis on sensory processing is intended to reflect evidence that the individual differences are not in the sense organs themselves but in the brain or the nerves leading to the brain or both (Patterson & Newman, 1993; Stelmack, 1990), causing certain individuals to be "geared to inspect" (Brebner, 1980, p. 13). As suggested previously, as a result of this longer inspection time, individuals with this trait will appear, through their hesitation or overarousal, to be shy or fearful. Indeed, I will review research that suggests that they may also be more affected by aversive experiences, making them more prone to actually become shy or fearful. But I am proposing that vulnerability, negative affect, fearfulness, or shyness are not as generally useful and accurate descriptors of this trait as sensitivity is. (As an analogy, "skin-cancer-proneness" is not as gen-

251

erally useful a descriptor of a blonde, blue-eyed person's major physical traits as "fair" or "fair complexioned" would be.)

Of course the concepts of shyness, fearfulness, negative affect, and the like are still useful and clinically important descriptors and apply both to some sensitive persons and many nonsensitive persons as well. But I believe that substantial harm has been done to our research and practice by confusing these traits. It is time to sort them out.

This chapter (1) explores the concept of sensitivity as others have observed it, directly or indirectly; (2) reviews my own research on the topic; (3) suggests how extreme shyness and fearfulness may in many cases arise from this fundamental trait rather than make up the fundamental trait; and (4) discusses the implications of this new understanding for developmental outcomes and treatment.

## A Vein of Sensitivity Within the Literature

This emphasis on sensory processing sensitivity will seem to many, rightly, to be a new dress for an old inherited trait, highlighting some aspects of it and relegating others to a new, secondary position. This old temperament trait is probably the most researched by psychology and utilized by the general public. It is variously called introversion (Eysenck, 1981; McRae & John, 1993); early, fearful shyness (Buss, 1980); and innate fearfulness—the latter including inhibitedness (Kagan, 1994), timidity (Wilson, Coleman, Clark, & Biederman, 1993), and reactivity (Suomi, 1991). (I am well aware that significant work has been done by Eysenck, 1981, and others to separate introversion from neuroticism and fearfulness and by Clark and Watson, 1991 to separate negative affect from lack of positive affect. Yet these distinctions are frequently blurred, especially in infant and animal research, as well as by the general public. Because those with the trait can be labeled in any of these ways, I too will blur the distinction here.) Whatever this focal trait or mixture of traits, it is the most easily recognized difference not only in human personality but also in many animals as well—for example, other primates (Higley & Suomi, 1989; Stevenson-Hinde, Stillwell-Barnes, & Zung, 1980; Suomi, 1983, 1987, 1991), many canids (Bekoff, 1977; Fox, 1972; Goddard & Beilharz, 1985; MacDonald, 1983; Scott & Fuller, 1965), rats (Blanchard, Flannelly, & Blanchard, 1986; Blizard, 1981), goats (Lyons, Price, & Moberg, 1988), and sunfish (Wilson et al., 1993). Researchers of individual differences in all of these areas tend to cite each other's work and to see themselves as studying facets of the same trait for which the evidence of heritability by humans and many other species is now considered overwhelming. The question is, What is the fundamental nature of this difference? Is it low sociability? High arousal? Fearfulness?

In discussing what they called the "shy-bold continuum," Wilson et al. (1993) discussed another possibility. Biological research suggests that this continuum represents two distinct survival strategies found within many species. The two strategies result not only in different ways of responding to threat but also in different foraging and mating strategies. Even the parasites hosted by the two groups can be different. Wilson et al. (1993) speculated that in some species an individual's phenotypic strategy is determined by genotypic polymorphism and in other species by the environmental context working on a phenotypic plasticity. Either way, having two phenotypic strategies permits a species to make broader use of the same environment. And one way to understand the two most observed broad strategies is that one, that of the majority, involves taking many relatively risky actions; that of the minority involves taking a few seemingly more selected actions. Thus, although fear or shyness could be an aspect of the strategy of taking more selected action, it seems just as likely that some difference in the processing of sensory information is at work, creating a greater awareness of consequences, both positive and negative.

Is there evidence for such a form of sensitivity? There is an extensive body of work on introversion and extraversion that has pointed to a sensitivity-like variable as a key distinguishing feature of introverts. For example, compared with extraverts, they evidence more sensitivity to low auditory frequencies (Stelmack & Campbell, 1974; Stelmack & Michaud-Achorn, 1985); to pain (e.g., Barnes, 1975; Haier, Robinson, Braden, & Williams, 1984; Schalling, 1971); and to electrocutaneous (e.g., Edman, Schalling, & Rissler, 1979), olfactory (e.g., Herbener, Kagan, & Cohen, 1989), and visual thresholds (e.g., Siddle, Morrish, White, & Mangan, 1969). A difference in sensitivity is almost always cited in reviews of the literature on introverts and extraverts—for example, in Koelega's (1992) meta-analysis; Stelmack's (1990) and Stelmack and Geen's (1992) reviews; and Kohn's (1987) discussion of arousability. That the difference involves the central processing of stimulation is suggested by introverts' greater capacity for learning without awareness (which was unrelated to a measure of sociability in Deo & Singh, 1973) and the complicated role of distraction (e.g., Geen, McCown, & Broyles, 1985; Harley & Matthews, 1992; Shigehisa, Shigehisa, & Symons, 1973; Shigehisa, 1974). Patterson and Newman (1993), having studied the differences in the learning and problem-solving styles of the two types (e.g., after making an error, introverts choose to take time to think; extraverts choose to try again immediately), refer to the cognitive aspects of introversion as reflectivity and those of extraversion as impulsivity and describe broad, systematic differences in how the two types process sensory information. Still, the difference may not be entirely in central processing, given a shorter latency for the auditory brainstem-evoked response (Stelmack & Wilson, 1982; for a review, see Stelmack, 1990), making reflectivity, flattering as it may be, seem like too narrow a term for the trait.

Others besides introversion researchers have seen sensory-processing sensitivity as a fundamental individual difference. Thomas and Chess (1977), in their early work on childhood temperament, observed low sensory threshold as one of the nine basic traits that distinguish children. It, together with other traits such as social withdrawal, described the "slow to warm up" child. Petrie's (1967) early work on "augmenters" of stimulation also captured the phenomenon well but was probably lost as a useful concept because of the use by Buchsbaum, Haier, and Johnson (1983) of the opposite term, "reducers" (of evoked potentials), for the same phenomenon. Fine (1972, 1973) argued that sensitivity differences best explain field dependence-independence, finding support for his view in the better performance of field independents on color and weight discrimination tasks. Finally, there is the pioneering work of Mehrabian (1976, 1991; Mehrabian & O'Reilly, 1980), who developed a measure of low stimulus screening and arousability that assumed arousability to be an effect, not a cause, of a greater sensitivity to stimulation.

Another researcher with very relevant data is the sociologist Gilmartin (1987), who studied "love-shyness" in 500 men, including 100 who were over 35 and still virginal, prevented by shyness from fulfilling strong desires for a heterosexual romantic relationship. Although noticing important environmental influences, Gilmartin was convinced of the role in his sample of a fundamental genetic trait and maintained that some kind of sensory sensitivity was central to that trait. He found that love-shy men reported a stronger startle response and far greater sensitivity to temperature extremes, loud or noxious noise, pain, scratchy clothing, bright sun, seasonal declines in ambient light, and subtle irritants, such as a grain of sand in their shoe. They also had more allergies and skin irritations, as has been found to be the case for inhibited children (Bell, 1992), seemingly an indication of a more sensitive immune system.

A related line of work has been conducted by medical researchers Boice and colleagues (1995) in their study of high- and low-reactive children (reactivity was measured as change from baseline of heart rate and immune reactivity when individuals were placed in a challenge situation). High-reactive children living and going to school under stressful conditions were more prone to illness and injury, but, when living and going to school in low-stress environments, high-reactive children evidenced the least illness and injury. Gannon, Banks, and Shelton (1989) found similar results for adolescents (according to their tables—they discussed only the increased illness and injuries under high stress). Trying to explain this unusual result, Boice and colleagues (1995) speculated that "children with a heightened sensitivity to psychosocial processes [might have superior health] under low-stress, nurturing, and predictable conditions, in which social cues denote encouragement and acceptance" (p. 419) because of "a heightened sensitivity to the character of the social world" (p. 420).

Finally, it is noteworthy that Japanese psychologists (e.g., Nagane, 1990; Satow, 1987; Shigehisa, 1974) have been researching sensory sensitivity for some time. For example, Satow (1987) factor analyzed a 60-item questionnaire and found factors he termed lower sensory threshold, more rapid perception of a stimulus, and lower tolerance for intense or prolonged stimulation. Variations in these were said to lead to four types of sensitivity.

## Sensory-Processing Sensitivity Studied Explicitly

Impressed by this vein of results that imply some kind of processing sensitivity, Arthur Aron and I (1997) carried out a series of seven studies that focused on identifying a core trait of sensitivity and its link with related variables. The first study was qualitative, seeking to explore whether the phenomenon existed and what it might be in a general way. We interviewed 40 individuals, ages 18 to 66, using an announcement that sought those who identified themselves as "highly sensitive"— "either highly introverted (for example, preferring the company of one or two people rather than a group) or easily overwhelmed by stimulation (such as noisy places or evocative or shocking entertainment)." (This announcement reflected our belief at the time that we might simply be studying introversion as it is subjectively experienced.)

About half the interviewees had already thought considerably about being highly sensitive; for the others the announcement brought their sensitivity into focus for the first time. Either way, over 70 percent reported (1) a sense of being very different from others, especially in regard to their need to take frequent breaks during busy days; (2) a conscious arrangement of their lives to reduce stimulation and unwanted surprises; (3) the importance of their spiritual and inner lives, including dreams; (4) the sense that difficulties that were not obviously the result of childhood experiences stemmed from fear of failing due to overarousal while being observed (e.g., on the job), when they thought they were being socially judged (e.g., dating or attending social functions), or when they had to compete with others (e.g., competitive school situations).

About half of these respondents reported having had good childhoods, and this group also reported greater success, either as students or in their careers, and saw many advantages to their sensitivity, even though their lives had been considerably shaped by its demands. Their relationship histories were also considerably better than those of individuals with troubled childhoods. Of those with difficult childhoods, about half had received extensive psychotherapy. The rest evidenced fairly severe adjustment or personality problems in adulthood, although not necessarily in ways obviously related to their sensitivity (e.g., two had eating disorders). But there was a sense in which their sensitivity also seemed more problematic, affecting school, career, and relationships much more and creating in them a sense of being vulnerable, handicapped, or flawed.

Of the 35 who completed the Myers-Briggs Type Indicator (MBTI; Myers, 1962), 24 were introverted intuitive, 7 were extraverted intuitive, and 4 were introverted sensing (leaving 0 extraverted sensing). The MBTI results corroborated my surprising finding that over one-fourth of the interviewees reported being outgoing, in spite of the notice having been explicitly biased toward introverts. Some of the sensitive extraverts grew up in highly social environments; some seemed to have adopted an extraverted persona as a defense and under pressure from family dynamics; others seemed to have adopted an extraverted attitude out of a kind of energetic, restless giftedness.

From these interviews we developed other questionnaires and ultimately a measure of sensory-processing sensitivity that was used in the next six questionnaire studies. Study 2 participants were 329 undergraduates at the University of California, Santa Cruz (UCSC). Study 3 participants were 285 undergraduates in statistics classes at seven North American universities. Study 4 was a random-digit-dialing telephone survey in Santa Cruz County, California, an area including two small cities and a surrounding rural population. Respondents in this study included 165 women and 134 men aged from 18 to 91, with a mean age of 43.4; professions were typical of the region. Studies 5 ($n = 119$ UCSC students), 6 ($n = 172$ SUNY-Stony Brook students) and 7 ($n = 109$ SUNY-Stony Brook students) focused on special issues.

These quantitative studies yielded five key results. First, in all six studies, sensitivity was consistently found to be a unidimensional construct with strong intercorrelations among seemingly quite heterogeneous self-reported sensitivities, including sensitivity to subtleties, to the arts, to caffeine, hunger, pain, change, overstimulation, strong sensory input, others' moods, violence in the media, and being observed. These diverse sensitivities, along with a variety of other self-reported features such as being easily overaroused, startling easily, and being highly conscientious, showed a consistent unidimensional factor structure and consistently adequate alphas. The latent commonality that appeared among these not obviously similar experiences is consistent with the theory that there is an underlying differentiating characteristic that distinguishes the way some individuals process stimuli, one that involves a greater sensory-processing sensitivity, reflectivity, and arousability.

The second key finding was that sensitivity was related to but not identical with social introversion, the variable most often seen as identical with or subsuming sensitivity. In all six quantitative studies, we found the partial independence of social introversion and sensitivity, employing four different measures of social introversion—the MBTI, various versions of our own questionnaire measure, Eysenck and Eysenck's (1968) EPI, and the Big Five inventory measure of extraversion/surgency. Correlations with introversion were small to moderate (.14 to .45), but all were clearly well below unity. In some studies, more than one measure of introversion was used, and in each of these cases the correlations between the introversion measures were clearly higher than was any introversion measure with the sensitivity measure. Yet another indication of the independence of sensitivity is that appropriate, more purely sensitivity variables, such as still being affected by films the day after seeing them and being sensitive to seasonal changes in daylight hours, had unique correlations with sensitivity, even after partialing out introversion measures. Finally, the same partial independence of sensitivity from introversion was found in all these ways, even when an alternative measure of sensitivity (Mehrabian's, 1976, scale) was employed.

Not surprisingly, among the various measures of introversion, sensitivity was most related to Eysenck and Eysenck's (1968) older scale, which mixes items on sociability with those on arousability and impulsivity—Eysenck's understanding of the underlying reason for extraversion-introversion differences (these questions now make up much of Eysenck's [1991; Eysenck & Eysenck, 1975] Psychoticism factor). Thus, for example, Campbell (1992) found, in breaking down Eysenck's measure of extraversion in this way, that noise sensitivity was as related to low impulsivity as it was to the low-sociability aspect of the extraversion scale. (Campbell noted that impulsivity might have correlated even more negatively with noise sensitivity if a more reliable measure of impulsivity had been used; or, I would add, had he used one designed to measure what may be the more basic phenomenon, sensitivity, rather than a mere lack of impulsiveness.) Thus it also makes sense that on a simple visual search task on which introverts are always found to excel, Newton, Slade, Butler, and Murphy (1992) found that low Psychoticism was more associated with accuracy than low Extraversion.

Fearful shyness and introversion so extreme that they exclude all relationships are serious clinical problems that deserve quality research. For that very reason, these concepts need to be better differentiated from sensitivity, and a clinical approach to them should probably include assessments for sensory-processing sensitivity, as well as for social and attachment traumas.

The third key finding is that, as with introversion, sensitivity is related to but not identical with negative emotionality. I believe sensitivity has been seriously confused with neuroticism (e.g., Howarth, 1986), fearfulness (Buss & Plomin, 1984; Gray, 1991), reactivity (Strelau, 1983), negative affect (Clark & Watson, 1991), or inhibitedness (Kagan, 1994), because in the face of novelty both the sensitive and the fearful will pause and possibly choose not to proceed and because the sensitive do indeed become fearful, overaroused, or more easily depressed than others, but only when they experience repeated aversive experiences while lacking social resources. In support of this view, these six studies consistently found a partial independence of sensitivity from negative emotionality, using two different measures of negative emotionality (our own and the Big Five Neuroticism scale). The correlations of sensitivity with negative emotionality were substantial (median = .54) but always far from perfect. Further, after partialing out negative emotionality, there remained consistent unique associations of sensitivity with other, more purely sensitive variables, such as sensitivity to alcohol and being affected by movies the day after viewing them.

It seems quite reasonable that sensitive persons should be more emotional, as they are aware of more and also more easily overaroused. Overarousal is probably not often experienced without a context, so that, depending on context, it is labeled as an emotion, such as anxiety, social fear, or shyness (Brodt & Zimbardo, 1981), or even romantic attraction (Dutton & Aron, 1974). But given that overarousal is the result of the trait, not the trait itself, it seems more accurate to think of it as sensitivity rather than emotionality. In particular, it should not be confused with negative emotionality or neuroticism. This is a mistake on several counts. First, in Study 5 we found that highly sensitive persons (HSPs) were also more prone to intense positive emotions. More important are the findings, discussed next, on the two clusters of HSPs, those with and without troubled childhoods.

(Should you be wondering, sensitivity is also not merely the linear or multiplicative combination of social introversion and emotionality—these do not account for all the variance in sensitivity, and sensitivity accounts for unique variance in appropriate variables after partialling out the combination.)

Returning to the third key finding, in each study with a sample size adequate for conducting appropriate analyses (Studies 2, 3, and 4), we found a consistent pattern of two clear clusters of HSPs (see figure 12.1), even though the three studies involved quite different samples. In each study the smaller cluster, consisting of about one-third of the HSPs, reported childhoods that were substantially more troubled (and, in two of the samples, more introverted and emotional). The larger cluster, on the other hand, although having virtually identical means on sensitivity, was much more similar to those who were not highly sensitive with regard to troubled childhood, introversion, and emotionality.

My interpretation of the cluster analysis solution is that, although all highly sensitive individuals have the same underlying temperament, the implications of this temperament for the rest of their lives depends on environmental factors—with a prime candidate being circumstances of childhood (as suggested by the ability of reported unhappy childhood to differentiate the two clusters and by what we found to be generally strong correlations between emotionality and unhappy childhood). Further, many of the other variables typical of the smaller cluster (e.g., cry easily, love intensity) that seem logically linked to emotionality or neuroticism also seem easily explained by childhood experiences. The impact of childhood experiences on adult neuroticism is suggested by Shaver and Brennan (1992), who found correlations between insecure attachment and Big-Five neuroticism. Still, one might argue that infant irritability (the usual first sign of a sensitive temperament; Kagan, 1994; Rothbart, Derryberry, & Posner, 1994) is causal here—it leads to insecure attachments (a tentative finding by van den Boom, 1989, among lower class mother-

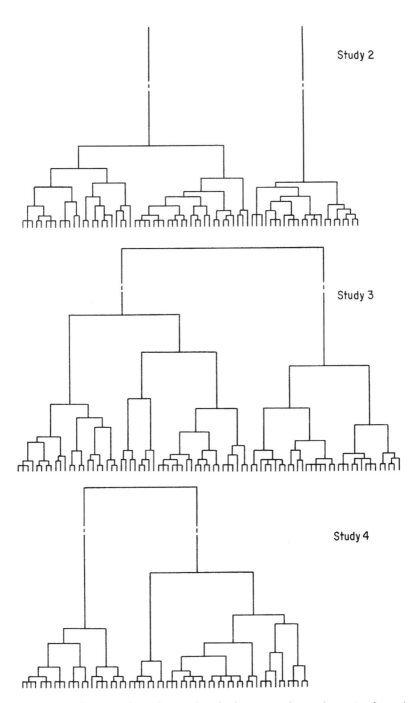

Figure 12.1. Dendograms from hierarchical cluster analyses from Study 2 (329 University of California, Santa Cruz students), Study 3 (285 students from universities around North America), and Study 4 (299 respondents to a random-digit-dialing community telephone survey). Note in each study the clear suggestions of a two-cluster pattern. From Aron and Aron (1997). Copyright 1997 by American Psychological Association. Reprinted by permission.

infant dyads) unless extra efforts are made by the mother to help the infant to feel secure. However, Main (1990) argued convincingly that evolution makes it a high priority that infants adapt to their caretakers rather than try to force caretakers to adapt to them, implying that infant temperament would be suppressed rather than actively creating a nonsecure attachment. There is also research reported by Gunnar (1994), discussed later, which suggests that sensitive children are not necessarily anxious in the face of novelty but become so when they perceive a lack of responsiveness from the caretaker accompanying them. This result suggests ways in which these individuals might be more affected than others by poor parenting.

The main point is that any overall association of negative emotionality, including fearfulness, with sensitivity or variables closely linked with it actually reflects two relatively distinct subpopulations. Hopefully, this finding will help undermine stereotypes of HSPs as universally emotional and neurotic and will also clarify the issue of whether shy people are or are not especially creative or aesthetic in orientation (Cheek & MacMillan, 1993; Cheek & Stahl, 1986; Ziller & Rorer, 1985) and generally admirable and underrespected (Gough & Thorne, 1986) or narcissistically self-preoccupied (Cheek & Melchior, 1985; Wink, 1991) and overly self-conscious (Buss, 1980). The answer appears to be that they are all of these things, depending on their environments.

The fourth and related key result was that an association between having a good parental environment and not experiencing an unhappy childhood appears to be stronger among HSPs (see figure 12.2), at least for men. This interaction was found over all subjects in Study 2 but for men only in Studies 3 and 4. The consistency, at least for males, over all three of the samples with sufficient *n's* is rather remarkable, given that it represents a quite complex pattern obtained with ad hoc and relatively indirect measures. On the other hand, the finding makes sense theoretically—again, those who are more sensitive to their environment will be more reactive to bad parenting.

Even if the interaction applies only to men, it is a quite provocative result from a developmental and clinical perspective, suggesting that highly sensitive boys (perhaps like all girls) are particularly affected by poor parenting (or that non–highly sensitive boys are particularly resilient). This should be a fruitful avenue for future research on individual differences thought to be associated with childhood environment.

Finally, in research done since Aron and Aron (1997), in two studies (Aron & Aron, 1999) using SUNY–Stony Brook students we found similar significant interactions (all $p < .05$). In the first $n = 113$), HSPs responding to the same set of questions about difficult childhood events as in Studies 2–4 (e.g., "Was alcoholism a problem in your immediate family while you were growing up?") were more likely to answer yes to the question, "Are you a shy person?" If they did not report such events, they were no more likely than those low on the HSP measure to report themselves to be shy. Using Cheek and Buss's (1981) shyness measure, the same interaction was found for men only.

In a replication ($n = 325$), the same interaction was found regardless of gender when using, for a measure of difficult childhood events, a checklist of the number of childhood traumas, and for shyness, a question on self-reported ability to speak up in a group when wishing to. Using Cheek and Buss's measure ($n = 157$), the same interaction was found, but as in the earlier study using this measure,

# Study 2

(All Participants)

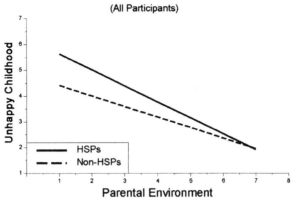

# Study 3

(Males Only)

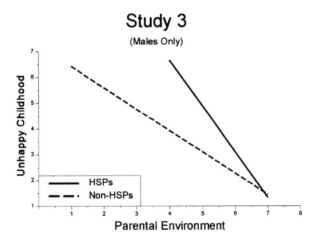

# Study 4

(Males Only)

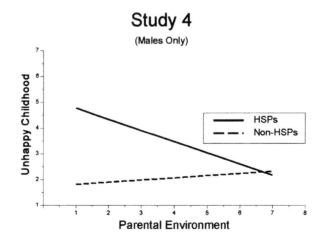

there was also a significant gender interaction such that the effect was only found for men.

These replicated interactions—and regression interactions are not generally easy to reproduce—strongly suggest that HSPs are indeed more likely to be shy, but only if they report difficult conditions in childhood. When these conditions are not reported, there appears to be little if any overall difference between HSPs and non-HSPs in self-reported shyness, and considering men only, little if any difference on the measure by Cheek and Buss (1981).

The last important result of these studies was the development of a 27-item questionnaire measure of high sensitivity that appears to have adequate psychometric properties for research applications. The measure has good content validity in terms of the conceptualization of high sensitivity as implying high levels of sensitivity both to subtle stimuli, such as the arts, and to being easily overaroused. Further, including both types of items also probably minimized social desirability bias by illustrating positive, as well as negative, consequences of the trait, compared with previous attempts at measuring constructs related to sensitivity. Finally, the measure's discriminant, convergent, and overall construct validity is supported by the entire set of studies.

This measure has obvious potential for the study of temperament and personality. Many findings based on extremes of introversion and extraversion in particular might benefit from replication that included the HSP Scale, which permits researchers to sort out variance due to low sociability or an avoidant attachment style from that due to sensitivity as we have distinguished it in these studies. Although the HSP Scale was not designed for clinical applications (and has not been evaluated in that context), it would also seem to have potential in this area. The identification of highly sensitive individuals seems important, since they can benefit greatly from counseling on issues such as the normalcy of their reactions to stimulation and their need to consider their sensitivity in regard to their vocations, relationships, health, and lifestyles (Aron, 1996a,b).

All of these results have limitations, of course. They involve no direct physiological study of this difference and no genetic research into its heritability, separate from what has already been done on introversion, shyness, inhibitedness, and low sensation-seeking, which we have argued are not quite the fundamental phenomenon. In addition, the results that suggest that the parental environment has a different impact on sensitive individuals, at least on males, is based on retrospective self-reports that were not really designed to explore the issue in depth.

---

Figure 12.2. Regression lines for highly sensitive persons (HSPs) and non–highly sensitive persons (non-HSPs) for parental environment on unhappy childhood. Note the pattern of an overall negative association between (positive) parental environment and the experience of an unhappy childhood and that the strength of the negative association is stronger for the HSPs. This pattern was observed for all participants in Study 2 (12.2 top; University of California, Santa Cruz students, *n* = 329). The pattern was qualified by significant gender interactions and observed only for males in Study 3 (12.2 middle; North American student sample; *n* = 50 males) and Study 4 (12.2 bottom; the random-digit-dialing community telephone survey; *n* = 134 males). From Aron and Aron (1997). Copyright 1997 by American Psychological Association. Reprinted with permission.

At the same time, this research program had key methodological strengths. It exemplifies what many methodologists (e.g., Campbell, 1975; Reichardt & Cook, 1979) describe as an ideal integration of qualitative and quantitative research. It employed a rare diversity of samples and methods. Over the six quantitative studies, the measurement of key variables (sensitivity, introversion, and emotionality) all employed at least two independent measures developed by different researchers. Most important, the major findings were replicated over a series of seven studies.

What will be important for the discussion which follows is that I, who am as steeped as anyone in thinking of the fundamental trait as embodying introversion and fearfulness and of their combination as shyness, found that sensory-processing sensitivity is independent of introversion and fearfulness to a surprising degree. For some individuals, sensitivity seems to be the basic difference, previously confused with and only known as introversion, shyness, or fearfulness.

## Some Possible Relationships between Sensitivity and Extreme Shyness and Fearfulness

Although the following discussion of two issues is based less directly on research and more on implications of research or on clinical experience, I think they are extremely important issues to explore in the context of this volume. The first question is, If sensitivity is the fundamental trait for some of those who are now seen as fearful and shy, how can their shy or fearful behavior be explained? The second is, If the observable behavioral consequences are inhibition or something that *looks* like shyness, fear, or timidity, why should we stop calling it that?

Regarding the first issue, how some sensitive persons become fearful or shy, I will begin with shyness and low sociability. Avoiding overstimulation would very likely be a central concern for individuals who are sensitive, since their sensitivity at the low end of stimulation gradients would seem to make them almost inevitably more easily overstimulated at the high end. Because much of the stimulation we receive is social, low sociability—specifically, preferring not to meet strangers or be in large groups—is a reasonable strategy for reducing unnecessary stimulation. Thus the first point to note, as many are now doing (e.g., Asendorpf, 1990), is that chronic shyness involves more than low sociability. A sensitive person can avoid groups and meeting strangers and be counted among the low sociables, but feel no fear of social situations or self-consciousness or low self-esteem about this behavior. Such persons may enter into situations they usually avoid in order to accomplish specific purposes, such as making new friends, but do not relish these situations or have high expectations about their performance in them. This behavior may be the result of a fear of overstimulation, but it is not social fear or shyness, although it may look like it or be called that by others.

It is possible, however, that not all sensitive persons have discovered this sort of strategy or accepted it for themselves, having been led to believe that they should behave like others and enjoy highly stimulating social situations (meeting strangers, being in large groups). These sensitive persons are likely to feel a conflict between wanting to interact in the style of everyone else and fearing unsuccessful interaction that is caused by overstimulation and overarousal. They may not realize that they largely fear the overstimulation itself. These sensitive persons are truly shy, but largely due to a misunderstanding about themselves. (Compared with shyness that is purely a response to aversive experiences, this kind of social discomfort can be more easily rectified by appropriate strategies and expectations—for example, meeting new people in familiar settings and not expecting to be as witty as others at parties.)

Another way of understanding how sensitive persons become shy is to think of a downward spiraling process. By avoiding social interaction, for whatever reason, they have fewer opportunities to practice social skills. Further, performance of any skill is adversely affected by overarousal. When sensitive persons enter social situations in which stimulation levels are high and their skills are rusty, especially if they have high expectations and worries about their own performance, they will certainly perform worse than others or than they hoped or expected. The next time they enter a social situation, all of these reasons for overarousal will be present, along with the memory of their last failure, deeply reflected on because of their sensory-processing proclivities. They will be even more overaroused and perform even worse, probably causing them to avoid most social situations in the future or to be deeply shy in them (a process I call the "slide into shy"; Aron, 1996b).

Of course sensitive persons often do report that they were seen as shy from birth. This perception seems to be the result of others mislabeling their trait due to the culture's preference for and preoccupation with a more outgoing style, making sociability/shyness a major focus for correction. This preoccupation may be the cause for the striking lack in North America, compared to other cultures, of adequate concepts for describing sensitivity (Chen, Rubin, & Sun, 1993). However, given the results of Aron and Aron (1999), the majority of cases of early and lasting shyness are probably due to negative family environments in childhood. This brings us to the issue of how sensitive persons become fearful in general, as well as how they become shy.

The most likely process is, again, an interaction between inherited sensory-processing sensitivity and childhood experiences, especially in the family environment. The results just reported from my own research found such an interaction, replicated with men, in studies with sufficient numbers of participants; in every case two clusters were found, those with troubled childhoods and negative emotionality and those without. Researchers who study children longitudinally have found a similar interaction. Hagekill (1996) reported that the most variance in children's neuroticism was accounted for by an interaction of temperament and negative life events such that children who evidence initial low sociability and experience more negative life events were more neurotic at later ages. Fox (1996) found that infants who evidenced greater negative emotionality and right hemisphere activity (signs of what I am calling sensitivity) had more variable outcomes at 4 years than those with more positive emotionality and left hemisphere activity in infancy. I have already mentioned the work of Boice et al. (1995) and Gannon et al. (1989), which found that sensitive children evidenced poorer health in a stressful environment but better health in a nonstressful one. Returning to adult samples, Gilmartin (1987), although he did not report interactions, also found that a negative family environment and other negative life experiences were important contributors to love-shyness, a trait which he also found had important inherited and sensitivity aspects. Finally, the experiments of Nachmias (1993) and Colton et al. (1992) and well discussed by Gunnar (1994) have nicely suggested some of the potential pathways to fearfulness for so-called inhibited children. In the laboratory, when 18-month-olds lacked social support (when they were with a mother with whom they were insecurely attached) while encountering a novel situation, they experienced the situation as threatening—that is, their cortisol levels rose. Uninhibited toddlers and inhibited toddlers with secure attachments did not experience any elevation in cortisol. "These data underscore the need to include 'quality of care' in making predictions about the sequelae of behavioral inhibition" (Gunnar, 1994, p. 185). Chronically high cortisol levels in sensitive children with insecure attachments must certainly contribute to the development of neuroticism. For example, cortisol disturbs sleep, which leads to still greater vulnerability in children especially (Weissbluth, 1989) and no doubt to lower serotonin levels, resulting in depression and anxiety.

Both common sense and clinical experience suggest that individuals who are more aware of subtleties and more easily overaroused will be affected more by a troubled family life. Besides being more aware of the difficulties around them, they would probably receive less useful guidance in controlling stimulation and containing and reframing emotions generated by stimuli in the media, family, or classroom—stimuli that might go unnoticed or unreflected on by other children.

Turning to the second issue, of what to call this trait if it looks like fearfulness and shyness, it seems that without aversive experiences and an unsupportive social environment, there might be little reason to call these individuals fearful, inhibited, or shy. Does it matter what we call them? In discussing the problem of naming the trait which has been his focus, Kagan (1994) claims that "nature is permissive with respect to the language we choose to name the forms in her garden of delights" (p. 270). I am not so certain. The name for a trait has to affect how we conceptualize research about it. Perhaps more important, it affects how clinicians and the public evaluate persons so named. I think there can be little doubt that in North American culture it is far more complimentary to be described as uninhibited. Thus I find it hard to agree with Kagan (1994) that the term *inhibited* "carries no evaluative connotations whatsoever" (p. 117). Terms such as *shy* or *fearful* are even more uncomplimentary.

Still, if fearful or anxious inhibition is the proper term for what has been inherited, it should be used. To examine the relation of sensitivity and fearfulness further, I turn to Gray (1981, 1985, 1991), who did most to legitimize the labeling of the trait as inhibition and anxiety. According to Gray, impulsivity is governed by the behavioral activation system (BAS) that comprises the pathways sensitive to catecholaminergic action, especially dopamine. The BAS is said to be sensitive to reward and escape from punishment, the source of goal-directed behavior and positive feelings in the presence of cues of impending reward, and especially active in what were formerly termed neurotic extraverts—what Gray termed *impulsives*—and relatively less active in stable introverts. Anxiety, as Gray used the term, is controlled by the behavioral inhibition system (BIS), consisting of the septohippocampal system, its monoaminergic afferents from the brainstem, and its neocortical projection in the frontal lobe. The BIS is said to be sensitive to punishment, nonreward, and novelty; affected by medications that alleviate anxiety; influenced more by serotonin; and especially active in neurotic introverts, whom Gray terms *anxious,* and less active in stable extraverts. However, if a greater activity of the BIS relative to the BAS is characteristic of the focal group, those I call highly sensitive, then two important problems arise with Gray's understanding of the BIS and therefore with calling this trait either anxiety (a high BIS) or *inhibitedness* (a low BAS).

First, Gray's model cannot, in his own words, explain the "good" evidence that "sensory thresholds are lower in introverts" (Gray, 1981, p. 270). According to Gray, his theory would have to explain greater sensory-processing sensitivity as being entirely due to a stronger BIS, which creates a greater awareness of the threat of punishment and nonreward; but such an explanation would, again in his words, "be tortuous, assuming it to be viable at all" (p. 270). Anxiety does not explain sensory-processing sensitivity.

Second, according to Gray, the "central task" of the BIS would be "to compare, quite generally, actual with expected stimuli" (1985, p. 8). To use his terms, this "checking" mode results in a temporary inhibition of activity, for which the system is named, unless there is a "mismatch"—the recognition of unexpected or aversive stimuli. Only then is there a complete cessation rather than a pause of the exploring behavior. But this pausing hardly sounds like fearfulness or anxiety. It is closer to unusual common sense. To label this process anxiety or even inhibition fails to emphasize the *purpose* of the inhibition, which is to pause and check. For individuals with greater sensory-processing sensitivity, processing is probably more complex and discriminating, creating a longer (but still temporary) pause; this pause becomes a very noticeable behavior that can be easily called inhibition or appear to be anxiety. But when Gray emphasizes anxiety and inhibition as the central aspect of this system, he misses his own two points about the greater sensory-processing sensitivity of these individuals and about the task of the BIS being to match the actual with the expected based on past experience. His first point, regarding their greater sensory-processing sensitivity, would seem to have to imply that for these individuals the matching task would be more time-consuming and complicated, causing a longer pause in behavior but hardly an inhibited or anxious personality. To prevent further confusion on this point, I would even go so far as to propose that this system be renamed the *pause-to-check system* (PCS).

I am not alone in questioning the equating of anxiety with this sort of pausing to check. McFatter (1994) concluded from his study of the interaction of mood and personality that there is little reason to associate the BIS with negative affects such as fear, arguing that a strong BIS means only a predisposition not to act—and, I would add, only a predisposition not to act without checking. Negative affect and a high BIS, according to McFatter, are associated only for neurotics, whom he suggests are neurotic due to conflict between pressures to act (due to a characteristically high arousal level) and not to act (due to their high BIS). "A high BIS individual does not simply pay little attention to reward; he or she could be very sensitive to whether a reward was present" (McFatter, 1994, p. 576). These criticisms call into grave question the current measure of the relative strength of the BIS and BAS by Carver and White (1994), which measures the BIS as nothing but strength of reaction to punishing experiences (fear, worry, upset, hurt feelings), not sensitivity to anything.

Kagan (1994) once observed that the inhibited individual's greater reactivity to novelty might be due to one of three possibilities—greater reactivity of the amygdala, more visceral feedback to limbic sites, or a special preparedness to detect subtle differences. It seems it is time to pay more attention to the third possibility. For at least some supposedly inhibited individuals, their hesitations are not due to fear or shyness but to sensitivity. Even if they have developed fearfulness or shyness over time, their fundamental trait is sensitivity.

## Implications for Developmental Outcomes and Treatment

When the reason for fearfulness or shyness is high sensitivity interacting with negative childhood experiences, treatment approaches change. This has been appreciated to some extent by those who study young children (e.g., Kochanska, 1993). But the simplest point about the developmental outcome of sensitive children is that they grow up, and no matter how shy or anxious some of them may be, they should not be labeled at any age as only or even primarily shy, neurotic, or fearful. These terms fail to supply sensitive persons with important information about themselves, and it has to be damaging to self-esteem. Further, seeing themselves as fearful, shy, or neurotic can only raise their arousal in evaluative situations, and high arousal already interferes too often with their performance. (One of the statements agreed to with significantly greater frequency by this group is, "When you must compete or be observed while performing a task, do you become so nervous or shaky that you do much worse than you would otherwise?"; Aron & Aron, 1997).

Like anyone, sensitive persons need experiences of success to feel good about themselves. When defeats due to overarousal continue to pile up, it is not sufficient to exhort them to give up self-defeating statements or stop thinking others are noticing. They are too sensitive to ignore the facts, including the fact that others definitely are noticing.

What then is helpful to sensitive persons? To summarize some of what I have written elsewhere (Aron, 1996a,b), first I have found that HSPs need accurate information about their trait—that it causes them to be aware of subtle stimulation and so inevitably also causes them to be overwhelmed by strong stimuli. It is a "package deal." But sensitive persons especially need to have the positive implications emphasized because of what they have learned about themselves thus far in a culture that has not appreciated them. (Indeed, it is helpful information in itself for them to know that other cultures do appreciate their trait, even though their own definitely does not—see Chen et al. 1992.) Examples of the assets associated with this trait come from questionnaire items that significantly distinguish sensitive persons from others and include being highly conscientious, aware of subtleties, careful to avoid mistakes, appreciative of the arts and music, and able to feel acute happiness, as well as having a rich, complex inner life and social and moral sensitivity (Aron & Aron, 1997). Other research has found them, for example, to be more reflective (Patterson & Newman, 1993), resulting in more accurate cognitive maps for problem solving. There is also the work already cited by Boice et al. (1995) and Gannon et al. (1989) that implies that once these people are living a suitable lifestyle, they can be healthier than others.

The second need of sensitive persons is help in cognitively reframing experiences that were humiliating or suggested incompetence (e.g., failing in an important contest or interview), as well as troubling life decisions such as not dating or marrying, choosing not to have children or a second child, or avoiding additional responsibility in their careers. Often these experiences can be understood entirely as due to overarousal or attempts to avoid overarousal. This reframing takes time but can greatly improve self-esteem and future self-care and life choices.

Third, sensitive persons need to learn a variety of methods to avoid, manage, and recover from the stress caused in their life by their greater tendency to become overaroused. Overarousal due to overstimulation can arise from any intense, prolonged, complex, or chaotic stimulation, even if it is positively valued. These individuals need to be guided in choosing a middle course in their exposure to stimulation, such that they are neither overprotecting themselves nor overexposing themselves for the sake of overcoming a perceived deficit or of being like others.

Fourth, they need to examine how their trait affects their personal relationships at home and on the job. For example, they need more downtime, but this need can cause others to see them as lazy, rejecting, aloof, or irritable. They also need to beware of the effect of going off alone at breaks or during lunch, so that they are not participating in informal work discussions during which many opinions are formed and decisions made. Often I find they want to believe that just doing a good job will suffice; then they find they are the first to be laid off. They can use their sensitivity to discern opinion trends if they will make the effort. Both at home and at work they also need to develop skills for communicating their needs appropriately in a way which both acknowledges the needs of others and models respect for their trait rather than revealing a sense of inferiority.

Fifth, many decide they must develop an entirely new life plan based on this information, one that better takes into account their assets, interests, and limits. They need considerable support during that process from a professional who appreciates the nature of their trait. Major life changes can be especially difficult for them but often seem to be desperately needed. In my experience the psychological and physical health benefits often repay the short-term costs of such support.

Finally, those who do exhibit shyness or fearfulness can benefit from all of the excellent knowledge already developed for helping these populations, through skills training, desensitization, cognitive relabeling of physiological cues, and the like. In cases in which there has been an acutely troubled childhood or in which there are signs of character disorder, they also frequently benefit from depth psychotherapy. But it is important to screen for the trait of sensitivity; and when that trait is present, it should be a major focus of treatment. Otherwise, when clients inevitably fail to meet therapeutic goals that would make them "like everyone else," they will again feel defective and hopeless rather than satisfied and even proud of their difference.

## Conclusion

The inherited trait generally assumed to give rise to extreme fearfulness and shyness may in many cases actually be a high level of sensory-processing sensitivity. Differences in sensitivity have been noted by those who study introversion, as well as other concepts of adult and child temperament. My own research has found that sensory-processing sensitivity cannot be equated with either introversion or negative emotionality. Nevertheless, it is reasonable that sensitive persons would be more prone than others to become less sociable or more shy or fearful; research does suggest such an interaction, as well as identifying the conditions under which variables such as an inadequate family environment can create these secondary features of fearfulness and shyness. Thus the relation of sensitivity to fearfulness and shyness is that some sensitive persons are fearful and shy but many are not, just as some fearful and shy persons are not sensitive. Equating sensitivity with fearfulness and shyness appears to be an error that has potential negative effects on research and practice, including at least six points to be considered when treating sensitive persons for chronic shyness or fearfulness.

*References*

Aron, E. N. (1996a). Counseling the highly sensitive person. *Counseling and Human Development, 28,* 1–7.
Aron, E. N. (1996b). *The highly sensitive person.* New York: Birch Lane Press.
Aron, E. N., & Aron, A. (1997). Sensory-processing sensitivity and its relation to introversion and emotionality. *Journal of Personality and Social Psychology, 73,* 345–368.
Aron, E. N., & Aron, A. (1999). *Interaction of sensory processing sensitivity and childhood experiences in predicting shyness.* Manuscript in preparation.
Asendorpf, J. B. (1990). Beyond social withdrawal: Shyness, unsociability, and peer avoidance. *Human Development, 33,* 250–259.
Barnes, G. (1975). Extraversion and pain. *British Journal of Social and Clinical Psychology, 14,* 303–308.
Bekoff, M. (1977). Mammalian dispersal and the ontogeny of individual behavioral phenotypes. *American Naturalist, 111,* 715–732.
Bell, I. R. (1992). Allergens, physical irritants, depression, and shyness. *Journal of Applied Developmental Psychology, 13,* 125–133.
Blanchard, R. J., Flannelly, K. J., & Blanchard, D. C. (1986). Defensive behaviors of laboratory and wild *Rattus norvegicus. Journal of Comparative Psychology, 100,* 101–107.
Blizard, D. A. (1981). The Maudsley reactive and nonreactive strains: A North American perspective. *Behavior Genetics, 11,* 469–489.
Boice, W. T., Chesney, M., Alkon, A., Tschann, J. M, Adams, S., Chesterman, B., Cohen, F., Kaiser, P., Folkman, S., & Wara, D. (1995). Psychobiologic reactivity to stress and childhood respiratory illnesses: Results of two prospective studies. *Psychosomatic Medicine, 57,* 411–422.
Brebner, J. M. T. (1980). Reaction time in personality theory. In A. T. Welford (Ed.), *Reaction times* (pp. 309–320). London: Academic Press.
Brodt, S., & Zimbardo, P. (1981). Modifying shyness-related social behavior through symptom manipulation. *Journal of Personality and Social Psychology, 41,* 437–449.
Buchsbaum, M. A., Haier, R. J., & Johnson, J. (1983). Augmenting and reducing: Individual differences in evoked potentials. In A. Gale & J. A. Edwards (Eds.), *Physiological correlates of human behavior: Individual differences and psychopathology* (Vol. 3, pp. 117–138). London: Academic Press.
Buss, A. H. (1980). *Self-consciousness and social anxiety.* San Francisco: Freeman.
Buss, A. H. & Plomin, R. (1984). *Temperament: Early developing personality traits.* Hillsdale, NJ: Erlbaum.
Campbell, D. T. (1975). Assessing the impact of planned social change. In G. M. Lyons (Ed.), *Social research and public policies* (pp. 3–45). Hanover, NH: University Press of New England.

Campbell, J. B. (1992). Extraversion and noise sensitivity: A replication of Dornic and Ekehammar's study. *Personality and Individual Differences, 13,* 953–955.

Carver, C. S., & White, T. L. (1994). Behavioral inhibition, behavioral activation, and affective responses to impending reward and punishment: The BIS/BAS Scales. *Journal of Personality and Social Psychology, 67,* 319–333.

Cheek, J. M., & Buss, A. H. (1981). Shyness and sociability. *Journal of Personality and Social Psychology, 41,* 330–339.

Cheek, J. M., & MacMillan, C. (1993, August). *Shyness: Aesthetic orientation or social anxiety?* Paper presented at the annual convention of the American Psychological Association, Toronto.

Cheek, J. M., & Melchior, L. A. (1985, August). Are shy people narcissistic? Paper presented at the annual convention of the American Psychological Association, Los Angeles.

Cheek, J. M., & Stahl, S. S. (1986). Shyness and verbal creativity. *Journal of Research in Personality, 20,* 51–61.

Chen, X., Rubin, K., & Sun, Y. (1992). Social reputation and peer relationships in Chinese and Canadian children: A cross-cultural study. *Child Development, 63,* 1336–1343.

Clark, L. A., & Watson, D. (1991). General affective dispositions in physical and psychological health. In C. R. Snyder & D. R. Forsyth (Eds.), *Handbook of social and clinical psychology: The health perspective* (pp. 221–245). New York: Pergamon Press.

Colton, M., Buss, K., Mangelsdorf, S., Brooks, C., Sorenson, D., Stansbury, K., Harris, M., & Gunnar, M. (1992, May). *Relations between toddler coping strategies, temperament, attachment and adrenocortical responses.* Poster presented at the 8th International Conference on Infant Studies, Miami, FL.

Deo, P., & Singh, A. (1973). Some personality correlates of learning without awareness. *Behaviorometric, 3,* 11–21.

Dutton, D. G., & Aron, A. (1974). Some evidence for heightened sexual attraction under conditions of high anxiety. *Journal of Personality and Social Psychology, 30,* 510–517.

Edman, G., Schalling, D., & Rissler, A. (1979). Interaction effects of extraversion and neuroticism on detection thresholds. *Biological Psychology, 9,* 41–47.

Eysenck, H. J. (1981). *A model for personality.* New York: Springer-Verlag.

Eysenck, H. J. (1991). Biological dimensions of personality. In L. A. Pervin (Ed.), *Handbook of personality* (pp. 244–276). New York: Guilford Press.

Eysenck, H. J., & Eysenck, S. B. G. (1968). *Manual for the Eysenck Personality Inventory.* San Diego, CA: EDITS.

Eysenck, H. J., & Eysenck, S. B. G. (1975). *Manual of the Eysenck Personality Questionnaire.* San Diego, CA: EDITS.

Fine, B. J. (1972). Field-dependent introvert and neuroticism: Eysenck and Witkin united. *Psychological Reports, 31,* 939–956.

Fine, B. J. (1973). Field dependence-independence as "sensitivity" of the nervous system: Supportive evidence with color and weight discrimination. *Perceptual and Motor Skills, 37,* 287–295.

Fox, M. L. (1972). Socioecological implications of individual differences in wolf litters: A developmental and evolutionary perspective. *Behaviour, 41,* 298–313.

Fox, N. A. (1996, October). *Continuities and discontinuities in behavioral inhibition.* Paper presented at the Eleventh Occasional Temperament Conference, Eugene, OR.

Gannon, L., Banks, J., & Shelton, D. (1989). The mediating effects of psychophysiological reactivity and recovery on the relationship between environmental stress and illness. *Journal of Psychosomatic Research, 33,* 165–175.

Geen, R. G., McCown, E. J., & Broyles, J. W. (1985). Effects of noise on sensitivity of introverts and extraverts to signals in a vigilance task. *Personality and Individual Differences, 6,* 237–241.

Gilmartin, B. G. (1987). *Shyness and love: Causes, consequences, and treatment.* Lanham, MD: University Press of America.

Goddard, M. E., & Beilharz, R. G. (1985). A multivariate analysis of the genetics of fearfulness in potential guide dogs. *Behavior Genetics, 15,* 69–89.

Gough, H. G., & Thorne, A. (1986). Positive, negative, and balanced shyness: Self-definitions and the reactions of others. In W. H. Jones, J. M. Cheek, & S. R. Briggs (Eds.), *Shyness: Perspectives on research and treatment* (pp. 205–225). New York: Plenum.

Gray, J. A. (1981). A critique of Eysenck's theory of personality. In H. J. Eysenck (Ed.), *A model for personality* (pp. 246–276). New York: Springer.

Gray, J. A. (1985). Issues in the neuropsychology of anxiety. In A. H. Ruma & J. D. Maser (Eds.), *Anxiety and disorder* (pp. 5–25). Hillsdale, NJ: Erlbaum.

Gray, J. A. (1991). The neurophysiology of temperament. In J. Strelau & A. Angleitner (Eds.), *Explorations in temperament: International perspectives on theory and measurement* (pp. 105–128). New York: Plenum.

Gunnar, M. R. (1994). Psychoendocrine studies of temperament and stress in early childhood: Expanding current models. In J. E. Bates & T. D Wachs (Eds.), *Temperament: Individual differences at the interface of biology and behavior* (pp. 175–198). Washington, DC: American Psychological Association.

Hagekill, B. (1996, October). *Influences of temperament and environment in the development of personality.* Paper presented at the Eleventh Occasional Temperament Conference, Eugene, OR.

Haier, R. J., Robinson, D. L., Braden, W., & Williams, D. (1984). Evoked potential augmenting-reducing and personality differences. *Personality and Individual Differences, 5,* 283–301.

Harley, T. A., & Matthews, G. (1992). Interactive effects of extraversion, arousal and time of day on semantic priming: Are they pre-lexical or post-lexical? *Personality and Individual Differences, 13,* 1021–1029.

Herbener, E. S., Kagan, J., & Cohen, M. (1989). Shyness and olfactory threshold. *Personality and Individual Differences, 10,* 1159–1163.

Higley, J. D., & Suomi, J. D. (1989). Temperamental reactivity in non-human primates. In G. A. Kohnstamm, J. E. Bates, & M. K. Rothbart (Eds), *Temperament in childhood* (pp. 152–167). Chichester, England: Wiley.

Howarth, E. (1986). Introversion and neuroticism: A persistent relationship. *Psychological Reports, 58,* 389–390.

Kagan, J. (1994). *Galen's prophecy: Temperament in human nature.* New York: Basic.

Kochanska, G. (1993). Toward a synthesis of parental socialization and child temperament in early development of conscience. *Child Development, 64,* 325–347.

Koelega, H. S. (1992) Extraversion and vigilance performance: 30 years of inconsistencies. *Psychological Bulletin, 112,* 239–258.

Kohn, P. M. (1987). Issues in the measurement of arousability. In J. Strelau & H. J. Eysenck (Eds.), *Personality dimensions and arousal* (pp. 233–250). New York: Plenum Press.

Lyons, D. M., Price, E. O., & Moberg, G. P. (1988). Individual differences in temperament of domestic dairy goats: Constancy and change. *Animal Behavior, 36,* 1323–1333.

Main, M. (1990). Cross-cultural studies of attachment organization: Recent studies, changing methodologies, and the concept of conditional strategies. *Human Development, 33,* 48–61.

MacDonald, K. (1983). Stability of individual differences in behavior in a litter of wolf cubs (*Canis lupus*). *Journal of Comparative Psychology, 97,* 99–106.

McFatter, R. M. (1994). Interactions in predicting mood from extraversion and neuroticism. *Journal of Personality and Social Psychology, 66,* 570–578.

McRae, R. R., & John, O. P. (1993) An introduction to the five-factor model and its applications. *Journal of Personality, 60,* 175–215.

Mehrabian, A. (1976). *Manual for the questionnaire measure of stimulus screening and arousability.* Unpublished manuscript, University of California at Los Angeles.

Mehrabian, A. (1991). Outline of a general emotion-based theory of temperament. In J. Strelau & A. Angleitner (Eds.), *Explorations in temperament: International perspectives on theory and measurement* (pp. 75–86). New York: Plenum Press.

Mehrabian, A., & O'Reilly, E. (1980). Analysis of personality measures in terms of basic dimensions of temperament. *Journal of Personality and Social Psychology, 38,* 492–503.

Myers, I. B. (1962). *Manual for the Myers-Briggs Type Indicator.* Princeton, NJ: Educational Testing Service.

Nachmias, M. (1993, March). *Maternal personality relations with toddler's attachment classification, use of coping strategies, and adrenocortical stress response.* Paper presented at the 60th annual meeting of the Society for Research in Child Development, New Orleans, LA.

Nagane, M. (1990). Development of psychological and physiological sensitivity indices to stress based on state anxiety and heart rate. *Perceptual and Motor Skills, 70,* 611–614.

Newton, T., Slade, P., Butler, N., & Murphy, P. (1992). Personality and performance on a simple visual search task. *Personality and Individual Differences, 13,* 381–382.

Patterson, C. M., & Newman, J. P. (1993). Reflectivity and learning from aversive events: Toward a psychological mechanism for the syndromes of disinhibition. *Psychological Review, 100,* 716–736.

Petrie, A. (1967). *Individuality in pain and suffering.* Chicago: University of Chicago Press.

Reichardt, C., & Cook, T. D. (1979). Beyond qualitative *versus* quantitative methods. In T. D. Cook & C. S. Reichardt (Eds.), *Qualitative and quantitative methods in evaluation research* (pp. 7–17). Beverly Hills: Sage.

Rothbart, M. K., Derryberry, D., & Posner, M. I. (1994). A psychobiological approach to the development of temperament. In J. E. Bates & T. D. Wachs (Eds.), *Temperament: Individual differences at the interface of biology and behavior* (pp. 83–116). Washington, DC: American Psychological Association.

Satow, A. (1987). Four properties common among perceptions confirmed by a large sample of subjects: An ecological approach to mechanisms of individual differences in perception. Part II. *Perceptual and Motor Skills, 64,* 507–520.

Schalling, D. (1971). Tolerance for experimentally induced pain as related to personality. *Scandinavian Journal of Psychology, 12,* 271–281.

Scott, J. P., & Fuller, J. (1965). *Genetics and the social behavior of the dog.* Chicago: University of Chicago Press.

Shaver, P. R., & Brennan, K. A. (1992). Attachment styles and the "Big Five" personality traits: Their connections with each other and with romantic relationship outcomes. *Personality and Social Psychology Bulletin, 18,* 536–545.

Shigehisa, P. M. J., Shigehisa, T., & Symons, J. R. (1973). Effects of intensity of auditory stimulation on photopic visual sensitivity in relation to personality. *Japanese Psychological Research, 15,* 164–172.

Shigehisa, T. (1974). Effect of auditory stimulation on visual tracking as functions of stimulus intensity, task complexity and personality. *Japanese Psychological Research, 16,* 186–196.

Siddle, D. A. T., Morrish, R. B., White, K. D., & Mangan, G. L. (1969). Relation of visual sensitivity to extraversion. *Journal of Experimental Research in Personality, 3,* 264–267.

Stelmack, R. M. (1990). Biological bases of extraversion: Psychophysiological evidence. *Journal of Personality, 58,* 293–311.

Stelmack, R. M., & Campbell, K. B. (1974). Extraversion and auditory sensitivity to high and low frequency. *Perceptual and Motor Skills, 38,* 875–879.

Stelmack, R. M., & Geen, R. G. (1992). The psychophysiology of extraversion. In A. Gale

& M. W. Eysenck (Eds.), *Handbook of individual differences: Biological perspectives* (pp. 227–254). Chichester, England: Wiley.

Stelmack, R. M., & Michaud-Achorn, A. (1985). Extraversion, attention, and auditory evoked response. *Journal of Research in Personality, 19,* 416–428.

Stelmack, R. M., & Wilson, K. G. (1982). Extraversion and the effects of frequency and intensity on the auditory brainstem evoked response. *Personality and Individual Differences, 3,* 373–380.

Stevenson-Hinde, J., Stillwell-Barnes, R., & Zung, M. (1980). Individual differences in young rhesus monkeys: Continuity and change. *Primates, 21,* 61–62.

Strelau, J. (1983). *Temperament, personality, activity.* San Diego, CA: Academic Press.

Suomi, S. J. (1983). Social development in rhesus monkeys: Consideration of individual differences. In A. Oliverio & M. Zappella (Eds.), *The behavior of human infants* (pp. 71–92). New York: Plenum Press.

Suomi, S. J. (1987). Genetic and maternal contributions to individual differences in rhesus monkey biobehavioral development. In N. A. Krasnegor, E. M. Blass, M. A. Hoffer, & W. P. Smotherman (Eds.), *Perinatal behavioral development: A psychobiological perspective* (pp. 397–419). San Diego: Academic Press.

Suomi, S. J. (1991). Uptight and laid-back monkeys: Individual differences in the response to social challenges. In S. E. Brauth, W. S. Hall, & R. J. Dooling (Eds.), *Plasticity of development* (pp. 27–56). Cambridge, MA: MIT Press.

Thomas, A., & Chess, S. (1977). *Temperament and development.* New York: Brunner/Mazel.

van den Boom, D. C. (1989). Neonatal irritability and the development of attachment. In G. A. Kohnstamm, J. E. Bates, & M. K. Rothbart (Eds.), *Temperament in childhood* (pp. 299–318). New York: Wiley.

Weissbluth, M. (1989). Sleep-loss stress and temperamental difficultness: Psychobiological processes and practical considerations. In G. A. Kohnstamm, J. E. Bates, & M. K. Rothbart (Eds.), *Temperament in childhood* (pp. 357–376). Chichester, England: Wiley.

Wilson, D. S., Coleman, K., Clark, A. B., & Biederman, L. (1993). Shy-bold continuum in pumpkinseed sunfish (*Lepomis gibbosus*): An ecological study of a psychological trait. *Journal of Comparative Psychology, 107,* 250–260.

Wink, P. (1991). Two faces of narcissism. *Journal of Personality and Social Psychology, 61,* 590–597.

Ziller, R. C., & Rorer, B. A. (1985). Shyness-environment interaction: A view from the shy side through auto-photography. *Journal of Personality, 53,* 626–639.

# 13

## Extreme Fear, Shyness, and Social Phobia

### *Treatment and Intervention*

Franklin R. Schneier

$A$lthough understanding of the biological underpinnings of states of shyness and extreme fear is growing, pharmacological treatments of associated disorders have been developed empirically for the most part. Established psychotherapies have been most influenced by cognitive-behavioral theory. Both pharmacological and psychotherapeutic interventions for social phobia have built on experience from treatments for better-studied disorders, such as depression. Treatment responses to specific drug classes have been used to confirm clinically defined borders of anxiety disorders and to support other biological evidence for specific pathophysiologies.

Over the past few decades, effective treatments for states of shyness and extreme fear have been targeted at increasingly specific diagnostic subgroups. Extreme fear is characteristic of a variety of clinical syndromes, and narrower diagnostic categories may offer advantages of superior diagnostic reliability and validity. Specific diagnoses hold the promise that homogeneous subgroups (and, ultimately, groups which are closely aligned with underlying pathophysiological and psychopathological states) will show superior response to specific treatments.

The trend toward diagnostic "splitting" has been counterbalanced by a growing recognition of commonalities across fear states. Temperamental constructs such as behavioral inhibition (Kagan, Reznick, & Gibbons, 1989) and harm avoidance (Cloninger, 1987) may cut across anxiety disorder boundaries. In children, anxiety diagnoses may be less distinct and less longitudinally stable than in adults (Pine, Cohen, Gurley, Brook, & Ma, 1998). Additionally, the most effective modalities of treatment, including cognitive and behavioral therapies, selective serotonin reuptake inhibitors (SSRIs), and benzodiazepines, have been shown to work across many anxiety disorders, with some specific modifications and exceptions.

This chapter will focus on the treatment of social phobia and will compare and contrast it with the treatment of panic disorder. Social phobia and panic disorder illustrate the duality between shared and specific features of fear states. Both of these disorders are characterized by episodes of extreme fear/panic, anticipatory anxiety, and avoidance, and both have been associated with behavioral inhibition in family studies (Rosenbaum et al., 1991). A variety of differences between these two disorders, however, has validated their diagnostic separation in adults. For example, social phobics tend to have an earlier age of onset (Mannuzza, Fyer, Liebowitz, & Klein, 1990), show a different pattern of physical anxiety symptoms (Amies, Gelder, & Shaw, 1983) and a different response to lactate infusions (Liebowitz, Fyer, et al., 1985), and report less anxiety sensitivity (Taylor, Koch, & McNally, 1992), and family studies suggest that each disorder tends to "breed true" (Fyer, Mannuzza, Chapman, Martin, & Klein, 1995; Mannuzza et al., 1995).

## Social Phobia in Adults

Social phobia is the disorder most closely associated with the concept of shyness and possibly with behavioral inhibition (Kagan, 1997). Although social phobia clearly overlaps with the more severe end of shyness, unlike shyness it is defined by specific criteria, and the two terms cannot be considered synonymous (Turner, Beidel, & Townsley, 1990). Social phobia is defined by a marked and persistent fear of social or performance situations due to fear of embarrassment or humiliation (Diagnostic and Statistical Manual of Mental Disorders [DSM-IV], American Psychiatric Association, 1994). The feared situations are avoided or endured with intense anxiety, and the phobia interferes significantly with the individual's functioning or causes marked distress. The generalized subtype of social phobia is defined by fear of most social situations, and this subtype has represented a large majority of participants in most of the treatment studies which have reported social phobia diagnosis by subtype.

### Biological Findings

A number of studies with widely varying methodologies have begun to link social phobia to underlying biological characteristics (see table 13.1), some of which have also been associated with shyness. Evidence for a genetic contribution to social phobia comes from twin studies, as has evidence for a genetic contribution to childhood behavioral inhibition (DiLalla, Kagan, & Reznick, 1994). Kendler, Neale, Kessler, Heath, and Eaves (1992) found a significant genetic contribution to the heritability of social phobia in 2,163 female twin pairs identified by the Virginia twin registry. A concordance rate of 24.4 percent for monozygotic twins versus 15.3 percent for dizygotic twins led to an estimation of a heritability index of 30 percent.

Autonomic Nervous System.    Although symptoms of autonomic nervous system arousal are hallmarks of social phobia and have led to the use of beta adrenergic blockers for discrete social phobias, studies that assess autonomic nervous system function in social phobia have yielded inconsistent results. Several studies have found that nongeneralized social phobic subjects have greater heart rate and/or greater heart rate increases during behavioral challenges than generalized social

Table 13.1  Some Positive Biological Findings in Social Phobia.

| Finding in Social Phobia | Method | Study |
|---|---|---|
| Genetic contribution (heritability of 30 percent) | twin study | Kendler et al., 1992 |
| Greater heart rate/ heart rate response to challenge | behavioral challenge | Heimberg et al., 1990 Hofmann et al., 1995 Levin et al., 1993 |
| R-sided activation, anterior temporal and lateral prefrontal brain regions | regional EEG | Davidson et al., in press |
| Cortical and subcortical gray matter abnormalities | proton magnetic resonance spectroscopy | Tuppler et al., 1997 Davidson et al., 1993 |
| Greater diminution of putamen volume with age | magnetic resonance imaging | Potts et al., 1994 |
| Increased dopamine reuptake site density in brain | SPECT | Tiihonen et al., 1997 |
| Lower CSF HVA levels in panic patients with SP | lumbar puncture | Johnson et al., 1994 |
| Augmented cortisol response to fenfluramine | neuroendocrine challenge | Tancer et al., 1995 |

phobic subjects (Heimberg, Hope, Dodge, & Becker, 1990; Hofmann, Newman, Ehlers, & Roth, 1995; Levin et al., 1993) and/or healthy controls (Davidson, Marshall, Tomarken, & Henriques, in press; Hofmann, Newman, Ehlers, & Roth, 1995; Levin et al., 1993), but two other studies reported no differences (Naftolowitz, Vaughn, Ranc, & Tancer, 1994; Turner, Beidel, & Townsley, 1992). Heart rate variability in social phobia has not been shown to consistently differ from that of healthy controls (Hofmann et al., 1995; Stein, Asmundson, & Chartier, 1994). Sympathetic nervous system activity, as measured by plasma epinephrine and norepinephrine, has not been shown to differ between social phobic subjects and normals during public speaking (Naftolowitz et al., 1994) or during autonomic function tests (Stein et al., 1994; Stein, Tancer, & Uhde, 1992).

Differences between the inconsistent findings of autonomic function in social phobia and evidence for high stable heart rates and sympathetic activation in behaviorally inhibited children have several possible explanations. Diagnostic criteria for social phobia, which emphasize self-reported cognitive features such as fear of embarrassment and do not require autonomic nervous system symptoms, may define a more heterogenous group in respect to autonomic nervous system activity than does the sample of behaviorally inhibited young children, which is defined by observed behavior. Alternatively, early childhood autonomic hyperreactivity might be a precursor of social phobia that becomes attenuated over time through normal maturation or end-organ down regulation in response to chronic hyperreactivity, with cognitive features of anxiety and self-consciousness becoming more prominent.

Electrocortical and Brain Imaging.  A single study of regional electroencephalography (EEG) in social phobia compared patients and healthy controls while they anticipated making a speech (Davidson et al., in press). Persons with social phobia showed a significantly greater increase in anxiety and negative affect during anticipation, and they showed a marked increase in right-sided activation of the anterior temporal and lateral prefrontal brain regions. Right frontal activation has also been associated with negative affect and high motor activity in infants (Calkins, Fox, & Marshall, 1996), with behavioral inhibition (Finman, Davidson, Colton, Straus, & Kagan, 1989; Fox et al., 1995), and with low sociability (but not shyness) in young women (Schmidt & Fox, 1994).

Brain imaging studies that utilized magnetic resonance imaging (Davidson, Krishnan et al., 1993; Potts, Davidson, Krishnan, & Doraiswamy, 1994) and proton magnetic resonance spectroscopy (Tuppler et al., 1997) have reported greater age-related reduction in putamen volumes in persons with social phobia. In the latter study, the most substantial metabolic differences between social phobic participants and controls were noted in cortical gray matter.

Monoamine Neurotransmitter Studies. Studies of various parameters of brain neurotransmitter function, along with response patterns to drugs that affect various neurotransmitter systems, have suggested that dopaminergic and possible serotonergic abnormalities may be associated with social phobia. Findings for dopamine system involvement in social phobia and related states include decreased density of dopamine reuptake sites in the brains of persons with social phobia (Tiihonen et al., 1997); lower levels of the dopamine metabolite homovanillic acid (HVA) in the cerebrospinal fluid of patients with social phobia, in addition to panic disorder (Johnson, Lydiard, Zealberg, Fossey, & Ballenger, 1994); a high rate of social phobia in patients with Parkinson's disease (Stein, Heuser, Juncos, & Uhde, 1990); and association of polymorphisms of the dopamine $D_2$ receptor and dopamine transporter genes in persons with avoidant personality traits (Blum et al., 1997). A neuroendocrine challenge study using levodopa as a probe, however, did not find differences between social phobic patients and healthy controls in respect to prolactin response or eyeblink rate, both of which are believed to be dopaminergically mediated (Tancer et al., 1995).

Corticotropin-Releasing Factor (CRF) and the Hypothalmic-Pituitary-Adrenal (HPA) Axis. The neuropeptide CRF and the HPA axis, which have been major areas of study in relationship to fear states in animals and depression in humans, have received relatively little attention in conjunction with social phobia and shyness. Animal studies suggest that CRF is an important mediator of the stress response, that it stimulates the locus coeruleus and has anxiogenic effects that are blocked by benzodiazepines (Nemeroff, 1992). Coplan et al. (1996; 1998) have noted that primates reared under stressful conditions tend to be socially submissive and to demonstrate persistently elevated cerebrospinal fluid (CSF) levels of CRF, somatostatin, and metabolites of serotonin and dopamine but depressed levels of cortisol. CSF concentrations of CRF have not been studied in social phobia, but concentrations in panic disorder patients have been found not to differ from normal controls in two studies (Fossey et al., 1996; Jolkkonen, Lepola, Bissette, Nemeroff, & Riekkinen, 1993).

Cortisol has been reported to be elevated in the saliva of behaviorally inhibited infants (Kagan, Reznick, & Snidman, 1988). Twenty-four hour urinary free cortisol levels in adults with social phobia, however, have been found not to differ from normals in two studies (Potts, Davidson, Krishnan, & Doraiswamy, 1991; Uhde, Tancer, Gelernter, & Vittone, 1994), in contrast to elevations found in depression and some panic disorder studies. Dexamethasone suppression test results were normal for social phobics in one study (Uhde et al., 1994).

In normal participants, plasma cortisol and ACTH have been shown to rise transiently during a public speaking task (Al'Absi et al., 1997), but social phobics did not differ from normals in plasma cortisol at baseline or 10–20 minutes after a public speaking task (Levin et al., 1993), and social phobics and panic disorder patients did not differ from normals in baseline plasma cortisol or cortisol response during pentagastrin-induced anxiety (McCann, Slate, Geraci, Roscow-Terrill, & Uhde, 1997). Tancer et al. (1995) did find an increased cortisol response to fenfluramine (believed to be serotonin-mediated) in social phobic subjects compared with healthy controls.

In summary, although most studies to date have not detected CRF and HPA axis abnormalities in social phobia, findings from animal studies and from human studies of fear and behavioral inhibition suggest that more work is needed to elucidate the functioning of this system. The treatment implications of possible abnormalities in CRF or in HPA axis function remain largely unexplored in social phobia. The adrenocoricotrophic hormone (ACTH)(4-9) analog Org 2766, which previously had been shown to increase social contact in a rat model of social anxiety, did not yield significant anxiolytic activity in a small double-blind, placebo-controlled trial in 12 persons with social phobia (Den Boer, van Vliet, & Westenberg, 1995).

In summary, a growing database of biological findings in persons with social phobia supports the validity of this diagnostic category, and it is consistent with findings of efficacy of medications that affect either peripheral autonomic nervous system activity or brain dopamine and serotonin function (as reviewed in the following section). Much remains to be clarified in respect to the specific nature of functional abnormalities in these and other biological systems in social phobia. Convergent and divergent biological findings for social phobia, in comparison with other classification systems such as behavioral inhibition and other measures of temperament, may help to sharpen definition of a clinical syndrome which is responsive to specific treatments.

## Pharmacological Treatments

The past decade has seen tremendous growth in the literature on both pharmacological and psychosocial treatments of social phobia. Pharmacological approaches to the treatment of social phobia are grounded in evidence suggesting that the disorder has a biological diathesis, either genetically programmed from birth or emerging through development, with or without additional environmental contributions.

Specific pharmacological treatment strategies for social phobia have grown out of the recognition of similarities with atypical depression on the one hand and with performance anxiety on the other. Atypical depression, with its characteristic hypersensitivity to rejection, had been shown to be responsive to monoamine oxidase inhibitors (MAOIs). Performance anxiety, with intense autonomic nervous system arousal and fear, as occurs in stage fright; precision athletic competitions; and test taking had been shown to be responsive to beta adrenergic blocking agents. Both classes of drugs have subsequently been utilized in social phobia. Although complete remission of social phobia sometimes occurs with treatment, successful therapy for this highly chronic condition is more usually measured by a functionally significant reduction of intensity of anxiety and of extent of avoidance. This review will focus on placebo-controlled short-term trials of medications for social phobia. (For a more comprehensive review, see Blanco, Schneier, & Liebowitz, in press).

Standard Monoamine Oxidase Inhibitors.    MAOIs, which were earlier shown to have specific efficacy for atypical depression, a condition characterized by hypersensitivity to rejection, appear to be the most efficacious of pharmacotherapies tested for social phobia. The standard MAOIs, of which phenelzine (trade name Nardil) has been best studied, work by inhibiting the enzyme monoamine oxidase in the brain. This inhibition diminishes the breakdown of several neurotransmitters, including dopamine, norepinephrine, and serotonin.

Four acute placebo-controlled trials (8 to 16 weeks duration) with treatment group sizes of 20–40 patients per cell, have demonstrated efficacy of phenelzine in nondepressed adults with a principal diagnosis of social phobia (Gelernter et al., 1991; Heimberg et al., 1998; Liebowitz et al., 1992; Versiani et al., 1992). Intent-to-treat response rates (including all participants randomized), with response most commonly defined by a score of 1 (very much improved) or 2 (much improved) on a 7-point Likert-type Clinical Global Impression–Change Scale, have run 50–80 percent in these studies versus placebo response rates of 12–30 percent. In these studies, phenelzine response was also superior by most measures to the beta blocker atenolol (Tenormin; Liebowitz et al., 1992) and by at least some measures to the benzodiazepine alprazolam (Xanax; Gelernter et al., 1991), the reversible MAOI moclobemide (Versiani et al., 1992), and cognitive-behavioral group therapy (Gelernter et al., 1991; Heimberg et al., 1998).

Despite their strong efficacy, MAOIs are often relegated to a second-line treatment because of the inconvenience to patients of maintaining a low tyramine diet. The diet is required to prevent a potentially serious hypertensive reaction, which could be precipitated by ingestion of most cheeses and alcoholic beverages, other aged foods, and sympathomimetic drugs, including epinephrine and decongestants. Less serious adverse effects are also common at effective doses of phenelzine (45–90 mg/d), including postural hypotension, sedation, sexual dysfunction, and weight gain.

Reversible Inhibitors of Monoamine Oxidase A.    A new generation of reversible MAOIs, represented by moclobemide and brofaromine, have recently also been shown to have efficacy in social phobia. These drugs differ from the standard MAOIs in that they bind monoamine oxidase (MAO) reversibly, resulting in a much lower risk of tyramine-induced hypertensive reaction and relaxing the need for dietary restrictions. Also, unlike the standard MAOIs, which inhibit both A and B isozymes of monoamine oxidase, these drugs inhibit only the A isozyme, which acts selectively on serotonin and norepinephrine but not on dopamine.

After moderate-sized placebo-controlled trials suggested good efficacy for moclobemide (Versiani et al., 1992) and for brofaromine (Van Vliet, den Boer, & Westenberg, 1992), these drugs were among the first to undergo testing for social phobia in industry-sponsored large multicenter placebo-controlled trials (International Multicenter Clinical Trial Group on Moclobemide in Social Phobia, 1997;

Lott et al., 1997; Noyes et al., 1997). The results of these multicenter studies and two other moderate-sized single center placebo-controlled studies of moclobemide (Schneier et al., 1998) and brofaromine (Fahlen, Nilsson, Borg, Humble, & Pauli, 1995) support the efficacy of these drugs for social phobia but temper initial enthusiasm with evidence that moclobemide, and possibly brofaromine as well, are substantially less effective than the standard MAOIs and possibly less effective than SSRIs or clonazepam (Klonopin). Brofaromine is not currently marketed, and moclobemide is not marketed in the United States. The apparently superior efficacy of the standard MAOIs to the MAO-A selective MAOIs suggests that inhibition of MAO-B, with its substrate of dopamine, may be important for maximal MAOI efficacy.

Benzodiazepines.    The high-potency benzodiazepines alprazolam (Xanax) and clonazepam (Klonopin), long known to have efficacy for generalized anxiety and panic disorders, have each subsequently been studied for social phobia in one placebo-controlled trial. Gelernter et al. (1991) found that a standing dose of alprazolam was not significantly different from placebo on a variety of outcome measures, although nonsignificantly more patients were rated unequivocal responders to alprazolam (38 percent) than to placebo (20 percent) or cognitive-behavioral therapy (24 percent).

Davidson, Potts, et al. (1993) reported robust efficacy, however, for clonazepam in a 10-week trial, with a 78 percent response rate on clonazepam (mean dose 2.4 mg/day) versus 20 percent on placebo. Benzodiazepines are believed to act centrally at the gamma aminobutyric acid (GABA) receptor complex. Clinically, they have the advantage of rapid onset of action, but due to relatively short duration of action, they require 2–4 times/day dosing. For patients with a history of sedative or alcohol abuse they pose a higher risk of abuse. Adverse effects may include sedation, memory impairment, unsteady gait, and anorgasmia.

Selective Serotonin Reuptake Inhibitors (SSRIs).    Following anecdotal reports of increased sociability in depressed patients given SSRIs, these drugs (paroxetine [Paxil], sertraline [Zoloft], fluoxetine [Prozac], and fluovoxamine [Luvox]) have also recently been demonstrated to be effective treatments for social phobia. After several reports of SSRI efficacy in open trials and in a small placebo-controlled trial (Van Vliet, den Boer, & Westenberg, 1994), several controlled studies have corroborated these findings. Stein et al. (1996) reported that responders to an acute trial of paroxetine who were randomly assigned to continue paroxetine fared significantly better than patients who were switched over to placebo. A subsequent large multicenter study of paroxetine in generalized social phobia demonstrated substantial efficacy (Stein et al., 1998). Katzelnick et al. (1995) demonstrated efficacy for sertraline in a small crossover-design placebo-controlled trial. SSRIs appear to be well tolerated by persons with social phobia, with relatively low severity of adverse effects such as nausea, insomnia, fatigue, and sexual dysfunction.

Beta-Adrenergic Blockers.    Beta-adrenergic blockers such as propranolol (Inderal) have been shown to be effective in single dose as-needed treatment of performance anxiety, with its marked symptoms of autonomic arousal, in nonpatient samples.

However, in two controlled trials, another beta blocker, atenolol (Tenormin) was ineffective in daily dosing of patients with mainly generalized social phobia (Liebowitz et al., 1992; Turner, Beidel, & Jacob, 1994). Although a controlled study of propranolol confirming its efficacy in patients diagnosed with nongeneralized social phobia remains to be done, beta blockers are widely used clinically for such forms of performance anxiety as public speaking phobias and stage fright (e.g., propranolol, 20–40 mg. taken 1 hour before performance). Beta blockers do not appear to be effective for generalized social phobia.

Summary.    The number of acute pharmacotherapy trials in social phobia, although still small, has become sufficient to develop some preliminary impressions of the relative efficacy of several drug classes. For example, mean drug-placebo differences in magnitude of change on one of the most common social phobia outcome measures, the Liebowitz Social Anxiety Scale (LSAS; Liebowitz, 1987), show relatively consistent results within drug classes across several acute (8–12 week duration) clinical trials (see figure 13.1).

Although the relative superiority of standard MAOIs for social phobia may be consistent with the idea that dopaminergic mechanisms operate in this disorder, as discussed previously, the efficacy of medications with a variety of mechanisms of actions at the level of neurotransmitters suggests the relevance of multiple neurotransmitter systems for social phobia and its pharmacotherapy.

## Psychosocial Treatments

The best researched psychosocial treatments involve a variety of behavioral or cognitive techniques, including social skills training, relaxation exercises, exposure to feared social situations, cognitive therapies, and combined cognitive-behavioral therapies (for a more comprehensive review, see Heimberg & Juster, 1995).

Social Skills Training.    Social skills training involves the teaching of appropriate and adaptive social behavior. Its use in social phobia is based on the premise that persons with social phobia have not developed adequate social skills (perhaps due to chronic avoidance of opportunities to hone such skills) and experience anxiety as a result of an awareness of these deficits. In social skills training, the therapist generally instructs the patient about target behaviors and demonstrates them, the patient rehearses the behavior in role-play with feedback from the therapist, and the patients practices the new behaviors in situations outside the therapy session until goals are achieved.

Several controlled and uncontrolled trials of social skills training have suggested that it may have efficacy in the treatment of social phobia (e.g., Öst, Jerremalm, & Johansson, 1981, Wlazlo, Schroeder-Hartwig, Hand, & Kaisar, 1990), whereas at least one well-controlled study Marziller, Lamberg, & Kellett (1976) failed to demonstrate efficacy. One possible problem with this approach is that the assumption that most persons with social phobia lack social skills is not well established. Many social phobics appear to have adequate skills but become unable to implement these skills when distracted or inhibited by their anxiety. There may be a subgroup of persons with social phobia, however, for whom social skills training is essential.

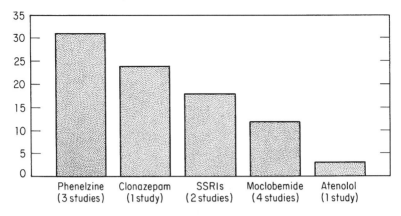

Figure 13.1. Mean drug-placebo difference in change in total social anxiety as measured by the Liebowitz Social Anxiety Scale (Adapted from Liebowitz, 1987).

Relaxation.    Relaxation therapies use techniques such as breathing retraining and progressive muscle relaxation to manage anxiety and physiological symptoms of arousal in social phobia. Results have been mixed and may be better for therapies that specifically apply these techniques to actual feared social situations (Öst et al., 1981).

Exposure.    Most psychosocial treatments for phobias and other anxiety disorders acknowledge the importance of exposure to successful therapy. Exposure therapies are based on the concept that phobic avoidance leads to temporary anxiety relief that serves to reinforce avoidance behavior. When prolonged exposure to the phobic situation is substituted for avoidance, anxiety reduction ensues within the phobic setting, attenuating the anxiety-avoidance cycle.

As applied to social phobia, exposure therapy involves development of a hierarchy of progressively more anxiety-provoking social or performance situations. The patient typically confronts these situations gradually, beginning with the least anxiety provoking. Specific therapies that have been studied vary widely in the ways in which exposure is done—with the therapist versus alone by the patient, by gradual versus more abrupt (flooding) exposure approaches, through imaginal versus in vivo exposure, in the duration and frequency of exposure sessions, and in the extent to which other modalities (cognitive therapy, relaxation, social skills training, medication) are combined with exposure. Controlled and uncontrolled studies of pure exposure (e.g., Hope, Heimberg, & Bruch, 1995) suggest that exposure is an effective treatment for social phobia.

Cognitive-Behavioral Therapies.    Cognitive therapists have noted several problems, however, with the application of pure exposure to social phobia (Butler & Wells, 1995). It may be difficult to assign graduated and repeatable social tasks because naturally occurring social situations are less controllable or less predictable than most other types of phobic situations. Butler and Wells (1995) have further noted that individuals with social phobia may successfully enter a feared situation, such as a party, yet then disengage by using subtle avoidance behaviors such as lack of eye contact or avoiding initiating conversations. Additionally, because the outcome of social interactions is often ambiguous, a bias toward negative interpretation of outcome may interfere with the anxiolytic effects of exposure (e.g., "Although I went to the party and participated in conversations, people didn't seem to enjoy talking with me.").

Based on the concept that negative cognitions contribute to avoidance behavior and need to be addressed directly, a variety of cognitive-behavioral approaches to social phobia have been widely studied. The most thoroughly studied approach has been a group therapy developed by Heimberg and associates (Heimberg, Juster, Hope, & Mattia, 1995). Cognitive-behavioral Group Therapy (CBGT) includes presenting patients a cognitive-behavioral model of social phobia; providing training in identifying maladaptive thoughts, disputing cognitive errors, and developing rational responses; exposure to simulated phobic situations in sessions; and homework assignments for in vivo exposure, coupled with use of cognitive coping skills.

CBGT has been shown to be superior to a control psychotherapy (Educational-Supportive Group Therapy) and to pill placebo (Heimberg et al., 1998). It was somewhat less effective than the MAOI phenelzine after 12 weeks of acute treatment (Heimberg et al., 1998), but proved more likely to lead to a response sustained 6 months after treatment was discontinued (Liebowitz et al., 1999). A variety of forms of cognitive-behavioral therapy have been shown to be effective in social phobia (e.g., Butler, Cullington, Munby, Amies, & Gelder, 1984). Although cognitive techniques appear to offer a useful adjunct to pure behavioral approaches, empirical studies have not demonstrated superior outcome for the combined approach (Feske & Chambless, 1995).

## Social Phobia in Children

Childhood-onset social phobia appears to be a common disorder with the potential to cause long-term impairment. Epidemiologic studies of social phobia in adults suggest an early mean age of onset in the mid-teens with a sizable subset of participants reporting social anxiety problems as early as they can remember (Schneier, Johnson, Hornig, Liebowitz, & Weissman, 1992). Treatment is often delayed; adults entering clinical trials for social phobia routinely report having experienced impairing symptoms for more than 10 years before seeking treatment. Early-onset shyness and social phobia is associated with rejection by peers (Strauss & Francis, 1989), missed opportunities to develop social competence (Rubin, LeMare, & Lollis, 1990) and long-term consequences of impairment in functioning (Caspi, Elder, & Bem, 1988).

Study of treatment interventions for social phobia or childhood shyness has grown out of several sources. Some established adult treatments, both psychosocial and pharmacological, have been adapted for use with children. Other interventions have grown out of the study of social anxiety and fear states in children. Because the formal diagnosis of social phobia has only recently been applied to children, this review will include treatments for social anxiety and avoidance states that are less specifically defined.

## Pharmacological Treatments

Studies of pharmacological treatment of children with social phobia are largely limited to case reports. An exception is the small literature on selective mutism, a condition which recently has been shown to overlap greatly with social phobia (Black & Uhde, 1992). Selective mutism is a relatively rare condition in which children with normal verbal capabilities refuse to speak with people outside the family in most or all unfamiliar social situations, especially when beginning school. This condition, which is often refractory to psychotherapy, has been the focus of two recent pharmacological trials that suggest that the SSRI fluoxetine may have efficacy (Black & Uhde, 1994; Dummit, Klein, Tancer, Asche, & Martin, 1996).

## Psychosocial Treatments

Behavioral methods used to treat social anxiety in children, including systematic desensitization, prolonged exposure, and modeling, have received little controlled study (see reviews by Barrios & O'Dell, 1989; Beidel & Morris, 1995). Systematic desensitization, which is based on the idea that social anxiety is a classically conditioned emotional response, involves pairing presentation of anxiety-provoking situations with relaxation training. It has been reported to have efficacy for adolescents and older children, especially for test or speaking anxiety (e.g., Leal, Baxter, Martin, & Marx, 1981). Reinforcement for appropriate social behavior may be used to shape behavior (e.g., Walker, Greenwood, Hops, & Todd, 1979). Other behavioral approaches have focused on the development of social skills through exposure and modeling, in which a child observes a filmed or live model or in which the therapist demonstrates appropriate coping strategies for a feared situation. The child then imitates the performance, and the therapist provides feedback and reinforcement. Social skills training has been utilized in which children receive instruction in performing specific behaviors (being introduced, holding conversations, making eye contact, etc.; e.g., Christoff et al., 1985).

Cognitive approaches have also been used in tandem with behavioral exposure with socially anxious children, as in a therapy for adolescents derived from Heimberg's model of cognitive behavioral therapy for adult social phobics (Albano, Marten, Holt, Heimberg, & Barlow, 1995). This approach has been studied in a format of 16 two-hour group sessions. The first eight sessions focus on educating the participants about social phobia and conducting skills training. Skills training includes cognitive restructuring, social skills, and problem solving, each taught via modeling, behavioral shaping, and role-playing. The second phase introduces in vivo exposure and practice.

Family interventions specifically designed for social anxiety have focused on education of parents and on training parents to be coaches who facilitate their child's application of the skills learned in cognitive-behavioral therapy (Albano et al., 1995). Parental behavior may also be a factor that contributes to the original development of social avoidance. Recent findings suggest that temperamentally fearful toddlers are more likely to be behaviorally inhibited if their mothers are highly involved yet insensitive to the toddler's needs in anxiety-provoking settings (Rubin, Hastings, Stewart, Henderson, & Chen, 1997). Interventions geared toward optimizing parenting behavior with socially anxious children need further study.

## Panic Disorder and Agoraphobia in Adults

Panic disorder is defined by the occurrence of at least one unexpected full-symptom panic attack, followed by recurrent unexpected attacks and/or persistent concern about having additional attacks, worry about consequences of the attacks or a change in behavior related to the attacks (DSM-IV, 1994). Agoraphobia often develops, with anxiety and avoidance related to places in which escape might be difficult in the event of a panic attack. Although some patients with panic disorder develop fears of embarrassment that someone might witness them having an attack, panic attacks are not limited to social situations, as is the case in social phobia. Although panic disorder is often a chronic condition, its natural course typically waxes and wanes more than does social phobia, and many patients are able to achieve a panic-free remission with treatment.

### Pharmacological Treatments

Since the discovery in the early 1960s that the tricyclic antidepressant imipramine (Tofranil) blocked panic attacks (Klein & Fink, 1962), several classes of drugs have been shown to have efficacy for panic disorder. Imipramine and clomipramine (Anafranil) are the best studied of the tricyclic antidepressants for panic disorder, their efficacy having been established in numerous placebo-controlled trials (e.g., Modigh, Westberg, & Eriksson, 1992; Zitrin, Klein, & Woerner, 1983). Interestingly, the apparent lack of efficacy of imipramine for social phobia helped stimulate recognition of social phobia as a condition distinct from panic disorder (Liebowitz, Gorman, Fyer, & Klein, 1985). Tricyclics have recently been displaced as the pharmacotherapy of choice for panic disorder by SSRIs, because tricyclics tend to be somewhat less well tolerated due to common occurrence of dry mouth, constipation, and other adverse effects and are more dangerous in the presence of cardiac disease and in overdose.

As in social phobia, SSRIs have recently been shown to be highly effective and well tolerated in the treatment of panic disorder (Boyer, 1995). Panic disorder patients do best with very low starting doses of these drugs to avoid an early hyperstimulation syndrome (Schneier et al., 1990) that is common in panic disorder but not social phobia.

The benzodiazepines alprazolam and clonazepam also have well-established efficacy in panic disorder (Ballenger et al., 1988; Beauclair, Fontaine, Annable, Holobow, & Chouinard, 1994). They carry the advantage of rapid efficacy and the disadvantages of sedation and dependence, as they do in social phobia.

MAOIs also appear to be highly effective in panic disorder (Sheehan, Ballenger, & Jacobsen, 1980), as they are for social phobia, although MAOIs are rarely used for panic disorder due to the long-available easier pharmacotherapy options of tricyclic, benzodiazepines, and now SSRIs.

Beta blockers have been shown to have only modest efficacy for panic disorder in a small number of controlled trials (Noyes et al., 1984). This contrasts with the clinical experience of beta blocker efficacy for performance anxiety and the nongeneralized subtype of social phobia.

Psychosocial Treatments

The literature on psychosocial treatment of panic disorder has recently grown even more dramatically than that on social phobia. Rather than attempting a comprehensive review of the literature, this review will focus on some key studies and compare them with studies of treatment of social phobia.

Early specific psychological approaches to treatment of agoraphobia conceptualized the problem as learned avoidance behavior and focused on in vivo exposure of phobic avoidance (Marks, 1969). During the 1970s and 1980s many studies of in vivo exposure established its acute effectiveness in comparison with no treatment or with a form of placebo and reported persistent gains after follow-up periods of several years (e.g. Burns, Thorpe, & Cavallaro, 1986; Cohen, Monteiro, & Marks, 1984).

During the 1980s and 1990s, reconceptualization of panic disorder to include unexpected panic attacks and catastrophic misinterpretation of bodily sensations led to behavioral therapies which incorporated exposure to anxiety symptoms and cognitive approaches to reduce sensitivity to anxiety (Barlow, Craske, Cerny, & Klosko, 1989; Clark et al., 1994). These developments paralleled consideration of the need for more attention to subtle avoidance behavior and catastrophic misinterpretation of social consequences in social phobia.

As in social phobia, there is some debate over the relative efficacy of pure behavioral versus cognitive-behavioral therapies for panic disorder. Cognitive-behavioral approaches have been widely studied. They have been shown to be superior to applied relaxation (Craske, Brown, & Barlow, 1991) and have demonstrated mixed results in comparison with acute drug treatments (Black, Wesner, Bowers, & Gabel, 1993; Klosko, Barlow, Tassinari, & Cerny, 1990) and superiority in respect to persistence of response after treatment is discontinued (Sharp et al., 1996). More recently, nondirective, psychodynamically based psychotherapies have also begun to be evaluated in controlled studies with some positive findings (Shear, Pilkonis, Cloitre, & Leon, 1994; Wiborg & Dahl, 1996).

Combined Psychosocial and Pharmacological Treatment

Several recent studies have examined innovative ways to combine medication and psychotherapy for panic disorder, such as by using behavior therapies to facilitate discontinuation of benzodiazepines (Spiegel & Bruce, 1997). In some studies, combined treatments have appeared to confer some benefits (deBeurs, van Balkom, Lange, Koele, & van Dyck, 1995), whereas in others combined treatment has not appeared superior to behavioral therapy alone, or adjunctive medication has appeared to diminish the efficacy of behavioral therapy (Brown & Barlow, 1995).

**Panic Disorder and Agoraphobia in Children**

Although onset of panic disorder typically occurs between late adolescence and the 30s, prepubertal onset appears uncommon, unlike in social phobia. Consequently, there has been little study of panic disorder in children. Some researchers have suggested a developmental relationship between childhood separation anxiety and later onset of panic disorder (Gittelman & Klein, 1984); however, subsequent studies have not consistently supported a specific relationship between these disorders (Pine, Cohen, Gurley, Brook, & Ma, 1998).

The literature on pharmacotherapy of panic disorder in children consists mainly of case reports of benzodiazepines and SSRIs (see review by Dummit & Klein, 1994). One small placebo-controlled study of the benzodiazepine clonazepam failed to demonstrate efficacy (Graae, Milner, Rizzotto, & Klein, 1994).

Psychosocial approaches to panic disorder have not been well studied with children. Uncontrolled reports have suggested the efficacy of cognitive and/or behavioral approaches (Drobes & Strauss, 1993).

## Conclusions

The literature on treatment of social phobia and panic disorder reflects similarities and differences between the two disorders. Both disorders are responsive to a variety of behavioral techniques, with in vivo exposure widely acknowledged as a powerful ingredient. Cognitive approaches have been tailored to each different focus of fear in each disorder, and use of cognitive-behavioral therapies has become increasingly common. These treatment findings are consistent with the notion that similar psychological processes govern both disorders, which differ most clearly in the nature of catastrophic cognitions and in the types of situations that are avoided.

Both social phobia and panic disorder have been shown to be responsive to several classes of medications, including serotonin reuptake inhibitors, benzodiazepines, and monoamine oxidase inhibitors. Tricyclic antidepressants, however, are highly effective for panic but disappointing for social phobia. Beta blockers appear effective for social phobia that is limited to performance anxiety, which with its prominent physical symptoms may most resemble panic disorder, yet beta blockers appear relatively ineffective for panic disorder or generalized social phobia. These differences in pharmacotherapy response may reflect differences in patterns of central neurotransmitter and peripheral autonomic activity in the two disorders, as has been suggested by differences in physical symptoms, response to lactate challenge, and preliminary brain imaging findings. Further elucidation of the pathophysiology of extreme fear states holds promise for the development of more specific targeted treatments.

It remains unclear to what extent these similarities and differences in treatment response are shaped by genetics, early environmental conditions, or other factors. Further work in these areas through longitudinal and family studies, as well as through more typical cross-sectional studies, is needed. Recognition and assessment of elements common to conditions of extreme fear may help elucidate factors which influence treatment response across these diagnostic categories and help refine the diagnostic categories of the future.

*References*

Al'Absi, M., Bongard, S., Buchanan, T., Pincomb, G. A., Licinio, J., & Lovallo, W. R. (1997). Cardiovascular and neuroendocrine adjustment to public speaking and mental arithmetic stressors. *Psychophysiology, 34,* 266–275.

Albano, A. M., Marten, P. A., Holt, C. S., Heimberg, R. G., & Barlow, D. H. (1995). Cognitive-behavioral group treatment for adolescent social phobia: A preliminary study. *Journal of Nervous and Mental Disease, 183,* 685–692.

American Psychiatric Association (1994). *Diagnostic and statistical manual of mental disorders.* (4th ed.). Washington, DC: Author.

Amies, P. L., Gelder, M. G., & Shaw, P. M. (1983). Social phobia: A comparative clinical study. *British Journal of Psychiatry, 142,* 174–179.

Ballenger, J. C., Burrows, G. D., DuPont, R. L., Jr., Lesser, I. M., Noyes, R., Jr., Pecknold, J. C., Rifkin, A., & Swinson, R. P. (1988). Alprazolam in panic disorder and agoraphobia: Results from a multicenter trial: I. Efficacy in short term treatment. *Archives of General Psychiatry, 45,* 413–422.

Barlow, D. H., Craske, M. G., Cerny, J. A., & Klosko, J. S. (1989). Behavioral treatment of panic disorder. *Behavior Therapy, 20,* 261–282.

Barrios, B. A., & O'Dell, S. L. (1989). Fears and anxieties. In E. J. Masn & R. A. Barkley (Eds.), *Treatment of childhood disorders* (pp. 167–221). New York: Guilford Press.

Beauclair, L., Fontaine, R., Annable, L., Holobow, N., & Chouinard, G. (1994). Clonazepam in the treatment of panic disorder: A double-blind, placebo-controlled trial investigating the correlation between clonazepam concentrations in plasma and clinical response. *Journal of Clinical Psychopharmacology, 14,* 111–118.

Beidel, D. C., & Morris, T. L. (1995). Social phobia. In J. S. March, (Ed.), *Anxiety disorders in children and adolescents* (pp. 181–211). New York: Guilford Press.

Black, B., & Uhde, T. W. (1992). Elective mutism as a variant of social phobia. *Journal of the American Academy of Child and Adolescent Psychiatry, 6,* 1090–1094.

Black, B., & Uhde, T. W. (1994). Treatment of elective mutism with fluoxetine: A double-blind, placebo-controlled study. *Journal of the American Academy of Child and Adolescent Psychiatry, 33,* 1000–1006.

Black, D. W., Wesner, R., Bowers, W., & Gabel, J. (1993). A comparison of fluvoxamine, cognitive therapy, and placebo in the treatment of panic disorder. *Archives of General Psychiatry, 50,* 44–50.

Blanco, C., Schneier, F. R., Liebowitz, M. R. (in press). Pharmacological treatment of social phobia. In D. J. Stein & E. Hollander (Eds.), *Textbook of Anxiety Disorders,* Washington, D.C., American Psychiatric Press.

Blum, K., Braverman, E. R., Wu, S., Cull, J. G., Chen, T. J. H., Gill, J., Wood, R., Eisenberg, A., Sherman, M., Davis, K. R., Matthews, D., Fischer, L., Schnautz, N., Walsh, W., Pontius, A. A., Zedar, M., Kaats, G., & Comings, D. E. (1997). Association of polymorphisms of dopamine $D_2$ receptor (DRD$_2$), and dopamine transporter (DAT$_1$) genes with schizoid/avoidant behaviors (SAB). *Molecular Psychiatry, 2,* 239–246.

Boyer, W. (1995). Serotonin uptake inhibitors are superior to imipramine and alprazolam in alleviating panic attacks: A meta-analysis. *International Clinical Psychopharmacology, 10,* 45–49.

Brown, T. A., & Barlow, D. H. (1995). Long-term outcome in cognitive behavioral treatment of panic disorder. *Journal of Consulting and Clinical Psychology, 63,* 754–765.

Burns, L. E., Thorpe, G. L., & Cavallaro, L. A. (1986). Agoraphobia eight years after behavioral treatment. *Behavior Therapy, 17,* 580–591.

Butler, G., Cullington, A., Munby, M., Amies, P., & Gelder, M. (1984). Exposure and anxiety management in the treatment of social phobia. *Journal of Consulting and Clinical Psychology, 52,* 642–650.

Butler, G., & Wells, A. (1995). Cognitive-behavioral treatments: Clinical applications. In R. Heimberg, M. Liebowitz, D. Hope, & F. Schneier (Eds.), *Social phobia: Diagnosis, assessment and treatment* (pp. 310–333). New York: Guilford Press.

Calkins, S. D., Fox, N. A., & Marshall, T. R. (1996). Behavioral and physiological antecedents of inhibited and uninhibited behavior. *Child Development, 67,* 523–540.

Caspi, A., Elder, G. H., Jr., & Bem, D. J. (1988). Moving away from the world: Life course patterns of shy children. *Developmental Psychology, 24,* 824–831.

Christoff, K. A., Scott, W., Kelley, M. L., Schlundt, D., Baer, G., & Kelly, J. A. (1985). Social skills and social problem-solving training for shy young adolescents. *Behavior Therapy, 16,* 468–477.

Clark, D. M., Salkovskis, P. M., Hackmann, A., Middleton, H., Anastasiades, P., & Gelder, M. (1994). A comparison of cognitive therapy, applied relaxation and imipramine in the treatment of panic disorder. *British Journal of Psychiatry, 164,* 759–769.

Cloninger, C. (1987). A systematic method for clinical description and classification of personality variants. *Archives of General Psychiatry, 44,* 573–578.

Cohen, S. D., Monteiro, W., & Marks, I. M. (1984). Two-year follow-up of agoraphobics after exposure and imipramine. *British Journal of Psychiatry, 144,* 276–281.

Coplan, J., Andrews, M. W., Rosenblum, L. A., Owens, M. J., Friedman, S., Gorman, J. M., & Nemeroff, C. B. (1996). Persistent elevations of cerebrospinal fluid concentrations of corticotropin-releasing factor in adult nonhuman primates exposed to early-life stressors: Implications for the pathophysiology of mood and anxiety disorders. *Proceedings of the National Academy of Science USA, 93,* 1619–1623.

Coplan, J., Trost, R. C., Owens, M. J., Cooper, M. A., Gorman, J. M., Nemeroff, C. B., & Rosenblum, L. A. (1998). Cerebrospinal fluid concentration of somatostatin and biogenic amines in grown primates reared by mothers exposed to manipulated foraging conditions. *Archives of General Psychiatry, 55,* 473–477.

Craske, M. G., Brown, T. A., & Barlow, D. H. (1991). Behavioral treatment of panic: A two-year follow-up. *Behavior Therapy, 22,* 289–304.

Davidson, J. R. T., Krishnan, K. R. R., Charles, H. C., Boyko, O., Potts, N. L. S., Ford, S. M., & Patterson, L. (1993). Magnetic resonance spectroscopy in social phobia: Preliminary findings. *Journal of Clinical Psychiatry, 54 (Suppl. 12),* 19–25.

Davidson, J. R. T., Potts, N., Richichi, E., Krishnan, R., Ford, S. M., Smith, R., & Wilson, W. H. (1993). Treatment of social phobia with clonazepam and placebo. *Journal of Clinical Psychopharmacology, 13,* 423–428.

Davidson, R. J., Marshall, J. R., Tomarken, A. J., & Henriques, J. B. (in press). While a phobic waits: Regional brain electrical and autonomic activity predict anxiety in social phobics during anticipation of public speaking. *Biological Psychiatry.*

deBeurs, E., van Balkom, A. J. L. M., Lange, A., Koele, P., & van Dyck R. (1995). Treatment of panic disorder with agoraphobia: Comparison of fluvoxamine, placebo, and psychological panic management combined with exposure and of exposure in vivo alone. *American Journal of Psychiatry, 152,* 683–691.

Den Boer, J. A., van Vliet, I. M., & Westenberg, H. G. M. (1995). Recent developments in the psychopharmacology of social phobia. *European Archives of Psychiatry and Clinical Neuroscience, 244,* 309–316.

DiLalla, L. F., Kagan, J., & Reznick, J. S. (1994). Genetic etiology of behavioral inhibition among two-year-old children. *Infant Behavior and Development, 17,* 401–408.

Drobes, D. J., & Strauss, C. C. (1993). Behavioral treatment of childhood anxiety disorders. *Child and Adolescent Psychiatric Clinics of North America, 2,* 779–794.

Dummit, E. S., & Klein, R. G. (1994). Panic disorder. In T.H. Ollendick, N. J. King, & W. Yule (Eds.). *International handbook of phobic and anxiety disorders in children and adolescents* (pp. 241–266). New York: Plenum Press.

Dummit, E. S., Klein, R. G., Tancer, N. K., Asche, B., & Martin, J. (1996). Fluoxetine treatment of children with selective mutism: An open trial. *Journal of the American Academy of Child & Adolescent Psychiatry, 35,* 615–621.

Fahlen, T., Nilsson, H. L., Borg, K., Humble, M., & Pauli, U. (1995). Social phobia: The clinical efficacy and tolerability of the monoamine oxidase-A and serotonin uptake inhibitor brofaromine. *Acta Psychiatrica Scandinavica, 92,* 351–358.

Feske, U., & Chambless, D. L. (1995). Cognitive behavioral versus exposure only treatment for social phobia: A meta-analysis. *Behavior Therapy, 26,* 695–720.

Finman, R., Davidson, R. J., Colton, M. B., Straus, A. M., & Kagan, J. (1989). Psychophysiological correlates of inhibition to the unfamiliar in children [Abstract]. *Psychophysiology, 26,* S24.

Fossey, M. D., Lydiard, B., Ballenger, J. C., Laraia, M. T., Bissette, G., & Nemeroff, C. B. (1996). Cerebrospinal fluid corticotropin-releasing factor concentrations in patients with anxiety disorders and normal comparison subjects. *Biological Psychiatry, 39,* 703–707.

Fox, N. A., Rubin, K., Calkins, S. D., Marshall, T., Coplan, R., Porges, S., Long, J., & Stewart, S. (1995). Frontal activation asymmetry and social competence at four years of age. *Child Development, 66,* 1770–1784.

Fyer, A. J., Mannuzza, S., Chapman, T. F., Martin, L. Y., & Klein, D. F. (1995). Specificity in familial aggregation of phobic disorders. *Archives of General Psychiatry, 52,* 564–573.

Gelernter, C. S., Uhde, T. W., Cimbolic, P., Arnkoff, D. B., Vittone, B. J., Tancer, M. E., & Bartko, J. J. (1991). Cognitive-behavioral and pharmacological treatments of social phobia: A controlled study. *Archives of General Psychiatry, 48,* 938–945.

Gittleman, R., & Klein, D. F. (1984). Relationship between separation anxiety and panic and agoraphobic disorders. *Psychopathology, 17,* 56–65.

Graae, F., Milner, J., Rizzotto, L., & Klein, R. G. (1994). Clonazepam in childhood anxiety disorders: Pilot study. *Journal of the American Academy of Child and Adolescent Psychiatry, 29,* 785–788.

Heimberg, R. G., Hope, D. A., Dodge, C. S., & Becker, R. E. (1990). Comparison of generalized social phobics and public speaking phobics. *Journal of Nervous and Mental Disease, 178,* 172–179.

Heimberg, R. G., & Juster, H. R. (1995). Cognitive-behavioral treatment: Literature review. In R. Heimberg, M. Liebowitz, D. Hope, & F. Schneier, (Eds.), *Social phobia: Diagnosis, assessment and treatment* (pp. 261–309). New York: Guilford Press.

Heimberg, R. G., Juster, H. R., Hope, D. A., & Mattia, J. I. (1995). Cognitive behavioral group treatment for social phobia: Description, case presentation and empirical support. In M. B. Stein (Ed.), *Social phobia: Clinical and research perspectives* (pp. 293–321). Washington, DC: American Psychiatric Press.

Heimberg, R. G., Liebowitz, M. L., Hope, D. A., Schneier, F. R., Holt, C. S., Welkowitz, L. A., Juster, H. R., Campeas, R., Bruch, M. A., Cloitre, M., Fallon, B., & Klein, D. F. (1998). Cognitive-behavioral group therapy versus phenelzine in social phobia: 12-week outcome. *Archives of General Psychiatry, 55,* 1133–1142.

Hofmann, S. G., Newman, M. G., Ehlers, A., & Roth, W. T. (1995). Psychophysiological differences between subgroups of social phobia. *Journal of Abnormal Psychology, 104,* 224–231.

Hope, D. A., Heimberg, R. G., Bruch, M. A. (1995). Dismantling cognitive-behavioral group therapy for social phobia. *Behaviour Research and Therapy, 33,* 637–650.

International Multicenter Clinical Trial Group on Moclobemide in Social Phobia (1997). Moclobemide in social phobia—A double-blind, placebo controlled clinical study. *European Archives of Psychiatry and Clinical Neuroscience, 247,* 71–80.

Johnson, M. R., Lydiard, R. B., Zealberg, J. J., Fossey, M. D., & Ballenger, J. C. (1994). Plasma and CSF HVA levels in panic patients with comorbid social phobia. *Journal of Biological Psychiatry, 36,* 426–427.

Jolkkonen, J., Lepola, U., Bissette, G., Nemeroff, C., & Riekkinen, P. (1993). CSF corticotropin-releasing factor is not affected in panic disorder. *Biological Psychiatry, 33,* 136–138.

Kagan, J. (1997). Temperament and the reactions to unfamiliarity. *Child Development, 68,* 139–143.

Kagan, J., Reznick, J. S., & Gibbons, J. (1989). Inhibited and uninhibited types of children. *Child Development, 60,* 838–845.

Kagan, J., Reznick, J. S., & Snidman, N. (1988). Biological bases of childhood shyness. *Science, 240,* 167–171.

Katzelnick, D. J., Kobak, K. A., Greist, J. H., Jefferson, J. W., Mantle, J. M., & Serlin, R. C. (1995). Sertraline for social phobia: a double-blind, placebo-controlled crossover study. *American Journal of Psychiatry, 152,* 1368–1371.

Kendler, K. S., Neale, M. C., Kessler, R. C., Heath, A. C., & Eaves, L. J. (1992). The genetic epidemiology of phobias in women: The interrelations of agoraphobia, social phobia, situational phobia, and simple phobia. *Archives of General Psychiatry, 49*, 273–281.

Klein, D. F., & Fink, M. (1962). Psychiatric reaction patterns to imipramine. *American Journal of Psychiatry, 119*, 432–438.

Klosko, J. S., Barlow, D. H., Tassinari, R., & Cerny, J. A. (1990). A comparison of alprazolam and behavior therapy in treatment of panic disorder. *Journal of Consulting and Clinical Psychology, 58*, 77–84.

Leal, L. L, Baxter, E. G., Martin, J., & Marx, R. W. (1981). Cognitive modification and systematic desensitization and relaxation of high test-anxious secondary school students. *Journal of Counseling Psychology, 16*, 446–451.

Levin, A. P., Saoud, J. B., Strauman, T., Gorman, J. M., Fyer, A. J., Crawford, R., & Liebowitz, M. R. (1993). Responses of "generalized" and "discrete" social phobics during public speaking. *Journal of Anxiety Disorders, 7*, 207–221.

Liebowitz, M. R. (1987). Social phobia. *Modern Problems in Pharmacopsychiatry, 22*, 141–173.

Liebowitz, M. R., Fyer, A. J., Gorman, J. M., Dillon, D., Davies, S., Stein, J. M., Cohen, B. S., & Klein, D. F. (1985). Specificity of lactate infusions in social phobia versus panic disorder. *American Journal of Psychiatry, 142*, 947–950.

Liebowitz, M. R., Gorman, J. M., Fyer, A. J., & Klein, D. F. (1985). Social phobia: Review of a neglected anxiety disorder. *Archives of General Psychiatry, 42*, 729–736.

Liebowitz, M. R., Heimberg, R. G., Schneier, F. R., Hope, D. A., Davies, S., Holt, C. S., Goetz, D., Juster, H. R., Lin, S.-H., Bruch, M. A., Marshall, R. D., & Klein, D. F. (1999). *Cognitive-behavioral group therapy versus phenelzine in social phobia: Long term outcome.* Manuscript submitted for publication.

Liebowitz, M. R., Schneier, F., Campeas, R., Hollander, E., Hatterer, J., Fyer, A., Gorman, J., Papp, L., Davies, S., Gully, R., & Klein, D. F. (1992). Phenelzine vs atenolol in social phobia: A placebo-controlled comparison. *Archives of General Psychiatry, 49*, 290–300.

Lott, M., Greist, J. H., Jefferson, J. W., Kobak, K. A., Katzelnick, D. J., Katz, R. J., & Schaettle, S. C. (1997). Brofaromine for social phobia: A multicenter, placebo-controlled, double-blind study. *Journal of Clinical Psychopharmacology, 17*, 255–260.

Mannuzza, S., Fyer, A. J., Liebowitz, M. R., & Klein, D. F. (1990). Delineating the boundary of social phobia: Its relationship to panic disorder and agoraphobia. *Journal of Anxiety Disorders, 4*, 41–59.

Mannuzza, S., Schneier, F. R., Chapman, T. F., Liebowitz, M. R., Klein, D. F., & Fyer, A. J. (1995). Generalized social phobia: Reliability and validity. *Archives of General Psychiatry, 52*, 230–237.

Marks, I. M. (1969). *Fears and phobias.* London, England: Heineman.

Marziller, J. S., Lamberg, C., & Kellett, J. (1976). A controlled evaluation of systematic desensitization and social skills training for socially inadequate psychiatric patients. *Behaviour Research and Therapy, 14*, 225–238.

McCann, U. D., Slate, S. O., Geraci, M., Roscow-Terrill, D., & Uhde, T. W. (1997). A comparison of the effects of intravenous pentagastrin on patients with social phobia, panic disorder and healthy controls. *Neuropsychopharmacology, 16*, 229–237.

Modigh, K., Westberg, P., & Eriksson, E. (1992). Superiority of clomipramine over imipramine in the treatment of panic disorder: A placebo-controlled trial. *Journal of Clinical Psychopharmacology, 12*, 251–261.

Naftolowitz, D. F., Vaughn, B. V., Ranc, J., & Tancer, M. E. (1994). Response to alcohol in social phobia. *Anxiety, 1*, 96–99.

Nemeroff, C. B. (1992). New vistas in neuropeptide research in neuropsychiatry: Focus on corticotropin-releasing factor. *Neuropsychopharmacology, 6*, 69–75.

Noyes, R., Anderson, D. J., Clancy, J., Crowe, R. R., Slymen, D. J., Ghoneim, M. M., & Hinrichs, J. V. (1984). Diazepam and propranolol in panic disorder and agoraphobia. *Archives of General Psychiatry, 41,* 287–292.

Noyes, R., Moroz, G., Davidson, J. R. T., Liebowitz, M. R., Davidson, A., Siegel, J., Bell, J., Cain, J. W., Curlik, S. M., Kent, T. A., Lydiard, R. B., Mallinger, A. G., Pollack, M. H., Rapaport, M., Rasmussen, S. A., Hedges, D., Schweizer, E., & Uhlenhuth, E. H. (1997). Moclobemide in social phobia: A controlled dose-response trial. *Journal of Clinical Psychopharmacology, 17,* 247–254.

Öst, L. G., Jerremalm, A., & Johansson, J. (1981). Individual response patterns and the effects of different behavioral methods in the treatment of social phobia. *Behaviour Research and Therapy, 19,* 1–16.

Pine, D. S., Cohen P., Gurley, D., Brook, J., & Ma, Y. (1998). The risk for early-adulthood anxiety and depressive disorders in adolescents with anxiety and depressive disorders. *Archives of General Psychiatry, 55,* 56–64.

Potts, N. L. S., Davidson, J. R. T., Krishnan, K. R. R., & Doraiswamy, P. M. (1994). Magnetic resonance imaging in social phobia. *Psychiatry Research, 52,* 35–42.

Potts, N. L. S., Davidson, J. R. T., Krishnan, K. R., & Doraiswamy, P. M. (1991). Levels of urinary free cortisol in social phobia. *Journal of Clinical Psychiatry, 52 (Supplement),* 41–42.

Rosenbaum, J. F., Biederman, J., Hirshfeld, D. R., Bolduc, E. A., Faraone, S. V., Kagan, J., Snidman, N., & Reznick, J. S. (1991). Further evidence of an association between behavioral inhibition and anxiety disorders: Results from a family study of children from a non-clinical sample. *Journal of Psychiatry Research, 25,* 49–65.

Rubin, K. H., Hastings, P. D., Stewart, S. L., Henderson, H. A., & Chen, X. (1997). The consistency and concomitants of inhibition: Some of the children, all of the time. *Child Development, 68,* 467–483.

Rubin, K. H., LeMare, L. J., & Lollis, S. (1990). Social withdrawal in childhood: Developmental pathways to peer rejection. In S.R. Asher & J.D. Coie (Eds.), *Peer rejection in childhood* (pp. 217–249). Cambridge: Cambridge University Press.

Schmidt, L. A., & Fox, N. A. (1994). Patterns of cortical electrophysiology and autonomic activity in adults' shyness and sociability. *Biological Psychology, 38,* 183–198.

Schneier, F. R., Goetz, D., Campeas, R., Fallon, B., Marshall, R., & Liebowitz, M.R. (1998). A placebo-controlled trial of moclobemide in social phobia. *British Journal of Psychiatry, 172,* 70–77.

Schneier, F. R., Johnson, J., Hornig, C., Liebowitz, M. R., & Weissman, M. M. (1992). Social phobia: Comorbidity and morbidity in an epidemiologic sample. *Archives of General Psychiatry, 49,* 282–288.

Schneier, F. R., Liebowitz, M. R., Davies, S. O., Fairbanks, J., Hollander, E., Campeas, R., & Klein, D. F. (1990). Fluoxetine in panic disorder. *Journal of Clinical Psychopharmacology, 10,* 119–121.

Sharp, D. M., Power, K. G., Simpson, R. J., Swanson, V., Moodie, E., Anstee, J. A., & Ashford, J. J. (1996). Fluvoxamine, placebo, and cognitive behaviour therapy used alone and in combination in the treatment of panic disorder and agoraphobia. *Journal of Anxiety Disorders, 10,* 219–242.

Shear, M. K., Pilkonis, P. A., Cloitre, M., & Leon, A. C. (1994). Cognitive behavioral treatment compared with nonprescriptive treatment of panic disorder. *Archives of General Psychiatry, 51,* 395–401.

Sheehan, D. V., Ballenger, J. C., & Jacobsen, G. (1980). Treatment of endogenous anxiety with phobic, hysterical, and hypochondriacal symptoms. *Archives of General Psychiatry, 37,* 51–59.

Spiegel, D. A., & Bruce, T. J. (1997). Benzodiazepines and exposure-based cognitive behavior therapies for panic disorder: Conclusions from combined treatment trials. *American Journal of Psychiatry, 154,* 773–781.

Stein, M. B., Asmundson, G. J. G., & Chartier, M. (1994). Autonomic responsivity in generalized social phobia. *Journal of Affective Disorders, 31,* 211–221.

Stein, M. B., Chartier, M. J., Haven, A. L., Kroft, C. B. L., Chale, R. A., Cote, D., & Walker, J. R. (1996). Paroxetine in the treatment of generalized social phobia: Open-label treatment and double-blind placebo-controlled discontinuation. *Journal of Clinical Psychopharmacology, 16,* 218–222.

Stein, M. B., Leibowitz, M. R., Lydiard, R. B., Pitts, C. D., Bushnell, W., & Gergel, I. (1998). Paroxetine treatment of generalized social phobia (social anxiety disorder): a randomized controlled trial. *Journal of the American Medical Association, 280,* 708–713.

Stein, M. D., Heuser, I. J., Juncos, J. L., & Uhde, T. W. (1990). Anxiety disorders in patients with Parkinson's disease. *American Journal of Psychiatry, 147,* 217–220.

Stein, M. D., Tancer, M. E., & Uhde, T. W. (1992). Physiologic and plasma norepinephrine responses to orthostasis in patients with panic disorder and social phobia. *Archives of General Psychiatry, 49,* 311–317.

Strauss, C. C., & Francis, G. (1989). Psychosocial impairment associated with anxiety in children. *Journal of Clinical Child Psychology, 16,* 235–239.

Tancer, M. E., Mailman, R. B., Stein, M. B., Mason, G. A., Carson, S. W., & Golden, R. N. (1995). Neuroendocrine responsivity to monoaminergic system probes in generalized social phobia. *Anxiety, 1,* 216–223.

Taylor, S., Koch, W. J., & McNally, R. J. (1992). How does anxiety sensitivity vary across anxiety disorders? *Journal of Anxiety Disorders, 6,* 249–259.

Tiihonen, J., Kuikka, J., Bergstrom, K., Lepola, U., Koponen, H., & Leinonen, E. (1997). Dopamine reuptake site densities in patients with social phobia. *American Journal of Psychiatry, 154,* 239–242.

Tuppler, L. A., Davidson, J. R. T., Smith, R. D., Lazeyras, F., Charles, H. C., & Krishnan, K. R. R. (1997). A repeat proton magnetic resonance spectroscopy study in social phobia. *Biological Psychiatry, 42,* 419–424.

Turner, S. M., Beidel, D. C., & Jacob, R. G. (1994). Social phobia: a comparison of behavior therapy and atenolol. *Journal of Consulting and Clinical Psychology, 62,* 350–358.

Turner, S. M., Beidel, D. C., & Townsley, R. M. (1990). Social phobia: Relationship to shyness. *Behaviour Research and Therapy, 28,* 497–505.

Turner, S. M., Beidel, D. C., & Townsley, R. M. (1992). Social phobia: A comparison of specific and generalized subtypes and avoidant personality disorder. *Journal of Abnormal Psychology, 101,* 326–331.

Uhde, T. W., Tancer, M. E., Gelernter, C. S., & Vittone, B. J. (1994). Normal urinary free cortisol and postdexamethasone cortisol in social phobia: Comparison to normal volunteers. *Journal of Affective Disorders, 30,* 155–161.

Van Vliet, I. M., den Boer, J. A., & Westenberg, H. G. M. (1992). Psychopharmacological treatment of social phobia: Clinical and biochemical effects of brofaromine, a selective MAO-A inhibitor. *European Neuropsychopharmacology, 2,* 21–29.

Van Vliet, I. M., den Boer, J. A., & Westenberg, H. G. M. (1994). Psychopharmacological treatment of social phobia: A double-blind, placebo-controlled study of fluvoxamine. *Psychopharmacology, 115,* 128–134.

Versiani, M., Nardi, A. E., Mundim, F. D., Alves, A. B., Liebowitz, M. R., & Amrein, R. (1992). Pharmacotherapy of social phobia: A controlled study with moclobemide and phenelzine. *British Journal of Psychiatry, 161,* 353–360.

Walker, H. M., Greenwood, C. R., Hops, H., & Todd, N. M. (1979). Differential effects of reinforcing topographic components of free play social interaction: Analysis and systematic replication. *Behavior Modification, 3,* 291–321.

Wiborg, I. M., & Dahl, A. A. (1996). Does brief dynamic psychotherapy reduce the relapse rate of panic disorder? *Archives of General Psychiatry, 53,* 689–694.

Wlazlo, Z., Schroeder-Hartwig, K., Hand, I., & Kaisar, G. (1990). Exposure in vivo vs. social skills training for social phobia: Long term outcome and differential effects. *Behaviour Research and Therapy, 28,* 181–193.

Zitrin, C. M., Klein, D. F., & Woerner, M. G. (1983). Treatment of phobias: I. Comparison of imipramine hydrochloride and placebo. *Archives of General Psychiatry, 40,* 125–138.

# Developmental Outcomes and Clinical Perspectives

Lynne Henderson & Philip G. Zimbardo

Our commentary focuses on key features of each of the chapters in this section, selecting those that raise interesting issues for future research or for treatment of shyness and extreme forms of social fear. In doing so, we interpose, wherever it is relevant to points being made by these authors, some of our own recent research with shy clients at our shyness clinic and with shy college students. We conclude with a brief presentation of the Social Fitness Model that is guiding our treatment of shyness in adolescent and adult shy clients. Although we both have been deeply involved with research and treatment of shyness for many years, our perspectives and knowledge have been broadened and enriched considerably by the vision and scholarship of these six authors.

## Beidel and Turner

Aspects of anxiety and sensitivity may appear in infancy and persist throughout the lifespan. Deborah Beidel and Samuel Turner provide an insightful, in-depth overview of research related to shyness, behavioral inhibition, social isolation, passivity, and fearfulness from infancy through adulthood. They explore the association of these constructs and the personal experiences that underlie them to anxiety disorders in adults. Zimbardo's earlier research demonstrated that shyness is an emotional state that is nearly universal (Zimbardo, 1986). We have wondered to what degree the labeling process itself is a major contributor to the induction of long-term impairment among those reporting early childhood shyness. It was interesting to note in the data presented by Beidel and Turner that children of both genders who became increasingly shy at 6 years old were those whose mothers rated them as less socially competent at 43 months. If parents and adults in the larger culture view temporary states of shyness as negative and label children in a negative manner, children will internalize the labels and experience a loss of self-esteem.

The authors speculate that different socialization patterns may account for the fact that early shyness in males is more predictive of later shyness than is the case for females in the Munich study (Engfer, 1993). This finding may also be related to differing cultural expectations for males, who are expected to be more dominant and autonomous in Western cultures than females or than males in Eastern cultures. It is evident that more data are needed to relate shyness to socialization patterns in collectivist cultures.

Shyness appears to be a more negative label for males in the United States and Western Europe where cultural norms emphasize individualism and autonomy with less regard for relationships and interdependence (Markus & Kitayama, 1991). In fact, cultural norms may be one of the core features that differentiate transient shyness from chronic and problematic shyness. However, the Swedish study differed from the American study in that shyness did not predict occupational impairment among adult males in Sweden. The samples differed in historic and cultural context, in that the Swedish cohort was studied in the 1950s, whereas the American cohort was studied in the 1940s (Caspi, Elder, & Bem, 1988). Furthermore, shyness is viewed more positively in Sweden, and more emphasis has been placed there on the equality of men and women, particularly since the 1960s (Kerr, Lambert, & Bem, 1996). Nevertheless, the authors also reported that shy women were less likely to work outside the home or to attend college; indeed, none of the shy women finished college. This lack of achievement-related behavior may be due to growing up in an earlier era dominated by more traditional cultural expectations for women. More aggressive women may have been less deterred by a traditional upbringing when increased opportunities became available.

Parental expectations are influenced by cultural expectations. In turn, parental expectations influence children's perceptions of appropriate social behavior and their self-perceptions. Expectation is particularly fascinating with regard to the Park finding regarding the stability of behavioral inhibition. Infant boys who were rated as high on negativity and low on positivity showed high inhibition as toddlers (Park, Belsky, Putnam & Crnic, 1997). Highly sensitive parents adjusted their behavior to meet the child's goals and needs, whereas insensitive parents imposed their own goals and agenda on the child. Because the insensitive parents used limit-setting and did not respond to their child's fretting, the development of fearful and inhibited behavior was lessened.

Children's behavior has been shown to be related to parental goals. In this case the child's undesirable behavior was reduced, which may benefit the child in the long run, particularly in the American culture. However, in recent years more emphasis has been placed on the importance of the emotional component of empathy, perhaps due in part to the realization of needing to deal with greater diversity in the United States and in the world at large. Shyness has been positively correlated with empathic concern; thus it is important to note the following parental characteristics that predict empathic concern: paternal involvement in child care, maternal tolerance of dependent behavior, inhibition of aggression, and maternal satisfaction with the role of mother (Davis, 1983; Koestner, Franz & Weinberger, 1990).

The authors do a fine job of acknowledging both temperament and environmental influence on the stability of the trait of behavioral inhibition. [They inform us that new research shows that childhood inhibition is negatively correlated with later social success but also positively correlated with a later departure from the family of origin (Gest, 1997).] This is further evidence for parental influence and the cumulative impact of family cultures. In some cases, more pressure to behave according to perceived norms outside the family and in other cases more responsiveness to the particular needs of the parents or a family culture resulted in a reduced focus on autonomy and individuality.

Although the authors report associations across several studies between childhood inhibition and adult psychopathology, the associations were not statistically significant and effect sizes were small. Beidel and Turner note that children who manifest both the physiological and behavioral aspects of inhibition are those who are also most likely to exhibit anxious behaviors. A possible explanation for this association may be that children, like college students we have studied, when they are both privately self-aware and describe themselves as fearful, blame themselves for negative interpersonal outcomes and then experience shame (Henderson, 1992). Negative internal states draw one's attention inward. If a child is less outgoing than other children and either becomes fearful when pushed beyond his or her comfort zone or becomes aware that others expect him or her to be more outgoing, vicious cycles may develop around negative thoughts and painful emotional states, escalating into a painful cognitive/affective spiral.

The role of blame in social anxiety is seen in part in the data of high school students who labeled themselves as shy but were not self-blaming. They did not report more social anxiety or fear of negative evaluation than did nonshy students (Henderson, 1993). Many inhibited children do not become shy and many become strategic about pushing themselves to be assertive when situations require it without viewing inhibition as a negative attribute. Because we are only beginning to elucidate the mechanisms by which problematic shyness and/or social phobia develop, there are many fruitful research avenues open to pursue.

We agree with the authors that social isolation in children may lead to skill deficits and clinical levels of anxiety. However, we have also observed clinically that many people who label themselves as extremely shy, some of whom meet criteria not only for generalized social phobia but also for avoidant personality disorder, demonstrate adequate, sometimes superior, social skills when they are exposed to other participants in a group situation (Henderson, 1994; St. Laurent, Henderson, & Zimbardo, 1997). Comparable behavior has been seen in previous research with lonely people (Vitkus & Horowitz, 1987). Furthermore, when shy clients do not feel judged negatively for a less extraverted interpersonal style they often become considerably less anxious (Henderson, Martinez, & Zimbardo, 1997).

Passive isolation appears stable from Grades 2 through 5 and appears to lead to depression and loneliness, particularly when it is accompanied by a negative self-perception of social competence (Rubin & Mills, 1988). We wonder about the extent to which such self-perception is related to the kinds of behavior that are valued in the classroom. With large class sizes and a public school system whose support and resources are not adequate to the demands of educating children, youngsters may need to become fairly competitive or aggressive to seize the teacher's attention. Useful research could be done in the area of relating different classroom cultures to the negative self-perceptions of less outgoing children.

On this score we recommend that readers review the innovative action research of social psychologist Elliot Aronson and his colleagues (Aronson, Blaney, Stephan, Sikes & Snapp, 1978) on creating "jigsaw classrooms." Children are assigned to work in small groups on a class presentation in which each group member has access to one essential set of information and must share it with the others in order for the group to be optimally effective. Children learn to listen and to encourage participation from each group member, even the usually nontalkative minority children and perhaps also the shy. Aronson's results clearly show enhanced self-esteem and grade improvement of most children working in these cooperative learning teams. Such a paradigm raises the basic issue of the value of reshaping shy or socially anxious children to fit into traditionally competitive classrooms versus reshaping the structure of the classroom to encourage fullest involvement of all students.

## Cheek and Krasnoperova

Of the many fascinating new findings presented in the chapter by Jonathan Cheek and Elena Krasnoperova, we start by highlighting their report that early-developing shyness appears to be more of an adjustment problem than does later-developing shyness, particularly for males. This corresponds to Buss's fearful shy group and Kagan's behaviorally inhibited children (Buss & Plomin, 1984; Cheek, Carpentieri, Smith, Rierdan, & Koff, 1986; Kagan et al., 1994). In line with their research, our study of Stanford students in 8-week treatment groups for shyness revealed that fearful shys were significantly higher in internal, global, stable, and self-blaming attributions in social situations with negative outcomes prior to treatment (Henderson, Martinez, & Zimbardo, 1997). They were also significantly higher in fear of negative evaluation, depression, and shame. However, of eight subjects with a shyness onset at 3 years or younger, only three were in the high-fear group, whereas four were in the low-fear group. Furthermore, the only variable that was predicted by age of onset was social anxiety, not fear, and age of onset did not predict fear of negative evaluation, depression, or shame. Of course this was a small treatment sample, and perhaps the discrepancy in outcomes is related to McDougall's (1963) position, which Cheek notes, that cognitive-affective sentiments replace biological propensities as behavioral influences during development. The critical issue may be when and how such replacements occur and for which kinds of children.

In an earlier effort to demonstrate empirically the existence of Buss's categories, Henderson hypothesized that self-conscious shyness would lead to a self-blaming attribution style and the emotion of shame in interpersonal situations with negative outcomes because self-conscious shy people were expected to be more self-critical in social situations (Henderson, 1992). Contrary to expectation, only fearfulness, not shyness or public self-consciousness, predicted self-blame, whereas both fear and shyness predicted shame. Perhaps these findings are suggestive of the ongoing increased discomfort in those who are fearful and shy rather than to differences in self-critical tendencies between the fearful and self-conscious shys. During treatment, fearful shy students obtained a greater reduction in subjective anxiety level than their low-fear counterparts.

Cheek and Krasnoperova also cite a study by Kendler and colleagues (Kendler, Health, Martin, & Eaves, 1987) that suggests there may be separate genetic factors involved in somatic and psychic anxiety. Gilmartin's finding, that shy men report precocious heterosexual sensitivity (Gilmartin, 1987), has also been observed clinically in our work. Shy men also report having been teased in elementary school by their peers about wanting to share activities with girls during recess. Again, an unresolved issue is to what degree their behavior is related to genetic programming and to what degree it is simply indicative of normal individual differences that are negatively sanctioned in our culture. Moreover, some shy male clients have identified with mothers and reported that fathers were either critical or distant. In these cases it may make most sense to assume that they have sought out females in elementary school due to more frequent contact with supportive or possibly overprotective mothers in their early years.

Cheek has continued to explicate a tripartite division of shyness into affect, cognition, and observable behavior. We find his three-component model of shyness compelling in the treatment of shyness. Our social fitness model divides his affect component into two parts, specific physiological complaints and specific emotions, particularly because the emotion of shame appears to be linked to the parasympathetic rather than the sympathetic nervous system and is associated with the subjective experience of fatigue and even relaxation (see table III.I.). We have felt it necessary to separate the two because physiological arousal (which includes sweaty palms, racing heart, and trembling) has been the component most often associated with the experience of problematic shyness. Having separated the two, clients are able to distinguish the emotion of shame and also to recognize that the relaxation associated with it may actually reinforce the avoidance pattern. If one becomes ashamed in a social interaction and begins to withdraw into that emotional state, the adrenaline level is reduced, but typically the continued social effort is reduced as well, whereas the negative cognition, particularly the negative attributions, continues to dominate and control social interactions.

Cheek and Krasnoperova also highlight the considerable heterogeneity in shyness and empirically demonstrate the existence of shy subgroups, including those with a dependent or avoidant interpersonal style. The difference between the ingratiating, compliant style and the avoidant style has been evident in our shyness clinic groups and has been confirmed by individual interviews and psychological testing using the Minnesota Multiphasic Personality Inventory (MMPI) and the Millon Clinical Multiaxial Inventory (MCMI). Treatment varies with personality style in individual clients. For example, for those who are dependent, treatment most frequently focuses on self-assertion, both in work and social settings; in contrast, for those who are avoidant, treatment often focuses on meeting people and working at the early stages of deepening relationships.

In order to compare more systematically our subjective clinical observation with data from our initial evaluation process, we conducted a comorbidity study of 114 shyness clinic clients. Initial data analyses revealed that 97 percent of the sample met criteria for generalized social phobia. Dependent personality disorder was present in 24 percent according to the MMPI and in 23 percent according to the MCMI (St. Laurent, Henderson, & Zimbardo, 1997). Avoidant personality disorder was present in 67 percent. These results are highly consistent with Cheek and Krasnoperova's findings. We have recently added the Inventory of

Table III.1  Description of Shyness Components and Vicious Cycles.

*Components of shyness*

- Behavior: inhibited, avoidant, overactive
- Physiology: high arousal, symptoms of fight-or-flight reaction triggered in sympathetic nervous system; heart racing, trembling, sweating; reactions were adaptive in evolution, now represent an overestimate of danger
- Cognitions: maladaptive automatic thoughts (ATs), attributions (ATTs), self-beliefs (SBs)
- Negative emotions: embarrassment, shame

*Vicious cycle #1, anxiety and escape*

- Subjective anxiety (SUDS, Subjective Units of Distress, measured from 0 to 100) leads to ATs, which lead to increased SUDS, which lead to behavioral avoidance, which leads to increased anxiety in next situation.

*Attribution style*

- How people assign responsibility for interpersonal interactions: positive and negative outcomes
- Self-enhancement bias: Most people take credit for success and externalize failure or attribute it to specific, temporary, and controllable factors.
- Self-enhancement bias reversed: Shy people take credit for failure and attribute success to specific, temporary, and uncontrollable factors.
- Failure as "characterological": Shy people see failure as internal, global, stable, uncontrollable; blame themselves.

*Vicious cycle #2, self-blame and shame*

- Self-blame for social failure produces shame, shame in turn produces more self-blame.
- Vicious cycle may lead to increased feelings of vulnerability when entering the next social situation.

*Self-concept distortions*

- Self-blaming attributions may lead to negative beliefs about the self, which organize information around the increased articulation of biases in the self-concept. These beliefs may be outside awareness, so successful goal completion is discounted, as is progress toward long-term goals.

*Vicious cycle #3, other-blame and anger*

- Shame is a painful affective state which may be reduced by blaming others, who are seen as more powerful and untrustworthy (which may be true in some cases).
- Other-blaming attributions lead to negative beliefs about others, which then interfere with reality-based hypothesis-testing and with forming and sustaining relationships.

*Role of Private Self-consciousness*

- Generally associated with seeing the self as others do.
- May contribute to perceptual distortion. During negative emotional states, such as fear or shame, private self-consciousness may contribute to perceptual distortions about one's behavior and about others' reactions due to increased awareness of negative emotions, thoughts, attributions, and beliefs.

Interpersonal Problems (Horowitz & Rosenberg, 1988) to our initial evaluation in order to attempt a more fine-grained future analysis.

The "shy-secure group," identified by Cheek and Krasnoperova, seems to correspond to a subgroup of our clients who come for treatment not because they have been particularly distressed but because they have been promoted to a position that requires more social interaction or visibility. They often want to practice new behaviors in a supportive environment before they tackle them in a more risky public arena. We speculate that their "double-risk group" corresponds to a subgroup at our clinic who score highly in overall distress as suggested by a cluster analysis of scores on a number of questionnaires (Henderson & Zimbardo, 1998). It is increasingly evident that future treatment of shy people demands more refined understanding of the various diagnostic categories into which they fit according to their development histories. This is as true of psychotherapies as it is of newer drug treatments, a point well made by Franklin Schneier in the final chapter in this section.

## Aron

Elaine Aron's discussion of "sensory-processing sensitivity" provides an interesting avenue for exploration of a phenomenon that both clinicians and researchers have been struggling to understand, namely the heightened interpersonal sensitivity seen so often in problematic shyness, generalized social phobia, and avoidant personality disorder. Quoting biological research that suggests two distinct survival mechanisms—risk-taking and "more selected action behavior"—Aron hypothesizes "a greater awareness of consequences, both positive and negative" among those who are sensitive. Aron supports her construct with several lines of interrelated research on the introversion/extraversion continuum (Eysenck, MacLeod & Mathews, 1987) and observed low sensory threshold as a basic trait (Thomas & Chess, 1977) and with Mehrabian's work on arousability as a consequence of greater sensitivity to stimulation (Mehrabian & Stefl, 1995). Parallel evidence is found in Boice's research with high-reactive children who are hypothesized to have a heightened sensitivity to the social world (Boice et al., 1995).

These findings are consistent with our clinical observation of many adults and adolescents who seek treatment for extreme shyness. A recent study found that the mean of an adult sample of Shyness Clinic clients was elevated on the Paranoia scale of the MMPI, which is purported to measure interpersonal sensitivity at moderate levels (Henderson, 1997). Furthermore, of two significantly different groups who have been identified in our clinic population using cluster analysis (high- and low-distress groups), the high-distress group showed markedly higher elevations in interpersonal sensitivity, in avoidance as measured on the Avoidance scale of the MCMI, in suppressed hostility, and also in emotional alienation (Henderson & Zimbardo, 1998; Spielberger, 1979). It is interesting that Aron's research revealed a partial independence of sensitivity from negative emotionality and greater levels of distress when sensitivity was associated with more stressful childhoods. These findings are consistent with the idea that sensitivity may only become problematic in children who are negatively affected by unsupportive family environments, culture, and negative conditioning events.

Aron's findings appear to support the theory that a fit between temperament and environment is the major factor that determines whether sensitivity will be a gift or a curse. That this may be more relevant to men is quite interesting, because men may get less support for their sensitivity in the world at large than women do; so if parents do not support boys' more sensitive temperaments, the world is less likely to compensate. Her notion that sensitive children develop conflicts if they believe that they should enjoy stimulating social situations is quite consistent with the clinical literature that abounds with examples of children who develop shame and rage when their basic attributes are unacceptable to parents and family (Scheff, 1987; Wurmser, 1981). It is also interesting that Boice's research reveals better health under emotionally supportive conditions among sensitive children than among the nonsensitive. This result fits well with that from Suomi's animal research with rhesus monkeys, in which a nurturing surrogate parent can create superior functioning in the timid young monkey (Suomi, 1987).

Aron's conceptualization of sensitivity as "complex and discriminating processing" and the likelihood that it could be mistakenly viewed as maladaptive inhibition or anxiety seems highly plausible. In fact, Henderson relabeled our shyness treatment "Social Fitness Training" in response to the stigma typically associated with shyness. Our shy clients exhibit a tendency to see themselves as defective in relation to other people, particularly in relation to more outgoing or extraverted people.

Initially, clients seemed to believe that they needed to be "cured" or "fixed" rather than to understand that if they want to be "world class social athletes" they must "work out," just like sports athletes. Anyone desiring to be a good sports or physical athlete must be willing to devote many hours of "working out" and training to perform appropriately according to the demands and rules of athletic games. The same holds true for social athletes. There are many social games to play and a huge variety of social settings in which to engage in them. The trick is to find the ones you enjoy and for which you have a natural affinity. Shy clients will often say to us, "What if I just don't have the talent?" The interaction of talent and effort is complicated. In fact, Bjorn Borg was told early in his career by one of his coaches that his swing was too idiosyncratic and "impossible" for competitive tennis. That was before he repeated his superb performance a number of times as the men's singles champion at Wimbledon. We also remind our male clients who use the current media image of the "hyper macho" male as their social comparison model that social "football" is not the only game in town. It is remarkable how many men who label themselves as shy are shocked by the notion that women have been known to find sensitive men attractive, as Aron could surely tell them. These men simply have to find the social game that is best suited for their talents. And they must learn through systematic, safe practice how to become "socially grammatical" by knowing what to do (content), how to do it (style), and when to do it (timing) as part of being an effective social athlete.

The social fitness metaphor allows for a much greater understanding and acceptance of individual differences in adaptive functioning. For many of our shy clients of both genders, it is the first time they have considered the freedom of deliberately choosing situations and companions to suit them rather than conforming passively to the wishes of others. As they have felt supported in a group setting, many demonstrate highly skilled social behaviors, particularly empathic behavior in response to other group members. Only when experiencing negative affective states, such as fear, insecurity, shame, guilt, or anger, do many appear to lose an empathic connection with others as their egocentric preoccupation takes precedence. In contrast, some shy adults have had fewer experiences of empathic responses and more experience with bullying and shaming by others. These individuals need training in perspective-taking and sensitively responding to the feelings of others by learning empathic concern.

## Schneier

Franklin Schneier's impressive review of the biological findings for social phobia reveals the nonobvious finding that heart rate variability does not consistently differ from that of healthy controls, nor does sympathetic nervous system activity in general. Schneier suggests "end-organ down regulation in response to chronic hyperactivity" as a possible explanation which could help account for the fact that shy clients demonstrate considerable variability in their reports of subjective anxiety during exposures in group psychotherapy. Furthermore, some clients consistently are described as calm and even soothing in an exercise in which adjectives that describe nonverbal behavior are selected as feedback by group members. During the initial evaluations with these particular clients, clinicians often describe their affect as blunted or flat. Schneier notes that social phobics showed an increase in right-sided activation of the anterior temporal and lateral prefrontal brain regions in anticipation of a public speaking task in the well-controlled research by Davidson and his colleagues (Davidson, Marshall, Tomarken, & Henriques, in press). Add to that result the further evidence that right frontal activation has been associated with behavioral inhibition. In view of these findings, it is curious that some shy clients report that instead of planning what they will say in a public speaking task, they do one of two things: either get negative mental images or just "go blank."

Although monoamine oxidase inhibitors (MAOI's) help reduce interpersonal hypersensitivity, most clients are reluctant to take them. Some clients who meet criteria for dysthymia and/or avoidant personality disorder benefit from serotonin reuptake inhibitors during cognitive-behavioral group treatment, particularly if they cannot bring themselves to enter feared situations due to considerable emotional discomfort associated with such action. Our clients have had less success with benzodiazepines, apparently due to the fact that their fear of unpleasant physiological arousal prevents desensitization and also prevents the realization that anxiety can be managed and reduced through cognitive restructuring. We have also had several cases in which clients were either abusing or had become dependent on the drugs. Because the data have shown so far that social phobics appear to maintain treatment gains better with cognitive-behavioral therapy, most of our clients prefer to use the cognitive-behavioral techniques alone unless their avoidance patterns preclude executing in vivo exposures between group sessions. Again there is an urgent call for more clinical studies of the utility of newer drug treatments for specific types of shy and social phobic clients, as an adjunct to various forms of psychotherapy and also as the primary treatment modality (since it will surely be the preferred mode paid for by the HMOs).

In summary, these six authors offer us a rich tapestry of new data, conceptual clarifications, research and clinically-based insights, and scholarly reviews of many issues previously neglected in the developmental study of shyness and a host of related syndromes. They add a vital lifespan and clinical orientation to previous research on shyness and social phobias that has been dominated in recent years by social, cognitive, and personality perspectives. We have seen how infantile social distress may eventuate in problematic shyness, anxiety disorders, and other types of psychopathology from childhood into adulthood. A new focus on gender issues, as well as cultural contributions, will further enrich the study of children's development of extreme social fears and shyness. The study of shyness continues to fascinate us, since it blends so much of what is central to the study of human nature: temperament, family, environment, culture, gender, lifespan development, attributions, emotions, cognitions, and psychopathology.

We conclude our commentary by outlining our social fitness program, which attempts to address many of the variables in extreme shyness that each of the authors of these four chapters raised in one way or another.

## The Social Fitness Training Program

The initial evaluation and assessment consists of at least three, and up to six, individual interviews. It is followed by 26 weeks of cognitive-behavioral treatment, which may be broken into modules for briefer treatment. Groups meet for 2 hours each week. The first 13 weeks are devoted to simulations of feared situations, accompanied by cognitive-attributional/self-concept restructuring and skills coaching. Clients practice challenging negative automatic thoughts, including attributions and negative self-beliefs, between sessions while doing in vivo exposures on their own. The second 13 weeks are devoted to continuing exposures and skills practice related to deepening relationships. We focus on interpersonal communication, with modeling and behavioral rehearsal. Clients practice one skill a week, among them self-disclosure, empathic listening, trust building, handling criticism, constructive conflict resolution, and anger management.

The development of the group parallels the way relationships develop, first with getting-acquainted skills and exposures to new people and situations, proceeding to skills in building friendships and professional relationships, to appropriate self-expression and assertiveness at work, and lastly to deepening intimacy with self and others, including romantic relationships.

In the final few weeks we provide assertiveness training using the DESC scripting model (Bower & Bower, 1976). The acronym refers to Describing behavior, Expressing feelings in response to it, Specifying the desired behavior, and Describing consequences (focusing primarily on the positive and using the negative only when necessary). We videotape the assertiveness scripts and play them back to our clients for their reactions, our constructive input, and group discussion. The safety of the therapeutic setting and the supportive atmosphere created for change and development of new skills combines with the therapist's "coaching" role to facilitate each client's optimal social fitness development.

*References*

Aronson, E., Blaney, N., Stephan, C., Sikes, J., & Snapp, M. (1978). *The jigsaw class-room.* Beverly Hills, CA: Sage.

Boice, W. T., Chesney, M., Alkon, A., Tschann, J. M., Adams, S., Chesterman, B., Cohen, F., Kaiser, P., Folkman, S., & Wara, D. (1995). Psychobiologic reactivity to stress and childhood respiratory illnesses: Results of two prospective studies. *Psychosomatic Medicine, 57,* 411–422.

Bower, S. A., & Bower, G. H. (1976). *Asserting yourself.* Menlo Park, CA: Addison-Wesley.

Buss, A. H., & Plomin, R. (1984). *Temperament: Early developing personality traits.* Hillsdale, NJ: Erlbaum.

Caspi, A., Elder, G. H., & Bem, D. J. (1988). Moving away from the world: Life course patterns of shy children. *Developmental Psychology, 24,* 824–831.

Cheek, J. M., Carpentieri, A. M., Smith, T. G., Rierdan, J., & Koff, E. (1986). Adolescent shyness. In W. H. Jones, J. M. Cheek, & S. R. Briggs (Eds.), *Shyness: Perspectives on research and treatment* (pp. 105–115). New York: Plenum.

Davidson, R. , Marshall, J. R., Tomarken, A. J., & Henriques, J. B. (in press). While a pho-bic waits: Regional brain electrical and autonomic activity predicts anxiety in so-cial phobics during anticipation of public speaking. *Biological Psychiatry.*

Davis, M. H. (1983). Measuring individual differences in empathy: Evidence for a mul-tidimensional approach. *Journal of Personality and Social Psychology, 44,* 113–126.

Engfer, A. (1993). Antecedents and consequences of shyness in boys and girls: A 6-year longitudinal study. In K. H. Rubin & J. B. Asendorpf (Eds.), *Social withdrawal, in-hibition and shyness in childhood* (pp. 49–79). Hillsdale, NJ: Erlbaum.

Eysenck, M. W., MacLeod, C., & Mathews, A. (1987). Cognitive functioning and anxi-ety. *Psychological Research, 49,* 189–195.

Gest, S. D. (1997). Behavioral inhibition: Stability and associations with adaptation from childhood to early adulthood. *Journal of Personality and Social Psychology, 72,* 467–475.

Gilmartin, B. G. (1987). Peer group antecedents of severe love-shyness in males. *Journal of Personality, 55,* 467–489.

Henderson, L. (1992, March). *Fear, private self-consciousness and self-blame.* Paper presented at the Anxiety Disorders Association of America, Houston, Texas.

Henderson, L. (1993, March). *Self-blame attributions in shys vs. non-shys in a high school sample.* Paper presented at the annual conference of the Anxiety Disorders Association of America, Charleston, South Carolina.

Henderson, L. (1994). *Social fitness training: A treatment manual for shyness and so-cial phobia.* Palo Alto: Shyness Institute.

Henderson, L. (1997). Mean MMPI profile of referrals to a shyness clinic. *Psychological Reports, 80,* 695–702.

Henderson, L., Martinez, A., & Zimbardo, P. G. (1997, July). *Social fitness training with attributional and self-concept restructuring: Preliminary data with a college stu-dent population.* Paper presented at the International Conference on Shyness and Self-Consciousness, Cardiff, Wales.

Henderson, L., & Zimbardo, P. (1998, March). *Shame and anger in chronic shyness.* Paper presented at the annual conference of the Anxiety Disorders Association of America, Boston, MA.

Horowitz, L. M., & Rosenberg, S. E. (1988). Inventory of Interpersonal Problems: Psychometric properties and clinical applications. *Journal of Consulting and Clinical Psychology, 56,* 885–892.

Kagan, J., Arcus, D., Snidman, N., Feng, W. Y., Hendler, J., & Greene, S. (1994). Reacti-vity in infants: A cross-national comparison. *Developmental Psychology, 30,* 342–345.

Kendler, K. S., Heath, A. C., Martin, N. G., & Eaves, L. J. (1987). Symptoms of anxiety and symptoms of depression: Same genes, different environments? *Archives of General Psychiatry, 44,* 451–457.

Kerr, M., Lambert, W. W., & Bem, D. J. (1996). Life course sequelae of chldhood shyness in Sweden: Comparison with the United States. *Developmental Psychology, 32,* 1100–1105.

Koestner, R., Franz, C., & Weinberger, J. (1990). The family origins of empathic concern: A 26-year longitudinal study. *Journal of Personality and Social Psychology, 58,* 709–717.

Markus, H. R., & Kitayama, S. (1991). Culture and the self: Implications for cognition, emotion, and motivation. *Psychological Review, 98,* 224–253.

McDougall, W. (1963). *An introduction to social psychology.* (31st ed.). London: Methuen (1st. ed. published 1908; 23rd ed., published 1936).

Mehrabian, A., & Stefl, C. A. (1995). Basic temperament components of loneliness, shyness, and conformity. *Social Behavior and Personality, 23,* 253–264.

Park, S. Y., Belsky, J., Putnam, S., & Crnic, K. (1997). Infant emotionality, parenting and 3-year inhibition: Exploring stability and lawful discontinuity in a male sample. *Developmental Psychology, 33,* 218–227.

Rubin, K. H., & Mills, R. S. L. (1988). The many faces of social isolation in childhood. *Journal of Consulting and Clinical Psychology, 56,* 916–924.

Scheff, T. J. (1987). The shame-rage spiral: A case study of an interminable quarrel. In H. B. Lewis (Ed.), *The role of shame in symptom formation* (pp. 109–149). Hillsdale, NJ: Erlbaum.

Spielberger, C. D. (1979). *State-trait Anger Expression Inventory (STAXI).* Odessa, Florida: Psychological Assessment Resources, Inc.

St. Laurent, T., Henderson, L., & Zimbardo, P. G. (1997, March). *Co-morbidity in a shyness clinic sample.* Paper presented at the annual conference of the Anxiety Disorders Association of America, New Orleans, Louisiana.

Suomi, S. J. (1987). Genetic and maternal contributions to individual differences in rhesus monkey biobehavioral development. In N. A. Krasnegor, E. M. Blass, M. A. Hoffer, & W. P. Smotherman (Eds.), *Perinatal behavioral development: A psychobiological perspective* (pp. 397–419). San Diego, CA: Academic Press.

Thomas, A., & Chess, S. (1977). *Temperament and development.* New York: Brunner/Mazel.

Vitkus, J., & Horowitz, L. (1987). Poor social performance of lonely people: Lacking a skill or adopting a role? *Journal of Personality and Social Psychology, 52,* 1266–1273.

Wurmser, L. (1981). *The mask of shame.* Baltimore: Johns Hopkins University Press.

Zimbardo, P. G. (1986). The Stanford shyness project. In W. H. Jones, J. M. Cheek, & S. R. Briggs (Eds.), *Shyness: Perspectives on research and treatment* (pp. 17–25). New York: Plenum Press.

# Epilogue

Louis A. Schmidt & Jay Schulkin

We live in a time of rapid expansion of biological information and knowledge. This accelerated knowledge touches many aspects of our lives and cuts across scientific inquiry that ranges from basic mechanisms of organs, cells, and genes to neurons and brain systems to ecosystems and natural habitat. Biological inquiry is broad based and at the heart of human possibilities.

In knowledge, the latter part of the twentieth century is to biological sciences what the early part of the twentieth century was to physics, the former symbolized by the Human Genome Project, the latter by the Manhattan Project. Both represent the awesome power of science. We believe that science is at its best when it seeks to understand a phenomenon from multiple disciplines, multiple levels, and multiple systems. We hope that this belief was evident in the pages of this book.

Recent theoretical and methodological advances in many disparate areas of scientific inquiry have expanded the study of complex brain/behavior relations. With the advent of animal analogs used to understand fear and anxiety and advances in neuroimaging techniques and molecular neurobiology, we are positioned to use the knowledge established by the new theories and techniques to more fully understand the origins and developmental course of extreme fear and shyness in humans than ever before.

For example, recent discoveries in molecular neurobiology have suggested that there are genes that turn on and off neurochemical systems implicated in some normal and atypical personality profiles. In addition, recent discoveries in behavioral neuroendocrinology have revealed relations among levels of corticotropin-releasing hormones (CRH) and fear-related behaviors in nonhuman primates. One recent study has reported that CRH levels correlated positively with acute and chronic social stress in nonhuman primates (Habib et al., in press). Another recent study by Ned Kalin and Richard Davidson and their colleagues at the University of

306

Wisconsin found that nonhuman primates that exhibited greater relative right frontal brain electrical activity (EEG) during baseline conditions also displayed more fear-related behaviors (Kalin, Larson, Shelton, & Davidson, 1998) and higher CRH levels (Kalin, Shelton, & Davidson, in press) than nonhuman primates that exhibited greater relative left frontal EEG activity. The subset of nonhuman primates reported by the Wisconsin group exhibiting greater relative frontal EEG activity and elevated CRH levels display many of the behavioral and physiological responses analogous to those observed in extremely fearful and shy children. Identifying the genes for CRH expression, their distribution and receptor sites in the brain, and the environmental conditions that activate CRH expression may be a first step toward identifying the origins of extreme fear and shyness in humans. This will, undoubtedly, have implications for providing effective intervention and treatment where and when appropriate. Hopefully, as this book attests, future research in this area will employ a systems neuroscience approach involving behavioral, physiological, neural, and molecular levels of analysis in the study of extreme fear and shyness.

We cannot, however, conclude this book without addressing one final point. We strongly believe that there are many positive qualities to some aspects of shyness and these should be accented. For example, children who are shy are nonimpulsive, reflective, compliant, and keenly aware of their own and others' feelings, to name a few. It is important to highlight this because with the increasing discoveries of genetic and biological contributions to shyness and anxiety that have occurred at the close of this century and will continue to occur into the twenty-first century, there will undoubtedly be the development of drugs used to treat many disorders of mind and personality. This raises a real danger in that, with the availability and easy access to drug therapy, many parents and educators may rush, or be encouraged, to treat with drugs normal personality characteristics in childen. We do not wish the readers of this book to think that we are "pathologizing" the child who is shy; rather, our goal is to understand the origins and mechanisms that underlie the phenomena of extreme fear and shyness. It is up to future research to decide how the knowledge established by basic research can be used most effectively. We caution future research, however, by noting that many individual differences in personality should be celebrated, not eliminated!

*References*

Habib, K. E., Weld, K. P., Schulkin, J., Pushkas, S., Listwak, S., Champoux, M., Shannon, C., Chrousos, G. P., Suomi, S., Gold, P. W., & Higley, J. D. (in press). Cerebrospinal fluid levels of corticotropin-releasing hormone positively correlate with acute and chronic social stress in non-human primates. *Society for Neuroscience Abstracts.*

Kalin, N. H., Larson, C., Shelton, S. E., & Davidson, R. J. (1998). Asymmetric frontal brain activity, cortisol, and behavior associated with fearful temperament in rhesus monkeys. *Behavioral Neuroscience, 112,* 286–292.

Kalin, N. H., Shelton, S. E., & Davidson, R. J. (in press). Individual differences in cerebrospinal fluid corticotropin releasing hormone levels are stable and are elevated in monkeys with patterns of brain activity associated with fearful temperament. *Proceedings of the National Academy of Sciences.*

# Index

acetylcholine, 140, 159
ACTH. *See* adrenocorticotrophic hormone
active-immature behavior, 213
Adalbjarnardottir, S., 215
adaptive responses, 141–42, 162, 194, 195
adolescents
  shyness types in, 224–43
  social phobia treatments, 283
adrenal gland, 100, 103–4, 126, 140, 150–51
  hormones, 174, 176–80
adrenal steroids, 105, 177–80, 181
adrenocortical system, 55, 57, 60, 177, 184
  attachment behaviors and, 31–42, 264
  *See also* hypothalamic-pituitary-adrenocortical system
adrenocorticotrophic hormone, 150, 151, 277
adults, 4, 50–51, 60–61, 70
  childhood behavioral inhibition effects, 211–12, 217
  childhood shyness effects, 3, 159, 205–6, 218, 226–28
  disorder treatments, 274–82, 284–85

fearful vs. self-conscious shyness in, 22–26
affective style, 67, 70, 79
affiliativeness, 92
age
  cognitive impairment and, 179, 182
  as shyness conception factor, 19–21
  *See also* adolescents; adults; children; infants
agoraphobia, 213, 284–86
Ainsworth, M. D. S., 30, 34–35, 39
alcoholism, 184, 195, 212, 279
aldosterone, 154
allergies, 185, 228, 254
allostasis, 181–82
allostatic load, 181–86
Allport, G. W., 242
alpha-melanocyte-stimulating hormone, 193
alprazolam (Xanax), 278, 279, 284
Alzheimer's disease, 184
amino acids, 179–80, 182
amygdala, 42, 82, 89, 90, 193, 265
  aversive fear conditioning and, 129–32, 153, 158–59
  brain development and, 181, 185
  CRH systems and, 101, 109, 111, 140, 151–53, 156, 158
  extended. *See* stria terminalis